PROTECTING CIVILIANS

Protecting Civilians

The Obligations of Peacekeepers

SIOBHÁN WILLS

OXFORD
UNIVERSITY PRESS

Great Clarendon Street, Oxford OX2 6DP

Oxford University Press is a department of the University of Oxford.
It furthers the University's objective of excellence in research, scholarship,
and education by publishing worldwide in

Oxford New York

Auckland Cape Town Dar es Salaam Hong Kong Karachi
Kuala Lumpur Madrid Melbourne Mexico City Nairobi
New Delhi Shanghai Taipei Toronto

With offices in

Argentina Austria Brazil Chile Czech Republic France Greece
Guatemala Hungary Italy Japan Poland Portugal Singapore
South Korea Switzerland Thailand Turkey Ukraine Vietnam

Oxford is a registered trade mark of Oxford University Press
in the UK and in certain other countries

Published in the United States
by Oxford University Press Inc., New York

First published 2009

British Library Cataloguing in Publication Data
Data available

Library of Congress Cataloging in Publication Data
Data available

Typeset by Newgen Imaging Systems (P) Ltd., Chennai, India
Printed in Great Britain
on acid-free paper by
the MPG Books Group

ISBN 978–0–19–953387–9 (Hbk.)

1 3 5 7 9 10 8 6 4 2

For Saskia

Table of Contents

Foreword

Peacekeeping and peace support operations have expanded considerably in scope and purpose, particularly over the last decade and a half. The complexity and, indeed, the contradictions attaching to these initiatives are often all too apparent, as Dr Wills shows in her timely study. Alive to the issues and concerns and solidly grounded in the experience of fifty or so years of missions throughout the globe, the analysis here reveals clearly the problems and the tension that can arise between national interests, humanitarian concerns, and international law, when mandates are ill thought-out, or lacking in political commitment.

For peacekeepers are no longer, if ever they were, simply guardians of the truce or observers of the cease-fire. They are now commonly enforcers of the peace or the settlement considered essential to present and future peace. Their liability to engage in combat for that greater good necessarily puts in issue their status—which cannot be that of belligerent and perhaps ought not either to be that of occupant, even in UN-run operations of long duration, such as Kosovo.

Dr Wills identifies and analyses closely the still worrying problems of the applicable law: Whether and to what extent UN operations are bound by international humanitarian law; how, if at all, rights and duties are transmitted through the legal responsibilities of troop-contributing nations; how relevant or important is the consent of the State where operations take place; and what impact does human rights law have on the conduct and accountability of States and troops.

Some of these questions have already come up before municipal courts, particularly if not exclusively in the United Kingdom. Here the House of Lords, finding jurisdiction in the fact of effective custody and control, has ruled on the extra-territorial reach of certain of the UK's human rights obligations, as provided for domestically by the Human Rights Act 1998. British and other military forces are even now reviewing and revising practices, training and manuals in the light of recent experience and the challenges thrown up at the sharp end, when peace support operations can call for war fighting, mediation, and civilian protection, all within a single mandate.

As Dr Wills clearly shows, it is at the point where peacekeepers enter into contact with civilians that the law—under the weight of political objectives and sometimes countervailing principles—must rise to the tasks of protection. It may be true, as she notes, that the Hague and Geneva conception of 'occupation law' is not obviously an appropriate setting for UN-mandated or UN-run operations with essentially humanitarian objectives. And yet, as she also shows, drawing on Australia's experience in Somalia, occupation law can provide the essential legal framework within which to maintain order and security and to rebuild civilian infrastructures.

Drawing on the rich history of the present and the recent past, this study pinpoints numerous inadequacies in the mandate, objectives, and implementation of various peace support operations—inadequacies, often compounded by lack of political will and purpose, which failed to stop or to do anything to prevent, not only the atrocities in Rwanda and Srebrenica, but also the daily violence, abuse and humiliation suffered by civilians at the hands of armed forces, militias, even peacekeepers themselves.

Too often, peacekeepers have not protected the vulnerable, but have been required to look the other way, or have done so for want of clear direction. Of course, as Dr Wills explains, the nature of conflict and the type and location of combatants are forever changing, and many parties, not just non-State actors, will manoeuvre in the spaces left by ambiguity. But if the principles of the UN Charter and the underlying spirit of the law are to mean anything, then the moral and political imperative to protect civilians ought indeed to have crossed the line to legal duty. The present and continuing challenge is implementation—finding effective ways to ensure that international peacekeepers and UN operations, in all their variety, do not become abusers of those entrusted to their protection; and that any immunity from process is legitimated by openness and accountability.

This important work lays down solid foundations for that programme of action. It is essential reading for students of these critical times, it gives legal content to the rhetoric of the responsibility to protection, and it will make a substantial and positive contribution to the doctrine of peace support operations in the years to come.

Guy S. Goodwin-Gill

All Souls College
Oxford

Preface and Acknowledgements

This book deals with the protection of civilians in peacekeeping and peace support operations. Since it went to press in September 2008 violence against civilians has once again become headline news, particularly the killings and rapes in the Democratic Republic of the Congo (DRC). In December, Amnesty International issued a press release in which it urgently called for more robust protection by the UN Mission in the Congo (MONUC) noting that 'the UN peacekeeping force, is badly overstretched but this is not an excuse for a less than robust approach to fulfil its protection mandate.'[1] The DRC is only one of many conflicts in which terrible violent crimes are constantly being perpetrated against civilians. Providing protection raises numerous practical problems, but mass killings, vicious rapes and other forms of sexual violence, and the conscription, terrorization[2] and abuse of children is an indicment of us all; especially when it takes place in the vicinity of United Nations' peacekeepers.

The book developed from my doctoral thesis and I would particularly like to thank my supervisor, Professor Guy Goodwin-Gill, for his critical advice and patience; Professor Sir Adam Roberts, who very kindly read some sections of the book and gave thoughtful and helpful comments; and my examiners Professor Nigel White and Mr Dapo Akande for their extremely useful insights and suggestions.

I would also like to thank Dr Ray Murphy of the Irish Centre for Human Rights, Dr Fiona de Londras of University College Dublin, Lieutenant Colonel Philip Wilkinson, and Lieutenant Colonel Alasdair Balgarnie, Staff Officer on Peace Support Operations and Mobility/Counter-Mobility, at the Ministry of Defence, Development, Concepts and Doctrine Centre, Shrivenham.

I also wish to thank John Louth, Chris Champion, Rebecca Smith, and especially Merel Alstein, of Oxford University Press, for their professional and supportive advice; all my colleagues at University College Cork for providing such a warm and stimulating environment; the fellows and staff at my former college at Oxford, Exeter, for their support during my time there; and all my family, especially my daughter, Saskia.

[1] Amnesty International, Press Release 'Democratic Republic of the Congo: Every Delay Costs Lives' 9 December 2008 http://www.amnesty.org/en/for-media/press-releases/democratic-republic-congo-every-delay-costs-lives-20081209.

[2] Amnesty International reports two children being kicked and beaten to death with wooden bats in front of other children 'as a lesson to all of us not to try to escape'. Amnesty International, *No End to War an Women and Children: North Kivu, Democratic Republic of the Congo*, AFR 62/005/2008 29 September 2008, 20.

Table of Cases

Introduction

This book deals with the civilian protection obligations of peacekeepers and other multi-national forces. These obligations are based on the mandates of such forces, and also on international humanitarian law (IHL) and human rights. The book assesses the extent to which troops' have obligations, under these laws, to intervene to stop the commission of serious abuses of human rights. It examines the meaning and practical consequences for peacekeepers and other multi-national forces, in terms of civilian protection, of the Article 1 duty to respect and ensure respect for the Geneva Conventions; of the duty to secure human rights (found in most international human rights treaties); and of the duty to restore law and order in an occupation. The book offers some guidelines for troops faced with egregious violations of human rights and humanitarian law, but the analysis is focused primarily on legal issues and is therefore only part of a much wider debate about the practical problems for peacekeeping forces in providing protection.

The analysis includes, but is not limited to, operations undertaken specifically to protect people from serious violations of human rights. The operations involved are of differing types and encompass peace operations and enforcement operations. Many, but not all, constitute 'peace support operations' a relatively new term which encompasses 'conflict prevention, peacemaking, peace enforcement, peacekeeping, peacebuilding and/or humanitarian operations.'[1] Although these operations do not all share the same legal basis they share some similar problems. Because the operations are often multi-national, they comprise contingents from different countries, each with their own different treaty commitments. In most cases the operations have been authorized by some international body whether the UN, NATO, or a regional organization. Where there has been no explicit UN authorization the States involved have usually argued that the action taken supports, or is supported by, Security Council resolutions concerning the conflict or security issues in question.

The need for clarification on the extent of the obligations of military forces to provide civilian protection has been a matter of concern since the 1960s when peacekeepers deployed to the Congo, under rules of engagement [ROE] that prohibited the initiation of the use of force, found themselves faced with massacres and other serious abuses of human rights. Hammarskjöld was torn between the need to act to support the norms of the Genocide Convention and the Universal Declaration of Human Rights,[2] and the need to remain impartial; recognizing

[1] UK Ministry of Defence, Joint Warfare Publication (JWP) 3.50 *The Military Contribution to Peace Support Operation* (n 5), Glossary 7.

[2] Annual Report of the Secretary-General on the Work of the Organization, June 16, 1960–June 16, 1961, 16th Session, UN Doc A/4800, 11.

that any action at all would be interpreted as aiding one side or another. At one point he even considered withdrawing the UN Mission to the Congo (ONUC) altogether on the grounds that 'complete passivity would have to be ruled out' but '[p]ractically every act of interposition in such a situation might lend itself to the interpretation that it was taken in order to help one side or the other.'[3] The peacekeeping problems in the Congo in the 1960s were long regarded as unique and sui generis; but after the Cold War when peacekeeping operations became more complex commentators began to note a recurrence of the same critical issues.

The mass killings in Rwanda and Srebrenica in 1994 and 1995, followed a few years later by the highly controversial bombing campaign of 1999 in Kosovo, prompted by fear of similar killings, resulted in sustained efforts by the then Secretary-General Kofi Annan to find someway of resolving the conflict between respect for State sovereignty and the protection of human security. What emerged was a new principle, the collective international 'responsibility to protect', which was first articulated by the International Commission on Intervention and State Sovereignty (ICISS) in 2001,[4] but has since rapidly acquired the status of a new norm against which the acts and omissions of the international community, through its representative organizations, are judged. Although it is primarily concerned with the responsibilities of States the 'responsibility to protect' has major implications for the responsibilities of peacekeepers and other multi-national forces deployed on behalf of the international community. The commitments by the General Assembly and the Security Council in 2005 and 2006, endorsing key aspects of the 'responsibility to protect' norm, has added to the already considerable pressure for improved clarity on peacekeepers' protection obligations.[5] Since 1999 (thus predating the ICISS report of 2001 but galvanized by the same humanitarian crises that prompted the setting up of the Commission), it has become the norm for the UN to include explicit authorization to provide civilian protection in peacekeeping mandates for UN missions and also in operations led by regional organizations such as the African Union, the Economic Community of West African States, and the European Union; but the carefully qualified language normally used to authorize protection leaves it unclear what peacekeepers are permitted to do and should do in response to attacks on civilians and other atrocities. There may be serious practical difficulties for troops in providing protection, particularly if the force is configured and deployed for another purpose, but a failure to provide protection may undermine the legitimacy of the mission

[3] Address to the General Assembly, GAOR, 15th Session, 975 plenary meeting, cited in Rosalyn Higgins, *United Nations Peacekeeping 1946–1967, Documents and Commentary, III, Africa* (Oxford University Press Oxford 1980), 50.

[4] International Commission on Intervention and State Sovereignty (ICISS) *The Responsibility to Protect* (Ottawa International Development Research Centre 2001).

[5] UK Ministry of Defence, Joint Warfare Publication (JWP) 3.50 *The Military Contribution to Peace Support Operation* (2nd edn, The Joint Doctrine and Concepts Centre Shrivenham 2004), [113]; S Breau, 'The Impact of the Responsibility to Protect on Peacekeeping' (2006) 11 Journal of Conflict and Security Law 3, 429.

in the eyes of the local community. In addition there is also widespread concern that peacekeeping may in itself be a source of human rights violations. Although only a minority of peacekeepers are involved, the problem of exploitation and abuse by peacekeepers is prevalent to some degree in almost all missions.

It is in the nature of peacekeeping that forces are generally deployed outside their own country. A State's jurisdiction is normally confined to that State's territory but there are exceptions. Where a peacekeeping force is in occupation of territory an extensive body of law governs the relationship with the local population. However, the applicability of occupation law to peace operations is controversial. Some commentators argue that it is only intended to apply in belligerent occupation and not to operations conducted on behalf of the local population or of the international community. Except where a peacekeeping force is in occupation of the territory, international law recognizes no general relationship between the inhabitants and a State that is contributing troops to a peacekeeping operation. Nevertheless peacekeepers (and other forces) may, in certain circumstances, have obligations towards the local population, under the domestic law of the contributing State, or under IHL or international human rights law. The draft replacement for the UK's current peace support operations doctrine notes that in assessing the force's obligations towards the local community commanders must take into account 'humanitarian & human rights law treaty obligations, customary international law, domestic law of the Troop Contributing Nations (TCN) and host-nation law, and meeting the principles of the UN Charter.' However, the doctrine does not discuss what these obligations are or the framework in which they arise. This book sets out to address this gap.

The Structure of the Book

Chapter 1 of this book analyzes the evolution of peacekeeping focusing in particular on the extent to which past peacekeeping operations have attempted to provide protection to civilians and the issues that this has raised.

Chapters 2 and 3 explore the extent to which international humanitarian law and international human rights law require peacekeepers to protect civilians from serious violations of the rights they protect.

Chapter 4 explores the issues regarding the potential applicability of occupation law to forces engaged in humanitarian or peacekeeping operations.

Chapter 5 draws on the analysis of the preceding chapters, and assesses the extent to which peacekeepers and other forces engaged in multi-national operations have an obligation to protect the local population from serious violations of human rights, focusing on three areas of protection responsibility: preventing attacks and abuse by peacekeepers; protecting people in peacekeepers' care from attacks and abuses by third-parties; and protecting the local population from attacks and abuses by third parties.

1

Historical Review of Civilian Protection by UN Peacekeepers

1. Introduction

Armed forces deployed into a conflict zone are subject to a range of laws, rules, and principles, derived principally from international law and the laws of the force's home State. Troops' protection obligations towards the local population are derived mainly from the humanitarian provisions of the laws of armed conflict and international human rights law, but troops' obligations, in particular the circumstances in which they may use force, are also governed by their Rules of Engagement (ROE), which, in turn, are governed by the operation's mandate in addition to international and domestic law. Whilst civilian protection obligations arise in relation to all military operations, the obligations of peacekeepers (broadly defined to include those engaged in peace support and peace enforcement operations) are of particular significance since they are normally deployed on behalf of organizations representing the international or a regional community. There is a high onus on peacekeepers to conduct themselves in a way that commands respect: standing by in the face of war crimes and crimes against humanity is incompatible with that aspiration.

This chapter explores the extent to which historically there has been an expectation on the part of the UN, the international community and local communities, that peacekeepers have some obligation to try and protect civilians from crimes against humanity, war crimes and other serious abuses of their human rights; and the extent to which this expectation was fulfilled. It discusses the theoretical development of peacekeeping and its evolution in practice, focusing in particular on the tension between on the one hand, respect for State sovereignty, the consensual nature of peacekeeping and the importance of remaining impartial as between the warring parties; and the need to be prepared to use force to protect civilians from crimes against humanity, war crimes and other serious abuses of their human rights, on the other hand. It explores the gradual evolution from consciously non-interventionist principles of peacekeeping, in which protection obligations were viewed as intrinsic to the nature of peacekeeping, in a similar way that they are to the work of firemen or policemen, but were not specifically addressed; to the explicit authorization of protection as the norm for peacekeeping mandates, albeit on highly qualified terms, but often with Chapter VII authorization (which allows the Security Council to override Member States' non-consent where it has determined that there is a threat to international peace and security). This development was triggered to a large extent by the international outcry at the repeated failures of the UN to prevent genocide and other terrible crimes against humanity during the 1990s in particular. It paralleled the gradual emergence and acceptance of the 'responsibility to protect' as a norm binding on international and regional organizations and their member States. The two developments have evolved in response to the same problems, and since peacekeeping is the main means by which the UN deploys forces it is inevitable that there are cross linkages between them, but the protection obligations of peacekeepers are distinct from the 'responsibility to protect' and they relate to different regimes of the law governing the use of force.

The *ius ad bellum*[1] concerns the law governing when it is permissible for a State or international organization to use force against another State; these rules are principally to be found in the United Nations' Charter. The *ius in bello* deals with the laws governing the conduct of an armed conflict. The law governing the conduct of armed conflict is unaffected by whether or not recourse to force is lawful under the *ius ad bellum*: however, this does not mean that the two realms are totally independent. The Charter restrictions on the use of force by States have played an important role in the development of the rules governing the use of force by troops, particularly in the context of peacekeeping. Peacekeeping was an innovation that developed after the adoption of the Charter in response to the inability of the permanent members of the Security Council to agree on anything, especially the use of military force, during the Cold War. Since peacekeeping was not envisaged at the time of the drafting of the Charter its principles were not debated and no rules governing it were included. Dag Hammarskjöld, who was Secretary-General when the very first peacekeeping operations were deployed, drafted some guiding principles and took care to try and ensure that they fitted within the Charter regime. They remain the bedrock of peacekeeping today; but they have evolved and have become qualified. One of the primary reasons for the changes in approach has been recognition that peacekeepers have a role in protecting the local community from deliberate attacks and atrocities.

2. The Early Development of Peacekeeping

Operations in the nature of peacekeeping have a long history predating the adoption of the Charter[2] but the articulation of general principles of peacekeeping,

[1] This body of law as it has developed since the Pact of Paris, August 27, 1928, (a treaty providing for the renunciation of war as an instrument of national policy) is sometimes referred to as the *ius contra bellum* since it outlaws the use of force other than in exceptional circumstances, primarily those set out in the UN Charter.

[2] N MacQueen, *Peacekeeping and the International System* (Routledge London & New York 2006), ch 2 'Peacekeeping before the UN'.

and recognition that it provides a distinct contribution to the maintenance of international peace and security, first arose in relation to operations authorized by the United Nations (UN).[3] Whilst peacekeeping in the second-half of the twentieth-century was dominated by the UN, today NATO and regional organizations, are increasingly likely to be involved.[4] In the first decade of the twenty-first century the African Union (AU), the Economic Community of West African States (ECOWAS), the European Union (EU), and the North Atlantic Treaty Organization (NATO) all deployed major operations of their own and are currently making efforts to increase their capacities in this area.[5]

Since peacekeeping is not provided for in the Charter and since every military operation is a unique response to particular circumstances, practice and doctrine have evolved (and continue to evolve), in response to each operation; consequently there is no universally agreed definition of peacekeeping.[6] As Major General Indar Jit Rikhye[7] has observed 'only the experience of the UN and regional organizations can establish the limits of the concept.'[8] The UN website on peacekeeping comments that:

> With the end of the Cold War, the strategic context for UN peacekeeping dramatically changed, prompting the Organization to shift and expand its field operations from 'traditional' missions involving strictly military tasks, to complex 'multidimensional' enterprises designed to ensure the implementation of comprehensive peace agreements and assist in laying the foundations for sustainable peace. Today's peacekeepers undertake a wide variety of complex tasks, from helping to build sustainable institutions of governance, to human rights monitoring, to security sector reform, to the disarmament, demobilization and reintegration of former combatants.[9]

However, whilst modern peacekeeping operations undertake a wide variety of tasks, many of which are civilian rather than military in nature, the military

[3] UN Peacekeeping evolved during the Cold War as an alternative means of managing relations between the Member States, because superpower opposition prevented the Security Council from reaching the consensus needed to authorize enforcement action. Military units were deployed to mitigate the effects of local violence and to assist the parties in maintaining peace, but only with the consent of the parties to the conflict. They were normally commanded and controlled by the Secretary-General. M Bothe 'Peacekeeping' in B Simma (ed), *The Charter of the United Nations: A Commentary* (2nd edn Oxford, Oxford University Press 2002), 662 [7]; M Berdal, 'The UN Security Council and Peacekeeping' in *The UN Security Council and War: The Evolution of Thought and Practice since 1945* (Oxford Oxford University Press 2008) eds V Lowe, A Roberts, J Welsh, D Zaum, 174, 176; United Nations Department of Peacekeeping Operations, *General Guidelines for Peacekeeping Operations* (United Nations New York 1995), [2–3].

[4] KP Coleman, *International Organizations and Peace Enforcement: The Politics of Legitimacy* (Cambridge University Press Cambridge 2007), 286.

[5] United Nations Peacekeeping Operations Principles and Guidelines, Capstone Doctrine, Consultation Draft 3, 29 June 2007, [18].

[6] JM Guehenno, 'On the Challenges and Achievements of Reforming the UN Peace Operations' (2002) 9 International Peacekeeping, 69, 69.

[7] Former military advisor to Secretary-Generals Dag Hammarskjöld and U Thant from 1957 to 1967and subsequently served as the Secretary General's Special Representative.

[8] IJ Rikhe, *The Theory and Practice of Peacekeeping* (C Hurst & Co, London 1984), 2.

[9] <http://www.un.org/Depts/dpko/dpko/>.

is still the dominant component of most missions. Various terminologies have been adopted to distinguish some of the more complex peacekeeping operations undertaken since the 1990s from those conducted during the Cold War, but there is no universal agreement on these new terminologies.[10] The UK's most recent *Draft National Doctrine on The Military Contribution to Peace Support Operations*, (which is intended to replace JWP 3–50, the doctrine adopted in 2004), distinguishes between peacekeeping (defined as an activity 'generally undertaken in accordance with the principles of Chapter VI of the UN Charter in order to monitor and facilitate the implementation of a peace agreement',) and peace enforcement, (defined as an activity which 'normally takes place under the principles of Chapter VII of the UN Charter... is coercive in nature and is conducted when the consent of all parties to the conflict has not been achieved or might be uncertain.') However, the draft doctrine notes that:

> the boundaries between PE and PK are blurred and the terms should not be used in isolation to rigidly enforce limits on the conduct of the PS [Peace Support] themed operation. Flexibility is required to avoid actors' thinking being unnecessarily constrained by terminology.[11]

Similarly the UN's Peacekeeping Operations Principles and Guidelines observes that the:

> boundaries between conflict prevention, peacemaking, peacekeeping, peacebuilding and peace enforcement have become increasingly blurred... Peace operations are rarely limited to one type of activity whether United Nations-led or conducted by non-United Nations actors.[12]

For the purposes of this study the broad definition of peacekeeping adopted by the International Peace Academy provides a useful base. Peacekeeping is:

> the prevention, containment, moderation and termination of hostilities between or within states through the medium of third party intervention, organised and directed

[10] This book does not discuss the various distinctions between classical peacekeeping; first, second and third generation peacekeeping; peace-support and peace-building, since these have been discussed in depth by numerous authors. The term peacekeeping will normally be used except where the context, or the terminology used in the source materials, render a different term appropriate. Peace enforcement differs from other types of peace operations in that it does not require the consent of the parties; it requires Chapter VII authorization; and it may involve the use of military force at strategic level. However civilian protection issues also arise in peace enforcement and moreover the distinction between robust peacekeeping and peace enforcement is not always clear: hence this study also looks at some peace enforcement operations where protection issues have been raised.

[11] Ministry of Defence UK, Development, Concepts and Doctrine Centre, *Draft UK National Doctrine that will replace JWP 3–50 The Military Contribution to Peace Support Operations* (MOD Shrivenham 16 April 2008) [0120–0122].

[12] United Nations Peacekeeping Operations, Principles and Guidelines (Department of Peacekeeping Operations Best Practices Unit New York 2008), 18.

internationally, using multinational military, police and civilian personnel to restore and maintain peace.[13]

From its inception peacekeeping was expected to fulfil a highly idealized role in the maintenance of international peace and security, a role that must be viewed within the context of the UN's undertaking 'to save succeeding generations from the scourge of war' and 'to reaffirm faith in fundamental human rights, in the dignity and worth of the human person, in the equal rights of men and women and of nations large and small.'[14] The choice of the term 'peacekeeping' is in itself aspirational, for traditionally peacekeepers were rarely given the power to *keep* the peace. Strict adherence to the operational principles laid down by Secretary-General Dag Hammarskjöld (which form the basis of what is generally referred to as traditional or classical peacekeeping), along with the limited capacity and resources of most missions, has meant that frequently peacekeepers have been able to do little more than *observe* the peace;[15] yet their role was envisaged in terms much greater than their capacity, mandates, and place in the scheme of international law, implied. Sir Pierson Dixon, who was the British Ambassador to the United Nations at the time of the creation of the first UN peacekeeping operation, the United Nations Emergency Force in Egypt (UNEF 1),[16] described it as 'a sort of peace brigade to put out world fires under the general direction of the head of the world organization.'[17] Peacekeepers were not expected to need to use force to secure compliance, partly because troops would only be deployed with the consent of the host State but also because it was assumed that their authority would be immediately respected on the basis that they are emissaries of the United Nations. A peacekeeping force was expected to achieve its goals 'not through military combat but by the simple fact of its presence.'[18] In keeping with their role as the world organization's 'firemen', it was envisaged that peacekeepers would treat all States, and their peoples, with equal respect and act impartially in their dealings with them. This task has proved more complex than was initially envisaged in part because of the failure to appreciate, or at any rate

[13] IJ Rikhye, *The Theory and Practice of Peacekeeping* (n 8) 1–2; Rikhye was founding president of the IPA from 1969 to 1989. During his presidency he focused the organization on the training of military and civilian professionals in peacekeeping, and it became the 'de facto UN peacekeeping training establishment': U Thant Institute <http://www.uthantinstitute.org/5-27-07-indar-jit-rikhye>.

[14] Charter of the United Nations, Preamble.

[15] JT O'Neill and N Rees, *United Nations Peacekeeping in the Post-Cold War Era* (Routledge Abingdon New York 2005) 30.

[16] Two earlier observer missions, theUN Truce Supervision Organization (UNTSO) deployed to the *Middle East* and the UN Military Observer Group in India and Pakistan (UNMOGIP), are also classified as peacekeeping operations.

[17] Telegram from Dixon to Foreign Office, Emergency Secret, 5 Nov. 1956, FO 371/121748 cited in WR Louis, 'The Suez Crisis and the British Dilemma at the United Nations' in *The United Nations Security Council and War: The Evolution of Thought and Practice since 1945* (n 3) 280, 295.

[18] R Thakur, *United Nations Peacekeeping In Lebanon: United Nations Authority and Multi-National Force* (Westview Press Boulder 1987), 57.

to acknowledge, the potential incongruity in a concept of equality that embraces States, peoples, and individuals on the same conceptual plane.[19]

3. Civilian Protection in UN Peacekeeping Operations during the Cold War

The United Nations Emergency Force (UNEF I), deployed along the Egypt–Israel border after the Suez Crisis, is generally regarded as the first UN peacekeeping operation although the term was not used at the time. The UNEF mission did not involve extensive civilian protection but because it established core peacekeeping principles it is key to understanding the approach taken by the UN when faced with protection issues in subsequent operations.

Deployment was authorized in November 1956 by the General Assembly[20] under the Uniting for Peace Procedure,[21] following the vetoing, by Britain and France, of Security Council resolutions calling for the withdrawal of Israeli forces from the Sinai.[22] This was the first time the Uniting for Peace procedure had been used. Mindful of Charter law governing enforcement action, Secretary-General Hammarskjöld was careful to ensure that the force was deployed with the consent of the States concerned and that its military functions did not exceed 'those necessary to secure peaceful conditions on the assumption that the parties to the conflict take all necessary steps for compliance with the recommendations of the General Assembly.'[23]

In October 1958, Hammarskjöld published a study of the lessons learned from the operation,[24] in which he set out, prescriptively, the 'basic principles and rules'

[19] The Preamble to the UN Charter refers to 'the equal rights of men and women and of nations large and small' in one phrase, as if these were parallel concepts.

[20] GA Res 1001 (ES-I) 7 November 1956; Also GA Res 1000 (ES-I) 5 November 1956.

[21] Under the Uniting for Peace resolution, the Assembly granted itself the power to deploy military force when this is 'necessary to maintain or restore international peace and security' and the Security Council, 'because of lack of unanimity fails to exercise its primary responsibility for the maintenance of international peace and security' (GA Res 377 (V), 5th Sess, 302nd Plen Meeting, 3 November 1950, A/PV. 302, 341 at 347), despite protests by the Soviet Union that this undermined Chapter VII of the Charter (GAOR 5th Sess, 301st Plen Meeting, 2 November 1950, at 328). The International Court of Justice subsequently advised that the Assembly had 'secondary' responsibility for peace and security and if use of the veto prevented the Council from acting, the Assembly could organize peacekeeping operations at the request or with the consent of the States concerned: *Certain Expenses of the United Nations*, Advisory Opinion of 20 July 1962, ICJ Reports 1962, 151, 163.

[22] Draft resolutions S/3710 + Corr.1 S/PV.749 and footnote 2 and S/3713/Rev.1; Official Security Council records S/PV.749 and S/PV.750/ Rev.1; *The United Nations Security Council and War: The Evolution of Thought and Practice since 1945* (n 3), Appendix 5.

[23] Second and Final Report of the Secretary-General on the plan for an emergency international United Nations force requested in resolution 998 (ES-1), adopted by the General Assembly on 4 November 1956 (UN Doc A/3302 of 6 November 1956), [9], [12]; UNEF was not deployed to the Israeli side of the border since Israel did not give its consent.

[24] After UNEF's initial objective of supervising the withdrawal of foreign forces had been completed, troop numbers were reduced but the force stayed on to help maintain stability in the region

that had been devised for UNEF as the basis for future peacekeeping operations, including those authorized by the Security Council.[25] These provide that peacekeeping operations should only be conducted with the consent of the parties to the conflict; that peacekeepers should be impartial; that force should only be used to the minimum extent necessary and that normally troops should only permitted to open fire in self-defence.[26] These principles reflected the concern of many UN Member States to ensure that the power of the Security Council to authorize coercive action in response to threats to international peace and security should not permit intervention into the internal affairs of a State, for fear that such power might be abused by strong States to advance their interests to the detriment of the independence of weaker States.

This concern featured strongly in debates in the General Assembly and other fora during the years of decolonization. In 1965 the General Assembly adopted a declaration stating that '[n]o State has the right to intervene, directly or indirectly, for any reason whatever, in the internal or external affairs of any other State.'[27] Similar affirmations were made in 1971 in the Declaration on Principles of International Law concerning Friendly Relations and Co-operation among States in Accordance with the Charter of the United Nations,[28] and again in 1975 in the Definition of Aggression.[29] Many of the less powerful States feared that human rights law, a relatively new body of international law that developed rapidly in the latter part of the twentieth century, might be used as a means of legitimizing intervention. The Declaration on the Inadmissibility of Intervention and Interference in the Internal Affairs of States, adopted in 1982, specifically condemns 'the distortion of human rights issues as a means of interference in the internal affairs of States.'[30]

In the context of these concerns it is unsurprising that the principles developed for peacekeeping placed heavy emphasis on consent; on constraining the use of force to self-defence; and on the need to be seen to be impartial. However, even as early as the mid-1960s there was already criticism of 'the disturbing lack of imagination . . . and a tendency towards repetitious rigidity' in the analyses of international peacekeeping 'structured heavily and rather inflexibly by

by providing a buffer between Israel and Egypt: N MacQueen, *Peacekeeping and the International System* (n 2), 73; DH Chapman, 'International Law: The United Nations Emergency Force: Legal Status', 57 *Michigan Law Review* 1 (Nov., 1958), 56, 57.

[25] Report of the Secretary-General: Summary Study of the Experience Derived from the Establishment and Operation of the Force, UN Doc A/3943 of 9 Oct. 1958.

[26] ibid [155], [166–167], [179].

[27] *Declaration on the Inadmissibility of Intervention in the Domestic Affairs of States and the Protection of Their Independence and Sovereignty*, annexed to GA Res. 2131 (XX) 21/12/1965. UN doc A/6014 (1965), 11–12, [1] [5].

[28] *Declaration on Principles of International Law concerning Friendly Relations and Co-operation among States in Accordance with the Charter of the United Nations* annexed to GA Res. 2625 (XXV) 24/10/1970 UN Doc A/8028 (1971), 121–124.

[29] *Definition of Aggression*, annexed to GA Res. 3314 (XXIX) 14/12/1974 UN Doc A/9631 (1975) [142–144].

[30] *The Declaration on the Inadmissibility of Intervention and Interference in the Internal Affairs of States*, annexed to GA Res. 36/103 9/12/1981 UN Doc A/36/51 (1982), 78–80.

a set of concepts, principles and practices stemming from the Hammarskjöld administration at the United Nations.'[31] The criticism stemmed in part from the experience of peacekeepers in the Congo in the early 1960s, a conflict in which Hammarskjöld himself lost his life on a visit to negotiate a truce in the civil war when the plane in which he was travelling crashed.[32] In contrast to most Cold War peacekeeping operations which were mainly tasked with monitoring ceasefires, maintaining buffer zones and undertaking border patrols, ONUC was deployed to deal with a disastrously managed decolonization process in which outside interests were heavily implicated.[33] Operating without explicit Chapter VII enforcement powers[34] troops found themselves having to deal with a number of problems that had not been anticipated in Hammarskjöld's study on the lessons learned from UNEF, in particular the need to provide human rights protection, the robust use of force in 'self-defence', and uncertainties with regard to consent following the secession of territory and the outbreak of civil war.

3.1 Civilian Protection by the United Nations Operation in the Congo (ONUC)

Shortly after the Security Council agreed to the deployment of ONUC, Hammarskjöld arranged that on first arrival in the Congo every member of the force was to be issued with a text setting out their impartial role and protective function, and informing them that:

> You serve as members of an international force. It is a peacekeeping force, not a fighting force... Protection against acts of violence is to be given to all the people, white and black. You carry arms, but they are *only* to be used in self-defence. You are in the Congo to help *everyone*, to harm no-one.[35]

Thus minimum use of force and protective duties were conceived as related elements central to the core concept of the force as peaceful, deployed to help mitigate

[31] OR Young, *Trends in International Peacekeeping* (Center on International Studies Princeton University 1966), 1 cited in R Gowen and I Johnstone, *New Challenges for Peacekeeping: Protection, Peace-building and the 'War on Terror'* (International Peace Academy 2007), 4.

[32] 17 September 1961.

[33] Just under twenty thousand troops were deployed at the height of the operation: *The United Nations Security Council and War: The Evolution of Thought and Practice since 1945* (n 3), Appendix 1.

[34] EM Miller, 'Legal Aspects of the United Nations Action in the Congo' (1961) 55 AJIL 1, 3–9; TM Franck, 'The United Nations Law in Africa: The Congo Operation as a Case Study' (1962) 27 Law & Contemporary Problems 632, 644.

[35] Press Release CO/15 July 19, 1960; GIAD Draper, 'The Legal Limitations Upon the Employment of Weapons by the United Nations Force in the Congo' (1963) 12 International and Comparative Law Quarterly 387, 399; U Thant in his Final Report to the Security Council on UNEF described the peacekeeper as a 'military man' who 'faced with a concept of soldiering which is entirely foreign to anything taught him in his national service' must demonstrate out of the ordinary qualities 'Though armed, he could use force only in the last resort in self-defence. He had no enemy. Under provocation he had to show discipline and restraint; his tasks had to be carried through with persuasion, tact, calm and soldierly bearing, but, if humanly possible, never by force.' United Nations, Final Report by Secretary-General U Thant on UNEF, UN Document A/6672 12 July 1967, [16].

the effects of violence, not to fight a war. Hammarskjöld's first report to the Council on the 18 July 1960, which drew heavily on his Summary Study of the UNEF experience, set out ONUC's use of force policy:

Men engaged in the operations may never take the initiative in the use of armed force, but are entitled to respond with force to an attack with arms, including attempts to use force to make them withdraw from positions they occupy under orders from their Commander, acting under the Security Council and within the scope of its resolution. The basic element involved is clearly the prohibition against any initiative in the use of force.[36]

Protection of civilians was to be achieved through the use of inter-positional strategies. Operations Directive No 6 of 28 October 1960 provided that if all attempts at peaceful settlement failed, 'threatened areas' may:

be declared as under UN protection by means of the deployment of UN troops... UN commanders will announce that the entry into such area of marauders or armed bands as the case may be, will be opposed by force, if necessary in the interests of law and order.

If, notwithstanding these warnings, attempts are made to attack, envelop or infiltrate the UN positions thus jeopardising the safety of UN troops, they will defend themselves and their positions by resisting and driving off such attackers with such minimum use of force, including firing, as may be necessary.

However, by mid-December 1960 as the conflict intensified, Hammarskjöld had concluded that if an 'acute civil war' was to develop peacekeepers might find themselves in a position in which they could not do nothing, nor could they act: passivity would be unacceptable but even an inter-positional strategy of providing protection would be interpreted, both locally and internationally, as supporting one or other side, which would violate the principle of non-intervention:

Should then the United Nations try to interpose itself? That seems to be what should follow from the general rule of non-interference, as the alternative of complete passivity would have to be ruled out... Practically every act of interposition in such a situation might lend itself to the interpretation that it was taken in order to help one side or the other—and that not only locally but in an international sense, due to the support that may be given from the outside to the various parties in the Congo. Also this would represent an impossible position for the United Nations.

He considered that in such a situation the only option would be to withdraw:

My conclusion is that, just as I have had to exclude the taking sides or passivity, I anticipate it would be impossible to pursue a policy of interposition. Therefore, were a situation for the United Nations of the kind I have described develop, I would have to put up to the Security Council the question whether the United Nations Force should not withdraw.[37]

[36] United Nations, First Report of the Secretary-General on the Implementation of Security Council Resolution S/4387 of 14 July 1960, UN Document S/4389, 18 July 1960, [179].

[37] Address to the General Assembly, GAOR, 15th Session, 975 plenary meeting, cited in R Higgins, *United Nations Peacekeeping 1946–1967, Documents and Commentary, III, Africa* (Oxford University Press Oxford 1980), 50; Herbert Nicholas, in a 1963 article published in International Organization, observed that 'no United Nations operation in the Congo could

However, when armed bands began killing civilians in the provinces of Kasai and Katanga (which had declared their independence), Hammarskjöld, without consulting with the Security Council[38] authorized ONUC to use force to stop the killings on the grounds that '[p]rohibition from intervention in internal conflicts cannot be considered to apply to the senseless slaughter of civilians or fighting arising from tribal hostilities.'[39] He even suggested that it might be necessary for ONUC to disarm military units in order to restore the law and order necessary to secure the protection of civilians:

> emphasis should be placed...on the protection of the lives of the civilian population in the spirit of the Universal Declaration of Human Rights and the Genocide Convention; that might necessitate a temporary disarming of military units which, in the view of the circumstances, were an obstacle to the restoration of law and order.[40]

ONUC succeeded in reducing the attacks against civilians (without undertaking disarmament)[41] by establishing protected areas and by interposing themselves between vulnerable civilians and armed attackers.[42] At least 35,000 people were protected within refugee camps and protected areas.[43]

After the murder of the Prime Minister, Patrice Lumumba, the Security Council began adopting more robust mandates[44] and ONUC's interpretation

possibly avoid contact with Congolese life at every point—and in circumstances where every contact (or indeed no contact) inevitably involved interference.' He concluded that 'in almost all the power contests of Congo politics the United Nations could not avoid taking decisions which favour[ed] one side or the other.' H Nicholas, 'UN Peace Forces and the Changing Globe: The Lesson of Suez and Congo' 17 International Organization 2 (1963), 321, 332, 338.

[38] During this period since the Security Council had become deadlocked, unable to agree on an appropriate response to the conflict, the General Assembly had taken responsibility under the Uniting for Peace Procedure. Hammarskjöld did however consult with the Congo Advisory Committee comprising all the troop contributing States: B Urquhart, *Hammarskjöld* (Harper Colophon Books New York 1984) 438.

[39] B Urquhart, *Hammarskjöld* (n 38), 438.

[40] Annual Report of the Secretary-General on the Work of the Organization, June 16 1960–June 16 1961, 16th Session, UN Doc A/4800, 11.

[41] Findlay observes that there are no reports of ONUC disarming military units or of it using significant force to protect civilians: T Findlay *The Use of Force in Peace Operations* (Oxford University Press Oxford 2002), 69.

[42] Operations Directive No 8 of February 1961 provided that 'Where feasible, every protection will be afforded to unarmed groups who may be subjected by any armed party to acts of violence likely to lead to loss of life. In such cases, UN troops will interpose themselves, using armed force if necessary, to prevent such loss of life. ONUC, Operations Directive No 8 February 1961, UN Archives DAG13/1.6.5.0.0. Ops Directives August 1960-January 1964, Box 3; Reproduced in T Findlay, *The Use of Force in Peace Operations* (n 41), Appendix 2, 414; United Nations, *The Blue Helmets: A Review of United Nations Peace-keeping* (3rd edn, UN Dept of Public Information New York 1996), 193.

[43] Section 9 of Operations Directive No 6 'Security and maintenance of law and order' 28 October 1960, UN Archives DAG13/1.6.5.0.0. Ops Directives August 1960–January 1964, Box 3; reproduced in T Findlay, *The Use of Force in Peace Operations* (n 41), Appendix 2 Rules of Engagement, 412.

[44] Following the murder of Prime Minister Patrice Lumumba in December 1960 the Council managed to patch up its differences sufficiently to take back responsibility for the

of 'self-defence' became virtually indistinguishable from enforcement action. In February 1961, the Council authorized ONUC to take 'all appropriate measures to prevent the occurrence of civil war in the Congo, including... the use of force, if necessary, in the last resort.'[45] In November 1961, following months of heavy fighting, the Council adopted a further resolution authorizing 'vigorous action' against all foreign military and paramilitary personnel and political advisors not under United Nations command.'[46] In December 1962, following attacks on its supply lines, ONUC took decisive action, which included air attacks,[47] to end the Katanganese secession.[48] Nevertheless Acting Secretary-General U Thant insisted that the measures taken came within the remit of self-defence:

The military action was forced upon the United Nations by a series of deliberate attacks on United Nations officials, soldiers and military officers in Katanga, involving wanton and brutal assault, cold-blooded murder and seizure of such personnel; the setting up of road-blocks impeding the freedom of movement in Elizabethville and attacks in strength on positions held by the United Nations elsewhere in Katanga, all of which were clearly part of a plan. The United Nations action was taken with the greatest reluctance... The purpose of the present military operations is to regain and assure our freedom of movement, restore law and order, and to ensure that for the future United Nations officials in Katanga are not subject to attacks; and meanwhile to react vigorously in self-defence to every assault on our present positions, by all the means available to us.[49]

Findlay comments that:

What is most extra-ordinary about the Congo experience is that, having obtained elements of what might today be considered a peace enforcement mandate, ONUC went on to actually conduct an enforcement operation—in the sense of defeating a breakaway regime and reasserting the authority of the central government—while all along

operation from the General Assembly; UN headquarters had refused Ghanian peacekeepers permission to take Lumumba into protective custody on the grounds that it would breach the principle of impartiality: Annual Report of the Secretary-General on the Work of the Organization, June 16 1960–June 16 1961, 16th Session, UN Doc A/4800, 27; A Sitowski, *UN Peacekeeping Myth and Reality* (Praeger Security International London & Westport 2006), 69–70;

[45] SC Res. 161 of 21 Feb. 1961; N MacQueen, *The United Nations since 1945: Peacekeeping and the Cold War* (Addison Westley Longman Ltd New York 1999), 41.

[46] SC Res. 169 of 24 Nov. 1961.

[47] AW Dorn and DJH Bell, 'Intelligence and Peacekeeping: The UN Operation in the Congo 1960–64' (Spring 1995) 2 *International Peacekeeping* 1, 11, 12.

[48] The secession ended in January 1963; ONUC operations were then slowly phased out during 1963 and withdrawal completed in June 1964, but largely for financial reasons; by September the violence and chaos had returned. T Findlay, *The Use of Force in Peace Operations* (n 41), 81; A Sitowski, *UN Peacekeeping Myth and Reality* (n 44), 73; JT O'Neill and N Rees, *United Nations Peacekeeping in the Post-Cold War Era* (n 15), 70–71.

[49] 10 December 1961 quoted by GIAD Draper, in 'The Legal Limitations Upon the Employment of Weapons by the United Nations Force in the Congo' (n 35), 406.

denying that it was doing more than acting in self-defence and preserving its freedom of movement.[50]

Gerald Draper, in a contemporaneous assessment, observed that it 'is a sobering thought to reflect how far beyond the limits' of Hammarskjöld's first directive to the troops[51] ONUC was subsequently compelled to go,[52] and argued that the expansion of the concept of self-defence to encompass the right to defend the force's freedom of movement:[53]

> amounted, in practice, to a considerable extension of the circumstances in which self-defensive force might be legitimately used by the United Nations Force. It cannot be over-emphasised that this right marked a notable departure from that of the individual soldier in the Force to defend his person and his weapons after he had been subjected to an attack upon him or them.
>
> We are thus confronted with a telling example of the expanding nature of the right of self-defence. It is an interesting and not entirely academic point to determine at what point that right has yielded up all that it can provide and the moment when it becomes necessary to invoke the right of the Force to take all military action necessary to carry out its mandate.[54]

The Congo operation 'was long regarded as a unique event that would never happen again' but 'that assumption, like so many others, has proven to be a casualty of the end of the Cold War.'[55] Nicholas Herbert's comments on ONUC, in a 1963 article, now seem highly prescient:

> It is often said that the Congo is *sui generis*. It certainly differs from any situation the United Nations had to tackle before, but is it so different from what may arise in the future?... it is true that the United Nations is not designed to cope with such situations;

[50] T Findlay, *The Use of Force in Peace Operations* (n 41), 86; Similarly Simon Chesterman comments that although the UN held that it acted entirely within the self-defence norm, the operation became 'in strategy and tactics, indistinguishable from a standard military campaign.' S Chesterman, *The Use of Force in UN Peace Operations*, External Study for the UN Department of Peacekeeping Best Practices Unit (New York Law School New York 2003), 7.

[51] Instructing them that they were in the Congo to 'help *everyone*' and that their arms were '*only* to be used in self-defence': Press Release CO/15 July 19, 1960; GIAD Draper, 'The Legal Limitations Upon the Employment of Weapons by the United Nations Force in the Congo' (n 35), 399.

[52] GIAD Draper, 'The Legal Limitations Upon the Employment of Weapons by the United Nations Force in the Congo' (n 35), 399.

[53] Granted ONUC by an Agreement between the United Nations and the Republic of the Congo (Leopoldville) relating to the legal status, facilities, privileges and immunities of the United Nations Organization in the Congo, New York, November 27 1961 S/5004, UNTS Vol 414, 229, [30].

[54] GIAD Draper, 'The Legal Limitations Upon the Employment of Weapons by the United Nations Force in the Congo' (n 35), 401.

[55] American Bar Association, Section of International Law and Practice Standing Committee on World Order under Law, Report to the House of Delegates, Safety of UN and Associated Personnel: Recommendation, 31 International Lawyer, 195, 197.

as an international organization it is built on the assumption that viable states are the entities with which it has to deal. This palliates failure but it cannot excuse inaction. Future Congos cannot be ignored simply because they were not dreamed of in the philosophy of San Francisco.[56]

Arguably, ONUC's lack of uniqueness in terms of many of the problems it faced surfaced much earlier than the end of the Cold War. Two operations first launched in the Cold War era are worth noting in the context of an analysis of civilian protection by peacekeepers: the UN Peacekeeping Force in Cyprus (UNFICYP), and the United Nations Interim Force in Lebanon (UNIFIL), both of which are still deployed. In the early years of the UNFICYP operation troops were frequently shot at, and killed, whilst trying to protect civilians using inter-positional strategies; but in comparison with the Congo, the conflict was relatively contained and is currently stable although the political situation remains unresolved.[57] UNIFIL, however, found itself deployed into a State where the government was unable to exercise any authority, where both foreign forces and local factions were engaged in conflicts on several fronts with high levels of violence, much of it against civilians, and which included massacres and deliberate destruction of homes and livelihoods. A decade on from the Congo conflict the right of self-defence, as applied to UN forces, had been formally expanded to encompass defence of the mission through Secretary-General Kurt Waldheim's 1973 Report on the Implementation of Security Council Resolution 340 (on UNEF II).[58] A number of commentators, including Trevor Findlay and Simon Chesterman, have observed that this Report represented a 'sea change' in UN doctrine on the use of force,[59] since allowing

[56] H Nicholas, 'UN Peace Forces and the Changing Globe: The Lesson of Suez and Congo' (n 37), 335.

[57] The major civilian protection issue faced by UNFICYP troops were kidnappings, taking of hostages and ethnic cleansing. Protection of civilians was achieved by creating and defending zones in which neither party's armed forces was permitted to enter and by interposing peacekeepers between the hostile groups. UNFICYP also provided escorts for essential civilians and supplies and patrols to protect harvesting and to guard government property and instituted procedures to ensure regularity of postal services and payment of social benefits: IJ Rikhe, *The Theory and Practice of Peacekeeping* (n 8), 95; KT Birgisson, 'United Nations Peacekeeping Force in Cyprus' in WJ Durch (ed), *The Evolution of UN Peacekeeping: Case Studies and Comparative Analysis* (St Martin's Press, New York 1993), 232; United Nations, *The Blue Helmets: A Review of United Nations Peacekeeping* (n 42), 157; UNFICYP was permitted to use force only self-defence, but, this included responding to attempts to forcibly prevent troops from carrying out their mission. Aide Mémoire of the Secretary-General concerning some questions relating to the function and operation of the United Nations Peacekeeping Force in Cyprus, 10 April 1964, UN Doc S/5653 of 11 April 1964, [16], [18], [20–21].

[58] United Nations, Report of the Secretary-General on the implementation of Security Council resolution 340 (1973), UN document S/11052/Rev.1, 27 October 1973; T Findlay, *The Use of Force in Peace Operations* (n 41), 100.

[59] T Findlay, *The Use of Force in Peace Operations* (n 41), 100; S Chesterman, *The Use of Force in UN Peace Operations* (n 50), 7.

peacekeepers to take positive action in defence of its mission 'is no different from allowing them to enforce it.'[60] However, this sea change has had little effect on UNIFIL, deployed the following year; even with a Chapter VII style mandate, which arguably it now has (since 2006), UNIFIL is in no position to enforce its mission.

3.2 The UN Interim Force in Lebanon (UNIFIL)

In March 1978 when Israel invaded Lebanon in Operation Litani the Security Council authorized the deployment of UNIFIL[61] at 'the request of the government of Lebanon'.[62] Israel eventually withdrew, although its influence remained through its proxy force the Southern Lebanon Army, but UNIFIL stayed to monitor the Israel-Lebanon armistice line and to assist 'the Government of Lebanon in ensuring the return of its effective authority in the area'[63] and to '[s]upervise the cessation of hostilities, ensure the peaceful character of the area of the operation, control movement and take all measures deemed necessary to assure the effective restoration of Lebanese sovereignty.'[64]

These expectations were unrealistically optimistic. UNIFIL was deployed on the unfounded assumption 'that the parties to the conflict w[ould] take all the necessary steps for compliance with the decisions of the Council.'[65] UNIFIL did not have the support of a consensus in the Security Council[66] or of the parties. The Lebanese government, which is not a party to the conflict, had requested the deployment of the force but it had virtually no authority in the country and hence could not guarantee the force's freedom of movement or its safe conduct.[67]

[60] WJ Durch, 'The UN Operation in the Congo: 1960–1964', in W J Durch (ed), *The Evolution of UN Peacekeeping: Case Studies and Comparative Analysis* (n 57), 315, 349.

[61] SC Res. 425 and 426 of 19 Mar. 1978.

[62] SC Res. 425 of 19 Mar. 1978;

[63] SC Res. 425 of 19 Mar. 1978.

[64] Report of the Secretary-General on the implementation of Security Council resolution 425 (1978) (UN Doc S/12611 of 19 March 1978), [6].

[65] ibid [4](d).

[66] China did not participate in the adoption of UNIFIL's mandating resolutions; the Soviet Union abstained and the United States was not prepared to pressure Israel. The Soviet Union refused to contribute to UNIFIL's funding for eight years and during the late 1980s the United States made only partial contributions to its funding; a number of Arab, Latin and African States were also in arrears with their contributions: M Ghali, 'United Nations Interim Force in Lebanon 1978-Present' in WJ Durch (ed), *UN Peacekeeping. American Policy and the Uncivil Wars of the 1990s* (n 57), 181, 188; N MacQueen, *Peacekeeping and the International System* (n 2), 122; IJ Rikhe, *The Theory and Practice of Peacekeeping* (n 8), 111–112; Many of the force's contingents were ill-equipped: IJ Rikhe, *The Theory and Practice of Peacekeeping* (n 8), 105; EA Erskine, *Mission with UNIFIL: An African Soldier's Reflections*, (St Martins Press New York 1989), 49. In addition UNIFIL's first force commander Lieutenant-General Emmanuel Erskine believed that there 'was no way that contributing countries would be prepared to receive sealed coffins from Naqoura at their respective international airports on a daily basis' EA Erskine, *Mission with UNIFIL: An African Soldier's Reflections* (ibid 115).

[67] M Ghali, 'United Nations Interim Force in Lebanon 1978–Present' in WJ Durch (ed), *UN Peacekeeping. American Policy and the Uncivil Wars of the 1990s* (n 57), 181, 190; N MacQueen, *Peacekeeping and the International System* (n 2), 122.

Neither the Palestinian Liberation Organization (PLO) nor Israel had given their full consent to the mission. Moreover, there was disagreement between them as to UNIFIL's authorized areas of operation.[68] The warring local militias were not supportive of UNIFIL either.[69] Norrie MacQueen argues that:

Arguably, what was required in southern Lebanon at that time was a large enforcement operation capable of intimidating the local factions into compliance with its instructions and punishing them militarily if they failed to do what was demanded of them... With détente in decline, however, this was simply not feasible.[70]

However, the troops provided extensive humanitarian assistance in helping recover the remains of the dead, and those who had been buried under the debris of houses, for reburial and cleared farms of unexploded bombs.[71] It also provided training workshops in stonemasonry, carpentry and plumbing, so as to provide young people with an alternative to the carrying of AK47s.[72]

In June 1982 Israel invaded again, ignoring the presence of UNIFIL,[73] which then became the first peacekeeping force to operate in territory under foreign occupation.[74] Thousands of civilians were killed, many of them in aerial bombardments.[75] The Security Council responded by authorizing the expansion of UNIFIL's mandate to include 'ensuring the security of all the inhabitants of the area without discrimination.'[76] Humanitarian assistance and protection

[68] SC Resolutions 425 and 426 were unclear on this point. Paragraph 2c of the Report of the Secretary-General on the implementation of Security Council resolution 425 (UN Doc S/12611 of 19 March 1978) states that 'The Force will establish itself in an area of operation to be defined in the light of subparagraph *b*.' Subparagraph *b* states that 'The Force will confirm the withdrawal of Israeli forces, restore international peace and security and assist the Government of Lebanon in ensuring the return of its effective authority in the area.' The Israelis believed the force should deploy to all of Southern Lebanon (excepting Israel's border enclave) and the Palestinians believed that the force should deploy only to areas previously controlled by the Israeli defence forces: EA Erskine, *Mission with UNIFIL: An African Soldier's Reflections* (n 66), 36; M Ghali, 'United Nations Interim Force in Lebanon 1978–Present' in WJ Durch (ed), *UN Peacekeeping. American Policy and the Uncivil Wars of the 1990s* (n 57), 181, 188; R Murphy, 'UN Peacekeeping in Lebanon and the Use of Force' (1999) 6 International Peacekeeping 2, 38, 39.

[69] B Jones, 'The Security Council and the Arab-Israeli Wars: Responsibility without Power' in *The United Nations Security Council and War: The Evolution of Thought and Practice since 1945* (n 3), 298, 311; N MacQueen, *Peacekeeping and the International System* (n 2), 122; JH Allan, *Peacekeeping: Outspoken Observations by a Field Officer* (Praeger Westport London 1996), 71.

[70] N MacQueen, *Peacekeeping and the International System* (n 2), 123.

[71] EA Erskine, *Mission with UNIFIL: An African Soldier's Reflections* (n 66), 89, 43.

[72] ibid 90.

[73] Some UNIFIL battalions put up obstacles, which were forcibly removed or bulldozed by the Israeli Defence Forces, whose tank barrels were trained on UNIFIL soldiers during the invasion: United Nations, *The Blue Helmets: A Review of United Nations Peace-keeping* (n 42), 101.

[74] R Thakur, *United Nations Peacekeeping In Lebanon: United Nations Authority and Multi-National Force* (n 18), 64; UN Doc S/16713, 24 August 1984, letter from the representative of Lebanon to the Security Council President calling on Israel to comply with the provisions of Geneva Convention IV, Relative to the Protection of Civilians in Time of War, 1949.

[75] Human Rights Watch, *Civilian Pawns Laws of War Violations and the Use of Weapons on the Israel-Lebanon Border* (Human Rights Watch New York 1996).

[76] S/RES 523 18 October 1982; Also S/RES 511 18 June 1982; S/RES 519 17 August 1982; S/RES 521 19 September 1982; Some months prior to the Israeli invasion the Council had approved

then became UNIFIL's principal tasks.[77] UNIFIL has intervened to prevent violence against civilians and to prevent the demolition of their houses by interposing themselves between the civilians and the Israeli Defence Forces and by stationing themselves on the roofs of houses targeted for destruction.[78] In 1986 the Israeli Defence Forces attempted to expel all of the Shiite residents of the village of Kunin, apparently in retaliation for the abduction of two of their soldiers; but UNIFIL successfully prevented them from attacking other villages that were also threatened.[79] In 1996, in a report that was subsequently approved by the Security Council, the Secretary-General, Boutros Boutros-Ghali, recognized that although 'there has been no progress towards the implementation of UNIFIL's mandate... the Force's contribution to stability on the area and the protection it is able to afford its inhabitants remain important',[80] a view reiterated by Secretary-General Kofi Annan in his report of 21 July 2006.[81]

Following the escalation of the conflict in 2006, which resulted in around 1200 Lebanese and 160 Israeli deaths, and the destruction of much of Lebanon's infrastructure,[82] the Security Council authorized an extension of UNIFIL's humanitarian assistance mandate and an increase in its capacity to 15,000 military personnel. Resolution 1701 also authorized UNIFIL's transformation to an 'almost' Chapter VII mission.[83] The resolution does not refer to Chapter VII and does not use the words 'all necessary means.' However, it does recognize the crisis in Lebanon as a threat to international peace and security and authorizes UNIFIL 'to take all necessary action... to ensure that its area of operation is not utilized for

an increase in the Force size bringing it to about 7000 troops: SC Res 501 25 February 1982; A non-UN peacekeeping operation the Multi-National Force, headed by the United States, was deployed in August 1992, which assisted 7,500 Palestinians to move out of Beirut. After its withdrawal (10–13 September 1982) more than 300 Palestinian men, women and children were massacred by Phalangist militias in the refugee camps of Sabra and Shatila on 16–18 September 1982. Eye witness accounts indicated Israeli complicity. A second MNF was deployed to support the Lebanese government but withdrew in 1983 following a series of suicide bomb attacks in October of that year, which killed over 300 US and French troops: R Thakur, *United Nations Peacekeeping In Lebanon: United Nations Authority and Multi-National Force* (n 18), 95–105; N MacQueen, *Peacekeeping and the International System* (n 2), 125.

[77] United Nations, *The Blue Helmets: A Review of United Nations Peace-keeping* (n 42), 102.

[78] T Findlay, *The Use of Force in Peace Operations* (n 41), 115; EA Erskine, *Mission with UNIFIL: An African Soldier's Reflections* (n 66), 108. The force has incurred 267 fatalities as of 6 October 2007 <http://www.un.org/Depts/dpko/missions/unifil/facts.html>.

[79] However in 1988 when resistance leaders were abducted in broad daylight from the Irish sector of UNIFIL's area of operations, it did not act: R Murphy, *UN Peacekeeping in Lebanon, Somalia and Kosovo* (Cambridge University Press Cambridge 2007), 268–269.

[80] Report of the Secretary-General on the United Nations Interim Force in Lebanon, 22 January 1996 (S/1996/45), [23] [27]; Approved in S/RES 1039 29 January 1996.

[81] Report of the Secretary-General on the United Nations interim Force in Lebanon, 21 July 2006 (S/2006/560) [42].

[82] Report of the Secretary-General on the Implementation of Security Council Resolution 1701 (2006), (S/2007/392), 28 June 2007, [2].

[83] One US official has described 1701 as a resolution that 'walks like, talks like and acts like a Chapter VII resolution' but is not quite one: KP Coleman, *International Organizations and Peace Enforcement: The Politics of Legitimacy* (n 4), 317.

hostile activities of any kind.'[84] UNIFIL's new ROE permit the use of deadly force in carrying out its mandate.[85] As with most UN peacekeeping operations launched since 1999, UNIFIL's new mandate also includes, in addition to humanitarian assistance, an explicit, albeit qualified, authority to protect civilians.[86]

Prior to its transformation in 2006 to a Chapter VII style operation, UNIFIL's twenty-eight year peacekeeping record, was criticized as 'dismal';[87] so 'futile' as to make its mandate appear 'absurd';[88] 'unlikely to be a model anyone would wish to emulate... forgotten and neglected until an incident or crisis arose';[89] and an attestation to 'the impotence and weakness of UN forces when these have been confronted with large-scale, offensive military actions.'[90] The 2006 mandate has not, at least as yet, had any significant transformative impact on UNIFIL's peacekeeping role.[91] Conversely there has been widespread and consistent praise for UNIFIL's humanitarian work, both prior to, and since, the Chapter VII-style transformation. Nigel White has observed that although 'the provision of humanitarian assistance is a function given to peacekeeping forces when wider, more ambitious aims have not been achieved... there is no doubt that despite the adverse publicity these limited operations attract they save thousands of lives.'[92] UNIFIL currently provides water, food, fuel, electricity, medicine,[93] dental care,

[84] S/RES 1701 11 Aug. 2006, [12].

[85] France also insisted, citing past experience of problems with the chain of command in Bosnia, that the force should report to military rather than civilian officials at UN headquarters: KP Coleman, *International Organizations and Peace Enforcement: The Politics of Legitimacy* (n 4), 318.

[86] S/RES 1701 11 Aug. 2006, [11].

[87] M Ghali, 'United Nations Interim Force in Lebanon 1978-Present' in WJ Durch (ed), *UN Peacekeeping. American Policy and the Uncivil Wars of the 1990s* (n 57), 181, 197.

[88] N MacQueen, *Peacekeeping and the International System* (n 2), 126–127; Bruce Jones also comments on the futility of UNIFIL: B Jones, 'The Security Council and the Arab-Israeli Wars: Responsibility without Power' in *The United Nations Security Council and War: The Evolution of Thought and Practice since 1945* (n 3), 298, 321.

[89] T Findlay, *The Use of Force in Peace Operations* (n 41), 119.

[90] M Berdal, 'The UN Security Council and Peacekeeping' in *The UN Security Council and War: The Evolution of Thought and Practice since 1945* (n 3), 175, 203.

[91] In May 2008 Hezbollah, responding to threats by the government (which is regarded as illegitimate by the opposition) to dismantle its secure communication system, took control of key areas of Lebanon (which it subsequently handed over to the army) during the course of which it turned its weapons on Sunnis, breaching a longstanding tradition in which it has portrayed itself as a resistance movement against Israel and not a sectarian movement: International Crisis Group Lebanon: *Hizbollah's Weapons Turn Inward* Middle East Briefing N°23 15 May 2008; The Secretary-General, Ban Ki Moon, did not mention UNIFIL in his 12 May 2008 statement on the violence that erupted: UN Press Release 12 May 2008 'Secretary-General strongly condemns those responsible for Lebanon violence' SG/SM/11560 <http://www.un.org/News/Press/docs/2008/sgsm11560.doc.htm>; Accessed 15 May 2008; Political leaders and the media also seem to have ignored UNIFIL's presence.

[92] N White, *Keeping the Peace* (Manchester University Press Manchester 1997), 276.

[93] UNIFIL's services proved so valuable that it caused the occasional complaint: after Irishbatt opened a clinic at Tibnin, a private medical doctor who had served the people of Tibnin before the invasion, but who had been absent for a year, returned and unsuccessfully demanded compensation from Irishbatt for the period that Irishbatt had been looking after his patients: EA Erskine, *Mission with UNIFIL: An African Soldier's Reflections* (n 66), 91.

hospital treatment, and equipment and services for schools and orphanages.[94] In addition UNIFIL's presence probably ensured a greater degree of compliance with fundamental principles of humanitarian law, which 'seemingly would otherwise have been disregarded.'[95]

3.3 Civilian Protection in UN Peacekeeping Operations during the Cold War: Summary

During the Cold War little attention was paid, at a theoretical level, to the potential clash between adherence to Hammarskjöld's peacekeeping principles and the need to use force to protect civilians. Protection was regarded as intrinsic to the nature of peacekeeping from the very beginning but the possibility that providing such protection might bring forces into conflict with one or more of the belligerent parties was not initially recognized. At the time peacekeeping was a new means of managing tensions between the major powers and the key focus was on constraining the potential escalation of disputes into inter-State wars. Where civilians came under deliberate attack then naturally peacekeepers would be expected to do something about it, but this aspect of peacekeepers' role was subsumed beneath their major task of keeping the peace (usually through monitoring compliance with agreed peace terms and the maintenance of buffer zones). This approach came under severe strain during the Congo crisis, which was also unusual in that it concerned an intra-state conflict but one in which with the interests of the major powers were heavily implicated. At one point Hammarskjöld considered withdrawing the force altogether, since requiring UN troops to ignore gross human rights abuses would be incompatible with the norms the UN is committed to upholding, but any kind of response, even inter-position, would be regarded as assisting one side or another. However, following massacres of civilians ONUC did provide protection through interposition and the creation of small protected areas and it succeeded in saving a significant number of lives. As the conflict progressed the force became engaged in action that was virtually indistinguishable from enforcement but that was described as self-defence. This was only possible because the political make-up of the Security Council tolerated it, despite the Soviet Union's furious criticism of the approach of the 'Western powers'.

Civilians were also targeted in Cyprus, at least in the early years of the conflict, and troops did engage in protection, largely through interposition techniques. UNFICYP was only permitted to use force in self-defence but in the light of the experience of ONUC, self-defence was explicitly stated to encompass responding to attempts by force to prevent troops 'from carrying out their responsibilities as

[94] M Ghali, 'United Nations Interim Force in Lebanon 1978–Present' in WJ Durch (ed), *UN Peacekeeping. American Policy and the Uncivil Wars of the 1990s* (n 57), 181, 200; Report of the Secretary-General on the United Nations interim Force in Lebanon, 21 July 2006 ((S/2006/560) [34].

[95] R Murphy, *UN Peacekeeping in Lebanon, Somalia and Kosovo* (n 79), 264.

ordered by their commanders' provided that 'when acting in self defence, the principle of minimum force was always to be applied.'[96] This broader approach to self-defence was taken further and officially authorized in 1973 in the Report on the Implementation of Security Council Resolution 340, for use in the second UNEF operation (which did not really need it as the mission had broad based support, but Secretary-General Waldheim considered that the opportunity afforded by the unusual levels of co-operation between Security Council members in relation to UNEF should not be missed). The broader concept of self-defence was much more relevant to the UNIFIL mission deployed in 1974. However, the political situation and the support relationships between Israel and key permanent members of the Security Council would have rendered a robust approach similar to that taken in the Congo impossible, even if such an approach had been practical, which is doubtful. But as with ONUC and UNICYP, UNIFIL provided protection through interposition. It also provided extensive humanitarian assistance.

During the Cold War awareness of the need for the Security Council to specifically address civilian protection had not yet come to a head. Massacres did occur in the Congo but ONUC had sufficient strength to be able to provide tolerable levels of protection through traditional techniques and in any case the Security Council was willing to support enforcement style action albeit under the banner of self-defence. In Cyprus and in Lebanon protection and humanitarian assistance were provided but this was never viewed as a primary mission objective. In Lebanon civilian protection and assistance became the main function of UNIFIL, but only because it was unable to carry out its peacekeeping objectives as set out in its mandate. Disagreements between Security Council members meant that no new operations were deployed until the very end of the 1980s. Thus the position at the end of the Cold War was that civilian protection was to be expected of peacekeepers but the possibility that this might entail departing significantly from traditional peacekeeping principles as originally formulated, was not seriously debated. The ONUC mission, which did raise the prospect of potential conflict, was regarded as a one off, unlikely to have implications for the future.

4. Peacekeeping in the Early 1990s: Humanitarian Objectives and Increased Interventionism

Between 1978 and 1987, during the period of the 'second cold war', no new UN peacekeeping operations were launched.[97] However, by the late 1980s, the thaw

[96] Aide Mémoire of the Secretary-General concerning some questions relating to the function and operation of the United Nations Peacekeeping Force in Cyprus, 10 April 1964, UN Doc S/5653 of 11 April 1964, [16], [18], [20–21].

[97] Although two major Cold War operations UNFICYP and UNIFIL, and two smaller observer operations, UNDOF and UNMOGIP, survived this drought and remain deployed today, they 'do not join the ranks of new peacekeeping simply by virtue of their longevity.' SR Ratner, *The New*

in superpower relations led, for a time at least, to greater co-operation between the permanent members of the Security Council.

The first major operation of this period was the United Nations Transition Group (UNTAG), deployed to Namibia in 1989 to help 'ensure the early independence of Namibia through free and fair elections under the supervision and control of the United Nations.'[98] It was the first UN peacekeeping mission to be headed by a civilian political leader, the Special Representative of the Secretary-General, Martti Ahrisaari. Despite initial problems that almost jeopardised the mission,[99] elections were successfully held in November[100] and Namibia became independent in March 1990. For the Secretary-General the success of the elections confirmed the possibilities for expanding the task portfolio of UN missions to include providing development aid, implementing arms control measures, organizing elections, and monitoring human rights violations; the Namibian model 'became the blueprint for UN multi-functional peacekeeping and peace support operations in Africa and other parts of the world.'[101]

During the decade that followed approximately twenty peacekeeping operations of significant size were deployed plus a number of smaller ones. The relaxation of the superpowers' control over their respective spheres of interest brought

UN Peacekeeping: Building Peace in Lands of Conflict After the Cold War (St Martins Press New York 1996), 20.

[98] SC Res. 632 of 16 Feb. 1989 implementing the plan set out in SC Res. 435 of 29 Sep. 1978.

[99] The principal tasks for UNTAG's military component were to monitor the ceasefire, ensure the various armed forces involved in the conflict remained in their bases, and to assist in the holding of elections. The success of the mission was seriously jeopardized when, before UNTAG was fully deployed, South West African Peoples' Organization (SWAPO) forces invaded from Angola. Around three hundred of them were killed when the Secretary-General, who felt he had no option given SWAPO's violation of the ceasefire agreement, allowed South African Defence forces to redeploy to the border to halt the invasion.

[100] SWAPO gained 57.2% of the vote and 41 out of the 72 seats: N MacQueen, *Peacekeeping and the International System* (n 2), 190 footnote 9.

[101] DJ Francis, 'Peacekeeping in Africa' in Rachel Utley (ed), *Major Powers and Peacekeeping: Perspectives, Priorities and the Challenges of Military Intervention* (Ashgate Aldershot 2006), 101, 104; Unlike the peacekeeping operations of the previous decades, many of the more complex operations since the end of the Cold War have not been UN-run operations commanded and controlled by the Secretary-General, but instead were conducted by coalitions of States acting under a UN mandate. This was because the US and other major military powers were unwilling to leave the direction of substantial military operations to the UN: M Bothe, 'Peacekeeping' in B Simma (ed), *The Charter of the United Nations: A Commentary* (n 3), 664, [12]; The Security Council's main mechanism for controlling operations that are UN-authorized, but not UN-run, comes in the form of the enabling resolution and a reporting system: ND White 'The Legality of Bombing in the Name of Humanity' 5 Journal of Conflict and Security Law 1, 31 The operation must be conducted within the terms of the mandate set out in the enabling resolution. The States that contribute forces to the mission are required to provide information to the Security Council, usually via the Secretary-General, on the military action they have taken to fulfil the mandate. However the States undertaking the operation are generally given a broad discretion to determine when and how the goals of the operation might be achieved: S Chesterman, *You, The People: United Nations Transitional Administration and State-Building* (Oxford University Press Oxford 2004), 102; Chesterman notes that reporting requirements, which have gradually been introduced during the 1990s have been only partially successful in improving accountability: S Chesterman, *Just War or Just Peace?* (Oxford University Press Oxford 2001), 187–189.

with it a much greater willingness on the part of the Security Council to accept that internal conflict, and certain humanitarian disasters,[102] may constitute a threat to international peace and security.[103] A second, and related development, was a greatly increased interventionist element in peacekeeping operations, resulting from less stringently applied consent requirements,[104] coupled in some cases with less stringently applied authorization requirements. The peacekeeping operation to northern Iraq, undertaken in 1991 by a coalition of States,[105] was seen as epitomizing the new approach. Operation Provide Comfort was the first peacekeeping operation to be explicitly deployed primarily for humanitarian purposes, and it was undertaken without the authorization of the Security Council. Its success in providing protection engendered widespread optimism that a new world-order had begun; the international community would no longer allow massive human rights abuses to be perpetrated behind the shield of State sovereignty.[106]

4.1 Protection of the Kurds: Operation Provide Comfort

In 1991 encouraged by US propaganda during the First Gulf War the Kurds in northern Iraq had rebelled and briefly taken control of several cities; the rebellion was brutally suppressed and as a result, large numbers of Kurds fled towards Turkey. Turkey, fearing an exacerbation of its own problems with Kurdish insurgents, refused them entry. The refugees became trapped in the mountains on the borders of Turkey and many were dying of exposure. Resolution 688, adopted in April 1991, demanded an end to:

> the repression of the Iraqi civilian population in many parts of Iraq, including most recently in Kurdish populated areas, the consequences of which threaten international peace and security.[107]

[102] Christopher Greenwood notes the willingness of the Security Council to view certain humanitarian disasters as constituting a threat to international peace and security (and therefore potentially subject to the Security Council's power to take enforcement action under Chapter VII of the Charter) even where the direct threat to other States appears to have been minimal, for example in response to refugee flows in Iraq and Haiti, and to a humanitarian crisis in Somalia: C Greenwood, 'International Law and the Conduct of Military Operations' in *International Law Across the Spectrum of Conflict, Essays in Honour of Professor LC Green on the Occasion of his Eightieth Birthday*, International Law Studies Vol. 75 ed Michael N Schmitt, US Naval War College, (Newport 2000) 178, 185.

[103] Findlay observes that freed 'of the shackles of Security Council vetoes and hypersensitivity to the sovereign affairs of states' peacekeeping 'suddenly became the conflict resolution tool of choice.' T Findlay, *The Use of Force in Peace Operations* (n 41), 124; S Chesterman, *Just War or Just Peace* (n 101), 129.

[104] A Roberts, 'The Crisis in UN Peacekeeping' (1994) 36 Survival 3, 93, 99.

[105] Led by the United States. United Kingdom forces were also deployed under the mission name Operation Safe Haven.

[106] The ending of the Cold War and the successful conclusion of Operation Desert Storm had already engendered a sense that this was the beginning of a new era in which the United Nations would at last be able to carry out the purposes for which it was established.

[107] SC Res 688, 5 April 1991.

The resolution required Iraq to allow immediate access by international humanitarian organizations to all those in need of assistance and requested:

the Secretary-General to use all the resources at his disposal, including those of the relevant United Nations agencies, to address the critical needs of the refugees and displaced Iraqi population.[108]

Resolution 688 broke new ground in determining that the humanitarian crisis was a threat to international peace and security but it was not adopted under Chapter VII and did not authorize a military intervention. However, in response to the plight of the refugees (which was relayed to television screens all around the world by the Gulf War journalists most of whom who had had not yet gone home), the US, the UK and France undertook to set up safe havens to provide protection and shelter so as to enable the Kurds to remain in Iraq or to return if they had fled.[109] The US, stressing that the intervention was carried out purely for humanitarian reasons, argued that it was 'consistent' with Resolution 688. In a Press Conference on the 16th of April, President Bush announced that:

Consistent with United Nations Security Council Resolution 688 and working closely with the United Nations and other international organizations and our European partners, I have directed the US military to begin immediately to establish several encampments in Northern Iraq, where relief supplies for these refugees will be made available in large quantities and distributed in an orderly way... Adequate security will be provided at those sites by US, British and French guard forces consistent with the UN Resolution 688... We intend to turn over the administration, and security for these sites as soon as possible to the UN'.[110]

France stated that the operation was in accordance with the 'esprit' of Resolution 688:

Provide Comfort se fonde dans son esprit sur la résolution 688, mais il n'y a pas de texte explicite des Nations Unies qui fixe cette zone d'exclusion... Il n'est pas illégal... mais ce n'est pas la légitimité du Conseil Sécurité.[111]

Despite the absence of explicit UN authorization most commentators viewed the operation in a favourable light. There is no doubt that many lives were saved

[108] SC Res 688, 5 April 1991.

[109] The operation was undertaken on primarily humanitarian grounds: H Adelman, 'Humanitarian Intervention in the Case of the Kurds' 1 Int'l J Refugee Law, 4; However Frelick argues that 'The needs of the refugees were a considerably lower priority than the need to cement political alliances.' (with Turkey in particular): B Frelick, 'The False Promise of Operation Provide Comfort: Protecting Refugees or Protecting State Power' Middle East Report, No 176, Iraq in the Aftermath (May–June 1992) 22, 25.

[110] Press Conference of President Bush 17 April 1991 cited in E Coltran, 'The Establishment of A Safe Haven for the Kurds in Iraq' in N Al-Naiumi and R Meese (eds), *International Issues Arising under the United Nations Decade of International Law* (Martinus Nijhoff Publishers The Hague 1995) 855, 867; *Keesing's Record of World Events* Vol 37 (1991) 38127.

[111] Statement of French Foreign Ministry 2/9/1996 cited in N Krisch, 'Unilateral Enforcement of the Collective Will' Max Planck UN Year Book 3 (1999) 59, 76.

and that the troops carried out a difficult humanitarian operation with skill and commitment.[112] To many people it showed what could be done to save people whose lives were at risk if there was the political will to do it.[113] Operation Provide Comfort 'drove a coach and horses through the three and a half century, Westphalian notion that a sovereign state was the supreme arbiter within its own borders',[114] a development that was regarded positively by many commentators. Professor Lawrence Freedman argued that:

> a new world order is in the making, not in some quasi-biblical sense of ushering in an age of universal peace and tranquillity, but in terms of creating the precedents through which the international community will govern itself.[115]

This optimism was reflected in the Security Council's first ever summit meeting held at the level of Heads of State and Government in January 1992,[116] at which the newly appointed Secretary-General, Boutros Boutros Ghali, spoke of a 'new era' and of a 'revolution' which 'derives its momentum and authenticity not from any outdated or recycled ideology but from the primal needs of people for freedom, for justice, for solidarity and for recognition of their identities.' Several States commented that human rights issues were an integral aspect of international peace and security.[117] Russia stated that human rights and fundamental freedoms are 'not an internal matter for States' but 'obligations under the United Nations Charter, international covenants and conventions' and that it hoped to see this approach 'become a universal norm.' France commented that '[h]uman rights have triumphed—and I hope it is no temporary triumph—in the ideological struggle of the cold war.' The United States argued that the world stood 'at a crossroads' and that 'for perhaps the first time since that hopeful moment at San Francisco, we can look at our Charter as a living breathing document.' China was the only major power to express concern that the human rights issue might be used to interfere in the internal affairs of other countries. Arguing that although

[112] P Alston, 'The Security Council and Human Rights: Lessons to be Learned from the Iraq-Kuwait Crisis and its Aftermath' (1992) 13 Australian Yearbook of International Law, 107, 151; Major General R Ross, 'Some Early Lessons From Operation Haven' [Winter 1991] Royal United Services Institute Journal, 19, 21.

[113] R Connaughton, *Military Intervention and Peacekeeping* (Ashgate Publishing Ltd Aldershot 2001), 103; B Boutros-Ghali 'Empowering the United Nations' (Winter 1992/3) 71 Foreign Affairs 5, 89, 98–99; L Freedman, 'A clear-cut case for action; unable to ignore the Kurdish plight, the international community is setting precedents for a new world order', *Independent* (London 12 April 1991); P Alston, 'The Security Council and Human Rights: Lessons to be Learned from the Iraq-Kuwait Crisis and its Aftermath' (n 112), 151; Major General R Ross, 'Some Early Lessons From Operation Haven' (n 11), 21.

[114] R Connaughton, *Military Intervention and Peacekeeping* (n 113), 103.

[115] L Freedman, 'A clear-cut case for action; unable to ignore the Kurdish plight, the international community is setting precedents for a new world order', *Independent* (n 113).

[116] S/PV.3046 January 31 1992.

[117] The President in his summing up of the meeting observed that the 'non-military sources of instability in the economic, social, humanitarian and ecological fields have become threats to peace and security.' S/23500 January 31 1992.

human rights should be universally respected and that they include social and economic rights as well as civil and political rights it stated that 'in essence, the issue of human rights falls within the sovereignty of each country.'

At the invitation of the Council the Secretary-General presented a report entitled *An Agenda for Peace, Preventive Diplomacy, Peacemaking and Peace-keeping (Agenda for Peace)*[118] setting out his recommendations on ways of strengthening and making more efficient the capacity of the United Nations for preventive diplomacy, for peacemaking and for peace-keeping, in which he said that:

> In these past months a conviction has grown, among nations large and small, that an opportunity has been regained to achieve the great objectives of the Charter—a United Nations capable of maintaining international peace and security, of securing justice and human rights and of promoting, in the words of the Charter, 'social progress and better standards of life in larger freedom.' This opportunity must not be squandered. The Organization must never again be crippled as it was in the era that has now passed.

Noting that peace-keeping 'is the deployment of a United Nations presence in the field, *hitherto* with the consent of all the parties concerned', he commented that the 'foundation stone' of the UN's work:

> is and must remain the State. Respect for its fundamental sovereignty and integrity are crucial to any common international progress. The time of absolute and exclusive sovereignty, however, has passed; its theory was never matched by reality. It is the task of leaders of States today to understand this and to find a balance between the needs of good internal governance and the requirements of an ever more interdependent world.[119]

A month after the Secretary-General had delivered *An Agenda for Peace*, the largest peacekeeping operation since ONUC, the UN Transitional Authority in Cambodia (UNTAC),[120] was deployed.

4.2 The UN Transitional Authority in Cambodia (UNTAC)

In February 1992 the Security Council authorized the deployment of UNTAC,[121] to assist in implementing the Paris Peace Accords.[122] Consent to the operation was

[118] An Agenda for Peace, Preventive Diplomacy, Peacemaking and Peace-keeping, Report of the Secretary-General pursuant to the statement adopted by the Summit Meeting of the Security Council on 31 January 1992, A/47/277–S/24111 17 June 1992.

[119] ibid [3] [16–17] Emphasis added.

[120] S/RES 745 28 Feb 1992; at its maximum, in June 1993, the Force had a strength of 15,991 military personnel and 3,359 civilian police: *The United Nations Security Council and War: The Evolution of Thought and Practice since 1945* (n 3), Appendix 1.

[121] SC Res 745 28 Feb 1992.

[122] The Paris Conference concluded four documents: the Final Act of the Paris Conference on Cambodia 23 October 1991, 31 ILM 180 (1992); the Agreement on a Comprehensive Political Settlement of the Cambodia Conflict 23 October 1991, 31 ILM 183 (1992); the Agreement Concerning the Sovereignty, Independence, Territorial Integrity and Inviolability, Neutrality and National Unity of Cambodia 23 October 1991, 31 ILM 200 (1992); the Declaration on the Rehabilitation and Reconstruction of Cambodia October 1991, 31 ILM 203 (1992).

tenuous. Cambodia's internal factions had reluctantly agreed to the peace plan not out of a commitment to peace but primarily because policy changes towards Cambodia on the part of Vietnam, China and the Soviet Union threatened their vested interests: as a result, peacekeepers were deployed into what was effectively a war scenario.[123] Part of UNTAC's mandate was similar to that of UNTAG in that it was tasked with monitoring the ceasefire; assisting in the cantonment, disarmament and demobilization of armed personnel; and organizing elections: but unlike UNTAG, UNTAC was also tasked with administrative oversight of the country;[124] protecting and fostering human rights; making arrangements for the return of refugees, and aiding economic reconstruction.[125] Article 16 of *The Agreement for a Comprehensive Political Settlement of the Cambodia Conflict*[126] provided that 'UNTAC shall be responsible during the transition period for fostering an environment in which respect for human rights shall be ensured.'

The Security Council mandating resolution was not adopted under Chapter VII.[127] However, because of the appalling human rights abuses that had been committed over the previous decades, particularly by the Khmer Rouge, for the first time in a UN operation, the ROE specifically permitted, the use of 'all available means', including armed force, to prevent 'crimes against humanity' such as executions, or attacks on refugee columns, or on cantonment areas or on other soldiers who had laid down their weapons.[128]

[123] SR Ratner, *The New UN Peacekeeping: Building Peace in Lands of Conflict After the Cold War* (n 97), 158–159.

[124] The parties had been in deadlock as to how to manage power-sharing during the transition to a new government. The three opposition parties insisted that the State of Cambodia (the Vietnamese backed government) should cede administrative control to an interim authority. The State of Cambodia agreed to do so provided that the authority was only advisory in nature. Australia had suggested, as a means of breaking the deadlock, that the UN would be able to offer impartial administration during the transition period. In September 1990 the Cambodian parties established the Supreme National Council (SNC) (with six representatives from the State of Cambodia and two each from the other parties), under the chairmanship of Prince Sihanouk. Under Article 6 of *The Agreement for a Comprehensive Political Settlement of the Cambodia Conflict* October 23, 1991 31 ILM 183 (1992) the SNC delegated to the United Nations all powers necessary to ensure the implementation of the agreement, in particular foreign affairs, national defence, finance, public security and information.

[125] S/RES 745 28 Feb 1992; *The Agreement for a Comprehensive Political Settlement of the Cambodia Conflict* October 23, 1991 31 ILM 183 (1992) ; see also *Letter dated 30 October 1991 from the Permanent Representatives of France and Indonesia to the United Nations addressed to the Secretary-General*, S/23177, 30 October 1991, Annex.

[126] *The Agreement for a Comprehensive Political Settlement of the Cambodia Conflict*, October 23, 1991 31 ILM 183 (1992); see also *Letter dated 30 October 1991 from the Permanent Representatives of France and Indonesia to the United Nations addressed to the Secretary-General*, S/23177, 30 October 1991, Annex.

[127] S/RES 745 28 Feb 1992; James Schear comments that the UN leadership was keenly aware of the low tolerance for casualties among UNTAC's troops contributors and the lack of support on the Council for mounting anything other than on a consensual basis: Schear J, 'Policing Cambodia: The Public Security Dimensions of UN Peacekeeping Operations' in RB Oakley, MJ Dziedzic, and EM Goldberg (eds), *Policing the New World Disorder* (Washington National Defense University Press Washington 1998), 69, 74.

[128] J Schear, 'Riding the Tiger: the UN and Cambodia' ed WJ Durch, *UN Peacekeeping. American Policy and the Uncivil Wars of the 1990s* (n 57), 145.

UNTAC conducted extensive human rights education and training campaigns; investigated human rights related complaints; monitored conditions in prisons and 'pressed local authorities to improve the situation to the extent possible within the means available to the prison authorities.'[129] From early 1993 UNTAC was also authorized to arrest, detain and prosecute suspects for human rights violations.[130] This authority was little used, as UNTAC's civilian administration considered it beyond its mandate and UNTAC's military component was unwilling to use force when making arrests; there was in any case no independent local court able to hear cases brought by the Prosecutor's office.[131] UNTAC was also tasked with a mine-clearance and education programme that has been variously praised for its successes,[132] and failures.[133] However, the primary focus of the mission was on ensuring that the elections that had been planned went ahead.[134] These were held on time;[135] initial surveys had concluded that elections could only take place during the dry season and therefore too long a delay would mean that the elections would have to be postponed for a whole year vastly increasing the costs of the mission.[136] 89.56% of the registered voters cast their vote, a success which earned UNTAC high praise internationally.[137]

The local population, however, rapidly came to intensely resent UNTAC.[138] There was a perception that the force, anxious not to do anything that might delay the elections, had sacrificed human rights protection in order to ensure their success.[139] Human Rights Watch observed that the peacekeeping period was 'marked by major human rights violations, among them the slaughter of ethnic Vietnamese residents of Cambodia, abuse of prisoners, and incidents of

[129] United Nations, *The Blue Helmets: A Review of United Nations Peace-keeping* (n 42), 475–476.

[130] The Special Representative issued a directive on January 1993 S/25124 establishing procedures for prosecution of persons responsible for human rights violations. He also established the office of the Special Prosecutor: United Nations, *The Blue Helmets: A Review of United Nations Peace-keeping* (n 42), 467.

[131] M Berdal and M Leifer, 'Cambodia' in *United Nations Interventionism 1991–2004* in M Berdal and S Economides (eds) (Cambridge University Press Cambridge 2007), 32, 51.

[132] KZ Marten, *Enforcing the Peace: Learning from the Imperial Past* (Columbia University Press New York 2004), 29; United Nations, *The Blue Helmets: A Review of United Nations Peace-keeping* (n 42), 459, 476.

[133] After the end of UNTAC's operation it has been estimated that 8–10 million mines remained:
M Berdal and M Leifer, 'Cambodia' in *United Nations Interventionism 1991–2004* (n 131), 32, 54.

[134] J Weschler, 'Human Rights' in D Malone, *The UN Security Council: From the Cold War to the 21st Century* (Lynne Rienner Boulder & London 2004), 55, 57.

[135] United Nations, *The Blue Helmets: A Review of United Nations Peace-keeping* (n 42), 471.

[136] M Berdal and M Leifer, 'Cambodia' in *United Nations Interventionism 1991–2004* (n 131), 32, 45.

[137] United Nations, *The Blue Helmets: A Review of United Nations Peace-keeping* (n 42), 469.

[138] M Berdal and M Leifer, 'Cambodia' in *United Nations Interventionism 1991–2004* (n 131), 32, 58.

[139] SR Ratner, *The New UN Peacekeeping: Building Peace in Lands of Conflict After the Cold War* (n 94), 181; United Nations, *The Blue Helmets: A Review of United Nations Peace-keeping* (n 42), 467.

politically motivated murder, assault and intimidation',[140] but UNTAC refused to protect vulnerable groups, despite explicit provision for it in the ROE.[141] It was also alleged, in what has now become a familiar complaint, that UN soldiers themselves committed abuses.[142] In 1992 a doctor from a medical NGO asserted that at one point a majority of the injured people in Prear Vihear hospital 'were young kids, the victims of sexual abuse by UN soldiers.'[143] Several units failed to maintain even minimum standards of discipline such that in 'the eyes of ordinary Cambodians, many UN soldiers appeared to be spending most of their time in bars and brothels or to be driving recklessly in UN vehicles.'[144] HIV infection, which had been largely unknown, rose dramatically during the time that the mission was deployed and the UN bureaucracy 'was exceptionally slow in taking preventive action.'[145]

The Secretary-General, in his 1993 report on the situation in Cambodia, concluded that 'real progress' had been made:

> with a marked decline in the number of political assassinations, the release of political prisoners and prisoners of war, and appreciable improvement in enjoyment of freedom of expression and association which has facilitated the emergence of human rights associations and political parties.[146]

However, Yasushi Akashi, The Secretary-General's Special Representative in Cambodia later commented that he did not think the operation had been:

> an unqualified success...I should be candid also to admit that the quality of our personnel has not been uniformly outstanding...If possible we should have more training period before we send peacekeeping forces and civilians to make them more sensitive and more attuned to the local and national cultures, manners and languages. I think civil administration was one area in which UN has no experience so it took a lot of time for us to develop our methodology and approaches.[147]

[140] *Asia Watch*, An Exchange on Human Rights and Peacekeeping in Cambodia, New York September 23, 1993; *Human Rights Watch*, The Lost Agenda: Human Rights and UN Field Operations, New York, 1993; United Nations, *The Blue Helmets: A Review of United Nations Peacekeeping* (n 42), 468–469.

[141] RM Jennar, UNTAC: 'International Triumph' in Cambodia? (1994) 25(2) Security Dialogue 145, 147.

[142] A Özerdem, 'Peacekeeping in Asia: Lessons Learned from Afghanistan, Cambodia and Timor-Leste' in Rutley (ed) *Major Powers and Peacekeeping: Perspectives, Priorities and the Challenges of Military Intervention* (Ashgate Aldershot 2006), 119, 122.

[143] RM Jennar, UNTAC: 'International Triumph' in Cambodia? (n 141), 154.

[144] M Berdal and M Leifer, 'Cambodia' in *United Nations Interventionism 1991–2004* (n 131), 32, 58.

[145] ibid 32, 59.

[146] The Secretary-General's report on The Right of Peoples to Self-Determination and its Application to Peoples under Colonial or Alien Domination: The Situation in Cambodia E/CN.4/1993/19, [80]; However Raoul Jennar argues that UNTAC 'failed to make any significant improvements in the general respect for human rights': RM Jennar, UNTAC: 'International Triumph' in Cambodia? (n 141), 147.

[147] Speech to the Phnomh Penh Foreign Correspondents Club 13 September 1993, quoted in RM Jennar, UNTAC: 'International Triumph' in Cambodia? (n 141), 155; In 1997 Second Prime

Over the next few months a series of missions was launched to Somalia, Rwanda and the Balkans. Unfortunately these too could have benefited from more training; clearer guidelines on how to deal with local cultural and political sensitivities; and clearer guidelines on the protection of civilians.

4.3 Peacekeeping Operations in Somalia 1992–1995

The UN operation in Somalia began as a humanitarian operation, accompanied by a peacekeeping presence,[148] but the lack of security, in a State where there was no longer a functioning government other than the power bases of local warlords, made it difficult to carry out these tasks.[149] The first UN Operation in Somalia (UNOSOM I) was, as Secretary-General Boutros-Ghali later observed, 'conceived as a peacekeeping mission even though, for the first time in the history of United Nations peacekeeping, one of its primary purposes was to make possible the delivery of emergency assistance to the civilian population.'[150] For Boutros-Ghali the disjunction he perceived between the peacekeeping nature of the mission and its humanitarian objective stemmed from the fact that 'peacekeeping operations use weapons only in self-defence',[151] but in 'the real world the division between interposition and enforcement will frequently be unclear.'[152] UNOSOM I was not equipped or resourced for enforcement.[153]

Given these difficulties, the Security Council unanimously adopted Resolution 794 on 3 December 1992 authorizing a Chapter VII peace-enforcement operation, the Unified Task Force (UNITAF), led by the United States[154] to operate alongside UNOSOM, with a mandate to use 'all necessary means to establish as soon as possible a secure environment for humanitarian relief operations in Somalia.' However, the US and the UN disagreed as to what means were in fact necessary. Boutros-Ghali believed that in order to create a secure environment the warlords would have to be disarmed[155] but the US was reluctant to undertake

Minister Hun Sen led a successful coup d'etat. Elections were held in 1998 which returned a government dominated by Hun Sen's Cambodian People's Party.

[148] As set out in Resolution 751 (24 April 1992) and subsequent Resolutions 767 (24 July 1992) and 775 (28 August 1992).

[149] SR Sloan, Peacekeeping and Conflict Management Activities: A Discussion of Terminology 4 (Congressional Research Service Report for Congress November 26, 1993) cited in American Bar Association, Section of International Law and Practice Standing Committee on World Order under Law, Report to the House of Delegates, Safety of UN and Associated Personnel: Recommendation, 31 International Lawyer, 195, 200; *The United Nations and Somalia 1992–1996* (UN Department of Public Information New York 1996), 29–30, [80–81].

[150] B Boutros-Ghali, 'Introduction' in United Nations, *The United Nations and Somalia 1992–1996* (UN Department of Public Information New York 1996), 24, [66].

[151] ibid.

[152] N MacQueen *The United Nations since 1945: Peacekeeping and the Cold War* (n 45), 85.

[153] United Nations, *The Blue Helmets: A Review of United Nations Peace-keeping* (n 42), 292.

[154] The coalition comprised over 38,000 troops from more than 20 countries but was dominated by 28,000 US troops.

[155] B Boutros-Ghali, *Unvanquished: A US-UN Saga* (Random House New York 1999) 59–60.

this task since everyone carried guns, it being a normal part of every day life in Somalia.[156] Moreover, because the objectives for the mission were primarily humanitarian (this was the first Chapter VII operation to be mandated on primarily humanitarian grounds), the Bush administration wanted to maintain the norm of non-interference in internal affairs;[157] it was hoping that a show of potential force would obviate any need to use it.[158] Therefore, despite its Chapter VII mandate, UNITAF operated largely in accordance with traditional peacekeeping principles.[159] Although the ROE authorized the use of 'deadly force' where 'armed elements, mobs, and/or rioters threaten human life' or where there was 'a clear demonstration of hostile intent' in the troops' presence,[160] non-governmental organizations in Mogadishu complained that UNITAF refused to come to their aid even when they were under direct attack.[161]

In May 1993, UNITAF/UNOSOM I handed over to a UN-led operation, UNOSOM II, which was given a Chapter VII mandate.[162] The mission was beset with problems, in part because of the disjointed command and control structure,[163] but also because neither UNITAF, nor UNOSOM II, was prepared for the complexities of operating in a failed State with no government. The reputation of the UN was also severely damaged as a result of the serious human rights violations committed by UN forces themselves.[164] The constant lawlessness and

[156] RG Patman, 'Disarming Somalia: The Contrasting Fortunes of United States and Australian Peacekeepers During United Nations Intervention 1992–1993' 96 African Affairs, 509, 512; JL Hirsch and RB Oakley, *Somalia and Operation Restore Hope: Reflections on Peacemaking and Peacekeeping* (US Institute of Peace Washington 1995) 103–106.

[157] RG Patman, 'Disarming Somalia: The Contrasting Fortunes of United States and Australian Peacekeepers During United Nations Intervention 1992–1993' (n 156), 512.

[158] T Findlay, *The Use of Force in Peace Operations* (n 41), 170.

[159] RG Patman, 'Disarming Somalia: The Contrasting Fortunes of United States and Australian Peacekeepers During United Nations Intervention 1992–1993' (n 156), 512.

[160] Rules of Engagement for Operation Restore Hope, Peace Operations FM 100–23 (Department of the Army Washington DC December 1994) Appendix D, [3]. The section goes on to give guidelines as to factors to consider in determining whether there is hostile intent, eg whether weapons are present; the size of the opposing force; the response of the opposing force to US; the response of the opposing force to unarmed civilians.

[161] T Findlay, *The Use of Force in Peace Operations* (n 41), 175; KM Kennedy 'The Relationship Between the Military and Humanitarian Organizations in Operation Restore Hope' (1996) 3 International Peacekeeping 1, 92, 105–7 (But outside of Mogadishu the relationship between the military and humanitarian organizations was good: ibid, 102).

[162] SC Res. 814 26 March 1993.

[163] The US continued to play a leading role in the UNOSOM II mission, retaining full command of its own troops and a parallel US chain of command was established that was intended to exist alongside, but independent from, the UN command structure: R Murphy, *UN Peacekeeping in Lebanon, Somalia and Kosovo* (n 79), 129–131; B Boutros-Ghali, *Unvanquished: A US-UN Saga* (n 155), 93.

[164] *R v Brocklebank* CMAC-383, April 2, 1996: J Simpson Law Applicable to Canadian Forces in Somalia 1992/93: Study Prepared for the Commission of Inquiry into the Deployment of Canadian Forces to Somalia (Minister of Public Works and Government Services Canada 1997) 28–30; Judgment of the Belgian Military Court regarding violations of IHL committed in Somalia and Rwanda Nr 54 AR 1997, 20 November 1997; Journal des Tribunaux 24 April 1998, 286–289 (French language): Comment by M Cogen (1998) 1 Yearbook of International

local violence resulted in a high level of casualties for both the UN mission and for Somali civilians. For the US, the killing of eighteen American peacekeepers and the subsequent parading of their bodies through the streets of Mogadishu proved 'a watershed in its policy towards UN Peacekeeping.'[165] In May 1994, President Clinton issued Presidential Decision Directive 25 sharply restricting future US involvement in peacekeeping.[166] UNOSOM II's operations were scaled down during 1994 and withdrawn by March 1995.

4.4 The United Nations Assistance Mission for Rwanda (UNAMIR)

In April 1994 genocide was perpetrated in Rwanda despite the presence of UN troops. In August 1993 the government of President Juvénal Habyarimana, and the Rwandan Patriotic Front (RPF), a rebel faction that had taken control of a significant part of northern Rwanda, had signed the Arusha Peace Accords. These provided for the deployment of a UN force to assist 'in catering to the security of civilians'; in 'tracking arms caches and in the neutralization of armed gangs throughout the country'; and 'in the recovery of all weapons distributed to or illegally acquired by the civilians' as well as monitoring the observance of hostilities. In September a joint government-RPF delegation to the Secretary-General had asked for a force of 4,260 to be deployed as soon as possible.[167] Resolution 872, adopted on the 5th October, agreed to the deployment of 2,548 personnel with a much more limited mandate than the parties had proposed: the United Nations Assistance Mission for Rwanda (UNAMIR) was to monitor observance of the hostilities but its mandate did not include 'catering to the security of civilians' or disarmament. The US, burned by their experience in Somalia, pushed strongly for the more limited mandate, notwithstanding that the Special Rapporteur of the Commission on Human Rights on extra-judicial, summary or arbitrary executions, Mr Waly Bacre Ndiaye, had stated in his report, published

Humanitarian Law 415–416; F Mégret and F Hoffman, 'The UN as a Human Rights Violator? Some reflections on the United Nations Changing Human Rights Responsibilities' 25 Human Rights Quarterly, 314, 327; Commission of Inquiry into the Deployment of Canadian Forces to Somalia, <http://www.dnd.ca/somalia/somaliae.htm>.

[165] Report of the Independent Inquiry into the Actions of the United Nations during the 1994 Genocide in Rwanda (New York United Nations 15 December 1999), 39; Department of State Publication 10161, May 1994; One Malaysian peacekeeper was also killed and 24 Pakistani peacekeepers were killed in June 1993.

[166] Presidential Decision Directive 25 stated that a primary consideration for US involvement in future peacekeeping operations was whether it advanced US interests and whether other countries would commit adequate resources. Other considerations to be taken into account were whether the US presence is essential to an operation's success; whether the risk to troops is acceptable; and whether the domestic and congressional support exists. Canada's contribution to peacekeeping has also markedly declined since 1994; whilst it was once a leader in peacekeeping by 2007 it ranked 62nd in UN troop contributions: T Othieno and N Samasuwo, 'A Critical Analysis of Africa's Hybrid Missions and Security Collaboration' (2007) 16 African Security Review 3, 25, 28.

[167] Report of the Independent Inquiry into the Actions of the United Nations during the 1994 Genocide in Rwanda (n 165) 3.

only a week after the signing of the Accords, that massacres and other serious human rights violations were taking place; that Tutsis were being targeted; and that he feared that there was a serious risk of genocide.[168]

In November 1993, one month after Resolution 872 had been adopted, the Force Commander Brigadier-General Romeo Dallaire, drafted ROE that took into account the possibility that UNAMIR might be faced with having to deal with crimes against humanity. Paragraph 17 of the ROE alerted troops to the fact that:

> There may also be ethnically or politically motivated criminal acts committed during this mandate which will morally and legally require UNAMIR to use all available means to halt them. Examples are executions, attacks on displaced persons or refugees.[169]

In early 1994, just prior to the genocide, Dallaire had received information on the location of weapons caches that were to be used in mass killings of Tutsis but the UN Secretariat refused to allow him to confiscate them stating that UNAMIR 'cannot, repeat, cannot take an active role... UNAMIR's role should be limited to a monitoring function.'[170] Headquarters insisted that 'the overriding consideration is the need to avoid entering into a course of action that might lead to the use of force and unanticipated repercussions.'[171] On 6 April 1994, the aeroplane carrying President Habyarimana was shot down; roadblocks were set up immediately and Tutsis were stopped and killed. Dallaire sought to use force to stop the killings, which were taking place at the rate of hundreds per day, mostly using machetes, but the Secretariat reminded him that 'UNAMIR is not, repeat not, to fire unless fired upon.'[172] Dallaire pointed out that the ROE allowed UNAMIR to use force to prevent crimes against humanity. He was told that 'UNAMIR was not to fire unless fired upon, we were to negotiate, and, above all else, avoid conflict.'[173] When Headquarters was informed that the people under UNAMIR's protection, including the Prime Minister, were being

[168] He recommended a series of steps to prevent further massacres but 'his report seems to have been largely ignored by the key actors within the United Nations system.': Report of the Independent Inquiry into the Actions of the United Nations during the 1994 Genocide in Rwanda (n 165), 3.

[169] Headquarters never formally responded to the Force Commander's request for approval of the ROE. The Report of the Independent Inquiry into the Actions of the United Nations during the 1994 Genocide in Rwanda notes that, 'to the Force Commander, in the absence of a formal reply, the Rules of Engagement must be considered approved and in effect, a conclusion which the Inquiry believes was reasonable.' The same draft ROE was sent again to Headquarters after the genocide began and again Headquarters did not object: *Report of the Independent Inquiry into the Actions of the United Nations during the 1994 Genocide in Rwanda* (n 165), (26) 32.

[170] R Dallaire, *Shake Hands with the Devil* (Arrow Press London 2004), 167; Report of the Independent Inquiry into the Actions of the United Nations during the 1994 Genocide in Rwanda (n 165), 12.

[171] Report of the Independent Inquiry into the Actions of the United Nations during the 1994 Genocide in Rwanda (n 165), 9.

[172] R Dallaire, *Shake Hands with the Devil* (n 170), 229.

[173] ibid 229.

attacked and it might be necessary to use force to save their lives, the instruction not to fire, unless fired upon, was repeated.[174] The Prime Minister was subsequently shot at the United Nations Volunteer compound where she had sought protection.[175] The Vice-President of the Liberal Party and Minister for Labour and Social Affairs, who had been the subject of propaganda threats on Radio Télévision Libre Mille-Collines, was also killed whilst under UN protection.[176] Two thousand refugees that had been sheltering at the camp of the Belgian contingent at the Ecole Technique Officielle, in Kicukiro, were massacred when the Belgians withdrew without informing the Force Commander of the presence of the refugees, or of the fact that the Interhamwe had been stationed outside the camp for days, machetes at the ready, waiting for their opportunity.[177] The dead included a prominent politician, Mr Ngulinzira, who had been brought from his house to the camp by his UNAMIR guards.[178]

Dallaire argued for a 'modest increase of troops and capability' and believes that if he had been given them he would have been able to stop the killings;[179] but on the 21st April, the Security Council, in Resolution 912, having noted the 'large-scale violence in Rwanda, which has resulted in the deaths of thousands of innocent civilians, including women and children', decided to reduce the number of UNAMIR troops from the 2,548 the Council had authorized the previous October[180] to 270.[181] Non-governmental organizations such as Oxfam, and UNAMIR itself, began referring to the killings as genocide from mid April on[182] but both the US and the UK lobbied to have Security Council resolutions drafted in ambiguous language, avoiding use of the word genocide.[183] On 10 May the

[174] ibid 233.

[175] Report of the Independent Inquiry into the Actions of the United Nations during the 1994 Genocide in Rwanda (n 165) 12.

[176] The family claimed that the Ghanaian troops guarding him had fled to a neighbouring property without giving him any warning or explanation: Ibid, 16.

[177] ibid 16–17.

[178] ibid 17.

[179] R Dallaire, *Shake Hands with the Devil* (n 170), 514; In Dallaire's assessment 5,000 troops deployed under a Chapter VII mandate, with air support and proper logistics could have prevented much of the killing. The Carnegie Commission in a subsequent conference of military experts agreed with this assessment: SR Feil, *Preventing Genocide: A Report to the Carnegie Commission on Preventing Deadly Conflict* (Carnegie Corporation New York 1998): Other commentators have disputed the Commission's findings: AJ Kuperman, 'Rwanda in Retrospect' (January/February 2000) 79 Foreign Affairs 1, 94; NJ Wheeler, *Saving Strangers: Humanitarian Intervention in International Society* (Oxford University Press Oxford 2000), 222–224.

[180] S/RES 872 5 October 1993.

[181] S/RES 912 21 April 1994; On 7 April 10 Belgian UNAMIR peacekeepers were murdered in a deliberate act to provoke their withdrawal—a plan which succeeded. Willy Claes, the Belgian foreign minister lobbied New York for immediate reinforcements and massive logistics supplies. These were refused and the Belgian contingent withdrew: *Report of the Independent Inquiry into the Actions of the United Nations during the 1994 Genocide in Rwanda* (n 165), 17.

[182] R Dallaire, *Shake Hands with the Devil* (n 168), 333

[183] *The Triumph of Evil*, Prods. M Robinson and B Loeterman PBS *Frontline* Documentary 26 January 1999 <http://www.pbs.org/wgbh/pages/frontline/shows/evil>; C McQueen, *Humanitarian Intervention and Safety Zones* (Palgrave Macmillan New York 2005), 115.

High Commissioner for Human rights, Ayala Lasso, reporting on a fact-finding mission, stated that genocide was taking place.[184] On 17 May in Resolution 918, the Security Council agreed to the expansion of UNAMIR to 5,500 troops and mandated it to conduct a Chapter VI peacekeeping operation to:.

> contribute to the security and protection of displaced persons, refugees and civilians at risk in Rwanda, including through the establishment and maintenance, where feasible, of secure humanitarian areas.[185]

But the resolution did not refer to genocide. It was not until 31 May in a report to the Security Council that the Secretary-General Boutros Ghali acknowledged that 'on the basis of the evidence that has emerged, there can be little doubt that it constitutes genocide.'[186] Nevertheless Member States failed to provide the troops or equipment necessary to implement Resolution 918. Therefore in June 1994, the Council accepted an offer by France, which had previously had a close relationship with the Hutu government, to lead a Chapter VII mission to establish a *zone humanitaire sûre* covering a large part of the country. Most of the killings had already taken place by then but nevertheless Operation Turquoise did save thousands of lives.[187] UNAMIR II did not enter Rwanda until August, and did not reach its authorized strength of 5,500 until November, by which time the genocide was over.[188]

4.5 The United Nations Protection Force (UNPROFOR) at the Fall of Srebrenica

A year after the genocide in Rwanda, UN forces were again present when genocide was committed, this time in Bosnia-Herzegovina. The United Nations Protection Force (UNPROFOR) was initially authorized in February 1992, to deploy to Croatia as 'an interim arrangement to create conditions of peace and security for

[184] R Dallaire, *Shake Hands with the Devil* (n 168), 339.

[185] SC Resolution 918, 17 May 1994.

[186] SG Report S/1994/640, 31 May 1994 [6].

[187] However, although the French did not purposefully hide, or facilitate the escape, of perpetrators of the genocide many were able to flee through the *Zone Humanitaire* to Zaire, now the Democratic Republic of the Congo (DRC), and other neighbouring countries. In the DRC they established a new base for insurgency operations which then became involved in the civil war there in 1996. Democratic Forces for the Liberation of Rwanda (FDLR) is a militia group founded by Hutu militia leaders who fled Rwanda in 1994, some of whom are wanted by the International Criminal Court. *Guardian* reporter Chris McGreal reports that child soldiers are being trained by FDLR to hate Tutsis (inyenzi, cockcroaches) and to plan for a re-conquest of Rwanda to establish in power a Hutu dominated government: C McQueen, *Humanitarian Intervention and Safety Zones* (n 183), 141, 145; Bruce D Jones 'Military Intervention in Rwanda's Two Wars' in BF Walter and J Snyder, *Civil Wars, Insecurity and Intervention* (Columbia University Press New York 1999), 116, 133; C McGreal, 'We have to kill Tutsis wherever they are' *Guardian* 16 May 2008.

[188] United Nations, Lessons Learned Unit, Department of Peacekeeping Operations, *Comprehensive Report on Lessons Learned from the United Nations Assistance Mission for Rwanda (UNAMIR) October 1993–April 1996* (December 1996), 1.

the negotiation of an overall settlement of the Yugoslav crisis.'[189] UNPROFOR was deployed in support of the UN High Commissioner for Refugees' humanitarian relief operations. UNPROFOR's mandate evolved as the war developed; it was extended to Bosnia in June[190] and to the Former Yugoslav Republic of Macedonia in December.[191] In October and November the Security Council also adopted several resolutions condemning the ethnic cleansing and other violations of human rights and humanitarian law that were being committed by both sides.[192] Special Rapporteur Tadeusz Mazowieki was appointed to investigate the human rights situation. The UN kept expanding the role of UNPROFOR in an attempt to deal with the critical humanitarian situation but there was no clear overall strategy; the force's tasks were expanded without any corresponding change in the force's configuration. In an attempt to maintain consensus on the Security Council UNPROFOR's mandate was revised in vague terms making it appear superficially more robust but without pinning down exactly what the changes meant. This was particularly the case in relation to the safe area policy adopted in 1993.

On 16 April 1993, following a promise made by UNPROFOR's commander, General Philippe Morillon, to the people of Srebenica,[193] the Security Council, acting under Chapter VII of the UN Charter, adopted resolution 819, requiring all parties to treat the town and its surroundings as a 'safe area' which should be free from any armed attack or any other hostile act.[194] A second Security Council resolution extended the safe area declaration to another five towns: Sarajevo, Tuzla, Zepa, Gorazde, and Bihac.[195] In June, again acting under Chapter VII, the Council authorized Member States to take, under the authority of the Security Council and subject to close co-ordination with the Secretary-General and the force, all necessary measures, through the use of air power, in and around the safe areas in Bosnia and Herzegovina, to support UNPROFOR in the performance of its mandate.[196] UNPROFOR was authorized:

> acting in self-defence, to take the necessary measures, including the use of force in reply to bombardments against the safe areas by any of the parties or armed incursion into them or in the event of any deliberate obstruction in or around those areas to the freedom of movement of the Force or of protected humanitarian convoys.[197]

General Sir Michael Rose has observed that the mandate 'explicitly eschewed the use of the words 'protect' or 'defend' and linked the use of force to the phrase

[189] SC Res 743 21 February 1992. [190] SC Res 758 5 June 1992.

[191] SC Res 795 1 December 1992.

[192] SC Res 779, 6 October 1992; SC Res 780, 6 October 1992; SC Res 787, 16 November 1992.

[193] Horrified by conditions in Srebrenica and prevented from leaving by the inhabitants, Morillon hoisted the UN flag from the local post-office and told the crowd 'You are now under the protection of the United Nations. I will never abandon you.' D Rohde, *Endgame: The Betrayal and Fall of Srebrenica: Europe's Worst Massacre since World War II* (Westview Press Boulder 1998) xv.

[194] SC Res 819, 16 April 1993. [195] SC Res 824, 6 May 1993.

[196] SC Res 836, 4 June 1993. [197] SC Res 836, 4 June 1993.

'acting in self-defence.'[198] The safe areas were large and were never completely demilitarized, raising questions as to the extent to which their safety could be assured within the concept of self-defence.[199] Moreover, despite the robust language of its mandate UNPROFOR was largely configured and equipped for traditional peacekeeping duties.[200] The Secretary-General subsequently observed that non-troop contributing countries wanted the force to confront the Serbs whereas the troop-contributing countries wanted to avoid this. As a result:

> resolutions were adopted in which some of the more robust language favoured by the non-troop-contributing nations was accommodated. Chapter VII was invoked with increasing frequency, though often without specifying what that implied in terms of UNPROFOR operations. In this way, the efforts of Member States to find compromise between divergent positions led to the UNPROFOR mandate becoming rhetorically more robust than the Force itself.[201]

Tadeusz Mazowieki, in his reports for the year 1994, drew attention to human rights violations by both sides that were taking place even within UN protected areas and UN 'safe areas.' In June 1994 he reported on massive human rights violations perpetrated by Bosnian Serbs in the 'safe area' of Gorazde and in his report of November 1994 he expressed concern over the ongoing violence, harassment and intimidation of minorities in the UN Protected Areas in Croatia.[202] In July 1995 Srebrenica was overrun. UNPROFOR troops did not try to stop them.[203] Dutchbat was in a much weaker position than the Serbs numerically and in terms of resources. Moreover, General Sir Michael Rose was acutely conscious of the local population's dependency on the UN for humanitarian aid and the consequent need for the UN to work with the Serbs.[204] The local commander

[198] Report of the Secretary-General pursuant to General Assembly Resolution 53/55: *The Fall of Srebrenica* UN Doc A/54/549 (15.11.1999), [79]; General Sir Michael Rose, *Fighting for Peace: Lessons from Bosnia* (2nd edn, Warner Books London 1999), 360.

[199] General Sir Michael Rose, *Fighting for Peace: Lessons from Bosnia* (n 198), 360.

[200] The former Special Representative of the UN Secretary General for the former Yugoslavia, Yasushi Akashi, wrote that 'the Security Council entrusted UNPROFOR with a mandate that it knew or should have known, was not only unrealistic, but impossible to implement. That the creation of the safe areas was a "quick fix" response to an immediate problem was evident in the Security Council's hesitation to provide UNPROFOR with the necessary resources to implement its mandate... the force was faced with a peculiar situation: on the one hand, there was a strongly stated commitment by the Security Council to protect the civilian populations in the safe areas, while on the other hand, none of the Security Council members, including those most supportive of the creation of the safe area mandate and some of whom already had troops within the UNPROFOR, were willing or able to provide the resources necessary to carry out the mandate.' Y Akashi, 'The Use of Force in a United Nations Peace-Keeping Operation: Lessons Learnt from the Safe Areas Mandate, 19 Fordham International Law Journal, 312, 315–316.

[201] Report of the Secretary-General pursuant to General Assembly Resolution 53/55: *The Fall of Srebrenica* (n 198), [43].

[202] United Nations, *The Blue Helmets: A Review of United Nations Peace-keeping* (n 42), 503.

[203] Norrie McQueene has described this as abandonment by the UN: N MacQueen, *The United Nations since 1945: Peacekeeping and the Cold War* (n 45), 74.

[204] General Sir Michael Rose, *Fighting for Peace: Lessons from Bosnia* (n 198), 354.

called for air strikes but 'those requests were not heeded by his superiors at various levels, and some of them may not have been received at all.'[205] After they took the town, the Serbs separated Muslim women and children from the men.[206] Their identity cards were removed, piled into a heap and destroyed. The men were taken away and executed. The UN Secretary General Kofi Annan called it 'a massacre on a scale unprecedented in Europe since the Second World War.'[207] Judge Riad of the International Tribunal for the Former Yugoslavia described it as:

> a truly terrible massacre of the Muslim population... The evidence tendered by the Prosecutor describes scenes of unimaginable savagery: thousands of men executed and buried in mass graves, hundreds of men buried alive, men and women mutilated and slaughtered, children killed before their mothers' eyes, a grandfather forced to eat the liver of his own grandson. These are truly scenes from hell, written on the darkest pages of human history.[208]

4.6 Civilian Protection in UN Peacekeeping Operations during the early to mid-1990s: Summary

UNTAG saw the start of more broadly based multi-functional peacekeeping operations that went beyond supporting parties to a conflict in maintaining peace agreements made between them and took on tasks relating to the establishment and securing of stable post colonization and/or post conflict States. In addition to the positivism engendered by the success of elections in Namibia, early in the decade Operation Provide Comfort, deployed to Iraq, raised hopes that a new world order had begun in which the United Nations would be 'capable of maintaining international peace and security, of securing justice and human rights and of promoting... social progress and better standards of life.'[209] However,

[205] Report of the Secretary-General pursuant to General Assembly resolution 53/55, *The fall of Srebrenica* (n 198), [471].

[206] Refugees at the UN base camp in Potočari were forced outside to where the Serbs were waiting for them. Major Franken, the acting commander, subsequently gave testimony in the *Kristic* trial at the ICTY. After Franken had acknowledged that he knew that the refugees would be killed, the judge asked him if 'to your knowledge there was no plan to foot at the UN to try to mobilize humanitarian organizations or anything to do anything once they got up to Potočari?" Franken replied that "No, seen the fact that we got orders to defend the Potočari perimeter even if necessary with defensive air support and two hours later we got orders to facilitate the deportation, it was obvious there was no plan on the UN side." Major Franken's testimony 04.04.2000: *Prosecutor v Radislav Krstic*, International Criminal Tribunal for the former Yugoslavia, Case No IT-98–33-T, P18 (Judgment 2 Aug., 2001).

[207] Press Release SG/SM/7489, Secretary-General Kofi Annan, United Nations, Srebrenica Tragedy Will Forever Haunt United Nations History, Says Secretary-General on Fifth Anniversary of City's Fall (10 July 2000), available at <http://www.un.org/News/Press/docs/2000/20000710.sgsm7489.doc.html>.

[208] Press release issued by the International Tribunal for the Former Yugoslavia (cc/PIO/026-E), The Hague, 16 November 1995.

[209] 'An Agenda for Peace, Preventive Diplomacy, Peacemaking and Peace-keeping' Report of the Secretary-General pursuant to the statement adopted by the Summit Meeting of the Security Council on 31 January 1992, UN Doc A/47/277–S/24111, [3].

although Secretary-General Boutros Ghali's *Agenda for Peace* acknowledged that 'the time of absolute and exclusive sovereignty... has passed'[210] this statement was made in the context of unusual Security Council co-operation, and in relation to operations that had broad based international support. Colonization had run its course and there was no support for anything other than independence for Namibia. Iraq's government was unable to resist coalition forces since it was recovering from defeat in the Kuwait war and had no allies on whom it could rely. But in the years that followed UN forces were deployed into highly complex conflict scenarios in which the UN's commitment to human security was sharply tested; and found wanting.

UNTAC, deployed at the height of enthusiasm for the UN's new role, was hailed as a success internationally for ensuring that elections went ahead and for the exceptionally high turn out on the day. However, within Cambodia itself, there was little support for the force whose conduct was regarded as ill disciplined, self-serving and in some cases seriously abusive; sexual exploitation, including of children, was a problem. In addition, NGOs reported that UNTAC was willing to turn a blind eye to massacres and ethnic cleansing rather than risk jeopardizing the elections.

At around the same time (1992) a UN mission was deployed to the failed State of Somalia. The UN force, and the US force that was deployed later that same year, were ill prepared for the chaotic and lawless environment they found there. High levels of casualties amongst civilians, the parties to the conflict and peacekeepers, together with serious abuses of human rights committed by peacekeepers as well as others, brought the operations there into disrepute. The killing of 18 soldiers prompted the US to adopt a new highly restrictive policy towards peacekeeping. Pressure from the US ensured that the response to the genocide in Rwanda in 1994 was slow and far too minimal for the scale and gravity of the human rights atrocities that took place. The approach to the humanitarian crisis in Bosnia-Herzegovina the following year was muddled. UNPROFOR's mandate was frequently revised but the desire for consensus, the fears and interests of the troop contributing States, and the need for the UN to be seen to be doing something, meant that there was no clarity as to what the mandate meant, a problem that was exacerbated by poor leadership and poor communication. As a result seven thousand men were massacred and nothing was done to stop it.

Thus by the mid 1990s the UN's record on civilian protection was at a shameful low. The implicit understanding in the peacekeeping doctrine drawn up by Hammarskjöld in the early days of the Cold War, that peacekeepers had an obligation to protect civilians (albeit as far as possible within the constraints of the self-defence norm), appears to have been forgotten. The euphoria arising from the initial post Cold War co-operation between Security Council members and the success of Operation Provide Comfort had raised hopes that the protection

[210] ibid [17].

of people from serious human rights abuses would no longer be subordinate to State sovereignty and State interests. This euphoria rapidly dissipated in the face of high peacekeeper casualties to be replaced by US withdrawal from peacekeeping and by an overly restrictive interpretation of Hammarskjöld's peacekeeping principles. Initial analyses of mission responses to the genocides by the UN Department of Peacekeeping Operations were slow to address the UN's failings, but the insistent pressure for inquiry and reform generated in response to the atrocities, eventually prompted a major change in attitudes towards the UN's role in civilian protection, and that of regional organizations.

5. Lessons Learned from the Failure to Prevent Genocide

In 1993 and 1994 the Security Council authorized the establishment of the International Criminal Tribunals for the former Yugoslavia, and for Rwanda, to prosecute those involved in perpetrating war crimes and crimes against humanity during these conflicts;[211] but it was slow to critically examine in its own role in failing to prevent the genocides. The UN's *General Guidelines for Peacekeeping*, published in October 1995, makes only one reference to the protection of civilians and it is critical not of the failure to protect, but of the attempt. The report notes that protecting civilians in safe areas was one of three aspects of peacekeeping in Somalia and Bosnia-Herzegovina that led peacekeeping forces to lose the consent of the parties to the conflict and 'to behave in a way that was perceived to be partial and/or to use force other than in self-defence.'[212] There are no references to genocide, massacres or crimes against humanity, in the forty page document.

In early 1995 the UN Department of Peacekeeping Operations established a Lessons Learned Unit (now renamed the Best Practices Unit) to produce reports on the successes and failures of its missions.[213] The Unit's 1996 general report *Multidisciplinary Peacekeeping: Lessons from Recent Experience*, although it does have a section entitled 'Relations with the Local Population', does not discuss

[211] SC Res 808 22 February 1993; SC Res 955 8 November 1994.

[212] United Nations Department of Peacekeeping Operations, *General Guidelines for Peacekeeping Operations* (n 3), [29]; The other two were protecting humanitarian operations during continuing warfare and pressing the parties to achieve national reconciliation at a pace faster than they were ready to accept. The Secretary-General Boutros Boutros-Ghali had made a similar point in January 1995 in his *Supplement to An Agenda for Peace*, in which he retreated from the stance adopted in his 1992 *An Agenda for Peace*. The latter had implied the possibility of future peacekeeping missions operating outside the consent of the parties: *Supplement to An Agenda for Peace* UN Doc A/48/403 A/50/60, S/19951, 3 January 1995, [34].

[213] The Unit's analyses of the failures of key missions of the early 1990s have been criticized as less than rigorous: *Comprehensive Review of the Whole Question of Peacekeeping Operations in all their Aspects*; Report of the Secretary-General on *Implementation of the Recommendations of the Special Committee on Peacekeeping Operations and the Panel on United Nations Peace Operations* A/55/977 1 June 2001, [65].

civilian protection or crimes against humanity at all.[214] Moreover, despite the horrific scale of the genocide in Rwanda, the Unit's report on UNAMIR did not engage in an in-depth analysis of how peacekeepers should respond to crimes against humanity. Whilst it is true that UNAMIR's force level was too small and the mission was not designed or equipped for a conflict situation, the Report's conclusion that therefore 'the Mission had neither the appropriate mandate nor the means to take any effective action',[215] is overly defensive. The significance of the provisions in the ROE allowing for the use of force in response to attacks on civilians was cursorily dismissed in a single paragraph:

Some people have advanced the argument that UNAMIR could have resorted to its rules of engagement, one paragraph of which was interpreted as authorizing the operation to take any necessary action, including the use of force, to protect civilians at risk. Other participants at the Comprehensive Seminar warned against any attempt to usurp the powers of the Security Council, which, under the Charter of the United Nations, is the only body authorized to decide on mandates of peacekeeping operations. Senior military officials of UNAMIR stated that, during that period, even if they had wanted to invoke that paragraph of the rules of engagement, they did not have the physical capability and the means to do so.[216]

The report is similarly dismissive of Dallaire's requests to confiscate weapons caches:

The discussion that occurred between UNAMIR and the Secretariat on the issue of searching for and confiscating weapons in early 1994 elucidates the relationship between a peacekeeping mission and the Secretariat. Interviews revealed that, on the one hand, it is the role of Headquarters to prod reluctant mission leaders to take action in conformity with the mission's mandate. Yet, on the other hand, it must temper the enthusiasm of the mission leaders who may either wish to stretch the mandate or believe that they have the means to carry out ambitious plans, although within the mandate, but not practical within existing means.[217]

The report notes that, despite its reduced presence, 'UNAMIR troops protected tens of thousands of Rwandese who took shelter at sites under their control.'[218] However, the report does not mention the massacre at Kicukiro or the deaths of political leaders whilst under UN protection. The report does mention the massacre of internally displaced people at the Kibeho camp in April 1995 but only to comment that '[m]any Rwandese believed that the United Nations was there to stop the genocide and were bitterly disappointed when this was not the case.'[219]

[214] Lessons Learned Unit, Department of UN Peacekeeping Operations, *Multidisciplinary Peacekeeping: Lessons from Recent Experience* (December 1996).

[215] United Nations, Lessons Learned Unit, Department of Peacekeeping Operations, *Comprehensive Report on Lessons Learned from the United Nations Assistance Mission for Rwanda (UNAMIR) October 1993–April 1996* (n 188), [10].

[216] ibid [11].

[217] ibid 32, [41].

[218] ibid 6, 32, [43].

[219] ibid 42, [87].

This extraordinarily insensitive understatement is then followed by the following observation:

It has been suggested that UNAMIR should have done much more to inform the public about its limited role and mandate early on, particularly for the protection of civilians at risk, so as not to give the people a false sense of security. This might also have averted disasters such as the Kibeho massacre, where internally displaced people in the Kibeho camp believed that UNAMIR soldiers would protect them from the RPA [Rwandan Patriotic Army].[220]

The UN's Department of Peacekeeping also produced a Peacekeeping Training Manual,[221] which provides guidelines to be used for training of peacekeepers in all Member States. However, although it is nearly 300 pages long, it does not refer to the protection of civilians or discuss responses to crimes against humanity. The latter part of the Manual consists of a serious of training exercises, using example situations. Exercise 4 deals with the use of force; none of the example situations relates to the protection of civilians.

5.1 The Independent Inquiries; the Brahimi Report; the Kosovo Report

It was not until the appointment of Kofi Annan as Secretary-General in 1997,[222] that the UN began to critically investigate its failure to react effectively to the 1994 and 1995 genocides.[223] Kofi Annan commissioned two high level inquiries into the UN's response to the genocides, one a UN inquiry into the Fall of Srebrenica,[224] and the other an Independent Inquiry into the Actions of the United Nations during the 1994 Genocide in Rwanda.[225] Both produced highly critical reports emphasizing the need for lessons to be learned. The *Report of the Independent Inquiry into the Actions of the United Nations during the 1994 Genocide in Rwanda*, published in 1999, praised the personnel courage of many UN personnel in Rwanda, but stated that a 'force numbering 2,500 should have been able to stop or limit massacres of the kind which began after the plane crash which killed the presidents of Rwanda and Burundi.'[226] UNAMIR's mandate

[220] ibid 42, [87].

[221] United Nations, *United Nations Peacekeeping Training Manual* (United Nations Department of Peacekeeping Operations, New York and the International Training Centre of the International Labour Organization, Turin; there is no date on the document but it was produced shortly after the establishment of the Centre at Turin in 1996).

[222] Kofi Annan was Under-Secretary General for Peacekeeping Operations from 1993–1995 and Special Representative of the Secretary-General to the former Yugoslavia from 1995–1996.

[223] The UN's human rights rapporteur, Tadeusz Mazowieski, visited Srebrenica within days of the massacre and immediately afterwards resigned his post.

[224] Report of the Secretary-General pursuant to General Assembly Resolution 53/55: *The Fall of Srebrenica* (n 198).

[225] Report of the Independent Inquiry into the Actions of the United Nations during the 1994 Genocide in Rwanda (n 165) <http://www.un.org/News/ossg/rwanda_report.htm>.

[226] ibid 28.

'was cautious in its conception' but it was also interpreted cautiously by the Secretariat.[227] Moreover, the effectiveness of the force was hampered by a lack of intelligence about the true nature of what was happening and by command and control problems.[228] The Report criticized the lack of political will on the Security Council and amongst Member States but also criticized the peacekeepers who, in some cases, 'by not resisting the threat to the persons they were protecting...showed a lack of resolve to fulfil their mission.'[229] In particular, the manner in which troops abandoned civilians at the Ecole Technique Officielle was said to be 'disgraceful.'[230]

The report on the *Fall of Srebrenica*, noted that none of the troop contributing States had been willing to provide any of the additional troops that would have been necessary to repel attacks against the safe areas by military force. UNPROFOR's major deterrent capacity was to flow from its presence in the safe areas and not from its military strength.[231] Whilst acknowledging the vulnerability of the 150 lightly armed Dutch UNPROFOR troops in Srebrenica (a besieged town, overburdened with huge numbers of displaced people and critically short of provisions, surrounded by approximately 2000 heavily armed Serb troops) the report concluded that if Dutchbat had engaged the Serbs when the safe area was attacked, events might have unfolded differently.[232] In the view of the Secretary-General the lesson to be learned from this is that:

> the United Nations must be aware that its presence in conflict areas also raises among those same civilians an expectation of protection which must be borne in mind when analysing the means necessary to conduct an operation. Whether or not an obligation to protect civilians is explicit in the mandate of a peacekeeping operation, the Rwandan genocide shows that the United Nations must be prepared to respond to the perception and the expectation of protection created by its very presence.[233]

In his concluding remarks on the report Kofi Annan urged Member States to engage in a process of reflection and to consider:

> issues such as the gulf between mandate and means; the inadequacy of a symbolic deterrence in the face of a systematic campaign of violence; the pervasive ambivalence within the United Nations regarding the role of force in the pursuit of peace; an institutional impartiality even when confronted with attempted genocide; and a range of doctrinal and institutional issues that go to the heart of the United Nations ability to keep the peace and help protect civilians from armed conflict.[234]

In September 1999 the Security Council adopted the first of a series of resolutions on the Protection of Civilians in Armed Conflict. Resolution 1265 stressed the need for UN personnel involved in peacemaking, peacekeeping

[227] ibid 30. [228] ibid 33.
[229] ibid 43. [230] ibid 43.
[231] Report of the Secretary-General pursuant to General Assembly Resolution 53/55: *The Fall of Srebrenica* (n 198), [95].
[232] ibid [472]. [233] ibid [502]. [234] ibid [505].

and peace-building activities to have 'appropriate training in international humanitarian, human rights and refugee law' and expressed the Council's 'willingness to consider how peacekeeping mandates might better address the negative impact of armed conflict on civilians.'[235] The following year in Resolution 1296 of 19 April 2000, on the Protection of Civilians in Armed Conflict, the Council affirmed:

its intention to ensure, where appropriate and feasible, that peacekeeping missions are given suitable mandates and adequate resources to protect civilians under imminent threat of physical danger, including by strengthening the ability of the United Nations to plan and rapidly deploy peacekeeping personnel, civilian police, civil administrators, and humanitarian personnel, utilizing the stand-by arrangements as appropriate.[236]

On the 7 March 2000 Kofi Annan convened a Panel on United Nations Peace Operations, chaired by Mr. Lakhdar Brahimi, to assess the shortcomings of the system under which UN peace operations are conducted. In August 2000 the Panel published its report, commonly referred to as 'the Brahimi Report', which aimed to make 'frank, specific and realistic recommendations for change.'[237] The opening paragraph set a strong tone:

Without significant institutional change, increased financial support and renewed commitment on the part of Member States, the United Nations will not be capable of executing the critical peacekeeping and peace-building tasks that the Member States assign it in the coming months and years. There are many tasks which the United Nations should not be asked to do. But when the United Nations does send its forces to uphold the peace, they must be prepared to confront the lingering forces of war and violence with the ability and determination to defeat them.[238]

The key conditions for success for any operation are 'political support, rapid deployment with a robust posture and a sound peace-building strategy.'[239]

The report set out a number of recommendations on preventive action and peace-building as well as recommendations for peacekeeping doctrine and

[235] S/RES/1265, 17 September 1999, [14], [11].

[236] SC Res 1296, 19 April 2000, [13]; A third resolution adopted in April 2006 reiterates and expands the earlier commitments: SC Res 1674 28 April 2006; Paragraph 16, 'reaffirmed' the Council's 'practice of ensuring that the mandates if United Nations peacekeeping, political and peace-building missions include, where appropriate and on a case by case basis provisions regarding (i) the protection of civilians, particularly those under imminent threat of physical danger, within their zones of operation (ii) the facilitation of humanitarian assistance and (iii) the creation of conditions conducive to the voluntary, safe, dignified and sustainable return of refugees and internally displaced persons and *expresses its intention* of ensuring that (i) such mandates include clear guidelines as to what missions can and should do to achieve these goals, (ii) the protection of civilians is given high priority in decisions about the use of available capacity and resources, including information and intelligence resources, in the implementation of mandates, and (iii) that protection mandates are implemented.

[237] Report of the Panel on United Nations Peace Operations A/55/305-S/2000/809 August 21, 2000, [2].

[238] ibid [1]. [239] ibid [4].

strategy.[240] In the opening section on peacekeeping doctrine it emphasized that the 'consent of the parties, impartiality, and the use of force only in self-defense should remain the bedrock principles of peacekeeping',[241] but observed that consent is not always what it seems: consent may be partial or temporary. It may be agreed to at some level but not by local militias, or agreed to in order to buy time but without any real commitment. A party 'may seek to limit a force's freedom of movement, adopt a policy of persistent non-compliance with the provisions of an agreement, or withdraw its consent altogether':[242]

In the past, the United Nations has often found itself unable to respond effectively to such challenges. It is a fundamental premise of the present report, however, that it must be able to do so. Once deployed, United Nations peacekeepers must be able to carry out their mandate professionally and successfully. This means that United Nations military units must be capable of defending themselves, other mission components and the mission's mandate. Rules of engagement should not limit contingents to stroke-for-stroke responses but should allow ripostes sufficient to silence a source of deadly fire that is directed at United Nations troops or at the people they are charged to protect and, in particularly dangerous situations, should not force United Nations contingents to cede the initiative to their attackers.[243]

The report stressed that 'impartiality is not the same as neutrality, or equal treatment of all parties in all cases.'[244] Since targeting of civilians may constitute a threat to international peace and security and therefore may trigger Security Council action, if a United Nations peace operation 'is already on the ground, carrying out those actions may become its responsibility and it should be prepared.'[245] Where civilians are being deliberately attacked troops 'may not only be operationally justified in using force but morally compelled to do so.' The report continues:

Indeed, peacekeepers—troops or police—who witness violence against civilians should be presumed to be authorized to stop it, within their means, in support of basic United

[240] United Nations, *Handbook on UN Multi-dimensional Peacekeeping Operations* (United Nations Department of Peacekeeping Operations Best Practices Unit New York 2003), 6–7.

[241] Report of the Panel on United Nations Peace Operations (n 237), [48].

[242] ibid [48]. [243] ibid [49].

[244] ibid [50]; Jean Pictet discussed the distinction in his Commentary to the Fundamental Principles of the Red Cross in which he states that 'we cannot say someone who does not act is impartial for this would be confusing impartiality with neutrality but we can say that he is impartial who, in taking action, does so without prejudice. Impartiality presupposes that a man called upon to take action has sufficient freedom. This freedom has a double nature, on the one hand it is freedom vis-à-vis himself and on the other, freedom vis-a-vis the outside world. In the latter sense, freedom refers to independence, which we shall discuss in another chapter. Interior freedom is perhaps even more difficult to achieve than freedom from external influences, since passion, psychic complexes and preconceived ideas influence human behaviour and, what is especially serious, do so mostly when we are unaware of the fact. Emphasizing the difficulty of impartiality, Goethe wrote in his Aphorisms, I can promise to be sincere, but not to be impartial.' J Pictet, Principles of the Red Cross: Commentary (ICRC 1979), Principle II Impartiality.

[245] Report of the Panel on United Nations Peace Operations (n 237), [50].

Nations principles and, as stated in the report of the Independent Inquiry on Rwanda, consistent with 'the perception and the expectation of protection created by [an operation's] very presence' (see S/1999/1257, p. 51).[246]

Thus the report potentially links peacekeepers' responsibilities on the ground with the Security Council's responsibility for maintenance of international peace and security but also states that peacekeepers should in any case be presumed to be authorized to stop serious human rights abuses 'in support of basic United Nations principles.'

In this context 'basic United Nations principles' would seem to be a reference to the human rights orientated ethos of the Charter rather than the Council's obligations in relation to international peace and security, since the latter is dealt with on a case by case basis whereas the report indicates a presumption that peacekeepers should generally be authorized to respond to human rights abuses. The report does not discuss what peacekeepers should do when they are faced with a moral responsibility to act but the Secretariat considers this to be beyond their mandate. It does, however, stress the need for Member States to summon the political will to support the United Nations and to accept that mounting a credible operation may involve the risk of casualties.[247] Noting that there are thousands of civilians potentially at risk of being attacked, the report warns that promising to extend protection to civilians 'establishes a very high threshold of expectation... If an operation is given a mandate to protect civilians, therefore, it also must be given the specific resources needed to carry out that mandate.[248]

In response to the report, the General Assembly convened an extraordinary session of the Special Committee on Peacekeeping Operations. Many of the delegates expressed concern at any evolution in peacekeeping, fearing that it would be used as an excuse to intervene in the internal affairs of Member States and also that resources for peacekeeping would be given priority over development issues.[249] In this the Committee was reiterating concerns regarding the concept of 'humanitarian intervention',[250] which it had voiced, in a report to the General Assembly in March 2000, in which it had emphasized that 'non-intervention in matters that are essentially within the domestic jurisdiction of any State, is crucial to common efforts, including peacekeeping operations, to promote international peace and security' and that 'respect for the basic principles of peacekeeping, such as the consent of the parties, impartiality and the non-use of force except in self-defence, is essential to its success.'[251]

[246] ibid [62]. [247] ibid [5], [52]. [248] ibid [63].

[249] 'Fourth Committee: Peacekeeping Reform' (2000) 37 United Nations Chronicle 4, <http://www.un.org/Pubs/chronicle/2000/issue4/0400p46.htm>.

[250] Special Committee on Peacekeeping Operations, Report on a 'Comprehensive review of the whole question of peacekeeping operations in all their aspects.' UN Doc A/54/839 20 March 2000, [21].

[251] ibid [51–52], [21].

Nevertheless, in response to the Brahimi report the Committee did take up a number of the Panel's recommendations, including measures for improving communications and co-ordination, for improving the speed at which troops can deploy, for ensuring the quality of mission leaders, for increasing staff levels in the UN's Department of Peacekeeping Operations, for improving pre-mission planning, and a call for increased resources so as to ensure that these are appropriate for the mission.[252] The Committee also stressed the need for 'clear, credible achievable mandates' and emphasized that once deployed peacekeepers 'must be capable of accomplishing the mission's mandate and of defending themselves and, where mandated, other mission components.' However, in the whole of the Committee's response there is no reference whatsoever to the protection of civilians.[253]

The absence of any reference to civilian protection despite two inquiries into genocide, the explicit recommendations of the Brahimi report, and Security Council Resolutions 1265 and 1296 on the Protection of Civilians in Armed Conflict, may be at least partially attributable to the high level of concern within the General Assembly aroused by NATO's intervention in Kosovo in June 1999 and the perceived threat to the inviolability of State sovereignty.[254] In September 1999 Kofi Annan had indicated that he thought that intervention was sometimes necessary where there were gross violations of human rights.[255] However, few states endorsed the Secretary-General's position and even fewer supported the Swedish position that 'the collective conscience of mankind demands action'.[256]

The following year the Independent International Commission on Kosovo recommended 'revising the so-called inviolability of sovereign states so that sovereignty becomes conditional on observance of certain minimal but universal and clear standards of behavior.'[257] The Commission concluded that because of the seriousness of the humanitarian catastrophe and the failure of the Security Council to respond effectively:

> the intervention was legitimate, but not legal, given existing international law. It was legitimate because it was unavoidable: diplomatic options had been exhausted, and two

[252] United Nations, Comprehensive Review of the whole question of peacekeeping operations in all their aspects, Report of the Special Committee on Peacekeeping Operations, UN Doc A/C4/55/6, 4 December 2000.

[253] ibid [8–9].

[254] UN General Assembly, Report of the Secretary-General on the implementation of the report of the Panel on United Nations Peace Operations (n 237), [7f] The Independent International Commission on Kosovo *The Kosovo Report* (Oxford University Press Oxford 2000), 296; Security Council, 4011th Meeting, 10 June 1999; W Durch and V Holt, *The Brahimi Report and the Future of UN Peace Operations* (Henry L Stimson Centre Washington 2003), 8.

[255] Kofi Annan's speech to the UN General Assembly on 20 September 1999 'Two Concepts of Sovereignty' UN Press Release SG/SM/7136 GA/9596 of 20 September 1999; text reprinted in K Annan, *The Question of Intervention: Statements by the Secretary-General* (UN Department of Public Information New York 1999); S Chesterman, *Just War or Just Peace?* (n 101), 183–4, 206.

[256] Address by Former President Nelson Mandela delivered at the Independent International Commission on Kosovo's final seminar, University of the Witwatersrand, South Africa, August 25, 2000 reprinted in *The Kosovo Report* (n 254), 15.

[257] The Independent International Commission on Kosovo *The Kosovo Report* (n 254), 291.

sides were bent on a conflict which threatened to wreak humanitarian catastrophe and generate instability through the Balkan peninsula. The intervention needs to be seen within a clear understanding of what is likely to have happened had intervention not taken place: Kosovo would still be under Serbian rule, and in the middle of a bloody civil war. Many people would still be dying and flows of refugees would be destabilizing neighbouring countries.[258]

The Commission went on to urge that:

The time is now ripe for the presentation of a principled framework for humanitarian intervention which could be used to guide future responses to imminent humanitarian catastrophes and which could be used to assess claims for humanitarian intervention.[259]

The Kosovo Report raised very different issues from those discussed in the Brahimi Report; the former dealt with intervention on humanitarian grounds, whereas the latter dealt with the responsibilities of peacekeepers already deployed. However, questions concerning the potentially robust use of force by peacekeepers and the overriding of consent requirements in the context of protection from serious abuses of human rights, were perceived to raise parallel, albeit separate, concerns over the threat to State sovereignty,[260] particularly in light of the fact that States are unlikely to be willing to contribute to robust peacekeeping operations unless they also serve State interests (an approach explicitly endorsed by the United States in Presidential Decision Directive 25).[261]

In his Millennium Report, Kofi Annan acknowledged that his implied support for the Kosovo intervention in his speech to the Assembly the previous year had caused anxiety among many UN Member States:

Some critics were concerned that the concept of 'humanitarian intervention' could become a cover for gratuitous interference in the internal affairs of sovereign states. Others felt that it might encourage secessionist movements deliberately to provoke governments into committing gross violations of human rights in order to trigger external interventions that would aid their cause. Still others noted that there is little consistency in the practice of intervention, owing to its inherent difficulties and costs as well as perceived national interests—except that weak states are far more likely to be subjected to it than strong ones.[262]

Kofi Annan went on to say that he recognized:

[258] ibid 289.

[259] ibid 10.

[260] W Durch and V Holt, *The Brahimi Report and the Future of UN Peace Operations* (n 254), 8.

[261] Presidential Decision Directive 25 stated that a primary consideration for US involvement in future peacekeeping operations was whether it advanced US interests and whether other countries would commit adequate resources. Other considerations to be taken into account were whether the US presence is essential to an operation's success; whether the risk to troops is acceptable; and whether the domestic and congressional support exists.

[262] Secretary-General Kofi Annan's Millennium Report, 'We The Peoples: The Role of the United Nations in the 21st Century' (New York April 3, 2000), 47 <http://www.un/org/millenium/sg/report/state/htm>.

both the force and the importance of these arguments. But to the critics I would pose this question: if humanitarian intervention is, indeed, an unacceptable assault on sovereignty, how should we respond to a Rwanda, to a Srebrenica—to gross and systematic violations of human rights that offend every precept of our common humanity?[263]

However, there is no evidence to suggest that had there been greater clarity over the doctrine of humanitarian intervention the Security Council might have been willing to authorize more robust protection in Rwanda and Srebrenica. The lack of clarity on the legality of humanitarian intervention did not prevent the intervention into Kosovo. UN troops were already deployed to Rwanda and Srebrenica when the genocides began. In the case of Rwanda, members of the Security Council appear to have believed that the Convention on the Prevention and Punishment of Genocide,[264] together with the prohibition on genocide as a *ius cogens* norm, obligates the Council, and UN Member States acting through the Council, to act in response to genocide; which is precisely why they delayed recognition that genocide was being perpetrated. Christine Shelley, the US State Department Spokesman at the time, consistently referred to 'acts of genocide' rather than 'genocide' when talking about the massacres in Rwanda and explained that:

there is a reason for the selection of words that we have made...There are obligations which arise in connection with use of the term [genocide].[265]

In the Balkans, crimes against humanity had been widely perpetrated before the genocide at Srebrenica and unlike UNAMIR, UNPROFOR did have a Chapter VII mandate in relation to the safe areas, although the scope of it was unclear. The reluctance to act to protect civilians in Rwanda and Srebrenica seems to have had more to do with political will and resources. In Bosnia-Herzegovina there was also concern that a robust response to the Serbs might prompt reprisals against civilians, or a refusal to allow humanitarian aid through.[266]

Whilst humanitarian intervention and peacekeepers' protection obligations are separate concepts involving different regimes of law (the *ius ad bellum* and *ius in bello* respectively), concerns relating to sovereignty overlap when peacekeepers cannot stop crimes against humanity without using force against the host State. As the UN, in its 2008 Principles and Guidelines for United Nations Peacekeeping, has pointed out:

While robust peacekeeping involves the use of force at the tactical level with the consent of the host authorities and/or the main parties to the conflict, peace enforcement may

[263] ibid.

[264] Convention on the Prevention and Punishment of the Crime of Genocide, Adopted by Resolution 260 (III) A of the United Nations General Assembly on 9 December 1948.

[265] *The Triumph of Evil*, Prods. M Robinson and B Loeterman, PBS *Frontline* Documentary 26 January 1999 <http://www.pbs.org/wgbh/pages/frontline/shows/evil>; C McQueen, *Humanitarian Intervention and Safety Zones* (n 183), 115.

[266] General Sir Michael Rose, *Fighting for Peace: Lessons from Bosnia* (n 198), 354.

involve the use of force at the strategic or international level, which is normally prohibited for Member States under Article 2(4) of the Charter unless authorized by the Security Council.[267]

However, the distinction may appear grey or blurred, at least to the parties, in situations where the attacks on civilians are perpetrated by the government of the host State, particularly where those attacks are part of the State's strategic domestic policy (for example to ethnically cleanse an area of a minority group that opposes the government's policies) or part of its strategic war aims (for example to ethnically cleanse an area of a minority group that has ethnic affiliations to the enemy). The Brahimi report argued that 'basic United Nations principles' provide peacekeepers with the authority to stop violence against civilians.[268] Basic United Nations principles are a permanent foundation for UN action, not something that varies on a case by case basis (although how to implement them may). However, 'basic United Nations principles' are also at the root of the expansion, in conceptual terms, of the UN's responsibility for the maintenance of international peace and security to encompass human security, an expansion now commonly referred to as 'the responsibility to protect.' That expansion will, and already has, impacted on the expectations of local populations, the international community and troops themselves, as regards the extent of peace keepers' obligations to provide protection.

5.2 The Emergence of the Responsibility to Protect Norm[269]

In response to the Secretary-General's Millennium challenge to find some means of resolving the potential conflict between respect for State sovereignty and the protection of human rights, Canadian Foreign Minister Lloyd Axworthy worked to establish the International Commission on Intervention and State Sovereignty (ICISS),[270] and succeeded in securing the participation of an impressive number of leading academics and diplomats from all parts of the world.[271] The ICISS report, *The Responsibility to Protect*, published in 2001, recommended the adoption of a new concept, 'the collective international responsibility to protect' which whilst emphasizing the responsibility of States to secure human rights and humanitarian norms allows room for humanitarian intervention should a

[267] United Nations Peacekeeping Operations, Principles and Guidelines (n 12), 19.

[268] Report of the Panel on United Nations Peace Operations (n 237), [62].

[269] It should be noted that the concept as a whole is much broader than the following analysis, which focuses on those aspects of the 'responsibility to protect' concept that have implications for the tactical use of force by troops to provide protection.

[270] International Commission on Intervention and State Sovereignty (ICISS) *The Responsibility to Protect* (Ottawa International Development Research Centre 2001).

[271] The ICISS comprised twelve commissioners drawn from a diverse range of regional backgrounds, views and perspectives. It was chaired by Gareth Evans and Mohamed Sahnoun. In addition to the commission meetings, eleven regional roundtables and national consultations were held to ensure that the commission heard the broadest range of opinions.

State fail to carry out its responsibilities in this regard. *The Responsibility to Protect* affirms that State sovereignty remains a core principle of international law, but with the added qualification that State sovereignty implies responsibility.[272] This 'imaginative approach was intended, at least in part, to "defang" the governments and individuals' who view discussion of intervention on humanitarian grounds as just another cloak for Western imperialism.[273] The essence of the Commission's argument is that 'the responsibility to protect' is a responsibility of all governments, first and foremost in their territories. The primary responsibility for the protection of the people in a State lies with the State itself.[274] But:

where a population is suffering serious harm, as a result of internal war, insurgency, repression or state failure, and the state in question is unwilling or unable to halt or avert it, the principle of non-intervention yields to the international responsibility to protect.'[275]

The ICISS argues that the 'collective international responsibility to protect' imposes obligations on the UN Security Council and also upon each and every individual State. There are a number of ways in which the UN and/or States may carry out this responsibility, ranging from diplomatic pressure and economic sanctions through to military action. Whilst the use of coercive measures, as a last resort, is only one aspect of the responsibility to protect, it is the most controversial. The report suggests that if non-forceful preventive measures are ineffective, coercive action by States or international organizations may be needed, preferably, but not necessarily, with the authorization of the Security Council. The Report suggested that should the Security Council fail to agree on action it

[272] ICISS, *The Responsibility to Protect* (n 270) XI; The Danish Institute of International Affairs also examined the issues and published a report in 1999, entitled Humanitarian Intervention: Legal and Political Aspects, in which it stated that 'The protection of human rights has become a 'shared responsibility' of the state and the international community. Under international law the state remains the prime [actor] responsible for the protection of individuals on its territory, but under international supervision. The responsibility of the international community to prevent and punish serious violations of human rights comes into play if the state is either unwilling to meet its international obligations or, in the case of "weak" or "failed" states, unable to prevent serious violations from being committed on its territory by private parties.' Similarly the Special Representative of the Secretary-General for Internally Displaced Persons, Francis Deng, had had also proposed the idea of 'sovereignty as responsibility' which 'means that national governments are duty bound to ensure minimum standards of security and social welfare for their citizens and be accountable both to the national body politic and the international community,' and a State that allows its citizens 'to suffer in a vacuum of responsibility' temporarily forfeits its moral claim to be treated as legitimate. Therefore its sovereignty and its right to non-intervention are suspended. F Deng, *Sovereignty as Responsibility* (Brookings Institution Washington, DC 1995); F Deng, 'Frontiers of Sovereignty' Leiden Journal of International Law 8 No 2 (1995) 249–286; F Deng Protecting the Dispossessed: A Challenge for the International Community (Brookings Institution Washington, DC 1993).

[273] DM Malone, Book Review of *Humanitarian Intervention: Ethical, Legal, and Political Dilemmas*, eds JL Holzgrefe and RO Keohane (Cambridge University Press, Cambridge 2003) in 97 AJIL, 999, 1001.

[274] ibid XI; *Vienna Declaration and Programme of Action* adopted by the UN World Conference on Human Rights on 25 June 1993 (UNHCHR Geneva) General Assembly A/CONF. 157/23 and 32 International Legal Materials 1661 (1993) [1].

[275] ICISS, *The Responsibility to Protect* (n 270), XI.

might be possible to seek support from the General Assembly in an Emergency Special Session utilizing the 'Uniting for Peace' procedure.[276] Alternatively collective intervention by a regional organization might be another possibility.[277] The ICISS, in summarizing its position, acknowledged the fears of many States that intervention without Security Council authorization, even where there were strong humanitarian grounds for the action, could nevertheless be exploited by the more powerful States to exercise unjustified control over weaker States: but it concluded that 'if the Security Council fails to discharge its responsibility to protect in conscience-shocking situations crying out for action, then it is unrealistic to expect that concerned states will rule out other means and forms of action.'[278]

The ICISS report has been extremely influential and 'has succeeded in provoking debate where it matters most: in the marketplace of ideas.'[279] In 2004 the Secretary-General's High Level Panel on Threats, Challenges and Change[280] endorsed:

> the emerging norm that there is a collective international responsibility to protect, exercisable by the Security Council authorizing military intervention as a last resort, in the event of genocide and other large-scale killing, ethnic cleansing or serious violations of international humanitarian law which sovereign Governments have proved powerless or unwilling to prevent.[281]

The efforts of Kofi Annan in speeches and in his report *In Larger Freedom*[282] succeeded in persuading the General Assembly, at the September 2005 World Summit, to formally endorse this aspect of the responsibility to protect, if necessary through Chapter VII measures. The Assembly undertook:

> to take collective action, in a timely and decisive manner, through the Security Council, in accordance with the Charter, including Chapter VII, on a case by case basis and in co-operation with relevant regional organizations as appropriate, should peaceful means be inadequate and national authorities are manifestly failing to protect their populations from genocide, war crimes, ethnic cleansing and crimes against humanity.[283]

This provision was affirmed by the Security Council in its third resolution on the Protection of Civilians in Armed Conflict, Resolution 1674 adopted unanimously on 28 April 2006.[284] In Resolution 1674 the Council also reaffirmed 'its

[276] ibid [6.29–6.30]. [277] ibid [6.31–6.35].

[278] ibid [6.40] Precautionary Principles.

[279] DM Malone, Book Review of *Humanitarian Intervention: Ethical, Legal, and Political Dilemmas* (n 273), 999.

[280] Report by the Secretary-Generals' High Level Panel on Threats, Challenges and Change '*A More Secure World: Our Shared Responsibility*' [201–203] <http://www.un.org//secureworld>.

[281] ibid 65–66, [201] [203].

[282] In Larger Freedom; towards development, security and human rights for all A/59/2005 21 March 2005, [135].

[283] A/RES/6/1, 24 October 2005, [139].

[284] S/RES/1674, 28 April 2006, [4]; In paragraph 26 The Council also noted 'that the deliberate targeting of civilians and other protected persons, and the commission of systematic, flagrant and

practice of ensuring that the mandates of United Nations peacekeeping, political and peacebuilding missions include, where appropriate and on a case-by-case basis, provisions regarding (i) the protection of civilians, particularly those under imminent threat of physical danger within their zones of operation.'[285]

The conceptual link between peacekeepers' protection responsibilities and the collective international 'responsibility to protect' was noted, impliedly at least, by a number of delegates to the Security Council Open Debate on the Protection of Civilians in Armed Conflict, in June 2006. The Argentinian delegate commented that:

> ... the Outcome Document of the 2005 Summit consolidated the rich debate of the previous years through the adoption of the concept of responsibility to protect populations from genocide, war crime, ethnic cleansing and crime against humanity. In this document our leaders indicated that they are ready to take collective action in a timely and decisive fashion through this Council against these grave situations. The second significant development of the issue was given by the approval by unanimity of resolution 1674 on the protection of civilians in armed conflicts by the Council, completing and updating the legal framework that was established by resolutions 1265 and 1296.[286]
>
> ... Both elements, the responsibility to protect and the new resolution of the Council on the protection of civilians are the start of a new phase regarding the actions to be taken by the international community in this subject.[287]

The majority of peacekeeping mission mandates, and the ROE for both UN and regional peacekeeping operations, now include reference to obligations of peacekeepers in relation to civilian protection, often in language that reflects the 'responsibility to protect' concept. Thus most mandates for multi-dimensional peacekeeping operations since 1999 provide that peacekeepers have authorization to provide protection but also include a statement to the effect that peacekeepers' responsibilities are subsidiary to the sovereign responsibilities of the host State to secure the human rights of their populations. However, the appearance of this

widespread violations of international humanitarian and human rights law in situations of armed conflict, may constitute a threat to international peace and security, and, *reaffirm[ed] in this regard* its readiness to consider such situations and, where necessary, to adopt appropriate steps'.

[285] S/RES 28 April 2006, [16]; A fourth resolution on the Protection of Civilians in Armed Conflict was adopted in December 2006, dealing mainly with protection of journalists: S/RES/1738 23 December 2006.

[286] S/RES/1265 (1999) deals with improving peacekeeping mandates so that they might better address 'the negative impact of armed conflict on civilians.' S/RES/1296 (2000) affirmed the Council's 'intention to ensure, where appropriate and feasible, that peacekeeping missions are given suitable mandates and adequate resources to protect civilians under imminent threat of physical danger.' S/RES/1674 (2006) affirms the UN's commitment 'to take collective action, in a timely and decisive manner, through the Security Council, in accordance with the Charter, including Chapter VII, on a case by case basis and in co-operation with relevant regional organizations as appropriate, should peaceful means be inadequate and national authorities are manifestly failing to protect their populations from genocide, war crimes, ethnic cleansing and crimes against humanity'.

[287] Security Council Open Debate on the Protection of Civilians in Armed Conflict, 28 June 2006.

format in the language of peacekeeping mandates predates the ICISS report and suggests a convergence of concerns stemming from a number of sources, including the inquiries into the 1994 and 1995 genocides, the Brahimi report, the ICISS report, the Secretary-General's High Level Panel on Threats, Challenges and Change, the World Summit Resolution of General Assembly and the Security Councils resolutions on the Protection of Civilians in Armed Conflict.

6. Civilian Protection in UN Peacekeeping Missions Since 1999

In 1999 the Security Council adopted the first of its resolutions on the Protection of Civilians in Armed Conflict in which it expressed the intention to 'better address the negative impact of armed conflict on civilians.'[288] However, whilst there have been some improvements, in many conflicts civilians still suffer appalling abuses despite the presence of international peacekeeping forces. Some of the problems that have arisen in implementing protection may be due to the exponential increase in the number of peacekeeping operations:[289] by early 2008 the UN was engaged in twenty operations, with between them approximately 100,000 personnel.[290] The number of personnel deployed is expected to rise to 140,000 by the end of 2008.[291] The African Union (AU) and the European Union (EU) are also engaged in peacekeeping operations in conjunction with UN missions. Both regional organizations have made strong commitments to civilian protection and if necessary and feasible to undertake military interventions for protection purposes.

For many years most African States were strongly opposed to humanitarian intervention fearing that it might provide cover for colonial style interference in their domestic affairs[292] but two years after the publication of the Kosovo report,

[288] S/RES/1265, 17 September 1999, [14], [11].

[289] The large number of peacekeeping operations deployed since 1999 precludes a detailed analysis of all of them in this chapter, therefore, although civilian protection has been an issue for most of these operations, this section will focus on key operations where civilian protection has been especially problematic.

[290] The UN peacekeeping budget doubled between 2001 and 2006, but this represents only one half of one percent of global military spending; Annual Report of the Secretary-General on UN Peacekeeping, 2007, UN Doc A/62/1 [51] ; William Lacy Swing, *The United Nations Mission in the Democratic Republic of the Congo (MONUC): Experiences and Lessons* (Institute for Security Studies Situation Report 23 November 2007), 4.

[291] United Nations Department of Peacekeeping Operations, *Peace Operations Year in Review, 2007*, 2.

[292] In August 2000 most participants (both African and non-African) at a seminar held by the South African Institute of International Affairs and the University of Witwatersrand in cooperation with the Independent International Commission on Kosovo, had criticized the doctrine of humanitarian intervention as a tool of Western powers. However they were also concerned that reliance on the Security Council was likely to leave African populations vulnerable in a humanitarian crisis since until recently the Council has been much more reluctant to authorize robust operations to

and a year after the publication of the ICISS report, the African Union (AU) adopted a new Constitutive Act, Article 4 of which provides for:

> the right of the Union to intervene in a Member State pursuant to a decision of the Assembly in respect of grave circumstances, namely: war crimes, genocide and crimes against humanity;[293]

The Constitutive Act is the first international treaty to recognize the right to intervene for a humanitarian purpose.

The Use of Force Concept for EU-led Military Crisis Management Operations also provides for intervention on humanitarian grounds. The Concept states that Military Crisis Management Operations may be deployed pursuant to permission or invitation of the host government; in self-defence; pursuant to authorization by the UN Security Council; pursuant to authorization by a competent regional arrangement in accordance with the UN Charter, and, 'if otherwise permitted under international law.' This last ground for the deployment of military force is listed separately from the other grounds enumerated above and is referenced to 'resolution A 3–0227/94 on the right of intervention on humanitarian grounds, adopted by the European Parliament at its session on 20 April 1994 (OJC 128, 9.5.1994, p. 225.'[294] The Use of Force Concept also suggests that since 'the law in Member States with regard to the use of force in self-defence varies in scope and nature' it may be necessary to issue 'Confirmatory ROE' whose purpose is to 'authorize the use of force in situations that for some EU-led forces would—even in the absence of these authorization—be acceptable within self-defence.'[295] These include a provision allowing minimum force, including deadly force, 'to defend other persons against attacks which endanger life or are likely to cause serious bodily harm.'[296] The inclusion of this in Confirmatory ROE indicates that there is no consensus, as yet, as to whether use of force in self-defence extends to a right to protect civilians from attacks deliberately perpetrated against them. However, this provision, along with the reference to humanitarian intervention

tackle human rights abuses in Africa than elsewhere: The Independent International Commission on Kosovo *The Kosovo Report* (n 254), 296; Address by Former President Nelson Mandela delivered at the Independent International Commission on Kosovo's final seminar, University of the Witwatersrand, South Africa, August 25, 2000 reprinted in *The Kosovo Report* (n 254), 15; Report by the Secretary-Generals' High Level Panel on Threats, Challenges and Change 'A More Secure World: Our Shared Responsibility', <http://www.un.org//secureworld>, 19, [41–42].

293 Constitutive Act of the African Union, Lome, Togo, (adopted 26 May 2001entered into force 11 July 2002) <http://www.africa-union.org/home/Welcome.htm>.

Following an amendment adopted by the Heads of State and Government of the AU at their First Extraordinary Session on 3 February 2003, in addition to interventions in response to war crimes, genocide and crimes against humanity, the AU may now intervene, upon the recommendation of the Peace and Security Council, when there is a serious threat to legitimate order for the purpose of restoring peace and stability in a member state of the AU.

294 Use of Force Concept for EU-led Military Crisis Management Operations EUMC DOC/CCD 02-14-06-OPS 16/2001 Final Draft (27/09/2002), 4.

295 ibid Annex A, 19.

296 ibid Appendix 6 to Annex A, 2.

as grounds for the authorization of use of force, suggests a strong commitment to human security protection.

6.1 West Africa

The first UN peacekeepers to be given an explicit protection mandate were those deployed to the conflict in West Africa that has encompassed Sierra Leone, Liberia and the Côte d'Ivoire with massive loss of civilian life. The UN Assistance Mission to Sierra Leone (UNAMSIL) was launched in 1999 as a Chapter VI mission, however, paragraph 14 of the mission's mandating resolution was adopted under Chapter VII. It provides:

> that in the discharge of its mandate UNAMSIL may take the necessary action to ensure the security and freedom of movement of its personnel and, within its capabilities and areas of deployment, to afford protection to civilians under imminent threat of physical violence, taking into account the responsibilities of the Government of Sierra Leone and ECOMOG [Military Observer Group of the Economic Community of West African States]'[297]

The mission rapidly foundered partly because of poor planning and training. The Chapter VII authorization for paragraph 14 proved to be of little significance to the way in which the operation was initially conducted. However, in 2000, after 500 peacekeepers were taken hostage by the Revolutionary United Front, British forces, deployed ostensibly to evacuate nationals, undertook to secure the capital Freetown and to organize and train UN troops and conduct joint patrols with them. The force adopted a robust approach which was subsequently adopted by UNAMSIL.[298] In February 2000 the operation was expanded to a full Chapter VII mission.[299] By January 2002 UNAMSIL had disarmed 72,490 combatants (including at least 6,845 children).[300] By April 2002 a joint government-UN committee had declared most areas safe for resettlement by internally displaced people and refugees and around 165,000 had returned home.[301] In May; 'the first truly non-violent' elections in Sierra Leone's history took place, made possible 'in large part because of the successful disarmament and the continued substantial presence of UNAMSIL peacekeepers.'[302] UNAMSIL completed its mandate in 2005. A public opinion survey conducted at that time showed strong support for

[297] S/RES/1270 22 October 1999, [14].

[298] Fourth Report of the Secretary-General Pursuant to Security Council Resolution 1270 (1999) on the United Nations Mission in Sierra Leone, UN Doc S/2000/455 (19 May 2000), [14].

[299] UNAMSIL's protection tasks were expanded to include providing security at key locations and Government buildings; facilitating the free flow of people, goods and humanitarian assistance along specified thoroughfares; and providing security in and at all sites of the disarmament, demobilization and reintegration programme: S/RES/1289, 7 February 2000, [10].

[300] M Malan, S Meek, T Thusi, J Ginifer, P Coker, *Sierra Leone—Building the Road to Recover* (Institute of Security Studies Monograph 80 March 2003 <http://www.iss.co.za>), 14.

[301] ibid 15.

[302] ibid 16.

the mission. 98% of respondents believed the security situation had improved during UNAMSIL's deployment and that the force had conducted itself professionally; 94% believed UNAMSIL had 'done a great job in raising awareness of human rights, holding workshops, establishing district human rights committees, human rights clubs, and intervening on behalf of victims.'[303]

From 2003 peacekeepers were also deployed to the neighbouring States of Liberia and Côte d'Ivoire. The UN Mission in Liberia (UNMIL) is authorized 'to...ensure the security and freedom of movement of its personnel and, without prejudice to the efforts of the government, to protect civilians under imminent threat of physical violence, within its capabilities.'[304] The ROE allow for the use of force 'up to and including deadly force...to protect civilians, including humanitarian workers, under imminent threat of physical violence, when competent local authorities are not in a position to render immediate assistance.'[305] Whilst the security situation in Liberia remains fragile, and violence against women in particular remains a serious problem, a public opinion survey conducted in 2006 indicated that 94% of respondents believed that the security situation had improved during UNMIL's deployment and 91% believed that the force conducted itself professionally. 88 percent believed that UNMIL had helped to improve human rights conditions in Liberia, 'by bringing peace to Liberia through increased security, disarmament, and enabling people to have freedom of movement' and also by raising awareness of human rights, holding human rights seminars, and intervening on behalf of victims.'[306]

The 2004 UN Mission to the Côte d'Ivoire (UNOCI), and the missions there in 2003 led by France and the Economic Community of South West Africa (ECOWAS), were authorized to protect civilians under imminent threat of physical violence, within their capabilities and areas of deployment 'without prejudice to the responsibilities of the Government of National Reconciliation.'[307] UNOCI's mandate has been renewed and extended several times. Resolution

[303] J Krasno, *Public Opinion Survey of UNAMSIL's Work in Sierra Leone*, Conducted January-February 2005 (External Study undertaken for the UN Department of Peacekeeping Operations City College of New York and Yale University July 2005), 4–6, 19, 26.

[304] S/RES/1509, 19 September 2003, [3]; The same paragraph also authorizes UNMIL to facilitate the provision of humanitarian assistance, including by helping to establish the necessary security conditions; to contribute towards international efforts to protect and promote human rights in Liberia, with particular attention to vulnerable groups including refugees, returning refugees and internally displaced persons, women, children, and demobilized child soldiers, within UNMIL's capabilities and under acceptable security conditions, in close cooperation with other United Nations agencies, related organizations, governmental organizations, and non-governmental organizations; to ensure an adequate human rights presence, capacity and expertise within UNMIL to carry out human rights promotion, protection, and monitoring activities.

[305] United Nations Mission in Liberia (UNMIL), Rules of Engagement—Soldiers Pocket Card. A starred postscript adds 'when and where possible, permission to use force should be sought from the immediate superior commander'.

[306] J Krasno, *Public Opinion Survey of UNMIL's Work in Liberia*, Conducted January 2006 (n 303), 5–6, 11–17.

[307] S/RES/1464, 4 February 2003 [9] S/RES/1528, 27 February 2004, [6].

1572 of 15 November 2004 mandates the establishment of a Committee to examine allegations of human rights abuses in Côte d'Ivoire. Under Resolution 1739 of 10 January 2007 UNOCI is specifically tasked with contributing to the protection and promotion of human rights, mainly by monitoring, investigating and reporting.[308] But there have been problems. The Secretary-General in his May 2007 Progress Report expressed concern over allegations of misconduct by some UNOCI troops and reports of 'instances when UNOCI troops in the western part of the country had failed to intervene when civilians in their areas of deployment were under attack, including cases of gender-based violence.'[309] In the same paragraph the Secretary-General 'stressed the need to take immediate action to ensure full compliance with the Secretary-General's zero tolerance policy',[310] which would seem to imply that the troops failure to intervene in gender-based violence may be a consequence of the peacekeepers own attitudes to sexual exploitation.

The Secretary-General's January 2008 Progress Report noted that violence against civilians, including sexual violence against children, remains widespread and is of serious concern, but he also noted that UNOCI has been actively promoting human rights through training and workshop sessions and the setting up of human rights clubs in schools.[311] Whilst human security remains fragile it is probably the case that UNOCI's presence has prevented major massacres of civilians.[312]

6.2 The Democratic Republic of the Congo

The UN also has major commitments to peacekeeping in central Africa, of which the largest and most complex is in the Democratic Republic of the Congo. The

[308] Human Rights Watch has criticized the UN on the grounds that it has failed to send a strong message that 'the era of impunity in Côte d'Ivoire is over' in particular by failing to make public a report on human rights abuses conducted under the auspices of the United Nations High Commissioner for Human Rights and submitted to the Council in 2005: Human Rights Watch, Letter to UN Security Council on Upcoming Mission to Africa, June 12, 2007.

[309] Thirteenth progress report of the Secretary-General on the United Nations Operation in Côte d'Ivoire, 14 May 2007, UN Doc S/2007/275, [30].

[310] ibid. 'Since 2004 the UN has been investigating a "shockingly large number" of peacekeepers that have engaged in sexual exploitation in the Democratic Republic of the Congo (DRC) and other missions and has declared a zero tolerance policy': UN News Centre 'UN will enforce 'zero tolerance' policy against sexual abuse, peacekeeping official says' 5 January 2007 <http://www.un.org/apps/news/story.asp?NewsID=21169&Cr=sex&Cr1=abuse>; *Report of the Secretary-General: A Comprehensive Strategy to Eliminate Future Sexual Exploitation and Abuse in United Nations Peacekeeping Operations*, UN Doc A/59/10 26 March 2005; Secretary-General's Bulletin on Special Measures for Protection from Sexual Exploitation and Sexual Abuse UN Doc ST/SGB/2003/13 9 October 2003.

[311] Fifteenth progress report of the Secretary-General on the United Nations Operation in Côte d'Ivoire, 2 January 2008, UN Doc S/2008/1, [2–3] [45–48].

[312] Susan C. Breau, 'The Impact of the Responsibility to Protect on Peacekeeping', 11 Journal of Conflict and Security Law 2006, 429, 449.

UN Mission in the Congo (MONUC) was initially deployed as a Chapter VI mission, involving mainly observers, but the mission was expanded to a full peacekeeping one in 2000. MONUC was authorized, by means of the addition of a Chapter VII clause, to 'take the necessary action, in the areas of deployment of its infantry battalions and as it deems it within its capabilities, to... protect civilians under imminent threat of physical violence'[313] However, the Secretary General in his report to the Council a few weeks earlier, after noting terrible atrocities committed against civilians, including an incident in which 15 women were buried alive,[314] emphasized that MONUC 'would not serve as an interposition force' and 'would not have the capacity to protect the civilian population from armed attack.'[315] They would be able to escort humanitarian assistance convoys 'only within the limits of their means and under favourable security conditions.'[316] Thus, despite the inclusion of the Chapter VII clause authorizing the force to provide protection 'as it deems within its capabilities', it was understood at the outset that MONUC's capabilities would not be sufficient to enable it respond to the terrible human rights atrocities that were being widely perpetrated.

The following year the Secretary-General reported massacres of civilians but reiterated that 'it is important to stress' that MONUC will not be able to provide protection to the local population.[317] In May 2002 a massacre of 160 civilians at Kisangani just a few kilometres from a camp of 1000 MONUC soldiers led to an international outcry. Resolution 1417 adopted a month later, explicitly reaffirmed, but without reiterating the reference to Chapter VII, the force's mandate 'to take the necessary action in the areas of deployment of its armed units and as it deems it within its capabilities... to protect civilians under imminent threat of physical violence';[318] but this did not lead to any change in the UN's cautious approach.[319]

In 2003 UNCHR expressed strong concern about the widespread prevalence and seriousness of the violations committed, which included massacres, mutilations, cannibalism, group rapes and the burning of homes.[320] In response to this and to the fall of Bunia (a town in the Ituri district, which, following two weeks of fighting, and despite the presence of MONUC, had come under the control of a rebel militia, the Union of Congolese Patriots) the Security Council authorized the deployment of an EU Interim Emergency Force. Operation Artemis was the

[313] S/RES/1291, 24 February 2000 [8].

[314] Report of the Secretary-General on MONUC, 17 Jan. 2000, S/2000/30, [35].

[315] ibid [67]. [316] ibid [67].

[317] Report of the Secretary-General on MONUC, 12 Feb. 2001, S/2001/128, [54–64] [77]; S/RES/1341 of 22 February 2002 does not explicitly reaffirm MONUC's authority to protect civilians, presumably because it was understood that it could not.

[318] S/RES/1417, 14 June 2002 [7].

[319] International Crisis Group, The Congo's Transition Is Failing: Crisis in the Kivus (ICG Africa Report N°91 30 March 2005), 23.

[320] Report of the United Nations High Commissioner for Human Rights to the Security Council on the situation on human rights in the Democratic Republic of the Congo, Feb 13, 2003, S/2003/, 216 [28] [14–27].

first EU operation to be mandated under Chapter VII; the first to operate outside the umbrella of NATO; and the first to operate outside Europe. Resolution 1484 of May 2003 authorized the French-led Force to 'ensure the protection of the airport, the internally displaced persons in the camps in Bunia and, if the situation requires it, to contribute to the safety of the civilian population, United Nations personnel and the humanitarian presence in the town' and to use 'all necessary measures' to carry out its mandate.[321] However, although the Interim Emergency Force was able to restore stability to Bunia it proved impossible to secure agreement to deploy outside of the town. The UN Department of Peacekeeping Best Practices Unit reported that the violence against civilians 'simply moved beyond the environs of the town, where atrocities continued.'[322]

In July 2003 the Security Council, acting under Chapter VII, reaffirmed MONUC's authorization to protect civilians under imminent threat of physical violence 'in the areas of deployment of its armed units, and as it deems it within its capabilities'[323] and in addition authorized the force to 'use all necessary means' in the Ituri district to help in 'stabilizing the security conditions and improving the humanitarian situation, ensuring the protection of airfields and displaced persons living in camps and, if the circumstances warrant it, helping to ensure the security of the civilian population and the personnel of the United Nations and the humanitarian organizations.'[324] But MONUC's ability to do this was limited by the vastness of the country and the impossibility of being able to deploy sufficient troops to all the vulnerable areas.[325] During the take-over of the town of Bukavu by rebels in May 2004, MONUC provided protection to several hundred civilians but was criticized for making no serious attempt to stop the killing, raping, and looting that took place after the rebel troops marched into the town.[326] At the time MONUC had only 600–700 troops in Bukavu whereas rebel leader General Nkunda had 4000.[327]

In October 2004 the Security Council authorized the increase of MONUC's strength from 10,800 to 16,700[328] and authorized it to 'use all necessary means, within its capacity and in the areas where its armed units are deployed' to 'ensure the protection of civilians, including humanitarian personnel, under imminent threat from physical violence.'[329] To 'ensure' is a strong choice of words and is stated without qualification. Resolution 1592 of March 2005 goes even further:

[321] S/RES/1484 30 May 2003 [1] [4].

[322] Operation Artemis: The Lessons of the Interim Emergency Multinational Force (DPKO Peacekeeping Best Practices Unit, Oct 2004) 14.

[323] S/RES/1493, 28 July 2003 [8] [12] [25].

[324] S/RES/1493, 28 July 2003 [26–27].

[325] Human Rights Watch, Human Rights Overview, Democratic Republic of the Congo, 2004 <http://hrw.org/english/docs/2005/01/13/congo9855.htm> accessed 17 April 2008.

[326] International Crisis Group, Pulling Back from the Brink in the Congo (ICG Africa Briefing 7 July 2004), 6.

[327] ibid 7; Human Rights Watch, DR Congo: War Crimes in Bukavu, Briefing Paper, June 12 2004 <http://hrw.org/english/docs/2004/06/11/congo8803.htm>.

[328] S/RES/1565 1 October 2004, [3].

[329] S/RES/1565 1 October 2004, [4] [6].

and *stresses* that, in accordance with its mandate, MONUC may use cordon and search tactics to prevent attacks on civilians and disrupt the military capability of illegal armed groups that continue to use violence in those areas;[330]

That same month, in order to stabilize the country in preparation for the first free and fair elections to be held for 40 years, MONUC began participating in joint operations with the Congolese army. An EU Force was also deployed to work with MONUC, and with the government of the DRC, in providing security.[331] Eufor RD Congo was authorized to take all necessary measures, within its means and capabilities, 'to contribute to the protection of civilians under imminent threat of physical violence in the areas of its deployment, and without prejudice to the responsibility of the Government of the Democratic Republic of the Congo.'[332] Elections were delayed by tensions caused by the arrival and settlement in the north east of the Lords Resistance Army, a Ugandan rebel militia, but were eventually held on 30 July 2006, with a second round on 29 October 2006.

Following the elections a degree of stability returned to the DRC but it remains fragile;[333] in late 2007 fighting broke out again in North Kivu, which is in the mineral-rich eastern part of the State. Resolution 1756 of May 15 2007 authorizes MONUC to 'use all necessary means, within the limits of its capacity and in the areas where its units are deployed' to 'assist the Government of the Democratic Republic of the Congo in establishing a stable security environment in the country' and, to that end, to '[e]nsure the protection of civilians, including humanitarian personnel, under imminent threat of physical violence';[334] to 'seize and collect arms, as appropriate.' It may also use all necessary means to '[d]eter any attempt at the use of force to threaten the political process from any armed group, foreign or Congolese... including by using cordon and search tactics to prevent attacks on civilians and disrupt the military capability of illegal armed groups that continue to use violence in those areas.' The force is also authorized to:

[a]ssist in the promotion and protection of human rights, with particular attention to women, children and vulnerable persons, investigate human rights violations with a view to putting an end to impunity, assist in the development and implementation of a transitional justice strategy, and cooperate in national and international efforts to bring to justice perpetrators of grave violations of human rights and international humanitarian law.[335]

Nevertheless human rights abuses continue to be widespread. Human Rights Watch reports that, in addition to massacres and forcible displacement:

[330] S/RES/1592 30 March 2005, [7].
[331] S/RES/1671 25 April 2006, [2]
[332] S/RES/1671 25 April 2006, [8].
[333] International Crisis Group, *Congo: Four Priorities for Sustainable Peace in Ituri*, Africa Report N°140 13 May 2008.
[334] S/RES/1756 15 May 2007, [2].
[335] S/RES/1756 15 May 2007, [2], [3].

In some cases soldiers or combatants raped women and girls as young as five years old as part of a more general attack in which they killed and injured civilians and looted and destroyed property. Their intent was to terrorize communities into accepting their control or to punish them for real or supposed links to opposing forces. In cases where there was no larger attack, individuals or small groups of soldiers and combatants also raped women and girls whom they found in the fields, in the forest, along the roads, or in their homes.[336]

Perpetrators include the Democratic Forces for the Liberation of Rwanda (FDLR), a militia founded by Hutu refugees from the Rwandan conflict, including a number wanted by the International Criminal Court for their part in the genocide; and General Nkunda, a renegade from Rwanda, who says he is fighting to protect Congo's Tutsis from the FDLR. One of the worst offenders is the Congolese army. In addition to sexual violence perpetrated by the army and treated with impunity by the government,[337] credible reports allege that Congolese soldiers have abducted civilians and forced them into slave labour working in mines (the minerals obtained are destined for multi-national corporations in Europe and North America),[338] transporting goods, and harvesting crops.[339] MONUC is deployed with the consent of the government to work alongside the army to restore order and is accused of having participated in joint operations in which the army attacked civilians and torched their homes, leaving some dead, some maimed, and hundreds internally displaced.[340] There have also been allegations that MONUC soldiers traded military information to local armed groups in return for gold.[341] Sexual exploitation and abuse by MONUC has been substantiated against all categories and levels of personnel; from support staff to senior managers, and from soldiers to commanding officers.[342] In north

[336] Human Rights Watch, Renewed Crisis in North Kivu (Vol. 19, 17a, October 2007), 25, 29.

[337] Major-General Patrick Cammaert, now retired but formerly General Officer Commanding the Eastern Division of MONUC, states that 'since 2005, the UN Mission provides the Government with a monthly report listing reported human rights abuses committed by the Government security forces. Through its good offices, the Mission regularly addresses the issue. However, the Government has hardly taken any action against the perpetrators.' P Cammaert, Wilton Park Conference 914 *Women Targeted or Afflicted by Armed Conflict: What Role for Military peacekeepers?* 27–29 May 2008, Text of Presentations, 7.

[338] Coltan, an ingredient of mobile phones found in few other places in the world; gold; and diamonds.

[339] Human Rights Watch, Human Rights News, DR Congo: Army Abducts Civilians for Forced Labor, Brussels 16 October 2006 <http://hrw.org/english/docs/2006/10/13/congo14387.htm> accessed 16 April 2006.

[340] Unreported World, The UN's Dirty War, Channel 4, 23 June 2006, 7.35pm; Aidan Hartley, UN accused over Congo village massacre, Observer, 18 June 2006.

[341] Human Rights Watch, Renewed Crisis in North Kivu (Vol. 19, 17a, October 2007), 79; Oxanne Escobales, *Guardian*, April 28 2008, UN peacekeepers 'traded gold and guns with Congolese rebels'. There have also been allegations of sexual exploitation by MONUC: S/RES/1592 30 March 2005, [11]; *Report of the Secretary-General: A Comprehensive Srategy to Eliminate Future Sexual Exploitation and Abuse in United Nations Peacekeeping Operations*, UN Doc A/59/10 26 March 2005; UN Doc A/60/640/Add.1, 29 December 2005, Implementation of the Special Committee on Peacekeeping Operations, [42].

[342] N Dahrendorf, *Sexual Exploitation and Abuse: Lessons Learned Study, Addressing Sexual Exploitation and Abuse in MONUC* (UN DPKO Best Practices Unit March 2006), [8];

Kivu civilians have demonstrated against MONUC for failing, in their view, to take sufficiently robust action to protect them although in other parts of the DRC there is more support for the UN Force.[343]

6.3 Darfur

Since violence began in Darfur in 2004 an estimated 200,000 to 400,000 people have died at the hands of government forces, Janjaweed militias, Darfur rebels and Khartoum-sponsored rebels from Chad and the Central African Republic.[344] Millions of others have been forced to flee their homes either to camps within Sudan or to neighbouring Chad.[345] USAID reports that since 2003, 4.2 million people have been affected by the emergency in Darfur and more than 2.4 million are now internally displaced.[346] Air raids on villages by government armed forces have become common and are often followed by Janjaweed raids pillaging and destroying the villages, and raping the women and girls.[347] A UN sponsored Commission of Inquiry concluded that the Sudanese government and the government-backed Janjaweed militias are responsible for crimes against humanity committed against the civilian population, including massacres, deliberate destruction of villages and of villagers' means of livelihood.[348] A civil society analyst has commented that '[w]hat we are witnessing in Darfur is a regionalised war against civilians. Both the Sudanese and Chadian governments are actively supporting competing militia groups on their sides of the border.'[349]

P Cammaert, Wilton Park Conference 914 *Women Targeted or Afflicted by Armed Conflict: What Role for Military peacekeepers?* (n 337), 11.

[343] Human Rights Watch, Renewed Crisis in North Kivu (n 336), 80; Human Rights Watch, Letter to JM Guéhenno, then UN Under-Secretary-General for Peacekeeping Operations, 23 July 2007.

[344] P Kagwanja and P Mutahi, 'Protection of civilians in African peace missions: The Case of the African Union Mission in Sudan, Darfur' (Institute for Security Studies Paper 139 May 2007), 2; The UN estimate is 200,000 <http://www.un.org/Depts/dpko/missions/unamid/background.html>; the 400,000 estimate comes from S Chin and J Morgenstein, 'No power to protect: the African Union Mission in Sudan,' (Refugees International 11 September 2005), 1.

[345] Chad and Sudan have been at war since December 2005 but on 13 March 2008 the two governments signed an agreement in Dakar, committing to normalizing their bilateral relations: Report of the Secretary-General on the deployment of the African Union-United Nations Hybrid Operation in Darfur, 14 April 2008, S/2008/24, [48].

[346] US Agency for International Development (USAID), The Humanitarian Situation in Sudan, <http://www.usaid.gov/locations/sub-saharan_africa/sudan/> visited 5 May 2008.

[347] Henry L Stimson Center, UNAMID, AU/UN Hybrid Operation in Darfur, Peace Operations Fact Sheet Series 2007 <http://www.stimson.org/fopo/pdf/AU_UN_Hybrid_Fact_Sheet_Aug_07.pdf> Visited 5 May 2008.

[348] Report of the International Commission of Inquiry on Darfur to the United Nations Secretary-General, Pursuant to Security Council Resolution 1564 of 18 September 2004 (Geneva, 25 January 2005).

[349] P Kagwanja and P Mutahi, 'Protection of civilians in African peace missions: The Case of the African Union Mission in Sudan, Darfur' (n 344), 3.

The AU mission in Darfur was a consequence, in part, of the UN's reluctance to intervene militarily,[350] and of the AU's new determination, endorsed by its Constitutive Act of 2002, to respond to war crimes, genocide and crimes against humanity committed in Africa.[351] The African Mission in Sudan (AMIS) was initially deployed as a monitoring mission but from October 2004 it was authorized to 'protect civilians whom it encounters under imminent threat and in the immediate vicinity, within resources and capability, it being understood that the protection of the civilian population is the responsibility of the GoS [Government of Sudan].'[352] The ROE on the use of force for civilian protection are relatively weak; the AU's AMIS website states that the force's:

> mandate via the Rules of Engagement allows AMIS troops to fire in self defense, but it is not to aggressively intervene between the parties for the protection of civilians. Likewise, neither the AMIS force or CIVPOL may arrest or detain Sudanese from any party unless they are directly threatening AMIS personnel or property controlled by AMIS, in which case they may be detained until such time as they are handed over to Government of Sudan law enforcement agencies.[353]

AMIS's principal protection tasks fell into two categories: deterrence through the force's physical presence, and 'soft protective security' involving liaison, monitoring, and verification.[354] In the first limb it has not been very effective: far from being deterred, militias, and rebels have frequently attacked both AMIS and humanitarian organizations in an effort to obtain arms.[355] At the

[350] Some Security Council members, particularly China, are reluctant to put pressure on President Omar Bashir. Moreover, the UN has had a mission in southern Sudan, UNMIS, since 2005, (which followed an advance UN-AU mission, UNAMIS, in 2004), and it was feared that intervention in Darfur might jeopardise the peace process in the south. In addition the UN has a number of large peacekeeping operations already deployed; MONUC, UNMIL, UNOCI.

[351] Constitutive Act of the African Union, Lome, Togo, (adopted 26 May 2001entered into force 11 July 2002) <http://www.africa-union.org/home/Welcome.htm>.

Following an amendment adopted by the Heads of State and Government of the AU at their First Extraordinary Session on 3 February 2003, in addition to interventions in response to war crimes, genocide and crimes against humanity, the AU may now intervene, upon the recommendation of the Peace and Security Council, when there is a serious threat to legitimate order for the purpose of restoring peace and stability in a member state of the AU.

[352] African Union—Communiqué of the Seventeenth Meeting of the Peace and Security Council (20 October 2004), [4].

[353] <http://www.amis-sudan.org/MilitaryComponent.html> Accessed 5 May 2008.

[354] P Rankhumise, 'Civilian (in) security in the Darfur region of Sudan' (Institute for Security Studies Occasional Paper 123, March 2006), 9.

[355] P Kagwanja and P Mutahi, 'Protection of civilians in African peace missions: The Case of the African Union Mission in Sudan, Darfur' (n 344), 8; Henry L Stimson Center, UNAMID, AU/UN Hybrid Operation in Darfur, Peace Operations Fact Sheet Series 2007 <http://www.stimson.org/fopo/pdf/AU_UN_Hybrid_Fact_Sheet_Aug_07.pdf> Visited 5 May 2008; The Security Council imposed an arms embargo on all non-governmental entities and individuals, including the Janjaweed, operating in Darfur on 30 July 2004 with the adoption of resolution 1556. The sanctions regime was strengthened with the adoption of resolution 1591 (2005), which expanded the scope of the arms embargo and imposed additional measures, including a travel ban and an assets freeze on four individuals—two rebel leaders, a former Sudanese air force chief and the leader of a pro-government militia: UN Department of Peacekeeping Operations, African

Forty-Sixth Meeting of the Peace and Security Council of the African Union in March 2006 the Council urged the Commission of the African Union to 'immediately take all necessary steps for the consistent, flexible, broad, and robust interpretation of the mandate... in order to ensure a more forceful protection of the civilian population';[356] but it was clear that AMIS did not have the capability to stop the attacks on villages. However, whilst AMIS's soft security measures have not prevented the massacres and destruction of villages they have made a difference to people's lives: peacekeepers have monitored and reported violations and escorted vulnerable women on trips to collect firewood in areas particularly known for rape attacks.[357] However, although this has been an effective measure to some degree, it has not been possible to provide escorts in all areas. Moreover '[r]egrettably, military peacekeepers have come to be seen as occasional perpetrators of sexual violence, and this has diverted attention from their primary role as protectors.'[358] In Darfur this problem has been exacerbated because firewood patrols generally include the much distrusted Government of Sudan police as well as peacekeepers. Alternatives, such as teams of men from the villages banding together and going out to collect the firewood, escorted in particularly dangerous areas by peacekeepers, do not seem to have been considered, presumably for cultural reasons.

In August 2006, at the request of the AU, the UN Security Council authorized the deployment of a UN Force of up to 17,300 military personnel and 3,300 police officers[359] to take over from AMIS but the government of Sudan rejected its deployment on the grounds that it was a 'colonialist' attempt to subjugate the country. President Omar al-Bashir threatened to turn Darfur 'into a graveyard for any foreign troops entering' and raised the prospect of 'another Iraq.'[360] The threats were sufficient to delay deployment and to force the UN to think again. In July 2007 after long-drawn out negotiations with President al Bashir, the Security Council, acting under Chapter VII but with the agreement of Sudan, adopted resolution 1769 mandating a hybrid AU-UN mission, the United Nations African Union Mission in Darfur (UNAMID) with up to 19,555 military personnel (plus up to 6, 432 civilian police officers and 5,105 other civilian personnel) under a single chain of command (Force Commander General Martin Luther Agwai, from Nigeria, reporting to the AU/UN Joint Special Representative General Rodolphe

Union-United Nations Hybrid Operation in Darfur <http://www.un.org/Depts/dpko/missions/unamid/background.html> Accessed 5 May 2008.

[356] African Union—Communiqué of the Forty-Sixth Meeting of the Peace and Security Council (10, March 2006), [4(b)(i)].

[357] Human Rights Component of the Mission <http://www.amis-sudan.org/HumanRight.html Accessed May 25 2005>.

[358] AM Goetz, Wilton Park Conference 914 *Women Targeted or Afflicted by Armed Conflict: What Role for Military peacekeepers?* (n 337), 6.

[359] S/RES 1706 31 August 2006.

[360] P Kagwanja and P Mutahi, 'Protection of civilians in African peace missions: The Case of the African Union Mission in Sudan, Darfur' (n 344), 10.

Adada, from the DRC) but comprised predominantly of African troops, many of them 're-hatted' from AMIS. UNAMID's mandate to protect civilians is virtually identical to that of AMIS.[361] Acting under Chapter VII, the Council in Resolution 1769 decided that UNAMID:

> is authorised to take the necessary action, in the areas of deployment of its forces and as it deems within its capabilities in order to:
>
> (i) protect its personnel, facilities, installations and equipment, and to ensure the security and freedom of movement of its own personnel and humanitarian workers,
> (ii) support early and effective implementation of the Darfur Peace Agreement, prevent the disruption of its implementation and armed attacks, and protect civilians, without prejudice to the responsibility of the Government of Sudan;[362]

As of March 2008 the total strength of UNAMID was 9,200 uniformed personnel (7,500 of which were military personnel, the remainder police) and 1,400 civilians.[363] This is not large enough for the size of Darfur and the force lacks a number of critical capabilities; it does not have sufficient helicopters or aerial reconnaissance ability to perform surveillance and monitor events on the ground.[364] UNAMID also needs land in the northern sector in order to build a base camp but permission for this has yet[365] to be granted by the Sudanese government.[366] The Sudanese government has reluctantly given UNAMID permission in principle to conduct night flights but continues to obstruct these by restricting flying hours.[367] The Secretary-General's conclusions on the situation, as of April 2008, are bleak:

> I am extremely disappointed at the lack of progress on all fronts in the efforts to address the situation in Darfur. The parties appear determined to pursue a military solution; the political process stalled; the deployment of UNAMID is progressing very slowly and continues to face many challenges; and the humanitarian situation is not improving. The primary obstacle is the lack of political will among all the parties to pursue a peaceful solution to the Darfur crisis....
>
> The implications of the current security situation for the people of Darfur are grave. Violence in Western Darfur during the reporting period has significantly impaired the humanitarian community's ability to provide the civilian population with the critical assistance they require and has increased the vulnerability of thousands of civilians. Additionally, the ongoing attacks on food convoys throughout Darfur have hampered

[361] Letter dated 5 June 2007 from the Secretary-General to the President of the Security Council, S/2007/307/Rev.1, 5 June 2007, [54(b)]; S/RES/1769 31 July 2007.

[362] S/RES/1769 31 July 2007, [15(a)].

[363] Report of the Secretary-General on the deployment of the African Union-United Nations Hybrid Operation in Darfur, 14 April 2008, S/2008/24, [26].

[364] ibid [35].

[365] As of April 2008.

[366] Report of the Secretary-General on the deployment of the African Union-United Nations Hybrid Operation in Darfur (n 363), [36].

[367] ibid [38].

the capacity of agencies on the ground to provide food aid to the population. Reports of a build-up of forces on the Chad-Sudan border during the reporting period offer a deeply troubling sign that the violence and instability will continue, to the detriment of the civilian populations on both sides of the border and in clear violation of the Ceasefire Agreement.[368]

Whilst all parties are engaged in attacks on civilians, the key to their protection lies with the Sudanese government. Darfur is a large area far from Khartoum and far from a port. Without the support of the government it is very difficult for a peacekeeping force so far from its supply lines to maintain sufficient strength and to be sufficiently well equipped to patrol the region and to robustly intervene to protect civilians; but this is of little consolation for the people of Darfur. Newsweek reported that in June 2008 Janjaweed had roamed through a camp in Tawila burning down the market and looting homes whilst 'peacekeepers watched.'[369] Henry Anyidoho, the deputy political head of the mission commented that 'the problem is the failure of the international community to give Unamid the equipment it needs to do its job. They expect too much, too quickly, even though they are not providing the means.'[370] In July 2008 UNAMID was ambushed by 200 assailants with horses and 40 trucks; 7 peacekeepers were killed and 22 wounded.[371]

Chad is also far from a port but the government there (which is accused of providing support to Darfur's rebel militias) is supportive of the European Union Mission to Chad and the Central African Republic (EUFOR TCHAD/RCA). EUFOR TCHAD/RCA was authorized, in July 2007, by the Security Council acting under Chapter VII, to 'contribute to protecting civilians in danger, particularly refugees and displaced persons.'[372] The ROE authorize the '[u]se of minimum force to prevent the commission of serious crimes that are occurring or are about to occur in the vicinity of EUFOR personnel.' Serious crimes are defined as those that bear the risk of serious harm or grave violations of human rights. EUFOR TCHAD/RCA may also use minimum force to detain persons 'where detention is necessary for mission accomplishment.' Minimum force is stated to include the authority to use deadly force, on the condition that it is necessary and proportionate. EUFOR is also authorized to:

> undertake operations outside the Area of Operations . . . under the following conditions. Force is authorized against spoilers, which have . . . committed a serious crime, which caused serious bodily harm, inhuman treatment or grave violations of human rights, and which have escaped outside the Area of Operations. EUFOR must inform appropriate local authorities and must have, within a reasonable time frame, indications that they are

[368] ibid [56–57].

[369] S Bloomfield, 'A Thin Coat of Blue' Newsweek Web Exclusive July 7 2008 <http://www.newsweek.com/id/144909>.

[370] ibid.

[371] L Polgreen, 'Peacekeepers in Sudan Lose 7 in Ambush' *New York Times*, 10 July 2008.

[372] S/RES/1778, 25 September 2007 [6].

unable or unwilling to act prior to operating outside the Area of Operations. Duration of EUFOR operation is limited to the absolute operational necessity and in any case must not exceed 100 km from the boundary line of the Area of Operations.[373]

As of May 2008 the force had not fully deployed but the prospects for protection of civilians may be better for the EU Force in Chad than for UNAMID, precisely because it has the co-operation of the government. However, the situation remains extremely volatile. In May 2008 one of the largest Sudanese rebel militias, the Justice and Equality Movement (JEM), attacked members of Government forces on the outskirts of Khartoum, the first time any Darfur militia has reached the capital. Since the Sudanese government believes that JEM is being assisted by Chad, tensions between the two States are high and there is a strong possibility that the situation in both States may deteriorate greatly (and it is already critical) during 2008. The former Under-Secretary-General for Peacekeeping Operations, Jean-Marie Guéhenno, warned that thousands of people in Darfur could be forcibly displaced from their homes in the next few months as a result of increased bombing attacks on villages and violence between militias and there could also be a rapid intensification of the proxy war between Sudan and Chad.[374]

6.4 Civilian Protection in UN Peacekeeping Missions since 1999: Summary

In 1999, in response to the atrocities perpetrated against civilians during the 1990s, and the UN's failure to prevent them even when it had forces present on the ground, the Security Council adopted the first of its resolutions on the Protection of Civilians in Armed Conflict in which it expressed the intention to 'better address the negative impact of armed conflict on civilians.'[375] Since then it has been normative practice to explicitly include provision for protection of civilians within the mission's areas of deployment, and within the framework of an acknowledgement that the protection of the civilian population is the responsibility of the host State's government, in peacekeeping mandates. Exactly what that acknowledgement signifies is unclear. The existence of a mandate to provide protection to civilians in imminent danger, even if poorly thought out and subject to constraints, may provide some protection, in terms of mitigation, to soldiers that, acting out of conscience, disobey orders in order to prevent atrocities happening before their eyes. However, in the majority of countries where peacekeeping forces have been deployed, the government has been patently failing in its protection responsibilities but Security Council mandates, being politically constrained, do not provide guidance as to how troops should respond. David

[373] ROE Authorization for the EU Operation Commander's Operation Plan for the European Union Military Operation in TCHAD and CAR—EUFOR/RCA.

[374] UN News Service 14 May 2008, 'Darfur conflict threatens to enter new cycle of violence—top UN official' <http://www.un.org/apps/news/story.asp?NewsID=26673&Cr=darfur&Cr1=#>.

[375] S/RES/1265, 17 September 1999, [14], [11].

Malone, commenting in 2003, argued that sometimes the protection tasks have been 'tacked on to mandates nearly as an afterthought by the Council' without proper planning for their implementation.[376] The Brahimi report states that troops should be presumed to be authorized to use force to protect people from deliberate attacks: but it acknowledged that such authorization would not be much use if the troops did not have the resources to be able to act.[377] In most scenarios, particularly where the country is very large and therefore difficult to patrol and where there are serious problems in managing supply links and troop security, or where a robust response significantly increase the risk of reprisals against other civilians (through for example blocking humanitarian aid), it is extremely difficult to provide protection without the co-operation of the government.

In some cases mandates have authorized troops to protect civilians (within their capabilities and areas of deployment) in resolutions that detail horrific abuses of human rights, even though the Secretariat and Security Council members were well aware that the troops deployed did not have the capabilities to provide the protection authorized. This was particularly evident in the early resolutions mandating MONUC and has been a feature of the AU and UN responses to Darfur. How much of an improvement this is from the situation where '[m]any Rwandese believed that the United Nations was there to stop the genocide and were bitterly disappointed when this was not the case',[378] is debateable. In Resolution 1674 of 2006 the Council indicated that there was a need to clarify the role of peacekeepers in implementing protection mandates. It reaffirmed its practice of ensuring that the mandates of United Nations peacekeeping missions include where appropriate provisions regarding:

(i) the protection of civilians, particularly those under imminent threat of physical danger within their zones of operation,
(ii) the facilitation of the provision of humanitarian assistance, and
(iii) the creation of conditions conducive to the voluntary, safe, dignified and sustainable return of refugees and internally displaced persons,

The Council then expressed its intention of ensuring that:

(i) such mandates include clear guidelines as to what missions can and should do to achieve those goals,
(ii) the protection of civilians is given priority in decisions about the use of available capacity and resources, including information and intelligence resources, in the implementation of the mandates, and
(iii) that protection mandates are implemented;[379]

[376] Executive Summary by DM Malone of "Cooperation in Peace Operations: The United Nations and Europe" 33rd Annual International Peace Academy Seminar, Vienna, Austria 4–6 July 2003 (Rapporteurs: Clara Lee and Dr Alexandra Novosseloff).

[377] Report of the Panel on United Nations Peace Operations (n 238), [48–64].

[378] United Nations, Lessons Learned Unit, Department of Peacekeeping Operations, *Comprehensive Report on Lessons Learned from the United Nations Assistance Mission for Rwanda (UNAMIR) October 1993 – April 1996* (n 188), [87]

[379] A fourth resolution on the Protection of Civilians in Armed Conflict was adopted in December 2006, dealing mainly with protection of journalists: S/RES/1738 23 December 2006.

Whilst there have been improvements in all three of the implementation objectives listed above there remains a considerable shortfall between goals and performance. Where missions have the support of the host State's government and a sufficiently large force, more robust approaches to protection have been possible, for example in the DRC, where the much expanded MONUC force was eventually in a position to take a strong line on protection, which has lead to an improvement in security for many vulnerable civilians. However, since the DRC government forces have themselves engaged in serious human rights abuses on a large scale, the UN's co-operation with them, particularly in the context of joint enforcement type actions, has left peacekeepers open to allegations that they have participated in the commission of war crimes.[380] The position of power created where troops have a robust mandate and are working alongside corrupt government forces may lead to exploitation by peacekeepers as well as by the State's own forces. Human Rights Watch has criticized a UN investigation into an alleged peacekeepers' smuggling ring as grossly inadequate stating that:

> [s]urely a report confirming illegal acts by UN peacekeepers is not the end of a process, but the beginning... When Human Rights Watch first brought information about gold-smuggling by peacekeepers to the attention of the United Nations in December 2005, our findings indicated that a ring of Congolese army officers, Kenyan traders, and Pakistani peacekeepers was involved in smuggling millions of dollars of gold from Ituri. A separate BBC investigation reached a similar conclusion. According to our research, this ring carried out at least two major trades in late 2005 benefiting from significant facilitation from Pakistani peacekeepers including accommodation, transportation, security, and access to UN flights. We were therefore surprised that the report concluded that only one peacekeeper was involved in aiding and abetting these illegal acts. It is our view that the assistance provided by Pakistani peacekeepers went well beyond one individual.[381]

Allegations of abuse of force by peacekeepers have also surfaced in relation to the operations in Haiti, where forces have been deployed for over a decade in a number of missions (involving the US and the UN) to help support the government in restoring order. In 1994, when US soldiers were ordered to stand by when Haitian police attacked civilians with tree limbs and iron pipes, the New York Times reported that the order was 'messing with the heads' of the young privates who believed they were there to protect the people:

> 'I think we're working with the wrong side here,' said 19-year-old Thomas Hasdorff, a private with the 10th Mountain Division. 'I don't believe they treat their own people this way. I can't believe it. And I can't believe I sit here and have to watch it happen. We're just images here, something to look at.'
>
> ...'It's messing up my head,' said Pvt. Greg Hendl, 20, also with the 10th Mountain Division. 'It's wrong. And every time you have to look into the faces of the people here,

[380] Unreported World, The UN's Dirty War, Channel 4, 23 June 2006, 7.35 pm.

[381] Human Rights Watch, Letter to JM Guéhenno, former UN Under-Secretary-General for Peacekeeping Operations, 23 July 2007.

the people who thought we were coming to save them from these guys, it breaks your heart.'[382]

It was not until the public outcry that followed television footage of US soldiers standing by whilst government forces beat pro-Aristide supporters, one of them to death, that the troops began to use force to protect civilians.[383]

More recently human rights organizations have accused the United Nations Stabilization Mission in Haiti (MINUSTAH) both of standing by and watching unarmed civilians being shot and of using excessive force on a number of occasions resulting in massacres. The ROE for MINUSTAH (as of May 2004) state that force beyond self-defence may only be used in specific circumstances, which include in order 'to protect civilians under imminent threat of physical violence, within its capabilities and areas of deployment, without prejudice to the responsibilities of the Transitional Government and of police authorities.'[384] In July 2005, shortly before planned demonstrations intended to coincide with ousted president Jean-Bertrand Aristide's birthday, MINUSTAH carried out an excessively forceful operation in the Cite Soleil area of Port-au-Prince. An After Action Report submitted to the US embassy in Port au Prince by MINUSTAH stated that 'the fire-fight lasted over seven hours during which time [UN] forces expended over 22,000 rounds of ammunition...given the flimsy construction of homes in Cite Soleil and the large quantity of ammunition expended, it is likely that rounds penetrated many buildings, striking unintended targets.'[385] It is alleged that peacekeepers subsequently refused to allow the Red Cross to enter the area.[386] It is also alleged that on 22 December 2006, after a protest by around 10,000 people demanding the return of President Jean-Bertrand Aristide, MINUSTAH killed at least 30 people, including women and children. Inter Press Service, which covered the incident immediately following the attack,

[382] R Bragg, 'Mission to Haiti: The Troops; GIs angry over orders to stand by' *New York Times*, 22 September 1994.

[383] DM Malone, *Decision-Making in the UN Security Council: The Case of Haiti, 1990–1997* (Clarendon Press, Oxford 1998), 113; T Findlay, *Use of Force* (n 41), 274.

[384] UN Department of Peacekeeping Operations, 'MINUSTAH-ROE: Rules of Engagement of the Military Component of the United Nations Stabilization Mission in Haiti (MINUSTAH)', UN Restricted, DPKO Military Division, 24 May 2004; Cited in VK Holt and TC Berkman, *The Impossible Mandate? Military Preparedness; the Responsibility to Protect and Modern Peace Operations* (Henry L Stimson Center September 2006)

[385] Haiti Information Project, 'Embassy in Haiti acknowledges excessive force by UN' January 4 2007 <http://www.haitiaction.net/News/HIP/1_23_7/1_23_7.html>; W Pierre and J Sprague 'Haiti: Poor Residents of Capital Describe a State of Siege' Inter Press Service February 28 2007 <http://ipsnews.net/news.asp?idnews=36772> Accessed 17 May 2008.

[386] W Pierre and J Sprague, 'Haiti: Poor Residents of Capital Describe a State of Siege' Inter Press Service February 28 2007 <http://ipsnews.net/news.asp?idnews=36772>; Haiti Information Project 'Evidence mounts of a UN massacre in Haiti' <http://www.haitiaction.net/News/HIP/7_12_5.html> Accessed 17 May 2008; ML Mendonça, 'UN Troops Accused of Human Rights Violations in Haiti' Americas Program, Center for International Policy (CIP), January 21, 2008.

reported finding high-calibre bullet holes in many homes.[387] Local human rights organizations report eye witness testimonies that UN troops shot unarmed civilians from helicopters.[388]

In Darfur the problem is the opposite. The government is opposed to the presence of peacekeepers and has only agreed to their deployment reluctantly and with numerous conditions that make it extremely difficult for any peacekeeping mission to function effectively, particularly given the large areas involved. AMIS has been unable to prevent the systematic destruction of villages and ethnic cleansing, although it has provided some protection to vulnerable women by escorting them on trips to gather firewood. UNAMID has similar difficulties and is constantly being obstructed by the government.

One of the difficulties for peacekeeping missions is that the drafters of mandates often seem not to have it clearly in their minds that peacekeepers are soldiers (the major component of peacekeeping missions is still the military one). Soldiers deal with people; for all the military hardware that exists, wars are primarily fought by people, for people, against people, using people. In the conflict zone, which is a place where people tend to get hurt, soldiers look out for each-other; they look out for the 'enemy' or, where there is no enemy, for 'spoilers'; they work in units and with allies; they patrol; they establish base camps; they expect to have weapons, equipment and transport. They look for rules and orders and they expect some degree of efficiency. Security Council mandates are intrinsically political and consequently their language tends to be nuanced rather than clear; a nuance is not particularly helpful to commanders trying to resolve problems in the field. Usually the protection provisions of mandates are worded so as to authorize peacekeepers to protect civilians that they encounter, if they under imminent threat and are in the immediate vicinity; providing protection is within the resources and capability of the force; 'it being understood that the protection of the civilian population is the responsibility of the government.' An authorization framed in this way leaves many questions open to be answered. What is an imminent threat; what is the immediate vicinity; how far can resources and capability be stretched; how does the government's responsibility towards the civilian population interact with the force's? Mandate ambiguity may be a useful tool in securing the consensus necessary to get a resolution adopted but:

> Mandate ambiguity, coupled with a fear of censure when mistakes are made, can create a disincentive to innovative action to protect civilians. Strong and specific mandates, backed by adequate resources, may stimulate strong and specific responses. The military after all, 'cannot operate in an environment of ambiguity'.[389]

[387] ML Mendonça, 'UN Troops Accused of Human Rights Violations in Haiti' Americas Program, Center for International Policy (CIP), January 21, 2008.

[388] Haiti Information Project 'UN in Haiti Accused of Second Massacre' January 21 2007 <http://www.haitiaction.net/News/HIP/1_21_7/1_21_7.html> Accessed 17 May 2008.

[389] Report on Wilton Park Conference 914 *Women Targeted or Afflicted by Armed Conflict: What Role for Military peacekeepers?* 27–29 May 2008, [30]. The report was sent to the Security Council

Ms Goetz, Chief Advisor on Governance, Peace and Security to the United Nations Development Fund for Women (UNIFEM) has noted that:

it is military peacekeepers now themselves that are demanding practical solutions to the types of conflict they encounter in theatre. They need much more effective means of protecting civilians, and in fact they also need means of coping with their own trauma.[390]

Yet 'mandates continue to be couched in unclear language susceptible to multiple interpretations, difficult to translate into operational orders.'[391] ROE put the mandate into more concrete terms but since their purpose is to define and to carefully control the degree and manner in which force is used,[392] they tend to deal with what troops are allowed to do and not allowed to do, rather than what is expected of them. Even where the ROE does suggest an obligation to act in certain circumstances (if it is possible), this is not always conclusive. In the case of Rwanda, Dallaire's ROE permitted UNAMIR to use all available means to halt ethnically or politically motivated criminal acts such as executions and attacks on displaced persons or refugees, and suggested that troops may be 'morally and legally' required to act.[393] However, the Secretariat took a more restrictive view of the mandate and insisted that UNAMIR was not to intervene.

The Secretary General's High Level Panel on Threats, Challenges and Change, published in 2004, whilst it affirms the right of peacekeepers to use force to protect civilians, offers little clarity on what this means in practice. The report acknowledges that there are distinctions between peacekeeping operations mandated under Chapter VI and VII, and between a peacekeeping operation with a Chapter VII mandate and a peace enforcement operation, but offers little guidance was as to what effect these distinctions may have on the rights and obligations of troops as regard civilian protection. The Panel emphasized that enforcement action differs from peacekeeping even where the peacekeeping operation has a Chapter VII mandate granting it enforcement powers, observing that there:

is a distinction between operations in which the robust use of force is integral to the mission from the outset (e.g., responses to cross-border invasions or an explosion of violence, in which the recent practice has been to mandate multi-national forces) and operations in which there is a reasonable expectation that force may not be needed at all (e.g., traditional peacekeeping missions monitoring and verifying a ceasefire or those assisting in implementing peace agreements, where blue helmets are still the norm).[394]

by the Chargé d' Affaires of the United Kingdom (S/2008/402) and discussed in the meeting (S/PV.5916) leading to the adoption of SC/RES 1820 19 June 2008.

[390] AM Goetz, Wilton Park Conference 914 *Women Targeted or Afflicted by Armed Conflict: What Role for Military peacekeepers?* (n 337), 7.

[391] ibid 5.

[392] R Murphy, *UN Peacekeeping in Lebanon, Somalia and Kosovo* (n 79), 162.

[393] *Report of the Independent Inquiry into the Actions of the United Nations during the 1994 Genocide in Rwanda* (n 367), (26) 32.

[394] Report by the Secretary-Generals' High Level Panel on Threats, Challenges and Change 'A More Secure World: Our Shared Responsibility' <http://www.un.org//secureworld>, [212].

However, the Panel goes on to observe that since 'even the most benign environment can turn sour' it is now the usual practice for a Chapter VII mandate to be given to all peacekeeping operations on the grounds 'that it is desirable for there to be complete certainty about the mission's capacity to respond with force, if necessary' should 'spoilers emerge to undermine a peace agreement and put civilians at risk.'[395] It would seem that 'complete certainty' is the key objective in granting Chapter VII powers for the Panel goes on to say that:

> the difference between Chapter VI and VII mandates can be exaggerated: there is little doubt that peacekeeping missions operating under Chapter VI (and thus operating without enforcement powers) have the right to use force in self-defence—and this is widely understood to extend to 'defence of the mission'.[396]

It might have been expected that, given that the report was published in 2004, ten years after the genocide at Rwanda, that the Panel could have provided a little more clarity on what is meant by 'defence of the mission' than mere reference to a 'widely understood' right to use force. Similarly the reference to the need for 'complete certainty' as the reason for granting Chapter VII mandates to peacekeeping operations implies that the distinction between troops' obligations in relation to enforcing/defending their mission, in a Chapter VII mandated operation, and one that is not, are more semantic than real. This is unlikely to have been the intention but the lack of clarity on this point (which probably reflects the fact that national interpretations of the circumstances in which force can be used in self-defence differ)[397] suggests that the desire for consensus has resulted in obscuring a critical issue.

The experience of peace operations in the 1990s, and the lack of cohesive guidance on how to respond to the kind of problems that arose in them, prompted a number of European States (among them, the UK, Sweden and the FINABEL group)[398] to develop, and subsequently adopt, military doctrines specifically designed to provide guidance on conducting 'Peace Support Operations.'[399] In July 2001 NATO also adopted a new Peace Support Operations Doctrine.[400] Meanwhile in Harare, in January 2000, a workshop was held at which a working

[395] ibid [213].

[396] ibid [213].

[397] Use of Force Concept for EU-led Military Crisis Management Operations EUMC DOC/CCD 04–06-OPS 16/2001 Final Draft (27/09/2002), Annex A, 19 and Appendix 6 to Annex A, 2.

[398] France, Italy, Netherlands, Germany (Allemagne), Belgium, Spain (Espagne) Luxembourg—and now also Portugal and Greece: Lt. Col. P. Wilkinson, 'Sharpening the Weapons of Peace: The Development of a Common Military Doctrine for Peace Support Operations' International Security Information Service (ISIS), Briefing Paper No 18 April 1998 <http://www.isis-europe.org/isiseu/english/no18.html>.

[399] The term is relatively recent and is used to encompass a wide range of operations ranging from traditional peacekeeping to peace enforcement, and drawing within its umbrella some other operations that do not fit within any of the more traditional categories.

[400] Allied Joint Publication (AJP) 3.4.1 *Peace Support Operations*, July 2001 <http://www.pronato.com/peacekeeping/AJP-3-4-1/index.htm>.

manual on Peace Support Operation Doctrine for Africa was drafted.[401] The Manual is not officially adopted but it is in use and carried in loose-leaf form by forces from an increasing number of African States.[402] The UK has revised its doctrine on peace support operations several times in this period, most recently in 2004,[403] and is currently in the process of revising it once more.[404] Considerable effort has been made to try and achieve an international consensus on the approach to be taken.[405] The drafters of the different State and regional doctrines held meetings and conducted consultations with the aim of achieving 'a near-universal, consistent, and more flexible doctrine' which 'may, in turn guide the actions of those seeking to uphold the principles of the UN Charter and contemporary conceptions of collective peace and security.'[406]

7. Developments in Military Doctrine

The UK doctrine on Peace Support Operations, defines a peace support operation as:

An operation that impartially makes use of diplomatic, civil and military means, normally in pursuit of United Nations Charter purposes and principles, to restore or maintain peace. Such operations may include conflict prevention, peacemaking, peace enforcement, peacekeeping, peacebuilding and/or humanitarian operations.[407]

NATO's Allied Joint Publication 3.41 defines peace support operations as:

multi-functional operations, conducted impartially, normally in support of an internationally recognised organisation such as the UN or the Organisation for Security and Co-operation in Europe (OSCE), involving military forces and diplomatic and

[401] *'Peace Support Operations: A Working Draft Manual for African Military Practitioners'*, DWM 1–2000 February 2000 <http://www.iss.co.za/Pubs/Other/PeaceSupportManualMM>, produced as a result of a workshop held at SADC Regional Peacekeeping Training Centre in Harare, Zimbabwe, 24–26 August 1999.

[402] Interview with Lt. Col. Philip Wilkinson OBE 25.03.04. Lt. Col. Wilkinson is a Senior Research Fellow at the Centre for Defence Studies, King's College, London. He led the development of UK and NATO doctrine on peace support and civil-military operations and co-authored the UK's first official document on military doctrine for PSO, *The Military Contribution to Peace Support Operations*, Joint Warfare Publication 3.50. He also chaired the workshop that led to the drafting of DWM 1–2000 *'Peace Support Operations: A Working Draft Manual for African Military Practitioners'* (n 401) and chaired the NATO meetings leading to the publication of NATO's doctrine AJP 3.4.1 *Peace Support Operations* (n 399).

[403] UK Ministry of Defence, Joint Warfare Publication (JWP) 3.50, *The Military Contribution to Peace Support Operations* (2nd edn, The Joint Doctrine and Concepts Centre Shrivenham 2004).

[404] Ministry of Defence, Development, Concepts and Doctrine Centre, *Draft UK National Doctrine that will replace JWP 3–50 The Military Contribution to Peace Support Operations* (n 11).

[405] Lt. Col. P. Wilkinson, 'Sharpening the Weapons of Peace: The Development of a Common Military Doctrine for Peace Support Operations' (n 398).

[406] JWP 3.50, *The Military Contribution to Peace Support Operation* (n 403), [123].

[407] ibid Glossary 7.

humanitarian agencies. PSO are designed to achieve a long term political settlement or other specified conditions. They include Peacekeeping and Peace Enforcement as well as conflict prevention, peacemaking, peace building and humanitarian relief.[408]

These definitions reflect the controversial nature of some peace operations. The statement that peace support operations are 'normally conducted in pursuit of United Nations principles and purposes'[409] suggests that there may be abnormal cases in which the operation is undertaken in pursuit of other objectives. Similarly the statement that peace support operations are 'conducted impartially, normally in support of an internationally recognised organisation such as the UN or the Organisation for Security and Co-operation in Europe' indicates that on occasion such operations are undertaken without explicit authorization and possibly even without the implicit authorization that States have sometimes claimed on the basis that operations have been undertaken 'in support' of Security Council resolutions.

Operations that have been significant in terms of bringing to the fore recognition of the need for a revised military doctrine for peace support operations include Operation Provide Comfort in Iraq in 1991; the operations in Bosnia-Herzegovina in the mid-1990s; and the deployment of KFOR following the NATO bombing campaign in 1999.[410] Some statements in current military doctrine could be interpreted as implying that peace support operations also encompass the Kosovo bombing campaign itself, although many commentators would not consider that to have been a peace operation because of the high level of force used. However, paragraph A29 of the UK doctrine on peace support operations states that:

In recent years, default to unilateral NATO action has received mixed reaction amongst the international community. Some saw events in Kosovo as illustrative of the flexibility that regional responses can offer, whilst others regarded the action as having set a dangerous precedent undermining the authority and credibility of the UN. Judged on the basis of its competence to implement and uphold a treaty or charter derived mandate, NATO capacity has been proven. NATO PSO doctrine has reached an advanced stage of evolution, and many assigned national force elements have undergone extensive interoperability training as well as amassing considerable field experience. Looking more widely, the viability of regional solutions is undoubtedly set to improve, however, the efficacy and operational viability of these arrangements remains inconsistent.[411]

Peace support operations encompass a broad category of operations that do not necessarily have the same legal basis. Traditionally the presence or absence of the consent of the host State, and the rules of engagement regarding permissible use of force, were key factors in distinguishing between peacekeeping operations and enforcement operations. Those distinctions have become increasingly blurred as

[408] Allied Joint Publication (AJP) 3.4.1 *Peace Support Operations* (n 400), [0202].
[409] JWP 3.50, *The Military Contribution to Peace Support Operations* (n 403), Glossary 7.
[410] ibid [110], [219]. [411] ibid [A29].

result of 'grey area operations' that allow for the use of force in a broader range of situations than was permissible under traditional peacekeeping. In the traditional peacekeeping of the 1950s, operations deployed only with the consent of the parties, use of force was limited to self-defence and forces had to remain neutral and impartial. However, the operations of the 1990s, particularly the failure to protect civilians from deliberate egregious attacks on a massive scale, led to changes in this approach. In a situation where forces are deployed to areas where there are serious violations of human rights the Security Council is increasingly likely to mandate the use of force for limited purposes, such as the protection of human rights.[412] It is possible that this could result in the forces carrying out tasks that do not have the consent of the government of the State in which they are deployed, though consent to a more limited operation may have been granted. Moreover consent is not necessarily consistent throughout a peace operation. It is possible that consent can be given and then withdrawn. In addition:

> Whilst there may be consent at the strategic level, (by virtue of national or party commitments to a peace agreement), at the tactical level there may be local groups who disagree violently with their leaders, and who may be hostile to the PSO [Peace Support Operation]. This may result in non-compliance by (para-) military elements of one or more of the parties, including (for example) attempts to restrict the freedom of movement of the PSF [Peace Support Force] . . . In the event of an intra-state conflict or civil war, the warring factions may be difficult to differentiate from the general population, making judgements concerning consent highly problematic. Consent from the warring factions may be minimal and amount to nothing more than a phoney tolerance of the operation, while the rest of the population may be desperate for intervention and assistance. Should the level of consent be uncertain, and the potential for opposition exist, it would be prudent to deploy a force capable of enforcing compliance and promoting consent from the outset.[413]

The 'Wider Peacekeeping doctrine' developed in the UK in the early 1990s responded to the volatility of the Balkans conflict by acknowledging the need for a peace support force to act when consent was lost.[414] However, 'adherence to strict impartiality and the use of minimum force were cast as essential underpinnings of consent.'[415] This approach has since been revised. The current (2004) UK doctrine JWP 3.50 comments that:

[412] As seen in the mandates of the United Nations Mission in Sierra Leone (UNAMSIL) (S/RES/1270 22 October 1999)), the United Nations Organization Mission in the Democratic Republic of the Congo (MONUC) (S/RES/1417 14 June 2002)), the United Nations Mission in Liberia (UNMIL) (S/RES/1509 19 September 2003)), the United Nations Operation in Côte d'Ivoire (UNOCI) (S/RES/1528 27 February 2004)) and the United Nations Operation in Burundi (ONUB) (S/RES/1545 21 May 2004)): Report of the Secretary-General to the Security Council on the protection of civilians in armed conflict' 28 May 2004 S/2002/431 [8].

[413] AJP 3.4.1, *Peace Support Operations* (n 385) [0304] [0309]; JWP 3.50, *The Military Contribution to Peace Support Operation* (n 400), [508].

[414] JWP 3.50, *The Military Contribution to Peace Support Operation* (n 403), [A13].

[415] ibid.

A central tenet of the [Wider Peacekeeping] doctrine viewed consent as a line or Rubicon dividing peacekeeping and '*Wider Peacekeeping*' from peace enforcement. Crossing the Rubicon was to be avoided and re-crossing to regain consent and impartiality was thought to be almost impossible. Once a PSO had transitioned to peace enforcement stance, operations would be conducted: 'in accordance with standard military principles predicated on the identification of an enemy.'[416] The perception created, therefore, was that once consent was lost military force would default to the use of war-fighting techniques,[417] and consequently, consent was unlikely to be regained.[418]

In 1995, General Rupert Smith adopted an increasingly robust stance in Bosnia in the course of which:

Progress was made towards a more flexible approach to the 'Grey Area' between peacekeeping and peace enforcement utilising the full spectrum of war-fighting skills... The implications of this and recent events in Afghanistan and the Middle East, have created a fundamental shift in the strategic context of PSO.[419]

Current doctrinal thinking rejects the 'the diplomatic convenience of considering mandates in terms of the chapter divisions of the UN Charter' because the restrictions this approach creates hampered the effectiveness of past peace operations.[420] The current view is that a 'one doctrine approach to military operations' should be adopted:[421]

Throughout the later part of the 20th Century the Peacekeeping Trinity, consent coupled with the linked principle of impartiality and limits on the use of force, remained relatively unaltered. However by the end of the millennium it was clear that doctrine had not kept pace with events. Critically, the extant doctrine offered little guidance on peace enforcement; a role, which in Bosnia and Iraq, the United Kingdom and coalition partners were now performing.[422]

The NATO doctrine observes that:

Intervention in the form of a PSO may be required during a crisis... where consent for intervention is high it may be possible to mount a 'traditional' peacekeeping operation. In this situation the capability of the intervening Force to use force need not be high.[423]

However, where the level of consent is less certain:

the capability of the Peace Support Force will need to increase in order to be able to react appropriately. As PSF capability increases to allow greater use of force its profile and

[416] ibid citing C Dobbie, 'A Concept for Post-Cold War Peacekeeping' [1994] 36 Survival No 3, 121.

[417] JWP 3.50 comments in a footnote to this passage that 'Great care must be used to differentiate between the use of war-fighting skills and capacity to undertake combat operations, and the use of the expression when describing participation in an interstate conflict. War-fighting skills are required within a PSO.' ibid, [A 14].

[418] ibid [A14]. [419] ibid [A17].

[420] ibid [108]. [421] ibid [216].

[422] ibid [110]. The role in Iraq refers to operations to protect minorities in the north and south of Iraq following atrocities after the First Gulf War (ibid ch 1, fn 14).

[423] AJP 3.4.1, *Peace Support Operations* (n 400), [0220].

activities become those for Peace Enforcement [PE] rather than PK. Levels of consent are highly unlikely to be uniform in time or in space and thus the intensity of the PSF actions may vary across the Joint Operations Area. This fluctuating level of consent could lead to danger of insufficient Force capability in localised areas and encourages the deployment of Forces with capability and authority to conduct PE activities in all but the most stable situations.[424]

JWP 3.50 distinguishes between 'deliberate or focused intervention', on the one hand and peace support operations, which aim 'to resolve conflict, through a process of long-term engagement by a complex of actors' on the other hand.[425] However, the borders between a robust peace support operation and a humanitarian intervention conducted according to war fighting principles are not razor sharp:

Uniquely, in PSO the strategic intention is to resolve conflict, through a process of long-term engagement by a complex of actors. In war, deliberate, or focused intervention, the intention is less ambitious focusing on short or near-term objectives. Despite these differences of intent, the application of military power in all instances can be soundly guided by adherence to war-fighting doctrine. However, this doctrine must be modified if PSO are to achieve the outcome sought.[426]

Over a period of time the nature of an operation may mutate so that at times it is clearly a peace support operation but at other times that definition does not seem so appropriate. NATO's military doctrine on peace support operations observes that:

Both the mandate from the appropriate international authority and the NAC [North Atlantic Council] decision should distinguish a PSO from any other enforcement action or war with a designated enemy by specifying a desired political end state rather than the achievement of military victory. An enforcement operation may attempt to change the correlation of local forces and impose a solution by force alone, and may be required as a precursor to a PSO. The objectives of a PSO will then refer to such issues as the restoration of peace and security, and support for the principles of the UN and International Humanitarian Law. In PSO, the active participation of the parties, in the formulation and achievement of the political end state will be essential. On the other hand, as military operations move towards war or enforcement, the need to engage the parties in dialogue will diminish until ultimately the specified strategic objectives and political end state could be imposed on the parties without consultation.[427]

The UK's proposed new doctrine, which is still at draft stage and has not yet been adopted, notes that 'operations are operations'; that is, 'all operations can be approached fundamentally in the same manner. This is because peacekeepers must expect to perform a wide range of potentially simultaneous activities across the whole spectrum of conflict from conflict prevention before a crisis to major combat.'[428]

[424] ibid.

[425] JWP 3.50, *The Military Contribution to Peace Support Operation* (n 402), A18.

[426] ibid. [427] AJP 3.4.1, *Peace Support Operations* (n 400), [0204].

[428] Ministry of Defence, Development, Concepts and Doctrine Centre, *Draft UK National Doctrine that will replace JWP 3–50 The Military Contribution to Peace Support Operations* (n 11), [0003].

The key factor that distinguishes a peace support operation from war is that peace support operations are not directed against an enemy. Their aim is to secure a political end-state rather than military victory. They may or may not be authorized by the Security Council (but they are normally conducted in pursuit of UN purposes and principles). They may or may not have the consent of the State in which the operation takes place (but even if there is consent, the nature and extent of that consent may be variable). They are generally multi-functional—their purpose may include humanitarian objectives but there will normally be others too. The UK doctrine, JWP 3.50, observes that peace support operations are complicated. It cites a comment by an experienced PSO officer that:

> [A PSO co-ordinates] The application of state power to direct or facilitate the movement of the social, economic and political affairs of others in the direction that the intervening states think they should go. The political objectives of the intervening states may be ill defined, transient, limited, variable and unpredictable. Politicians may exercise tight control. A clear finite mission statement and final political end state is unlikely. PSOs evolve; success or failure opens or closes doors of opportunity. The environment is often one of deep-rooted mistrust, suspicion and reluctance to make concessions, unpredictable and intransigent. This could be true even after the signing of the peace agreement. The bad guy may become the good guy and vice versa. It is a complex and fluid situation.[429]

If this blunt assessment, made in 2001, remains to any degree accurate, it would not be surprising that peacekeepers are confused as to the nature of their relationship with the local population and the extent of their responsibilities in that regard.

7.1 Peace Support Doctrine on Protection of Civilians

The increased interventionism during the 1990s on humanitarian grounds, and the subsequent emergence of the 'collective international responsibility to protect' as an increasingly accepted norm, has strongly influenced military thinking with regard to the conceptual basis of peace support operations. The UK doctrine, in its introductory chapter under the heading 'The Need for A Contemporary Peace Support Operations Doctrine', comments that:

> There are occasions when a national government or sub-national organs of government fail to uphold international norms. They may be unable or unwilling to prevent abuse, or perhaps prove to be the sponsors of abuse; they may be unable or unwilling to prevent a faction or group being subject to or threatened with, significant harm. When this happens, a 'fundamental dissociation' may have occurred. Consequently, a responsibility to provide protection may fall upon the international community...To respond to those changes, and the associated responsibilities, those who are tasked with, or choose to assist

[429] ibid [302] citing remarks by Major General Wilson, UK Royal Marines, on completion of his tour as COS KFOR December 2001.

with, upholding, renewing or restoring acceptable governance need an expansion of the concepts and doctrine that guide their actions.[430]

It is therefore striking that despite the considerable effort made to try and achieve an international consensus on the peace support operations guidelines to be adopted,[431] and to arrive at 'a near-universal, consistent, and more flexible doctrine',[432] the approach to troops' obligations with regard to the protection of civilians is far from consistent across the various doctrines. In part this may be due to a lack of clarity as regards the legal status of many peace support operations. This lack of clarity stems from the erosion of some traditional peacekeeping principles that have proved ineffective in the type of operations in which forces have been deployed, and also from the uncertain legal status of some interventions that have been undertaken without Security Council authorization, for example those in Iraq in 1991 and Kosovo in 1999.[433]

Nevertheless, even allowing for discrepancies as a result of uncertainties regarding the legal status of some peace support operations, there are marked differences in the approach taken to serious human rights abuses. The West African peace support operations doctrine states that:

> The protection of a non-combatant's basic right to life and dignity is a fundamental element of all military operations. Should members of a PSF who are designated as combatants witness war crimes, but take no action to stop them, they themselves become party to that war crime.[434]

Even where the mandate of forces is limited to self-defence:

> not to intervene when confronted by wide spread abuses to basic human rights and ethnic cleansing, may be regarded as a dereliction of military duty.[435]

Thus under the West African doctrine, troops that are engaged as combatants (and therefore not restricted by the limitations on the use of force that may apply in certain peacekeeping operations, particularly those operating under 'traditional' peacekeeping principles) but fail to intervene to prevent war crimes could face prosecution for participation in a war crime. Even where troops are not engaged as combatants there may still be a duty to act.

NATO's approach to the issue is more cautious. Nowhere does it suggest any legal obligation to intervene. On the contrary the comments dealing with responses to attacks on civilians are preceded with a warning that intervention is

[430] JWP 3.50, *The Military Contribution to Peace Support Operation* (n 403), [113].

[431] Lt. Col. P. Wilkinson, 'Sharpening the Weapons of Peace: The Development of a Common Military Doctrine for Peace Support Operations' above (n 398).

[432] JWP 3.50, *The Military Contribution to Peace Support Operation* (n 403), [123].

[433] The UK Peace Support Operations doctrine notes that 'the legal position of a PSO is not always clear cut' ibid, [436].

[434] DWM 1–2000, '*Peace Support Operations: A Working Draft Manual for African Military Practitioners*' (n 401), [0245].

[435] ibid [0346].

not permitted unless provided for by the applicable Rules of Engagement or the mandate:

> The sensitive issue for PSO is whether to intervene in response to human rights abuses directed at 'civilians on the ground.' Any authorization to do so would be found in applicable ROE [Rules of Engagement]. Such an intervention would only be legally permissible if authorized by applicable ROE and/or mandate.[436]

However, like the West African manual it acknowledges that, to many people, observing and reporting without any attempt to intervene seems a totally inappropriate response to war crimes and crimes against humanity.[437]

The UK doctrine adopts guidelines that are somewhere between the West African and NATO approaches. It states that 'military forces have a moral and legal responsibility to prevent violations' of IHL and human rights but gives no specific guidance as to what these obligations entail.[438] However, the UK's proposed replacement for JWP 3.50 place much greater emphasis on the protection of civilians than its current version. This may well be a consequence of the development in the concept of the collective international 'responsibility to protect' since 2004. In the intervening years the concept has been endorsed by both the General Assembly and the Security Council and has been widely accepted by the UN and regional organizations as a core norm forming part of the international community's responsibilities with regard to the maintenance of international peace and security. The draft for the new JWP 3.50 comments that whilst an operation may have a number of military objectives, the strategic objective 'will normally relate to the establishment of a secure, stable and self-sustaining environment for the local population, the nation and the region' and therefore:

> ... the real or actual success of the operation is related to the human security of the local populace and achieving a situation in which violence is reduced to levels that are acceptable to the local population or within the normal levels for the society or region we are dealing with.[439]

In addition, the inclusion of a section on the physical protection of civilians in the appendices to the draft replacement for JWP 3.50 is a significant new development. It argues, correctly in my view, that military responsibility for the physical protection of civilians can be divided into two areas: a general responsibility to protect and mission responsibility to protect.[440] Under the general responsibility to protect the draft doctrine notes that:

[436] AJP 3.4.1, *Peace Support Operations* (n 400), [0322].

[437] ibid.

[438] JWP 3.50, *The Military Contribution to Peace Support Operation* (n 403), [560].

[439] Ministry of Defence UK, Development, Concepts and Doctrine Centre, *Draft UK National Doctrine that will replace JWP 3–50 The Military Contribution to Peace Support Operations* (n 11), [0112–0113].

[440] ibid [3A22].

All PS themed operations contain general elements of expectation and responsibility for the military to protect civilians; both civilians in the indigenous population and civilians participating in the international response to the crisis. These general responsibilities should be factored into the comprehensive plan for the PS themed operation. The relative importance of these elements will vary during and between PS themed operations but they include:

a. A need to have the appropriate ROE and contingency plans to deal with: international humanitarian & human rights law treaty obligations, customary international law, domestic law of the TCN [troop contributing nation] and host-nation law, and meeting the principles of the UN Charter.
b. Meeting mandates within a UN Security Council resolution that involve or imply the protection of civilians.
c. An effect generated by the application of military capability through the deterrence, neutralisation or defeat of spoilers within the laws of armed conflict.
d. Establishing security thus allowing humanitarian organisations to operate effectively.[441]

A footnote to paragraph (b) gives examples of provisions in mandates that involve the protection of civilians such as 'to protect civilians under imminent threat of physical violence', 'contribute to the protection of the civilian population' and 'respond appropriately to deliberate violence to life and person'. The note comments that:

Such mandates usually come with constraints such as 'without prejudice to the responsibilities' of the host government, 'within capabilities' and 'within area of deployment.' They are not normally given the highest priority within the overall UN Security Council resolution.[442]

By contrast mission responsibility to protect is triggered where an operation is given a primary specified task of responsibility for the physical protection of civilians:

This will probably be for Peace Enforcement only, as the consent of all actors is unlikely to be present and the robust use or credible threat of significant lethal military force may be required.[443]

Military success in this type of operation 'depends upon: a clear mandate and mission; willingness of TCN [Troop Contributing Nations] to actively participate; and robust authority and capacity to act.'[444] Decisions that must be made at the outset include: whether priority should be given to short-term effects (eg stopping all the killing as quickly as possible) or longer-term goals (eg establishing a stable, self-sustaining, peaceful society); whether indigenous security forces should contribute to protection and if so the degree and scope of responsibilities that they should have; whether protection should be provided through dispersed

[441] ibid [3A23].
[442] ibid [3A23 footnote].
[443] ibid [3A24].
[444] ibid.

security or through force concentration in selected areas. Finally 'where pervasive security cannot be maintained, e.g. due to limited resources, a decision must be made on who should be protected and thus who may be left vulnerable when all other options have been exhausted.'[445]

The UK's proposed new doctrine is a significant advance on earlier versions in that it acknowledges some of the critical difficulties peacekeepers are likely to face in protecting civilians; difficulties that have tended to be glossed over in the past. As the doctrine notes, all peacekeeping forces have civilian protection obligations, not just those specifically undertaken pursuant to the 'responsibility to protect.' The very presence of peacekeepers raises the expectation that if civilians are deliberately and brutally attacked troops will do their best to stop it. The suggestion proposed by the UN DPKO Lessons Learned Unit in its *Comprehensive Report on Lessons Learned from the United Nations Assistance Mission for Rwanda*, that it would have been better if UNAMIR had advised the local population that it would not protect them so as not to raise expectations[446] is completely unworkable (quite apart from the moral issues it raises). How is a peacekeeping force going to build a positive relationship with the local community and sustain 'campaign authority'[447] if it goes around telling people that if they are attacked it will not come to their aid? However, the nature and extent of civilian protection obligations in an operation where protection is not the main objective is less than clear. Certainly they 'will vary during and between PS themed operations' and the draft doctrine lists a range of elements to be taken into account, including international humanitarian and human rights law treaty obligations, customary international law, domestic law of the TCN and host-nation law, and meeting the principles of the UN Charter and the need for appropriate ROE. The elements listed are not simple issues; each one is linked to a whole complex of principles, rules, and factors to be taken into account, that no commander, or even his or her legal advisor, could be expected to process in the heat of a crisis. Moreover in the operations with 'mission responsibility to protect', where protection is the stated primary goal, it is unlikely to be the only objective. As Adam Roberts has observed 'it is extremely difficult to envisage any international order in which

[445] ibid [3A24].

[446] United Nations, Lessons Learned Unit, Department of Peacekeeping Operations, *Comprehensive Report on Lessons Learned from the United Nations Assistance Mission for Rwanda (UNAMIR) October 1993 – April 1996* (n 188), [11].

[447] 'Campaign Authority' also known as 'Perceived Legitimacy' is defined in JWP 3.50 as 'the amalgam of four related and inter-dependent factors: the perceived legitimacy of the international mandate that establishes a PSO; the perceived legitimacy of the freedoms and constraints, explicit or implicit in the mandate, placed on those executing the PSO; the degree to which factions, the local population and other actors subjugate themselves to the authority of those executing the PSO; from unwilling compliance to freely given consent; and the degree to which the activities of those executing the PSO meet the expectations of the factions, local population and others.' UK Ministry of Defence, Joint Warfare Publication (JWP) 3.50, *The Military Contribution to Peace Support Operation* (n 403), Glossary-1.

outside forces would be willing to intervene in humanitarian crises primarily on the basis of the urgent needs of threatened peoples.'[448]

The other key problem that peacekeepers face in the context of their general responsibility to protect is, as the draft replacement JWP 3.50 notes, that although nearly all peacekeeping mandates now authorize the protection of civilians they 'usually come with constraints such as 'without prejudice to the responsibilities' of the host government, 'within capabilities' and 'within area of deployment."'[449] What exactly is meant by 'without prejudice to the responsibilities' of the host government? The Brahimi report recommended that 'peacekeepers—troops or police—who witness violence against civilians should be presumed to be authorized to stop it, within their means, in support of basic United Nations principles.'[450] Does the phrase 'without prejudice to the responsibilities' of the host government qualify the authorization to protect civilians from violence where the violence that troops witness (such as necklace killings, rapes, beating with iron bars) is being perpetrated by the host government police or army personnel? Would it be different if the violence comes within the description 'excessive force'? Does the phrase have implications for the division of responsibilities regarding patrolling duties, or disarmament procedures, in a situation where massacres are anticipated? In order to train peacekeepers in how to carry out general civilian protection responsibilities, forces and their commanders, legal advisors, training school personnel and all the other actors involved in preparing a force for duty, need to know how this phrase should be interpreted in terms of general principles and not just in terms of the politics specific to a particular mission. They need to know in advance of a situation arising what the appropriate response or range of responses should be; rather than discover on the day that different key actors have different views on the matter, as occurred in Rwanda and Srebrenica.[451]

In what circumstances may a force commander faced with successive brutal attacks on civilians, take proactive action? Security Resolution 1756 authorizes MONUC, (which can probably be characterized as having 'mission responsibility to protect') to '[e]nsure the protection of civilians... under imminent threat of physical violence' and to this end it authorizes the force to 'seize and collect arms, as appropriate' and to use 'cordon and search tactics to prevent attacks on civilians and disrupt the military capability of illegal armed groups that continue to use violence in those areas.'[452] But such specific provisions are unusual. Moreover

[448] A Roberts, 'The So-Called 'Right' of Humanitarian Intervention' (2000) 3 Yearbook of International Humanitarian Law, 3, 41.

[449] Ministry of Defence UK, Development, Concepts and Doctrine Centre, *Draft UK National Doctrine that will replace JWP 3–50 The Military Contribution to Peace Support Operations* (n 11), [3A23 footnote].

[450] Report of the Panel on United Nations Peace Operations (n 238), [62].

[451] In the latter case the mandating resolution was drafted in deliberately obscure terms: SC Res 836, 4 June 1993.

[452] S/RES/1756 15 May 2007 [2] [3].

MONUC was working in co-operation with the DRC government forces and hence conflicts over the sovereign responsibility of the DRC government could more easily be resolved. Unfortunately the DRC army itself has a record of abuse of civilians, a fact that has tarnished MONUC's reputation. Dag Hammarskjöld when considering what response should be taken to the attacks on civilians in the conflict in the Congo in the 1960s, noted that 'the protection of the lives of the civilian population in the spirit of the Universal Declaration of Human Rights and the Genocide Convention ... might necessitate a temporary disarming of military units which, in the view of the circumstances, were an obstacle to the restoration of law and order.'[453] At the time ONUC was operating under the General Assembly's authorization under the Uniting for Peace Procedure and outside the control of the Security Council all together so there was no Security Council mandate, Chapter VII or otherwise, authorizing such action. In the event the force did not resort to disarmament but later, when the Security Council retook control and authorized increasingly robust mandates, the ONUC mission gradually mutated from peacekeeping to enforcement. Enforcement action of the kind used by ONUC to quell the secession in Katanga may be politically unacceptable and may undermine the reputation of UN peacekeeping operations by exposing them to the charge that they are merely a vehicle for carrying out the interventionist aims of powerful States.

Commanders may also need to take into account the potential interaction between the force's general responsibility to protect and its mission responsibility to protect. As regards mission responsibility to protect the draft doctrine notes that one of the decisions that must be made at the outset is '[w]hether priority should be given to short-term effects (e.g. stopping all the killing as quickly as possible) or longer-term goals (e.g. establishing a stable, self-sustaining, peaceful society).' If priority is given to longer term goals does that affect the force's general responsibility to protect? If, for example, the force is focusing on securing elections as part of a mission responsibility to establish a stable society, as was the case for UNTAC, does that relieve it of its general protection obligations where civilians are being attacked, as the Vietnamese were in Cambodia?

8. Conclusion

From very early in the history of peacekeeping, most notably with the ONUC mission, there has been an expectation that troops should protect civilians from massacres and crimes against humanity. Even in the early missions protection of civilians was regarded as a proper function of peacekeepers correlative with their impartial role in keeping the peace between the parties to a conflict and helping

[453] Annual Report of the Secretary-General on the Work of the Organization, June 16, 1960–June 16, 1961, 16th Session, UN Doc A/4800, 11.

'everyone', 'white and black'.[454] The difficulty arises when providing protection brings peacekeepers into conflict with the war aims of one or more parties, as Hammarskjöld foresaw in the 1960s when he considered withdrawing ONUC. In the civil wars of the 1990s ethnic cleansing and genocide were frequently used by the parties to the conflict as war-fighting techniques to gain control of territory or to eliminate the need to make political concessions to minority groups; such tactics remain common.

The concept of the collective international 'responsibility to protect' resolves, to some degree, the conflict between respect for State sovereignty and respect for human security, at the level of intervention, but in doing so it introduces a vertical relationship between the intervening organization or State and the protected population that does not in fact exist in law, at least on a general level. According to the ICISS report, 'the international responsibility to protect' bridges the divide between State sovereignty (encompassing the responsibility of the sovereign to protect its people) and intervention (the practical manifestation of the responsibility of the international community to protect those people should the sovereign fail to do so). This suggests that once a State exercises its 'responsibility to protect' through intervention, a new relationship should come into being between the protected population and its protectors. If not, the population that the humanitarian action is intended to benefit are left exposed. Their own government has abdicated its responsibility to protect them, but the intervening actors (notwithstanding the new banner 'responsibility to protect' under which their intervention is justified) have not taken on that responsibility. However, even in the context of an intervention pursuant to the 'responsibility to protect' the legal obligations of States in the international field still operate predominantly on a horizontal plane. Except where intervening forces are in occupation of the territory,[455] there is no relationship (of a general nature) recognized in international law, between the inhabitants of one State and an intervening State or organization, although rights and obligations may arise under international humanitarian law (IHL) and human rights treaties in certain circumstances. Thus the emerging practice of intervention pursuant to the collective international 'responsibility to protect' allows for the creation of a de facto relationship between States and foreign citizens living outside its borders—but there is only a very rudimentary legal regime to regulate it.

The Brahimi report and the peace support doctrines developed in Europe, Africa, and by NATO, suggest that there is a moral, and in the view of some

[454] Press Release CO/15 July 19, 1960; GIAD Draper, 'The Legal Limitations Upon the Employment of Weapons by the United Nations Force in the Congo,' (n 35), 399.

[455] In certain circumstances states may have obligations under human rights law when they are exercising authority or control over territory outside their national borders. These are similar criteria to that used for determining whether there is an occupation under IHL. However the two concepts are not necessarily entirely synonymous. *The Queen on the application of Mazin Jumaa Gatteh Al-Skeini and others v Secretary of State for Defence* [2005] EWCA Civ 1609, 21 December 2005, [124–127], [195–197].

States, legal, obligation on troops to stop attacks on civilians, whether the force is engaged in a mission specifically deployed to protect civilians or not; but at the same time they reflect some uncertainty as to how this obligation is to be interpreted, particularly in the context of operations conducted under a limited mandate. Brahimi posited a distinction between 'neutrality' and 'impartiality', arguing that taking a stand against the actions of one or other party would not infringe the obligation to remain impartial provided that the Force was acting evenly in seeking the parties' compliance with terms of the UN mandate:

> Impartiality for such operations must therefore mean adherence to the principles of the Charter and to the objectives of a mandate that is rooted in those Charter principles. Such impartiality is not the same as neutrality or equal treatment of all parties in all cases for all time, which can amount to a policy of appeasement. In some cases, local parties consist not of moral equals but of obvious aggressors and victims, and peacekeepers may not only be operationally justified in using force but morally compelled to do so.[456]

However, the loss of neutrality has serious consequences for peacekeepers as it increases the likelihood that they will be attacked, notwithstanding that the force's impartiality remains intact. Equally critical is the potential effect of loss of neutrality (in the eyes of a party to the conflict at least) on other civilians for whom the UN has protection or humanitarian responsibilities. During the Srebrenica crisis, General Sir Michael Rose was acutely conscious of the local population's dependency on the UN for humanitarian aid, observing that '[e]very time I called for NATO air strikes, the movement of aid across Serb-held territory was halted and people died.'[457]

These kinds of problems cannot be avoided in modern warfare, particularly given that peacekeepers are now routinely mandated with a complex range of tasks that frequently encompass humanitarian assistance and peace-building efforts, as well keeping the peace. In order to make these decisions commanders need a clearer legal framework as regards the use of force for protection. The antinomies that exist as regards forceful protection of civilians within the self-defence norm, or even within a limited Chapter VII mandate, are not easily reconciled: but it is clear that following the endorsement, by the UN and regional organizations, of the 'responsibility to protect' there has been a doctrinal shift towards stronger protection of civilians from direct attack, as an aspect of decision-making in all peace operations. The UK's intended replacement for JWP 3.50 states that since the nature of peace support is such that the strategic objectives will normally relate to the establishment of a secure environment for the local population, the nation and the region, 'the real or actual success' of a peace support operation (whatever its other objectives and whether or not the operation is undertaken pursuant to the 'responsibility to protect') is 'related to the human security of the

456 Report of the Panel on United Nations Peace Operations (n 238), [50].

457 General Sir Michael Rose, *Fighting for Peace: Lessons from Bosnia* (n 198), 354.

local populace and achieving a situation in which violence is reduced to levels that are acceptable to the local population or within the normal levels for the society or region we are dealing with.'[458]

The UK's intended replacement for JWP 3.50 also addresses the implications of the responsibility to protect for peace operations in more depth than its earlier doctrines. It separates the responsibility to protect into two aspects; a 'general responsibility to protect', which has been a function of peacekeeping missions for at least half a century, but has been thrown into stronger relief by the emergence of the second aspect, 'mission responsibility to protect', which is more directly associated with the emerging and evolving 'collective international responsibility to protect' norm. It is assumed that general protection obligations do not disappear where there are also 'mission responsibility to protect' obligations, thus for all peacekeeping missions it is essential that troops understand what their general protection obligations are. Currently this is difficult because of the lack of clarity surrounding this issue. The draft replacement for JWP 3.50 lists a number of elements that commanders must take into account when their obligations in this regard. These include international 'humanitarian & human rights law treaty obligations, customary international law, domestic law of the TCN and host-nation law, and meeting the principles of the UN Charter.' This is a vast area of law. Unless the protection obligations arising under these laws are understood there is little point in noting the need to address them. The following chapters explore the protection obligations arising under the first two heads: humanitarian and human rights law treaties and customary international law.

[458] Ministry of Defence UK, Development, Concepts and Doctrine Centre, *Draft UK National Doctrine that will replace JWP 3–50 The Military Contribution to Peace Support Operations* (n 11) [0112], [0113].

2

The Extent to which Peacekeeping and other Multi-national Forces have a General 'Responsibility to Protect' under International Humanitarian Law

1. Introduction

This chapter examines the extent to which international humanitarian law (IHL) may be applicable to peacekeeping forces and the extent to which this encompasses positive obligations that would require troops to protect the local population from serious abuses of certain of their human rights.

2. Applicability of International Humanitarian Law

IHL was developed to regulate the conduct of parties engaged in an armed conflict or military occupation.[1] Its purpose is to enable the parties to wage war, whilst at the same time providing protection to people that are not involved in the conflict (primarily civilians) and limiting suffering by prohibiting the use of excessively cruel weapons or methods of combat. The lack of clarity regarding the application of IHL to UN peace operations stems from the unusual position of UN forces, which are often deployed into situations where violence reaches a high degree of intensity, but are not party to the armed conflict. The Institut de Droit International declared in a 1971 resolution that '[t]he humanitarian rules of the law of armed conflict apply to the United Nations as of right, and they must be complied with in all circumstances by

[1] Article 2 common to Geneva Convention I for the Amelioration of the Condition of the Wounded and Sick in Armed Forces in the Field, 75 UNTS 31; Geneva Convention II for the Amelioration of the Condition of the Wounded, Sick and Shipwrecked Members of the Armed Forces at Sea, 75 UNTS 85; Geneva Convention III Relative to the Treatment of Prisoners of War, 75 UNTS 135; Geneva Convention IV Relative to the Protection of Civilians in Time of War, 75 UNTS 287 (all adopted Geneva, 12 Aug 1949, came into force 21 October 1950).

United Nations Forces which are engaged in hostilities.'[2] However, whilst the UN has never claimed outright exemption from the laws of war,[3] for a long time the UN was reluctant to recognize that IHL applied to its peacekeeping forces. For example, in relation to the Congo conflict of the 1960s, a dispute, which was never resolved, arose between the ICRC and the UN as to whether common Article 3 applied to ONUC forces engaged in combat in Katanga. GI Draper, discussing this in 1965, suggested that it 'is not an impossible solution that Article 3 applies as between the Government and rebel forces, but not as between the UN Force and either of the other contending elements.'[4] Common Article 3 is largely concerned with ensuring compliance with the most basic humanitarian standards.

Daphna Shraga, Senior Legal Officer, Office of the Legal Counsel, Office of Legal Affairs, the United Nations, writing in her personal capacity, in an article published in the American Journal of International Law in 2000, commented that for:

> nearly half a century, the United Nations was disinclined to recognize the applicability of international humanitarian law or to abide by its provisions.[5]

The ICRC, in a statement to the General Assembly on the 16 November 1995, observed that:

> [t]he ICRC has always taken the view that all the provisions of international humanitarian law are applicable when United Nations contingents resort to the use of force, whereas the United Nations has held the view that it is bound only by the 'principles and spirit' of the humanitarian law treaties. These respective positions have been restated many times.[6]

Richard Glick,[7] in a 1995 article in the Michigan Journal of International Law, argued that although officers of the United Nations 'concede that UN forces are subject to some form of customary international humanitarian law' in practice 'the United Nations treats the subject as a political issue and not as a fundamental legal obligation.'[8]

[2] Institut de Droit International 'Conditions of Application of Humanitarian Rules of Armed Conflict to Hostilities in which United Nations Forces May be Engaged' Session of Zagreb—1971, [2].

[3] D Bowett, *United Nations Forces: A Legal Study of United Nations Practice* (Steven & Sons London 1964), 56.

[4] GIA Draper, *The Geneva Conventions of 1949*, 14 Receuil des cours 1, 59, 95.

[5] D Shraga, 'UN Peacekeeping Operations: Applicability of International Humanitarian Law and Responsibility for Operations-Related Damage' (2000) 94 AJIL 406, 406.

[6] United Nations, General Assembly 50th Session (1995), Fourth Committee, Agenda item 86, Thursday 16 November 1995, statement by the International Committee of the Red Cross.

[7] Then a Senior Fellow at the Center for International Studies, New York University School of Law.

[8] RD Glick, 'Lip Service to the Laws of War: Humanitarian Law and United Nations Armed Forces' (1995) 17 Michigan Journal of International Law 53, 54.

However, because of the complexity of modern conflicts UN troops are now often deployed into scenarios where there presence has not been consented to by the warring parties (or not all of them). In Somalia there was no government capable of giving consent.[9] In addition it is now general practice for the Security Council to give peacekeeping forces mandates to use force in situations other than self-defence, for example in order to protect civilians from deliberate attack or in defence of the mandate.[10] As a result of these changes, and of changes in patterns of warfare, peacekeeping forces may now find themselves engaged in robust action. Evidence of serious misconduct by UN troops put further pressure on the UN to develop, in a series of conventions, agreements, declarations and bulletins, a special legal regime that applies to UN forces,[11] that is intended both to protect troops and to ensure high standards of conduct. This regime is based in IHL but provides additional safeguards intended, among other things, to minimize the risk of peacekeepers being attacked. These safeguards include the 'Convention on the Privileges and Immunities of the United Nation'[12] and the 'United Nations Convention on the Safety of United Nations and Associated Personnel.'[13]

2.1 The Specialized Regime that Applies to UN Forces

The UN is not a party to any IHL treaties, and moreover, since it is not a State it cannot become a party. Since it is not a State it does not have the legislative and judicial mechanisms of a State and therefore would not be able to carry out all the obligations contained in the IHL treaties. Nevertheless it has always accepted that UN forces are bound to respect the 'principles and spirit' of the laws of war.[14]

[9] The UN Operation in Somalia (UNOSOM I) began as a humanitarian operation, accompanied by a peacekeeping presence as mandated by S/RES 751 (24 April 1992), S/RES 767 (24 July 1992) and S/RES 775 (28 August 1992). On 3 December 1992 the Security Council adopted Resolution 794 authorizing a Chapter VII peace-enforcement operation, the Unified Task Force (UNITAF), led by the United States. S/RES 814 (26 March 1993) mandated UNOSOM II, a peace enforcement operation authorized under Chapter VII of the Charter.

[10] As seen in the mandates of the United Nations Mission in Sierra Leone (UNAMSIL) (S/RES/1270 22 October 1999)), the United Nations Organization Mission in the Democratic Republic of the Congo (MONUC) (S/RES/1417 14 June 2002)), the United Nations Mission in Liberia (UNMIL) (S/RES/1509 19 September 2003)), the United Nations Operation in Côte d'Ivoire (UNOCI) (S/RES/1528 27 February 2004)) and the United Nations Operation in Burundi (ONUB) (S/RES/1545 21 May 2004)): Report of the Secretary-General to the Security Council on the protection of civilians in armed conflict' 28 May 2004 S/2002/431 [8].

[11] ibid 59.

[12] Convention on the Privileges and Immunities of the United Nations, 13 February 1946, 1 UNTS 15.

[13] Convention on the Safety of UN and Associated Personnel (adopted 19 December 1994, entered into force 15 January 1999) 34 ILM (1995).

[14] UN Doc A/46/185 of 23 May 1991 [28]; A Roberts and R Guelff, *Documents on the Laws of War* (3rd edn Oxford University Press Oxford 2000) 625, 723; D Shraga and R Zacklin 'The Applicability of International Humanitarian Law to United Nations Peace-Keeping Operations: Conceptual, Legal and Practical Issues' in U Palwankar (ed), *International Committee of the Red Cross Symposium on Humanitarian Action and Peacekeeping Operations* (International Committee of the Red Cross Geneva 1994) 39, 44; PC Szasz, 'UN Forces and International Humanitarian Law' in

Roberts and Guelff argue that the obligation on UN forces to respect the principles and spirit of IHL applies to traditional peacekeeping as well as combatant forces, a view reflected in Bulletins issued by the Secretary-General from 1957 to 1964 and in the 1991 UN Model Agreement between the UN and Member States Contributing Personnel and Equipment to UN Peacekeeping Operations.[15] However, when allegations were made that UN forces in Somalia violated IHL, a number of military tribunals held in contributing States disputed that the operation was one to which the laws of armed conflict applied at all.

The Canadian Courts Martial Appeals Court held in *R v Brocklebank*[16] that Private Brocklebank (who was arrested for aiding and abetting the torture of a Somali teenager) had no legal obligation to ensure the safety of a prisoner, because neither the Geneva Conventions nor their Additional Protocols applied to peacekeeping operations. Hence they did not apply to Canadian Forces in Somalia. A Belgian Military Court investigating violations of IHL also concluded that IHL did not apply to the UN peacekeeping forces in Somalia.[17] This resulted in strong criticism of the national courts. In addition 'a lingering feeling remained that the United Nations was being let-off a little too easily.'[18] The government of Canada set up a public Commission of Inquiry but it was unable to properly complete its investigations because on 10 January 1997, while Parliament was adjourned, the Minister of National Defence announced that Cabinet had decided that the Inquiry had gone on long enough, that all hearings must be cut off on 31 March 1997, and that a report with recommendations was required by 30 June 1997.[19] The Commission was scathing in its criticism of this decision stating that:

> [t]he unexpected decision to impose a sudden time constraint on an inquiry of this magnitude is without precedent in Canada. There is no question that it has compromised and limited our search for the truth.[20]

The Commission also said that:

> we must also record with regret that on many occasions the testimony of witnesses was characterized by inconsistency, improbability, implausibility, evasiveness, selective

MN Schmitt (ed), *International Law across the Spectrum of Conflict, Essays in Honour of Professor LC Green on the Occasion of His Eightieth Birthday* (US Naval War College Newport 2000) 507, 516.

[15] A Roberts and R Guelff, *Documents on the Laws of War* (n 14), 625, 722–723.

[16] *R v Brocklebank* CMAC-383, April 2, 1996: J Simpson *Law Applicable to Canadian Forces in Somalia 1992/93: Study Prepared for the Commission of Inquiry into the Deployment of Canadian Forces to Somalia* (Minister of Public Works and Government Services Canada 1997) 28–30.

[17] Judgment of the Belgian Military Court regarding violations of IHL committed in Somalia and Rwanda Nr 54 AR 1997, 20 November 1997; Journal des Tribunaux 24 April 1998, 286–289 (French language): Comment by M Cogen (1998) 1 Yearbook of International Humanitarian Law 415–416.

[18] F Mégret and F Hoffman, 'The UN as a Human Rights Violator? Some reflections on the United Nations Changing Human Rights Responsibilities' 25 Human Rights Quarterly, 314, 327.

[19] *Commission of Inquiry into the Deployment of Canadian Forces to Somalia*, <http://www.dnd.ca/somalia/somaliae.htm>.

[20] ibid Final Report, Vol 0, Executive Summary.

recollection, half-truths, and plain lies... Perhaps more troubling is the fact that many of the witnesses who displayed these shortcomings were officers, non-commissioned officers, and senior civil servants—individuals sworn to respect and promote the values of leadership, courage, integrity, and accountability.[21]

The Commission observed that '[l]ittle attention was paid to Law of Armed Conflict training'[22] and that:

soldiers did not even seem to know whether they had a general duty to prevent harm to a prisoner if they were not tasked specifically to guard the prisoner at the time. In short, training prior to deployment on how to treat a prisoner after capture was virtually non-existent and therefore grossly inadequate.[23]

Despite the scandal created by the misconduct in Somalia and the failure to hold troops accountable, three years later there were shocking reports of gross misconduct by a minority of troops deployed to Srebrenica. It was alleged that soldiers had thrown sweets into fields that they suspected were mined in order to encourage the children to 'test' for them; that soldiers paid children to explore trenches for mines; that soldiers had given poisoned sweets to children; and that on at least one occasion soldiers driving an armoured vehicle and coming across a crowd of civilians in the road, (among them many children), made bets with each other as to how many they could hit. Pressure from the Dutch public led to a number of investigations, none of which were sufficiently thorough to meet the gravity of the allegations.[24]

[21] ibid. [22] ibid Vol 4, Brigadier General Ernest Beneto n 38.
[23] ibid Vol 4, Colonel Serge Labbé n 34.
[24] Netherlands Institute for War Documentation *Srebrenica 'A Safe Area': Reconstruction, Background, Consequences and Analyzes of the Fall of a Safe Area,'* (2002) ch 9, s7 'Misconduct', Section 8 'Back to square one: misconduct after all?' and Section 9 'Conclusions on misconduct?'; Following numerous damaging press reports, the Ministry of Defence requested the Commander in Chief of the Land Army Forces, Van Baal, to carry out an investigation. Van Baal sent his report to the Minister of Defence on 12 May 1995. Van Baal's report consists of a letter with two attachments. The first attachment contains the report of an investigation carried out by local commanders and headed by the commander in chief, Colonel Karremans. It consists of interviews with soldiers and local people who might have been witnesses. The second attachment consists of a report by an internal commission of inquiry that had analyzed the allegations and made discrete inquiries of former officers and colleagues. All of the soldiers interviewed denied that they had done any of these things, although some admitted that they had heard about other soldiers doing them. One soldier was particularly heavily interrogated but denied any wrongdoing. In his letter to the Minister of Defence, Van Baal wrote that, no further information other than the rumours already circulating in the media could be found. He advised the Minister not to request the public prosecutor to start a criminal investigation into the behaviour of Dutchbat forces. Given the seriousness of the allegations and the persistence of the rumours it is questionable whether the inquiries conducted were sufficient: *Letter from Commander in Chief of the Land Army Forces, A. van Baal to the Minister of Defence Joris Voorhoeve*, 12 May 1995 <http://www.nrc.nl/W2/Lab/Srebrenica/baal.html>. (In Dutch: I am grateful to Martijn van Kogelenberg for translating this for me). Under pressure from the Dutch public another investigation was carried out in 1998. A report was published on the 29 September 1998 entitled 'About Srebrenica.' The report acknowledged 'shortcomings and oversights' but held that there was no deliberate cover up or malicious intent: 29.09.1998 'Defence Ministry's Srebrenica Information Supply amateurish' <http://www.nisnews.nl/dossiers/

Professor Siekmann, in an article published in the 1998 Yearbook of International Humanitarian Law, argued that as Dutchbat was a UN peacekeeping force and was not engaged in combat, IHL did not apply to it.[25] Therefore, whether or not the allegations made against Dutchbat were true, '[a]ccording to the present state of public international law, the Dutch soldiers have not committed a punishable act.'[26] In short 'the behaviour of Dutchbat surrounding the fall of Srebrenica can, notwithstanding moral and ethical considerations, stand the test of legal criticism.'[27] To date not one Dutch soldier has been prosecuted in connection with the events in Srebrenica,[28] although three soldiers were fined approximately $200 dollars for walking around Srebrenica, in the days after it was overrun by the Serbs, wearing T-shirts depicting a UN soldier grabbing a Muslim child by the throat, and further antagonizing the local population by making Nazi-style salutes.[29]

2.2 Pressure for a Formal Undertaking that UN Forces Must Comply with International Humanitarian Law

Following the events in Somalia and subsequently in Bosnia-Herzegovina, and the resultant disputes over the applicability of IHL, the ICRC argued that 'principles and spirit' was not enough: there should be a formal undertaking from the UN that it would comply with IHL. Therefore in 1999 the Secretary-General promulgated a Bulletin on the Observance by UN forces of International Humanitarian Law.[30] However, the Bulletin does not cover all situations. It states that:

> The fundamental principles and rules of international humanitarian law are applicable to UN forces when in situations of armed conflict they are actively engaged therein as

srebrenica/195_290998.htm>. However, suggestions of a cover-up surfaced again a year later, when the Minister of Defence was forced to acknowledge that no less than 100,000 documents relating to the events in Srebrenica had been destroyed by officials in the Ministry of Defence; 15.07.1999 'Mid Sackings: Srebrenica Cover-up By Shadowy Secret Service' <http://www.nisnews.nl/dossiers/srebrenica/217_150799.htm>.

[25] RCR Siekmann, 'The Fall of Srebrenica and the Attitude of Dutchbat from an International Legal Perspective', 1 Yearbook of International Humanitarian Law, 301, 311.

[26] ibid 310. [27] ibid 312.

[28] A Knoops. Professor of International Criminal Law at the University of Utrecht, Speaking at the Irish Centre for Human Rights NUI Galway, 29 November 2004.

[29] NRC Handelsblad, March 20, 2001 (In Dutch); 31 July 1999 'Srebrenica: Dutch Regularly Gave Nazi-salutes' <http://www.nisnews.nl/dossiers/srebrenica/.htm>; 14 July 1999 'Top Military Information Service Resigns On Srebrenica' <http://www.nisnews.nl/dossiers/srebrenica/.htm>; Netherlands Institute for War Documentation *Srebrenica 'A Safe Area': Reconstruction, Background, Consequences and Analyzes of the Fall of a Safe Area,'* (2002) pt II, ch 8, s 15 'The extent of anti-Muslim behaviour' and ch 9 s 11'Right-wing extremist behaviour in B-Company'.

[30] Secretary-General's Bulletin on Observance by UN Forces of International Humanitarian Law (date of promulgation 6 August 1999, entered into force 12 August 1999) UN Doc ST/SGB/1999/13. The Bulletin is an internal document of the UN. It is binding on UN troops but does not in itself create direct legal obligations for States: Report of Experts Meeting on Multi-National Operations, 11–12 December 2003 (ICRC Geneva), 2.

combatants, to the extent and for the duration of their engagement. They are accordingly applicable in enforcement actions, or in peacekeeping operations when the use of force is permitted in self-defence.[31]

The Bulletin draws a clear distinction between forces engaged as combatants and forces that are not engaged as combatants. The reason for this was to ensure compatibility with the 1994 Convention on the Safety of UN and Associated Personnel (Safety Convention).[32] This Convention makes it a crime under international law to attack peacekeepers that are not engaged as combatants.[33] Similarly, Article 8 of the Statute of the International Criminal Court provides that attacks on peacekeepers may be prosecuted at the Court.[34] UN forces that are not engaged as combatants remain entitled to the protection of the Safety Convention.[35] Because IHL applies between parties to the conflict and permits combatants to attack and kill one another, it was felt that the UN forces could not be subject to IHL and entitled to the protection of the Safety Convention at the same time. It is a cardinal principle of IHL that combatant forces are treated equally.[36] Therefore the Bulletin provides that IHL applies to UN forces 'when

[31] ibid.

[32] Convention on the Safety of UN and Associated Personnel (adopted 19 December 1994, entered into force 15 January 1999) 34 ILM (1995). Article 2, (2), provides that the Convention 'shall not apply to a UN operation authorized by the Security Council as an enforcement action under Chapter VII of the Charter of the UN in which any of the personnel are engaged as combatants against organized armed forces and to which the law of international armed conflict applies.' Christopher Greenwood points out that the line between those UN operations to which the law of armed conflict applies and those which are subject to the Safety Convention, 'is far from straightforward...While most of the operations in which UN personnel become engaged as combatants against organized armed forces are likely to fall under Chapter VII of the Charter, that will not always be the case. Even a force established by the Security Council or the General Assembly without reference to Chapter VII of the Charter is entitled to use force in self-defense. The United Nations has traditionally interpreted this right of self-defense very broadly, so as to justify not only the use of force to protect United Nations and associated personnel and property from attacks, but also to justify the use of force in response to armed resistance to the discharge of the force's mandate. A peacekeeping force which exercized this right of self-defense might well find itself engaged in protracted hostilities with organized armed forces, which would be subject to the law of armed conflict. The Safety Convention would, however, also apply. Moreover, Article 2(2) only removes an operation from the scope of the Safety Convention in a case where personnel are engaged as combatants in a situation to which the law of international armed conflict applies.' C Greenwood 'Protection of Peacekeepers: The Legal Regime', 7 Duke Journal of Comparative & International Law, 185, 198–199.

[33] ibid Article 9.

[34] Article 8 of the Rome Statute gives the ICC jurisdiction over serious violations of the laws and customs applicable in international armed conflict including under 8(b)(iii) 'intentionally directing attacks against personnel, installations, materials, units or vehicles involved in humanitarian assistance or peacekeeping mission in accordance with the Charter of the United Nations, as long as they are entitled to the protection given to civilians or civilian objects under the international law of armed conflict.' 1998 Rome Statute of the International Criminal Court (adopted 17 July 1998 entered into force 11 April 2002) UN Doc A/CONF.183/9.

[35] Convention on the Safety of UN and Associated Personnel (n 32), Article 2 (2)

[36] A Roberts and R Guelff, *Documents on the Laws of War* (n 14), 625. It is feared that if the principle of equal application is undermined, all respect for the 1949 Geneva Conventions may be destroyed:

in situations of armed conflict they are actively engaged therein as combatants, to the extent and for the duration of their engagement.' However, the Bulletin does not make clear the obligations of non-combatant troops. Determining at what point peacekeepers become combatants may be difficult: soldiers may find themselves using some level of force in self-defence and yet not be considered combatants.[37] Moreover since attacks on peacekeepers are prohibited under the Safety Convention but permissible under IHL, it is likely that a high level of force must be reached before UN authorities will concede that their troops are now engaged as combatants. Hence a high level of force may be required before UN forces become subject to IHL.[38]

The Secretary-General's Bulletin only applies to forces that are UN commanded and controlled.[39] Many peace support operations are UN authorized but not UN-commanded and controlled. Sometimes UN-run and non-UN-run peace operations operate in the same vicinity, as occurred in Bosnia-Herzegovina. In addition a number of peace operations have been undertaken that have not been authorized by the Security Council at all; for example Liberia and Sierra Leone where Security Council authorization came after the operation had been initiated. The humanitarian interventions into Iraq in 1991 and Kosovo in 1999 also did not have explicit UN authorization.

NATO's military doctrine on Peace Support Operations (2001) implies that IHL is not formally applicable to most NATO peace support operations. The section entitled 'The Law of Armed Conflict' is quite brief; it states that:

> The Law of Armed Conflict (LOAC) is the body of international law that governs the conduct of hostilities during an armed conflict. The PSF [Peace Support Force] will not generally be a party to the conflict, yet certain LOAC principles may be applied. Individual civilians along with the civilian population must never be purposefully targeted unless they have taken active part in the armed conflict. When military force is used, every effort should be taken to minimise the risk of civilian casualties.[40]

Thus the basic premise of NATO doctrine is that IHL is not applicable to most peace support operations yet certain principles 'may be applied': primarily the principle of distinction and the principle of proportionality. The paragraph taken as a whole is problematic. In the first half it states that IHL does not generally apply. But in the second half it makes it plain that forces are likely to be engaged in action that to most of us would seem indistinguishable from armed

C Greenwood, 'Protection of Peacekeepers: The Legal Regime' 7 Duke Journal of Comparative & International Law (n 32), 186.

[37] A Roberts and R Guelff, *Documents on the Laws of War* (n 14), 625.

[38] ibid 627; C Greenwood 'Protection of Peacekeepers: The Legal Regime' (n 32), 186, 202.

[39] Secretary-General's Bulletin on Observance by UN Forces of International Humanitarian Law (n 30), Introductory paragraph.

[40] Allied Joint Publication (AJP) 3.4.1 *Peace Support Operations*, July 2001 <http://www.pronato.com/peacekeeping/AJP-3-4-1/index.htm>, Annex 4B Legal Considerations, Section III 'The Law of Armed Conflict'.

conflict. There would be no need to warn that civilians must not be deliberately targeted, if NATO did not anticipate that its peace support forces would be targeting someone or something. Nor would there be any need to remind that effort must be made to minimize civilian casualties, if NATO did not anticipate that there would be some civilian casualties. Yet these cases are given as examples of principles that may be applied even though IHL in general does not apply. This suggests that NATO anticipates that the threshold level of violence that needs to be reached before peace support forces become engaged as combatants, and so subject to IHL, may be a very high one. The difficulty in determining at what point peacekeepers become engaged as combatants is in any case very difficult to gauge. This issue has become even more pertinent with changes in peace supports operations doctrine that eschew sharp divisions between categories of operation, and instead view peace operations as operating on a continuum from traditional peacekeeping through to enforcement, with a similarly flexible approach to the use of force and requirements of consent.

2.3 Applicability of International Humanitarian Law to Civilians

The traditional approach to the applicability of IHL is that it is intended to be applicable to combatants only. (This is reflected in the Secretary-General's Bulletin and current peace support operations doctrine). However, recent developments suggest that there is a growing consensus that IHL is also binding on civilians. In 2001, the Court of Appeal for the International Criminal Tribunal for Rwanda held, in the *Akayesu* decision, that common Article 3 of the Geneva Conventions is binding on all actors, including civilians, and that there is no requirement of a nexus between a perpetrator and a party to the conflict. The case concerned the prosecution of a bourg-mestre, who was not a member of the armed forces but had actively incited killings and brutal treatment of Tutsis. The Trial Chamber had reiterated the established position on the applicability of IHL, which was that the Geneva Conventions are binding primarily on the parties to the conflict:

> The four Geneva Conventions—as well as the two Additional Protocols—as stated above, were adopted primarily to protect the victims as well as potential victims of armed conflicts. This implies thus that the legal instruments are primarily addressed to persons who by virtue of their authority, are responsible for the outbreak of, or are otherwise engaged in the conduct of hostilities. The category of persons to be held accountable in this respect then, would in most cases be limited to commanders, combatants and other members of the armed forces.[41]

However, the Trial Chamber noted that it 'is, in fact, well-established, at least since the Tokyo trials, that civilians may be held responsible for violations of

[41] *The Prosecutor v Jean Paul Akayesu* Case no ICTR 94-4-1 Judgment, 22 September 1998, [630].

international humanitarian law' and pointed to a number of World War II trials where civilians were held liable where they had had a link or connection with a Party to the conflict. It referred in particular to the Zyklon B case in which the Court said that:

The decision of the Military Court in the present case is a clear example of the application of the rule that the provisions of the laws and customs of war are addressed not only to combatants and to members of state and other public authorities, but to anybody who is in a position to assist in their violation. [...] any civilian who is an accessory to a violation of the laws and customs of war is himself also liable as a war criminal.[42]

The ICTR Trial Chamber commented that:

The principle of holding civilians liable for breaches of the laws of war is, moreover, favored by a consideration of the humanitarian object and purpose of the Geneva Conventions and the Additional Protocols, which is to protect war victims from atrocities. Thus it is clear from the above that the laws of war must apply equally to civilians as to combatants in the conventional sense.[43]

Nevertheless, the Trail Chamber considered that for Akayesu to be held criminally responsible for violations of common Article 3 it would have to be proved that:

by virtue of his authority, he is either responsible for the outbreak of, or is otherwise directly engaged in the conduct of hostilities. Hence, the Prosecutor will have to demonstrate to the Chamber and prove that Akayesu was either a member of the armed forces under the military command of either of the belligerent parties, or that he was legitimately mandated and expected, as a public official or agent or person otherwise holding public authority or *de facto* representing the Government, to support or fulfil the war efforts.[44]

The Trial Chamber held that this could not be proved beyond reasonable doubt.

The Prosecution appealed arguing that the Trial Chamber 'erred in law in applying a 'public agent of government representative test' in determining who can be held responsible for serious violations of common Article 3 and Additional Protocol II. In response the Appeals Chamber stated that it was:

of the opinion that international humanitarian law would be lessened and called into question if it were to be admitted that certain persons be exonerated from individual criminal responsibility for a violation of common Article 3 under the pretext that they did not belong to a specific category.

Commenting on the Trial Chamber's decision, the Appeal Court stated that:

the Trial Chamber found that the four Conventions 'were adopted primarily to protect the victims as well as potential victims of armed conflicts'. It went on to hold that '[t]he

42 Zyklon B Case, I Law Reports of Trials of War Criminals, 103.

43 *The Prosecutor v Jean Paul Akayesu* Case no ICTR 94-4-T Judgment, 22 September 1998, [631–633].

44 ibid [640].

category of persons to be held accountable in this respect then, would in most cases be limited to commanders, combatants and other members of the armed forces'. Such a finding is *prima facie* not without reason. In actuality authors of violations of common Article 3 will likely fall into one of these categories. This stems from the fact that common Article 3 requires a close nexus between violations and the armed conflict. This nexus between violations and the armed conflict implies that, in most cases, the perpetrator of the crime will probably have a special relationship with one party to the conflict. However, such a special relationship is not a condition precedent to the application of common Article 3 and, hence of Article 4 of the Statute. In the opinion of the Appeals Chamber, the Trial Chamber erred in requiring that a special relationship should be a separate condition for triggering criminal responsibility for a violation of Article 4 of the Statute.[45]

The ICRC now takes the view that '[e]veryone in situations of armed conflict: states, organised armed groups, multi-national forces, civilians and the staff of private military/security companies' is bound by international humanitarian law.[46] This development in the ICRC approach is partly fuelled by concern regarding the applicability of IHL to civilian private military companies, which are now a well established feature of modern warfare.

In contrast to the approach taken by national military tribunals in the 1990s, it is unlikely that today governments or tribunals would put forward the argument that IHL was not applicable to peacekeeping forces deployed into a situation of armed conflict. The UK's 2008 draft peace support doctrine that is to replace *JWP 3–50 The Military Contribution to Peace Support Operations*, notes that all peace support themed operations 'are conducted with a degree of restraint, particularly through adherence to the issued Rules of Engagement (ROE) and observance of the Law of Armed Conflict.'[47] However, controversy could arise if peacekeepers were to be deployed into conflicts where the applicability of IHL to the situation is in dispute because the type of conflict differs from those envisaged by the drafters of the Geneva Conventions. Non-international armed conflict is governed by common article 3 of the Geneva Conventions, Protocol II (for the Contracting States), and relevant customary international law.[48] The Institut de Droit International adopted a resolution on 25 August 1999 on the *Application*

[45] *The Prosecutor v Jean Paul Akayesu* Case no ICTR 94-4-A Judgment, I June 2001, [443–444].

[46] FAQ 'International humanitarian law and private military/security companies' <http://www.icrc.org/Web/eng/siteeng0.nsf/html/pmc-fac-230506>; the point is also made in a number of articles in issue No 843 of the International Review of the Red Cross, which is on the theme 'Private Military Companies' (2006) 88 International Review of the Red Cross 843

[47] Ministry of Defence UK, Development, Concepts and Doctrine Centre, *Draft UK National Doctrine that will replace JWP 3–50 The Military Contribution to Peace Support Operations* (MOD Shrivenham 16 April 2008) [0109].

[48] *Military and Paramilitary Activities in and against Nicaragua (Nicaragua v United States of America)*, Merits, Judgment, ICJ Reports (1986), 14, [114] (June 27); The ICRC in its extensive study of *Customary International Humanitarian Law* cites common Article 3 frequently, especially in the chapter on Fundamental Guarantees:J-M Henckaerts and L Doswald-Beck, *Customary International Humanitarian Law* (Cambridge University Press Cambridge 2005), 299–383.

of International Humanitarian Law and Fundamental Human Rights in Armed Conflicts in which Non-State Actors Are Parties, that extends also to 'internal armed conflicts in which peacekeeping forces intervene', which states that:

> All parties to armed conflicts in which non-State entities are parties, irrespective of their legal status, as well as the United Nations, and competent regional and other international organizations have the obligation to respect international humanitarian law as well as fundamental human rights. The application of such principles and rules does not affect the legal status of the parties.
>
> Respect for international humanitarian law and fundamental human rights constitutes an integral part of international order for the maintenance and reestablishment of peace and security, in particular in armed conflicts in which non-State entities are parties.[49]

The resolution stated that the international law applicable to armed conflicts in which non-State entities are parties includes:

> Article 3 common to the Geneva Conventions of 1949 as basic principles of international humanitarian law; Protocol II and all other conventions applicable to non-international armed conflicts; customary principles and rules of international humanitarian law on the conduct of hostilities and the protection of victims applicable to internal armed conflicts; the principles and rules of international law guaranteeing fundamental human rights; the principles and rules of international law applicable in internal armed conflicts, relating to war crimes, crimes against humanity, genocide and other international crimes; the principles of international law 'derived from established custom, from the principles of humanity and from dictates of public conscience'.[50]

The resolution was not aimed at conflicts between one State's armed forces and non-State entities operating within a different State. However, the US Supreme Court in *Hamdan v Rumsfeld* held that any armed conflict that is not governed by the laws of international armed conflict falls within the law applicable to non-international armed conflict.[51] In light of the acceptance that common article 3 constitutes a customary law 'minimum yardstick'[52] applicable in both international and non-international armed conflicts and the current view that IHL applies to all actors in an armed conflict, it is unlikely that the UN would dispute the applicability of common article 3 to its forces deployed into an armed conflict, whatever its nature, particularly given that common article 3 is largely limited to prohibiting the most egregious forms of abuse.

Problems may arise where the situation does not reach the level of armed conflict. The rules applicable in non-international armed conflict do not apply

[49] The Institut de Droit International adopted a resolution on 25 August 1999 on the Application of International Humanitarian Law and Fundamental Human Rights in Armed Conflicts in Which non-State Actors Are Parties (Fourteenth Commission, Berlin Session 1999, 25 August 1999), I, II.

[50] ibid III.

[51] *Hamdan v Rumsfeld* 126 S Ct. 2749 (2006).

[52] *Military and Paramilitary Activities in and against Nicaragua (Nicaragua v United States of America)*, Merits (n 48), [114].

to 'situations of internal disturbances and tensions, such as riots, isolated and sporadic acts of violence or other acts of a similar nature.'[53] Some threshold level of force must be crossed before peacekeepers are regarded as combatants; some use of force in self-defence would not necessarily mean that the threshold has been crossed. Determining at what point IHL becomes applicable may become even more complex if the scope of 'legitimate' intervention is to be extended to non UN-authorized operations, as might be the case were recent proposals for 'a league of democracies' prepared to override the resistance of the UN to interventions in cases of humanitarian need, were to come to fruition.[54] UN troops are protected under the Convention on the Safety of United Nations and Associated Personnel which makes attacks on peacekeepers that are not engaged as combatants an international crime, a provision that is reiterated in the Rome Statute.[55] The Rome Statute limits this protection to operations conducted 'in accordance with the Charter of the United Nations.'[56] Intervention without Security Council authority cannot be ruled out as a matter of practice. But in considering the legitimacy or lawfulness of such interventions, it is important to examine how changing the basis of the authority to intervene, may affect operations further down the line (in the field). How are local forces supposed to distinguish between a peace support force led by a 'coalition of the willing' lawfully deployed with the authorization of the Security Council and a peace support force led by a 'coalition of the willing,' 'legitimately' deployed without the authorization of the Security Council? Why should local forces respect the status of the UN if the Member States themselves do not? If coalitions of some Member States are willing to send protecting forces, without the authorization of the Security Council, and argue that such interventions are 'lawful/legitimate,' why should local groups see any difference between UN-authorized and non UN-authorized interventions?

3. Common Article 1: The Obligation to Ensure Respect for the Conventions

The Secretary-General's Bulletin acknowledges that IHL is applicable to peacekeepers engaged as combatants in a situation to which the law of international armed conflict applies. There is also a strong argument that IHL is binding even

[53] 1998 Rome Statute of the International Criminal Court (adopted 17 July 1998 entered into force 11 April 2002) UN Doc A/CONF.183/9, Art 8(2)(d).

[54] Prominent figures on both sides of the Republican/Democrat divide, campaigning in the summer of 2008 in preparation for the presidential elections, have proposed the idea of a US-led 'league of democracies', willing to act where the UN does not.

[55] Convention on the Safety of United Nations and Associated Personnel (adopted 9 Dec. 1994, entered into force 15 December 1999) 34 ILM (1995) 482; Rome Statute of the International Criminal Court (adopted 17 July 1998, entered into force 11 April 2002) UN Doc A/CONF.183/9, [8(III)].

[56] Rome Statute of the International Criminal Court (n 55), [8(III)].

when troops are not engaged as combatants, on the basis that IHL applies to all actors in an armed conflict including civilians; alternatively the UN has always accepted that peacekeepers are bound by the principles and spirit of IHL in all circumstances. However, the basis of the extent of troops' obligations under IHL is less clear; does it extend to positive obligations of protection, or is it limited to troops' own conduct?

The most significant provision of IHL that could be construed as obliging troops to take action to prevent serious abuses of human rights being committed by third parties is Article 1, common to the four Geneva Conventions. Article 1 provides that the High Contracting Parties undertake to 'respect and ensure respect' for the provisions of the Conventions 'in all circumstances.' This obligation applies to both the contracting States and their troops, who may be individually liable, if they breach their obligations.[57] Originally Article 1 only applied in international armed conflicts and occupation, but since it is now considered to constitute customary international law it will also apply in internal armed conflict.[58] The International Court of Justice in the Nicaragua case stated that the United States was obligated:

in the terms of Article 1 of the Geneva Conventions, to 'respect' the Conventions, and even to 'ensure respect' for them 'in all circumstances,' since such an obligation does not derive only from the Conventions themselves, but from the general principles of humanitarian law to which the Conventions merely give expression.[59]

Laurence Boisson de Chazournes and Luigi Condorelli argue that Article 1 not only derives from general principles of humanitarian law, it:

belongs to a select group of norms and principles held by the international community to be of cardinal importance for the promotion of 'elementary considerations of humanity'. Such norms play what may be termed a 'constitutional role' in a system of collective security where humanitarian values have become a reason for the adoption of a large number of measures.[60]

The nature of the obligation 'to ensure respect' has been much disputed but it is clear that the obligation continues during peacetime:

The Contracting Parties do not merely undertake to respect the Convention, but also to *ensure respect* for it. The wording may seem redundant. When a state contracts an

[57] A Roberts and R Guelff, *Documents on the Laws of War* (n 14), 19.

[58] The Institut de Droit International, The Application of International Humanitarian Law and Fundamental Human Rights in Armed Conflicts in Which non-State Actors Are Parties (n 48), Preamble; Anne Ryniker 'Respecting and Ensuring Respect for Humanitarian Norms' in *Forum, War and Accountability* (ICRC Geneva 2002) 30, 32.

[59] *Military and Paramilitary Activities in and against Nicaragua (Nicaragua v United States of America)*, Merits (n 48), [220].

[60] L Boisson de Chazournes and L Condorelli, 'Common Article 1 of the Geneva Conventions revisited: protecting collective interests' [2000] International Review of the Red Cross 837, 67, 85–86.

engagement, the engagement extends to all those over whom it has authority, as well as to the representatives of its authority; and it is under an obligation to issue the necessary orders. The use in all four Conventions of the words 'and to ensure respect for' was however deliberate: they were intended to emphasize the responsibility of the Contracting Parties... It would not be enough for example for a state to give orders or directions to a few civilian or military authorities, leaving it to them to arrange as they please for their detailed execution. It is for the state to supervise the orders it gives. Furthermore if it is to fulfil the solemn undertaking it has given, the state must of necessity prepare in advance, that is to say in peacetime, the legal material or other means of ensuring the faithful enforcement of the Convention when the occasion arises.[61]

The ICRC Commentary to the Conventions suggests that Article 1 obliges the contracting State to make preparations during peacetime to ensure compliance with the Conventions and to supervise both civilian and military authorities to see that its orders in this regard are carried out.

The drafters of the Conventions may never have been intended to imply any further legal obligation.[62] However, the ICRC Commentary suggests that the obligation also extends to ensuring that third parties comply with the Conventions:

in the event of a Power failing to fulfil its obligations, the other Contracting Parties (neutral, allied or enemy) may and should, endeavour to bring it back into an attitude of respect for the Convention. The proper working system of protection provide by the Convention demands in fact that that the contracting Parties should not be content merely to apply its provisions themselves, but should do everything in their power to ensure that the humanitarian principles underlying the Conventions are applied universally.[63]

Kalshoven is convinced that the authors of the ICRC Commentary:

never meant to suggest that contracting states not party to an armed conflict are under an affirmative international obligation to 'ensure' that belligerent parties respect the Conventions. And once again, even had they wished to do so, their suggestion could not have carried that effect.[64]

However, a number of commentators, including the president and vice-president of the ICRC,[65] argue that whether or not it was originally intended to do so, the meaning of Article 1 today now encompasses obligations on parties not involved

[61] J Pictet (ed), *The Geneva Conventions of 12 August 1949. Commentary IV Geneva Convention* (ICRC Geneva 1958), Article 1.

[62] F Kalshoven, 'The Undertaking to Respect and Ensure Respect in All Circumstances: From Tiny Seed to Ripening Fruit' 2 Yearbook of International Humanitarian Law 3, 21–23, 59–60; Adam Roberts, 'The Laws of War: Problems of Implementation in Contemporary Conflicts' 6 Duke J. Comp. & Int'l L. 11, 29–30.

[63] J Pictet (ed), *The Geneva Conventions of 12 August 1949. Commentary IV Geneva Convention* (n 61), 16 (The other 3 commentaries contain similar statements).

[64] F Kalshoven, 'The Undertaking to Respect and Ensure Respect in All Circumstances: From Tiny Seed to Ripening Fruit' (n 62), 38.

[65] Official Statement by ICRC President Dr Jacob Kellenberger, 'The Two Additional Protocols to the Geneva Conventions: 25 years later – challenges and prospects', 26th Round Table, San Remo, 5/9/2002 <http://www.icrc.org/Web/Eng/siteeng0.nsf/iwpList74/EFC5A1C8D8D8DD70B9C1256C3600>.

in a conflict to ensure that the four Conventions are respected by all parties that are engaged in conflict.[66] An ICRC forum on Accountability in War, held in May 2002 at Wolfsberg, also affirmed that Article 1 imposes obligations on parties not involved in a conflict to ensure that the belligerents respect humanitarian law.[67] Laurence Boisson de Chazournes and Luigi Condorelli argue that the Article 1 commitment is now almost 'a basic norm of behaviour' for the UN in the 'management of crises and armed conflicts.'[68] Both the Security Council and the General Assembly have adopted resolutions calling upon States to abide by their commitments under the Geneva Conventions and have cited common Article 1 as the basis for their demand. Common Article 1 is referred to in Resolution XXIII adopted at the Tehran Conference on Human Rights, 1968,[69] which urges States to take steps to ensure that other States respect humanitarian law. The preamble states that:

> States parties to the Red Cross Geneva Conventions sometimes fail to appreciate their responsibility to take steps to ensure respect of these humanitarian rules in all circumstances by other States, even if they are not themselves directly involved in the conflict.[70]

In 1990 the Security Council adopted Resolution 681 in which, 'gravely concerned at the dangerous situation of all the Palestinian territories occupied by Israel since 1967,' it called upon the High Contracting Parties to Geneva Convention IV to ensure respect by Israel, for its obligations under the Convention. It also requested the Secretary-General, in co-operation with the ICRC, 'to develop further the idea' of 'convening a meeting of the High Contracting Parties to discuss possible measures that might be taken by them.'[71] On 5 December 2001 a Conference of High Contracting Parties to Geneva Convention IV published

ICRC Vice-President Jacques Forster, Address to the Ninth Annual Seminar on International Humanitarian Law for Diplomats accredited to the United Nations, Geneva, 8–9 March 2000, <http://www.icrc.org/Web/Eng/siteeng0.nsf/iwpList74/4066C7BDB40DE831C1256B66005>.

[66] L Boisson de Chazournes and L Condorelli 'Common Article 1 of the Geneva Conventions revisited: protecting collective interests' (n 60), 70; HP Gasser 'Ensuring Respect for the Geneva Conventions and Protocols: the Role of Third States and the United Nations' in H Fox and MA Meyer (eds), *Armed Conflict and the New Law: Volume II 'Effecting Compliance'* (The British Institute of International and Comparative Law London 1993) 16, 24–25; U Palwankar, 'Measures available to States for fulfilling their obligation to ensure respect for international humanitarian law' (1994) 298 International Review of the Red Cross, 9, 10; K Sachariev, 'States' entitlement to take action to enforce humanitarian law' (1989) 270 International Review of the Red Cross, 177, 186.

[67] ICRC International Humanitarian Forum on War and Accountability, 23–24 May 2002, Wolfsberg, <http://www.icrc.org/Web/Eng/siteeng0.nsf/iwpList499/2B4A74F0962E312DC1256BCE005DBB44, R Gutman, 'Conclusion' in *Forum, War and Accountability*, (ICRC Geneva 2002) 80, 85.

[68] L Boisson de Chazournes and L Condorelli, 'Common Article 1 of the Geneva Conventions revisited: protecting collective interests' (n 60), 77.

[69] Resolution XXIII on 'Human Rights in Armed Conflicts' 12 May 1968 A/CONF.32/41.

[70] ibid [9].

[71] S/RES 681, 20 December 1990 [5–6] A conference of the High Contracting Parties was held on the 15 July 1999 but adjourned quickly.

a declaration, which called upon Israel to respect its obligations under the Convention and states that the High Contracting Parties:

encourage the initiatives by State Parties, both individually and collectively, according to art. I of the Convention and aimed at ensuring respect for the Convention, and they underline the need for the parties, to follow up on the implementation of the present Declaration.[72]

The ICJ in its Advisory Opinion concerning the Legal Consequences of the Construction of a Wall in the Occupied Palestinian Territory' also affirms that Article I entails third party obligations, stating that:

It follows from that provision that every State party to that Convention, whether or not it is a party to a specific conflict, is under an obligation to ensure that the requirements of the instruments in question are complied with.[73]

If this is the case, the fact that peacekeeping forces are generally not party to the conflict would not in itself exculpate the State that has deployed the force from an obligation to ensure that the belligerents respect IHL. The extent of the obligation to 'ensure respect' must surely be linked to the contracting party's ability to effect the belligerents' conduct which would be greater for a State that has forces deployed than one that doesn't, particularly if the mandate authorizes protection, as is now the norm. Certainly the ICJ in interpreting the scope of the obligation to prevent genocide under Article 1 of the 1948 Convention on the Prevention and Punishment of the Crime of Genocide held that the obligation of State parties is 'to employ all means reasonably available

[72] Conference of the High Contracting Parties to the Geneva Convention: Declaration, Geneva, 5 December 2001. The conference was called following General Assembly Resolution ES-10/6 of 9 February 1999, calling for the High Contracting Parties to call a conference pursuant to their obligation under Article I to ensure respect for the Convention. A meeting was held on 15 July 1999 but adjourned rapidly 'on the understanding that it will convene again in the light of consultations on the development of the humanitarian situation in the field.' (Statement issued by High Contracting Parties at the meeting on 15 July 1999) The High Contracting Parties reconvened in December 2001.

[73] *Advisory Opinion concerning the Legal Consequences of the Construction of a Wall in the Occupied Palestinian Territory*, ICJ, 9 July 2004, [158]. However, Judge Koojimans, in his separate opinion, stated that he had difficulty in accepting the Court's findings on this point: Separate Opinion Judge Koojimans, [46–47]; This is a much stronger affirmation that Article I entails third party obligations than the statement made in the Nicaragua case where the ICJ held that the requirement to respect and ensure respect for the Geneva Conventions entailed 'an obligation not to encourage persons or groups engaged in the conflict in Nicaragua to act in violation of the provisions of Article 3 common to the four Geneva Conventions.' *Military and Paramilitary Activities in and against Nicaragua (Nicaragua v United States of America)* (n 48), [220]. Kalshoven has argued that this 'amounts to little more than a confirmation of the well-established principle of non-intervention.' F Kalshoven, 'The Undertaking to Respect and Ensure Respect in All Circumstances: From Tiny Seed to Ripening Fruit' (n 62), 56–57. Meron believes that 'The fundamental obligation implies that each state must exert efforts to ensure that no violations of the applicable provisions of humanitarian law (ie 'to respect') are committed, at the very least by third parties controlled by that state' T Meron, *Human Rights and Humanitarian Norms as Customary Law* (Clarendon Press Oxford 1989), 30–31.

to them so as to prevent genocide as far as possible.'[74] A similar logic would surely apply to the High Contracting Parties obligations to 'ensure respect' for the Geneva Conventions; but the extent and nature of troops' obligations, as distinct from those of the contributing State, remain unclear. Commanders, and sometimes the troops themselves, must make decisions in relation to events on the ground and their perception of the extent of IHL violations and the appropriate response may be quite different from that of their governments' at home; how far can a commander take decisions in defiance of superior orders in order to prevent genocide, ethnic cleansing, other crimes against humanity, and war crimes?

The ICRC cited common article 1 in its 2001 'position statement' on humanitarian intervention in which it argued that:

> Under Article 1 common to the Geneva Conventions, there is an individual and collective obligation to 'respect and ensure respect for' international humanitarian law. If grave violations of that law are committed, the States are obliged to take action jointly or separately, in co-operation with the United Nations and in accordance with the UN Charter (Protocol I additional to the Geneva Conventions, Article 89).[75]

But:

> The question of what measures are to be taken by the States and United Nations in order to put an end to those breaches is not dealt with by humanitarian law but by the UN Charter.[76]

The reason for this 'division of labour' is that the Geneva Conventions as a whole, including article 1, deal primarily with the *ius in bello*, (that is with rules governing the conduct of war), and the right of a State or international organization to intervene militarily to uphold the Geneva Conventions is governed by the *ius ad bellum*, (which deals with those rules and principles governing when a State, or an international organization, may resort to armed conflict). As one commentator has observed:

> Article 1, by imposing an obligation on States, inevitably brings in politics... any effective attempt by a State to ensure respect for international humanitarian law, especially in the event of massive violations, would be difficult, if not impossible, without the political support of the community of States, and the United Nations is one of the most widely used vehicles for such support in the contemporary world.[77]

[74] ICJ, Application of the Convention on the Prevention and Punishment of the Crime of Genocide (Bosnia and Herzegovina v Serbia and Montenegro) Judgment of 26 February 2007, [430].

[75] A Ryniker, 'The ICRC's Position on Humanitarian Intervention' 83 International Review of the Red Cross 482, 527, 530.

[76] ibid.

[77] U Palwankar, 'Measures available to States for fulfilling their obligation to ensure respect for international humanitarian law.' (n 66), 18.

In the view of the ICRC, Article 1 obliges States to respond to violations of humanitarian law, or at the very least it creates an 'obligation for governments to consider seriously whether there is something they might do in respect of the situation.'[78] But the decision as to what response is appropriate falls outside the scope of IHL. Serious violations of humanitarian law may trigger coercive action on the part of the UN but the legal justification for armed intervention 'lies outside the frontiers of humanitarian law and should be sought elsewhere, notably in Chapters VI and VII of the Charter.'[79] Thus the Article 1 obligation to respect the principles and rules of IHL and the UN reliance on Article 1 in the 'management of crises and armed conflicts' belong to two different regimes of law, one governing the immediate obligations of forces at ground level and the other involving world politics. This makes it difficult for troops, and their commanders, to assess the scope of the force's Article 1 obligations: commanders need to make decisions based on the realities on the ground; world politics is an entirely different concern.

An argument can be made that since the Geneva Conventions were conceived as predominantly concerned with the *ius in bello* any developments with regard to the scope of Article 1 *ius ad bellum* should also be considered to apply *ius in bello*, since the *ius ad bellum* implications of Article 1 are subsidiary to its predominantly *ius in bello* function. Conversely, since the nature of the response of High Contracting Parties to violations of IHL is governed by the Charter and not by Article 1, it could be argued that in assessing how to carry out their obligation under Article 1 to ensure respect for the Geneva Conventions, force commanders and their troops should be guided by the nature of the operation as it has been determined by the Security Council or other mandating authority. But to take this approach is to blur *ius ad bellum* and *ius in bello* principles further. Moreover, given that mandates tend to be drafted in deliberately vague terms so as to secure consensus amongst Security Council members, such an approach is likely to increase confusion as to the nature of the force's obligations.

4. Conclusion

It is now largely accepted that Article 1 of the Geneva Conventions carries third-party obligations for State parties at a general level; but it is not clear what this implies for States that contribute to peacekeeping operations or for the peacekeepers themselves. One of the problems in the past has been the uncertainty

[78] Yves Sandoz, in an interview with Fritz Kalshoven: F Kalshoven, 'The Undertaking to Respect and Ensure Respect in All Circumstances: From Tiny Seed to Ripening Fruit' (n 62), 61.

[79] ICRC 'Official statement on 'Humanitarian Intervention and International Humanitarian Law', J. Forster, ICRC Vice President, 9th Annual Seminar on International Humanitarian Law for Diplomats accredited to the United Nations, Geneva, 8–9 March 2000, *ICRC Annual Report* (ICRC Geneva 2000).

regarding the extent to which IHL is applicable to peacekeeping forces. The Secretary-General's Bulletin of 1999 was intended to clarify the obligations of UN forces but it failed to properly address issues relating to the responsibilities of non-combatant forces to comply with IHL. Likewise the difficulties inherent in determining at what point use of force by troops triggers the applicability of IHL were not addressed. Who determines that a confrontation between UN troops and others has reached a sufficient threshold that the participants may be regarded as combatants? The American Bar Association considered that 'it is asking too much for a Somali clan warrior or Bosnian militiaman' to understand the distinctions in levels of conflict.[80] This issue has become even more pertinent with changes in peace support operations doctrine that eschew sharp divisions between categories of operation, and instead view peace operations as operating on a continuum from traditional peacekeeping through to enforcement, with a similarly flexible approach to the use of force and requirements of consent, guided by the needs of the operation rather then the divisions of the UN Charter. However, case law of the ICTR and statements of the ICRC since 2001, provide support for a broad interpretation of the applicability of IHL, which holds that it is applicable to civilians as well as combatants. The UK's draft revision of its current peace support operations doctrine, affirms that peacekeeping forces must observe the Law of Armed Conflict,[81] without any of the 'principles and spirit' phraseology that characterized earlier statements on the applicability of IHL to peacekeepers.

Nevertheless, even where it is accepted that the Geneva Conventions are applicable it is not clear what Article 1 means for troops. The Conventions, including Article 1, are binding not only on the High Contracting Parties but also on each and every soldier in all circumstances to which IHL applies. If peacekeepers are engaged as combatants, they are required by Article 1 to ensure respect for the Conventions. The Conventions do not define how they are supposed to implement this obligation. Even if they are not engaged as combatants they are obliged to respect the principles and rules of IHL, which would include the obligations encompassed by Article 1. Article 1 also constitutes customary international law. As noted above, the ICJ has stated that the obligation to 'respect' and 'to ensure respect' for the Conventions 'does not derive only from the Conventions themselves, but from the general principles of humanitarian law to which the Conventions merely give specific expression.'[82] The ICRC, the ICJ, and the UN Security Council and General Assembly, have all made statements that imply

[80] American Bar Association, Section of International Law and Practice Standing Committee on World Order under Law, Report to the House of Delegates, Safety of UN and Associated Personnel: Recommendation, 31 International Lawyer, 195, 200

[81] Ministry of Defence UK, Development, Concepts and Doctrine Centre, *Draft UK National Doctrine that will replace JWP 3–50 The Military Contribution to Peace Support Operations* (n 47) [0109].

[82] *Military and Paramilitary Activities in and against Nicaragua (Nicaragua v United States of America)*, Merits (n 48), [220].

that the Article 1 obligation 'to ensure respect' extends to conduct by other parties, not just that of the contracting party's own forces and is binding whether or not the State is involved in the conflict. An obligation on troops to 'ensure respect' would entail at an absolute minimum an obligation to report war crimes immediately so that even if the force itself is not in a position to take action, the contributing State and the international community can take steps to respond. However, given that the Security Council is essentially a political body (whose primary function is the maintenance of international peace and security through consensus decision-making) it is difficult to determine the nature of *its* legal obligation (if any) to provide the troops and resources to enable forces deployed in UN mandated operations to carry out *their* legal obligations under Article 1.

One of the difficulties in analysing the extent of obligations under Article 1 stems from the close correlation between Article 1 as it applies to the contracting States, and the development of the 'responsibility to protect' norm. The 'responsibility to protect' norm has its roots in customary international law, the UN Charter, the 1948 Genocide Convention, international humanitarian law (including common article 1 of the Geneva Conventions) and human rights law. However, whilst there has been strong endorsement of the idea that States, and the international organizations through whom they act, have an obligation to respond to serious human rights violations affecting human security on a large scale, there is considerable anxiety in some quarters at the idea that peacekeepers, and States that contribute forces, should be held accountable to the affected populations for their actions and omissions. There is a fear that States would stop contributing forces altogether. This means that whilst on the one hand there is increasing pressure on States to act in situations that give rise to the 'responsibility to protect,' there is a paradoxical countervailing pressure to ensure that Contributing States are not held accountable for their forces' actions, including failure to act, once deployed.[83] For example the European Court of Human Rights in *Behrami and Behrami v France* and *Saramati v France, Germany and Norway*,[84] and a number of subsequent cases, has refused to hear claims concerning allegations of human rights violations by forces deployed under a Chapter VII mandate on the grounds that to do so would undermine the Security Council's role in the maintenance of international peace and security.

Louise Arbour, citing the 1948 Genocide Convention, the ICJ judgement in the Case Concerning the Application of the Convention on the Prevention and Punishment of the Crime of Genocide (Bosnia and Herzegovina v Serbia and

[83] Relying principally on Article 105 of the UN Charter, which provides that the UN 'shall enjoy in the territory of each of its members such privileges and immunities as are necessary for the fulfilment of its purposes' and the Convention on the Privileges and Immunities of the United Nations, 13 February 1946, 1 UNTS 15.

[84] European Court of Human Rights *Behrami and Behrami v France* and *Saramati v France, Germany and Norway* Application nos. 71412/01 and 78166/01 2 May 2007 and subsequent cases. (Discussed in Chapter 3).

Montenegro),[85] and Security Council resolution 1674 of 2006, has suggested that the 'responsibility to protect' entails a legal, and not merely moral, obligation on States to respond to serious human rights abuses, at the very least to genocide. The ICJ held that legal responsibility is incurred 'if the State manifestly failed to take all measures to prevent genocide which were within its power, and which might have contributed to preventing the genocide.'[86] Moreover 'the possibility remains that the combined efforts of several States, each complying with its obligation to prevent, might have achieved the result—averting the commission of genocide—which the efforts of only one State were insufficient to produce.'[87] Arbour argues:

> Might the judgment [in the Case Concerning the Application of the Convention on the Prevention and Punishment of the Crime of Genocide (Bosnia and Herzegovina v Serbia and Montenegro] however, also carry responsibilities not only for Serbia and its surrogates in Bosnia Herzegovina, but also to other States parties to the Convention, and indeed to the wider international community? Certainly, the logic of the judgment would suggest such an assumption. In concrete terms, might it thus be suggested that all such tools as are at a State's disposal—in all areas of State authority, be it economic, political, diplomatic, or other—must be reasonably utilised, consistently with international law, in ways which might reasonably contribute to preventing genocide or deterring perpetrators? The Serbia example demonstrates that at least these tools of authority must be employed by neighbouring or regional States which are well positioned to exert influence and are likely to possess information about the reality of the relevant risks. But what about other States, those that because of their pre-eminence, global reach and capabilities may also be in a position to act?...
>
> I posit that because of the power they wield and due to their global reach, the members of the Security Council, particularly the Permanent Five Members (P5) hold an even heavier responsibility than other States to ensure the protection of civilians everywhere. If their responsibility were to be measured in accordance with the International Court of Justice's analysis, it would seem logical to assume that a failure to act could carry legal consequences and even more so when the exercise or threat of a veto would block action that is deemed necessary by other members to avert genocide, or crimes against humanity.[88]

If this the case, surely a positive failure to protect would encompass not only a veto of an intervention (where the prospects of success outweighed the potential harm to the civilian population) but also an insistence (through the use of a veto for example) on ensuring that only an emasculated force be deployed, without the appropriate mandate or resources or training. A contributing State's

[85] ICJ, *Case Concerning the Application of the Convention on the Prevention and Punishment of the Crime of Genocide (Bosnia and Herzegovina v Serbia and Montenegro)*, General List, no 91, 26 February 2007, available at: <http://www.icj-cij.org/docket/files/91/>.

[86] ibid [403].

[87] ibid [430].

[88] L Arbour, 'The responsibility to protect as a duty of care in international law and practice' 34 Review of International Studies (2008), 445, 453.

control of its forces might also give rise to a positive failure to protect if that State issues commands directly to its commanders requesting the force not to provide protection or not to oppose belligerents that clearly intend harm to the civilian population.[89]

Whilst the scope of States' legal obligations under the 'responsibility to protect' have yet to be clarified (Louise Arbour's comments suggest that the debate as at an early stage) States are certainly responsible under the Geneva Conventions for ensuring that their forces adhere to Convention standards. If States fail to ensure that their troops are properly trained in IHL they will have breached this obligation. As the ICRC in its 1958 Commentary observed 'if it is to fulfil the solemn undertaking it has given, the state must of necessity prepare in advance, that is to say in peacetime, the legal material or other means of ensuring the faithful enforcement of the Convention when the occasion arises.'[90] Nonetheless IHL is often treated as a:

> marginal item in military training programmes. Consequently these rules of law are not as well known or understood as they should be by those who must apply them, especially members of the armed forces.[91]

The evolution in the interpretation of Article 1 has implications for the obligations of contributing States because they must now ensure that troops deployed into a situation where grave violations of human rights are being perpetrated are sufficiently prepared to be able to ensure compliance with the conventions by all parties, not just themselves. Defence departments in a number of States have done a great deal of work to resolve some of the potential problems that arise for commanders in the context of the evolving responsibility to protect norm (for example by drafting new peace support operations doctrines), but the need for a consistent and coherent approach to the developments taking place in the *ius in bello* and *ius ad bellum* has not captured the attention of decision-making bodies at the political level. Governments make decisions at UN level and in their own parliaments regarding deployment of troops, frequently citing human security and human rights as the basis for their decisions, but seem slow to recognize that their undertakings entail radical revision of troop training, as well as resource implications, if the States are to comply with their international humanitarian law obligations.

[89] The plaintiffs in *Mothers of Srebrenica Foundation et al v The State of the Netherlands and the United Nations* have claimed that the Netherlands deliberately blocked requests for air support and also 'consciously made no reports on war crimes in the light of the safety of the Dutchbat soldiers held by the Bosnian Serbs.' *Mothers of Srebrenica Foundation et al v The State of the Netherlands and the United Nations* LJN: BJD6796 *Rechtbank 's-Gravenhage*, 295247/ HA ZA 07-2973 Hearing 18 June 2008, Writ of Summons, [374].

[90] J Pictet (ed), *The Geneva Conventions of 12 August 1949. Commentary IV Geneva Convention* (n 60), Article 1.

[91] R Murphy, 'International humanitarian law training for multi-national peace support operations—lessons from experience', 840 International Review of the Red Cross, 953, 961.

3

The Extent to which Peacekeeping and other Multi-national Forces have a General 'Responsibility to Protect' under International Human Rights Law

1. Introduction

One of the difficulties in determining the extent to which peacekeepers are required to uphold human rights standards, arises from the fact that today they are very likely to find themselves engaged in armed combat. In traditional peacekeeping the right to engage in armed conflict was limited to self-defence but the role of peacekeeping forces was also largely limited to consensual operations involving comparatively straightforward tasks such as monitoring compliance with peace agreements and acting as a buffer zone between the belligerents so as to reduce the likelihood of conflict being re-ignited. Modern peace operations generally involve more complex tasks and mandates usually provide for use of force in a wider range of situations than pure self-defence, such as defence of the mandate and prevention of serious war crimes and crimes against humanity. Use of force and the conduct of forces engaged in armed conflict are governed primarily by the laws of armed conflict. Although the General Assembly has adopted a number of resolutions that suggest it views IHL as a category of international human rights law,[1] IHL does not operate in the same way as the human rights laws that derive from human rights treaties because it was intended for use in very different circumstances.[2] Hence the two regimes do not fit together as symbiotically as some of those resolutions imply.

The primary purpose of IHL is to minimize the infliction of suffering and harm in the course of waging war. It is conceived in terms of the obligations required

[1] General Assembly Resolutions 2444 (1968); 2675, 2676 , 2677 (1970), 2853 (1971); GIAD Draper, 'The Relationship Between the Human Rights Regime and the Law of Armed Conflict' Israel Yearbook on Human Rights, 206.

[2] Pictet argues that to 'say that the law of Geneva is the offspring of human rights is a strange reversal of paternity. Besides that idea only emerged at the International Conference on Tehran in 1968.' J Pictet, *Le Droit Humanitaire des Victimes de la Guerre* (English translation Henry Dunan Institute Leiden 1975), 14.

of parties to an armed conflict (including individual combatants as well as State parties). Under Article I common to the Geneva Conventions parties must not only respect, but also ensure respect for, the Conventions.[3] However, although obligations under IHL may give rise to rights, they are not presented in terms of rights. IHL is principally concerned with the rules and principles that the parties to the conflict must undertake to apply in conducting their campaign, so as to balance the prevention of unnecessary suffering against military necessity and to minimize any harm caused to those that are not party to the conflict. Infliction of suffering beyond that needed to achieve military objectives is prohibited. Since IHL is primarily concerned with obligations, jurisdiction is less of an issue: the parties to the conflict must abide by their obligations wherever they are.[4]

By contrast the primary purpose of human rights law is to protect individuals from abuses perpetrated against them by their own government,[5] and it is conceived in terms of rights of individuals exercisable against the State (although the obligations are not exclusively limited to those between citizen and State). The rights of individuals give rise to obligations on the State to defend those rights through institutionalized means, for example through its legislative, administrative and judicial systems. Most human rights treaties encompass both negative and positive obligations, either explicitly or implicitly. Article 2 of the International Covenant on Civil and Political Rights (ICCPR) requires State parties to 'ensure' the rights recognized in the Covenant.[6] The Convention against Torture and other Cruel, Inhuman or Degrading Treatment or Punishment requires a State to take steps to prevent acts of torture 'in any territory under its jurisdiction.'[7] The International Covenant on Economic, Social and Cultural Rights (ICESCR) does not contain an equivalent provision but the Committee on Economic, Social and Cultural Rights has held that State Parties have an obligation to prevent violations of the rights contained in the Covenant by private actors (for example in relation to the right to water and the right to food).[8] The

[3] The extent to which the obligation 'to ensure respect' in Article I of the Geneva conventions entails an obligation to ensure respect by third parties is unclear. This is discussed in Chapter 2.

[4] However the obligations that apply in international armed conflict are considerably more extensive than those that apply in internal armed conflict. Therefore in determining a party's obligations it may be necessary to determine whether or not the conflict is international or internal, an issue that has been difficult in some conflicts, for example in the Balkans.

[5] J Patronogic, Commentary: Human Rights and Humanitarian Conflict—Confluence or Conflict (1985) 9 *Australian Yearbook of International Law* 109, 109.

[6] International Covenant on Civil and Political Rights 1966 (ICCPR) annexed to General Assembly Resolution 2200A (XXI) UN Doc A/6316 (1966) (entered into force 23 March 1976) 999 UNTS 171, art 2.

[7] Convention against Torture and other Cruel, Inhuman or Degrading Treatment or Punishment 1984 (adopted by General Assembly Resolution 39/46 on Dec. 10 1984 UN Doc A/39/51 (1984) and entered into force 26 June 1987)1465 UNTS 85, art 2.

[8] CESCR, Substantive Issues Arising in the Implementation of the International Covenant on Economic, Social and Cultural Rights: General Comment No 15 'The Right to Water', UN ESCOR, 29th session, Agenda Item 3, [23] UN Doc E/C.12/2002/11 (2002); CESCR, Substantive Issues Arising in the Implementation of the International Covenant on Economic, Social and Cultural Rights: General Comment No 12 'The Right to Adequate Food', UN ESCOR, 20th Session, Agenda Item 7, [27] UN Doc E/C.12/1999/5 (1999).

European Convention on Human Rights and Fundamental Freedoms (ECHR) requires States to secure to everyone within their jurisdiction the rights it protects.[9] The American Convention on Human Rights (ACHR) requires States to 'ensure to all persons subject to its jurisdiction the free and full exercise' of the rights and freedoms it recognizes.[10] Thus:

> [a]n illegal act which violates human rights and which initially is not directly imputable to a State (for example because it is the act of a private person or because the person responsible has not yet been identified) can lead to international responsibility of the State, not because of the act itself, but because of the lack of due diligence to prevent the violation or to respond to it as required by the Convention.[11]

If a State exercises no authority over the legislative, administrative and judicial systems of the territory in which its forces are deployed it is impossible for it to secure to the population the full range of rights protected under human rights treaties to which it is a party. Any attempt to do so would almost certainly infringe the sovereignty of the State in which the force is deployed. Hence the question of whether human rights laws are applicable in armed conflict is of most significance in internal armed conflict or where the State is in occupation, although some aspects of human rights laws may be relevant even where the State does not exercise governmental authority.

2. The Applicability of Human Rights Law to Armed Conflict

2.1 The Perspective from International Human Rights Law

The *travaux préparatoires* to the ICCPR suggests that the drafters intended that it should remain applicable in armed conflict, although some concern was expressed as to the possibility of a conflict with the laws of war.[12] During the 1947 to 1952

[9] European Convention on Human Rights and Fundamental Freedoms (ECHR), (signed 4 November 1950, came into force 3 September 1953), Article 1.

[10] American Convention on Human Rights, (ACHR) (signed 22 November 1969 came into force 18 July 1978), Article 1.

[11] *Velásquez Rodriguez Case*, Inter-Am Ct HR (Ser C) No 74, Judgment of July 29 1988, [172]. The responsibility of a State for an internationally wrongful act or omission is not dependent on whether it is has violated an applicable human rights (or other) treaty. However '[s]omething more needs to be shown' to bring the 'victims' of such an act within the jurisdiction of the State for the purposes of a human rights treaty. For example in *Banković v Belgium and 16 Other Contracting States* European Court of Human Rights (52207/99) (2001), the ECtHR held inadmissible the applicants' claims against NATO States for violations of their human rights as a result of the bombing of the Serb embassy in Belgrade in 1999, on the grounds that bombing the occurred in territory outside of the 'legal space' of the ECHR and so was not within the jurisdiction of the State for the purposes of the ECHR. However the US did accept responsibility for the 1999 bombing of the Chinese embassy in Belgrade and paid compensation: P Rowe, *The Impact of Human Rights Law on Armed Forces* (Cambridge University Press Cambridge 2006), 127.

[12] China and the Phillipines observed that if war broke out the rules of war would be applicable:
UN Doc E/CN. 4/SR. 126, 8, and UN Doc E/CN.4/SR.127, 5 cited in A Svensson-McCarthy, *The International Law of Human Rights and States of Exception: With Special Reference to the Travaux*

debates held by the drafting committee, the UK proposed a derogation clause so as to allow States to derogate from the full extent of their obligations during wartime on the grounds that it would prevent States 'from arbitrarily derogating from their obligations in respect of human rights in time of war.'[13] The majority of delegates were in favour[14] but thought that reference to war might be inappropriate in a UN Convention given that the UN Charter was intended to prevent war. The text finally adopted in 1966 reads:

In time of public emergency threatening the life of the nation and the existence of which is officially proclaimed, the State parties to the present Covenant may take measures derogating from their obligations under the present Covenant to the extent strictly required by the exigencies of the situation, provided that such measures are not inconsistent with their other obligations under international law and do not involve discrimination solely on the ground of race, colour, sex, language, religion or social origin.[15]

The Commission on Human Rights, commenting on the various proposals that had been discussed during the course of the drafting process, stated that:

The present wording is based on the view that the public emergency should be of such magnitude as to threaten the life of the nation as a whole. While it was recognized that one of the most important public emergencies was the outbreak of war, it was felt that the covenant should not envisage, even by implication, the possibility of war, as the United Nations was established with the object of preventing war.[16]

Derogation is only permitted to 'to the extent strictly required by the exigencies of the situation.'[17] Similar criteria apply to derogations from regional human rights instruments. Article 15 of the ECHR, adopted in 1950, provides that:

Préparatoires and Case Law of the International Monitoring Organs (International Studies in Human Rights, Martnus Nijhoff Publishers The Hague 1998), 205–206

[13] UN Doc E/CN.4/AC.3/SR.8, 10 and UN Doc E/CN.4/SR.42, 4–5 cited in A Svensson-McCarthy, *The International Law of Human Rights and States of Exception: With Special Reference to the Travaux Préparatoires and Case Law of the International Monitoring Organs* (n 12), 201.

[14] The US proposed that instead of a derogation clause Article 4 should read 'The rights and freedoms set forth in the Covenant shall be subject only to such limitations as are pursuant to law and reasonably necessary for the protection of the rights and freedoms of others or for national security or for general welfare': E/CN. 4/170 (USA) cited in M Bossuyt, *Guide to the 'Travaux Préparatoires' of the International Covenant on Civil and Political Rights* (Martinus Nijhoff Publishers Dordrecht 1987), 86. Although this proposal was not adopted, the final draft does allow for limitations to some protected rights even in peacetime, provided it is done according to law, where this is necessary in a democratic society to achieve certain defined goals relating to the administration of the State, eg in the interests of national security or public safety, public order, the protection of public health and morals or the protection of the rights and freedom of others: ICCPR (n 6). The ECHR and the ACHR also allow for restriction of certain rights and adopt similar criteria.

[15] ICCPR (n 6), Art 4.

[16] M Bossuyt, *Guide to the 'Travaux Préparatoires' of the International Covenant on Civil and Political Rights* (n 14), 86.

[17] ICCPR (n 6), Art 4; It is for the Human Rights Committee to determine whether an emergency in the sense of Article 4 exists and whether the acts by way of derogation are strictly required in the exigencies of the situation: Human Rights Committee, General Comment No 29, 'States of Emergency (Article 4)' CCPR/C/21/Rev.1/Add.11, 31 August 2001, [2]; DJ Harris, 'The

In time of war or other public emergency threatening the life of the nation any high Contracting Party may take measures derogating from his obligations under this Convention to the extent strictly required by the exigencies of the situation, provided that such measures are not inconsistent with its other obligations under international law.[18]

The ACHR, adopted two years after the ICCPR, provides that:

In time of war, public danger or other emergency threatening the independence or security of the State Party, it may take measures derogating from its obligations under the present Convention to the extent and for the period of time strictly required by the exigencies of the situation, provided that such measures are not inconsistent with its other obligations under international law and do not involve discrimination on the ground of race, color, sex, language, religion or social origin.[19]

The African Charter on Human and Peoples Rights[20] does not permit derogation at all. The African Commission on Human and Peoples Rights, in a decision relating to violation of freedom of expression through suppression of the press, has commented that:

In contrast to other international human rights instruments, the African Charter does not contain a derogation clause. Therefore limitations on the rights and freedoms enshrined in the Charter cannot be justified by emergencies or special circumstances. The only legitimate reasons for limitations of the rights and freedoms of the African Charter are found in Article 27(2), that is, that the rights of the Charter 'shall be exercised with due regard to the rights of others, collective security, morality and common interest.'

The justification of limitations must be strictly proportionate with and absolutely necessary for the advantages which follow. Most important, a limitation may not erode a right such that the right itself becomes illusory.[21]

Even in those treaties where derogation is provided for, certain rights are non-derogable at all times.[22] These vary between the conventions but the right to life and to freedom from torture and to freedom from slavery, are non-derogable under all. The ECHR is the only human rights convention to specifically acknowledge that the laws of war treat the right to life differently. Under the ECHR, States may derogate from the right to life in respect of deaths resulting from lawful acts of war, provided that the Secretary General of the Council of Europe has been fully informed of the derogation measures and that these do not

International Covenant on Civil and Political Rights and the United Kingdom: An Introduction' in *The International Covenant on Civil and Political Rights and the United Kingdom* (eds) DJ Harris and S Joseph (Clarendon Press Oxford 1995), 1, 8.

[18] ECHR (n 9), Article 15.

[19] ACHR (n 10), Art 27.

[20] African Charter on Human and Peoples Rights 1981 (adopted on 17 June 1981 by the Eighteenth Assembly of the Heads of State of the Organization of African Unity, entered into force 21 October 1986) OAU Doc CAB/LEG/67/3 rev.5, 21 ILM 58 (1982).

[21] African Commission on Human and Peoples Rights, *Constitutional Rights Project v Nigeria*, Communication Nos 140/94, 141/94, 145/98, [41–42].

[22] ICCPR (n 6) Art 4(2); ACHR (n 10), Art 27(2); ECHR (n 9), Art 15(2).

exceed what is strictly required by the exigencies of the situation.[23] The UK had proposed a similar exception for the ICCPR but this was not adopted by 4 votes to 4 with 5 abstentions.[24] However, the Commission, in its comments regarding the debates on paragraph two of the derogation clause, did note that the representative from New Zealand had pointed out that:

> since 'public emergency,' as defined by Article 4, must be understood to include a state of war, lawful acts of war could not be regarded as barred even though the article dealing with the right to life (article 6) was not subject to derogation in times of emergency.[25]

To date no derogation notices have been issued under any human rights treaty in respect of an international armed conflict, with the exception of states of emergency brought about by border incidents.[26] Nor has any State derogated from a human rights treaty in respect of its participation in a peace operation (regardless of whether or not IHL was considered applicable to the operation).[27]

2.2 The Perspective from International Humanitarian Law

By contrast to the debates on the applicability of human rights laws to armed conflict that took place during the drafting process of the principal human rights conventions, very little discussion on the topic took place during the drafting process of the Geneva Conventions. The absence of references to human rights standards in the Conventions is partly explicable on the grounds that the human rights law regime was in its infancy whereas the Geneva Conventions were building on substantial treaty-based law already in existence, but it was also a reflection of States' reluctance to submit to international regulation of the methods they used to quell insurgencies in their own State. Because of jurisdictional limitations on human rights treaties it is in internal armed conflict that the two regimes, IHL and human rights law, are most likely to be applicable concurrently: but the delegates to the *Diplomatic Conference of Geneva 1949* were reluctant to adopt any rules at all, other than those prohibiting the most egregiously inhumane conduct, that would limit a State's powers to take whatever steps it considered necessary to

[23] ECHR (n 9), Art 15; In contrast to the ICCPR and the ACHR, which prohibit the arbitrary killing, Article 2(2) of the ECHR sets out definitively the circumstances in which life may be taken.

[24] E.CN.4/365 (GB) and E/CN.4/SR.195, [130]; A similar proposal by the Netherlands was not voted on E/CN.4365 (NL); all quoted in M Bossuyt, *Guide to the 'Travaux Préparatoires' of the International Covenant on Civil and Political Rights* (n 14), 92.

[25] Third Committee, 18th Session (1963) A/5655, [53] and A/C.3/SR.1260, [7] (NZ) quoted in M Bossuyt, *Guide to the 'Travaux Préparatoires' of the International Covenant on Civil and Political Rights* (n 14), 95.

[26] P Rowe, *The Impact of Human Rights Law on Armed Forces* (n 11), 121; *Banković v Belgium and 16 Other Contracting States* (n 11), [62].

[27] F Naert, 'Detention in Peace Operations: The Legal Framework and Main Categories of Detainees' (Paper presented at the International Society for Military Law and the Law of War, XVIIth International Congress, The Hague 16–19 May 2006) Text to footnote 100.

quell an armed rebellion. Prior to the adoption in 1977 of Protocol II (Additional to the Geneva Conventions 1949), the only provisions of IHL that applied in internal armed conflict were Article 3 common to the Geneva Conventions (which requires parties to the conflict to refrain from the most severe abuses of human life and dignity and to care for the wounded and sick) and rules of customary international law. Draper argues that:

Article 3 represented the maximum restraint that States were prepared to accept in 1949, in international law, in the manner of quelling of armed rebellion.[28]

The IHL rules governing international armed conflict are much more extensive than those governing internal armed conflict, but even Geneva Convention IV, which is largely concerned with the protection of civilians, makes little reference to human rights standards. Occupation law becomes applicable when the contracting party is in effective control of the territory and it entails an obligation to administer the territory.[29] Therefore the jurisdictional problems inherent in the extra-territorial application of human rights treaties to territory where the State has no authority or control are much easier to overcome; but this is not reflected in the Convention.

Under Article 43 of the Hague Regulations, as supplemented by Article 64 of the Fourth Geneva Convention, occupants are required to respect local laws. An occupant may only make changes to local laws where it is absolutely necessary to do so in order to fulfil obligations under the Geneva Conventions, or to maintain the orderly government of the territory, or to ensure the occupant's own security and that of its forces.[30] No mention is made of human rights. At the *Diplomatic Conference of Geneva 1949* which resulted in the adoption of the Geneva Conventions, Mr de Alba, the delegate for Mexico, proposed modifying Article 64 to allow the occupant to change the legislation of an occupied territory if the legislation in question violated the principles of the 'Universal Declaration of the Rights of Man.'[31] His proposal appears to have attracted little interest, in part because the debate arose in the context of a US proposal to allow occupants to change any of the local laws without restriction or the need for a justification, a proposal that aroused fierce criticism; and a proposal from the USSR that would restrict the right to modify local law to 'cases where this constitutes a menace to the security of the Occupying Power,' a proposal considerably more restrictive

[28] GIAD Draper, 'The Status of Combatants and the Question of Guerilla Warfare', 45 BYIL,173, 218.

[29] Regulations annexed to Hague Convention IV Respecting the Laws and Customs of War on Land, (Hague Regulations) (signed at The Hague, 18 Oct 1907, came into force 26 January 1910) UKTS 9 (1910) Cd. 5030, Article 43; The Geneva Conventions (adopted Geneva, 12 Aug 1949, came into force 21 October 1950), 75 *UNTS* (1950), common Article 2.

[30] Geneva Convention IV Relative to the Protection of Civilians in Time of War, 287 (n 37), Article 64.

[31] *Final Record of the Diplomatic Conference of Geneva 1949*, Vol. II a, 670–2; *The Universal Declaration of Human Rights* was adopted by the General Assembly on the 10 December 1948, UN Doc A/811; *The American Declaration of the Rights of Man* was adopted by the Ninth International Conference of American States in 1948 *Acta y Documentos*, 297, OAS Res XXX.

than that adopted in the final draft.[32] Nevertheless had the debate arisen today it is inconceivable that Mr de Alba's proposal would have attracted no comment worthy of putting on record.[33]

2.3 Developments in Both Regimes since the 1960s

The 1960s saw a change in perspective triggered by public pressure to ensure that the human rights of peoples caught up in the colonial struggles for independence, and in the conflict in the Middle East, were not ignored. The Proclamation of Teheran, adopted at the end of the Teheran International Conference on Human Rights in 1968, has been described by Walter Kälin as part of a development characterized by a growing 'synthesis between human rights and humanitarian law.'[34] The Proclamation explicitly linked violations of human rights with armed conflict, stating that:

> Massive denials of human rights, arising out of aggression or any armed conflict with their tragic consequences, and resulting in untold human misery, engender reactions which could engulf the world in ever growing hostilities. It is the obligation of the international community to co-operate in eradicating such scourges[35]

A series of Security Council and General Assembly resolutions adopted during the late 1960s and early 1970s asserted unequivocally that the protection of human rights remained relevant during armed conflict.[36] However, it is not entirely clear from these resolutions to what extent the protections provided by human rights treaties (as distinct from those provided by IHL) are applicable in

[32] The UK suggested that modifying the first paragraph of the article (Article 55, which became Article 64 in the final draft) to allow for changes to tribunals where it was necessary to ensure the 'effective administration of justice' would be sufficient to resolve the dispute. The text finally adopted was 'in accordance with the spirit of the amendments submitted by the United Kingdom and the Soviet Delegations.' *Final Record of the Diplomatic Conference of Geneva 1949*, Vol. IIa, 670–2, 771; Vol. III, 139–140.

[33] Kelly argues that the failure to accept the Mexican delegates proposal indicates that it 'was clearly the intention of the participants in the GC IV process that additional human rights and standards over and above what was already laid out in the Convention were inappropriate': MJ Kelly, 'Iraq and the Law of Occupation: New Tests for an Old Law', 6 Yearbook of International Humanitarian Law, 127, 136.

[34] W Kälin, *Human Rights in Times of Occupation: The Case of Kuwait* (Law Books of Europe Berne 1994), 79.

[35] Proclamation of Tehran, Final Act of the International Conference on Human Rights, Tehran 22 April–13 May 1968, UN Doc A/CONF 32/41, [10]; Similarly the Vienna Declaration and Program of Action adopted by the World Conference on Human Rights on June 25, 1993, declared that 'Effective international measures to guarantee and monitor the implementation of human rights standards should be taken in respect of people under foreign occupation, and effective legal protection against the violation of their human rights should be provided, in accordance with human rights norms and humanitarian law, particularly the Geneva Convention relative to the Protection of Civilian Persons in Time of War, and other applicable norms of humanitarian law.' UN Doc A/CONF.157/23, [3].

[36] Eg Security Council Resolution 237 (1967) and General Assembly Resolutions 2443, 2444 (1968); 2675, 2676, 2677 (1970); 2852, 2853 (1971).

armed conflict: some of the resolutions suggest that the human rights that apply in armed conflict are those protections that arise out of the humanitarian provisions of IHL. Security Council resolution 237 of June 1967 states that 'essential and inalienable human rights should be respected even during the vicissitudes of war' and recommends to the governments concerned 'in the area of conflict in the Middle East' the:

> scrupulous respect of the humanitarian principles governing the treatment of prisoners of war and the protection of civilian persons in time of war contained in the Geneva Conventions of 12 August 1949

The implication is that the 'essential and inalienable human rights' that apply in armed conflict are largely encompassed by IHL. Similarly, General Assembly resolution 2853 of December 1971 states that 'effective protection for human rights in situations of armed conflict depends primarily on respect for humanitarian rules.'

However, in other resolutions the language suggests that human rights law and IHL may apply simultaneously. General Assembly Resolution 2443 of December 1968 on 'Respect for and implementation of human rights in occupied territories' called upon the Government of Israel 'to respect and implement the Universal Declaration of Human Rights and the Geneva Conventions of 12 August 1949 in occupied territories' and affirms:

> the inalienable rights of all inhabitants who have left their homes as a result of the outbreak of hostilities in the Middle East to return home, resume their normal life, recover their property and homes, and rejoin their families according to the provisions of the Universal Declaration of Human Rights.

General Assembly Resolution 2675 of 9 December 1970 on 'Basic principles for the protection of civilian populations in armed conflicts' also refers to 'the Universal Declaration of Human Rights' and 'other international instruments in the field of human rights.'

In addition to resolutions asserting that human rights remain applicable during armed conflict there was also pressure to develop new rules of IHL incorporating higher standards of human rights protection. In Resolution 2677 of 9 December 1970 the General Assembly reaffirmed 'its desire to secure the full observance of human rights applicable in armed conflicts pending the earliest possible termination of such conflicts.' It remained convinced:

> of the continuing value of existing humanitarian rules relating to armed conflict, in particular the Hague Conventions of 1899 and 1907, the Geneva Protocol of 1925 and the Geneva Conventions of 1949

However, it realized:

> that because existing humanitarian rules do not adequately meet all contemporary situations of armed conflict it is necessary to develop the substance of these rules and procedures for their implementation.

The Geneva Conference 1974–77 resulted in the adoption of two Protocols intended to supplement the Geneva Conventions. Protocol I, which concerns international armed conflict, contains provisions providing for a minimum standard of human rights protection for persons 'who are in the power of a Party to the conflict and who do not benefit from more favourable treatment under the Convention.'[37] Protocol II, which concerns non-international armed conflict, 'contains virtually all the irreducible rights' of the ICCPR:[38]

It also reiterates the judicial guarantees which are not part of that minimum protection, but which are of particular importance in situations of armed conflict... [These] include the presumption of innocence, the right of the accused to be present at his trial, and the principle that no one can be compelled to testify against himself... Thus there is some homogeneity between these fundamental rules of protection in the Protocol and in the Covenant.[39]

Ratification of the Protocols is far from universal[40] but many of the provisions of Protocol II are now considered to reflect customary international law.[41] The ICRC, in its 2005 study on Customary International Humanitarian Law, states that it is also a principle of customary law that human rights law 'applies at all times' including armed conflict except to the extent of permissible derogations and provided that the State party's jurisdiction under the relevant Convention extends to the situation.[42] Thus human rights law has both influenced the development of IHL and may also be applicable in its own right. A State's jurisdiction is normally limited to its territory but in certain circumstances may extend beyond it.

3. The Extra-territorial Jurisdiction of Human Rights Treaties

For the most part human rights treaties were originally thought to apply within the State party's territory only. All the principal human rights treaties contain articles

[37] Article 75 provides that such persons shall be treated humanely. Murder; torture of all kinds whether physical or mental; corporal punishment; mutilation; outrages upon personal dignity, in particular humiliating and degrading treatment, enforced prostitution and any form of indecent assault; the taking of hostages; collective punishments; and threats to commit any of the foregoing acts, are all prohibited. It also guarantees a minimum standard of treatment for detainees and rights to a fair trial.

[38] ICRC, *Commentary on the Additional Protocols of 8 June 1977 to the Geneva Conventions of 12 August 1949* (Y Sandoz et al. eds., ICRC Geneva 1987), 1365–66 [4509–45011].

[39] ibid.

[40] As of 22 May 2006, 163 States are parties to Additional Protocol I and 159 are parties to Additional Protocol II. Non parties include India, Pakistan and the United States <http://www.icrc.org>.

[41] T Meron, Crimes of War Project: The Book <http://www.crimesofwar.org/thebook/customary-law.html>; International Committee for Human Rights, Humanitarian Law and War Crimes <http://www.ichr-law.org/english/expertise/areas/hum_law.htm>.

[42] J-M Henckaerts and L Doswald-Beck, *Customary International Humanitarian Law* (Cambridge University Press Cambridge 2005), 299–305.

limiting their applicability to cases arising within the 'jurisdiction' of the State. Under general principles of international law jurisdiction is primarily, but not exclusively, territorial.[43] The ICCPR explicitly limits jurisdiction to 'all individuals within its territory and subject to its jurisdiction.'[44] The *travaux préparatoire* indicate that the territorial requirement in the Covenant was included because:

> it was not possible for the state to protect the rights of persons subject to its jurisdiction when they were outside its territory; in such cases action would be possible only through diplomatic channels.[45]

The Human Rights Committee in *Delia Saldias de Lopez v Uruguay*[46] recognized that in certain circumstances jurisdiction could be extended outside the State's territory where to do so would not infringe on the sovereignty of another State. The communication concerned the kidnap in Argentina of a citizen of Uruguay, by Uruguayan and Argentinian agents. The Committee held that it would be unconscionable to interpret the responsibility under Article 2 of the Covenant in such a way as to permit a State party to perpetrate violations of the Covenant on the territory of another State that it could not perpetrate on its own territory.[47] However, there was no suggestion that the applicability of the Convention might go beyond the regulation of misconduct by State agents. Judge Tomuschat argued that to deny extra-territorial jurisdiction for this type of offence would be incompatible with the Convention: the territorial limitation was included in recognition of the fact a State would not be able to guarantee rights of citizens when they were within the jurisdiction of another State. However, in his view, the Covenant was not intended to apply to situations such as military occupation:

> To construe the words 'within its territory' pursuant to their strict legal meaning as excluding responsibility for conduct occurring beyond the national boundaries

[43] Jurisdiction 'concerns essentially the extent of each State's right to regulate conduct or the consequences of events' Oppenheim, R Jennings and A Watts (eds), *Oppenheims' International Law* (Longman Harlow 1992), 456; 'The legal rules and principles governing jurisdiction... are concerned with the allocation between States, and other entities such as the European Union, of competence to regulate daily life—that is, the competence to secure the differences that make each State a distinct society. Inasmuch as they determine the reach of each State's laws, they may be said to determine the boundaries of that State's particular public order... State practice is consistently based upon the premise that it is for the State asserting some novel extra-territorial jurisdiction to prove that it is entitled to do so.' V Lowe, 'Jurisdiction' in MD Evans (ed), *International Law* (Oxford University Press, Oxford 2003) 329, 330, 335; DJ Harris, *Cases and Materials on International Law* (6th edn, Sweet & Maxwell London 2004), 266.

[44] ICCPR (n 6), Article 2(1).

[45] UN GAOR Annexes, UN Doc A/2929, part II, ch. 5, [4] (1955); Thomas Buergenthal, 'To Respect and to Ensure: State Obligations and Permissible Derogations' in Louis Henkin (ed), *The International Bill of Rights: The International Covenant on Civil and Political Rights* (Columbia University Press New York 1981) 72, 74.

[46] *Delia Saldias de Lopez v Uruguay*, United Nations Human Rights Committee, Communication No 52/1979 (29 July 1981) UN Doc CCPR/C/OP/1 at 88 (1984).

[47] *Delia Saldias de Lopez v Uruguay* (n 46), [12.3] ; *Lilian Celiberti de Casariego v Uruguay*, Communication No R.13/56, UN Doc Supp No 40 (A/36/40) at 185 (1981), [10.3].

would, however, lead to utterly absurd results. The formula was intended to take care of objective difficulties which might impede the implementation of the Covenant in specific situations. Thus, a State party is normally unable to ensure the effective enjoyment of rights under the Covenant to its citizens abroad, having at its disposal only the tools of diplomatic protection with their limited potential. Instances of occupation of foreign territory offer another example of situations which the drafters of the Covenant had in mind when they confined the obligation of State parties to their own territory. All these factual patterns have in common, however, that they provide plausible grounds for denying the protection of the Covenant.[48]

Unlike the ICCPR, the ECHR and the ACHR do not specifically limit jurisdiction to national territory but there is little evidence to suggest jurisdiction was intended to encompass military operations abroad. It is true that the original text of the ECHR, which provided that the contracting parties were to secure rights 'to all persons residing within their territories,' was rejected as being too narrow and that the words 'residing within' were replaced by 'within its jurisdiction.'[49] But the revised wording does not seem to have been prompted by any sense that the Convention might be applicable extra-territorially. The Committee of Experts when it approved the proposal to change the wording to 'within its jurisdiction' considered that:

The term 'residing' might be considered too restrictive. It was felt that there were good grounds for extending the benefits of the Convention to all persons within the territory of the signatory States, even those who could not be considered as residing there in the legal sense of the word. This word, moreover, has not the same meaning in all national laws. The Committee therefore replaced the term 'residing' by the words 'within their jurisdiction', which are also contained in Article 2 of the draft Covenant of the United Nations Commission.[50]

However, there is now a consensus that in certain circumstances a State's obligation to respect and ensure human rights extends to acts or omissions outside its territorial boundaries. From the early 1990s on, human rights institutions have been consistent in holding that a State's responsibility for respecting and ensuring the rights protected by any human rights treaties to which they are party extends outside their national boundaries to all territory under their effective control, regardless of whether the law of international armed conflict is also applicable. In its 1991 Report for its 46th Session, the Human Rights Committee expressed its concern at Iraq's failure to give information on the situation in Kuwait following its invasion, stating that Iraq had a 'clear responsibility under international

[48] *Delia Saldias de Lopez v Uruguay* (n 46), Appendix: Individual Opinion of Judge Tomuschat.

[49] ECHR (n 9), Art 1.

[50] AH Robertson (ed), *Collected Edition of the 'Travaux Préparatoires' of the European Convention on Human Rights* (Martinus Nijhoff Publishers Hague 1975), Vol. 3 *Committee of Experts 2 February–10 March 1950*, 260 (15 Feb 1950).

law for the observance of human rights during its occupation of that country.'[51] The 1992 report by the UN Special Rapporteur of the Commission on Human Rights 'on the situation of human rights in Kuwait under Iraqi occupation,' confirmed that Iraq was responsible for the observance of the ICCPR, without regard to the nationality of the victims, whether or not the victims' governments were parties to it.[52] The UN Special Rapporteur on the situation of Human Rights in Afghanistan, in his interim report of 1998, called on 'on all parties to respect international human rights, including the rights of women, and humanitarian law' and called:

> on all sides to put an immediate end to the armed conflict, to show restraint and respect for human rights, including the right to life and security of all persons, and to refrain forthwith from any acts that may constitute violations of human rights of both the civilian population and combatants, including those based on ethnicity and religion.[53]

Similarly the Human Rights Committee and the UN Commission on Human Rights (now the Human Rights Council) have consistently confirmed that the ICCPR is applicable in the Occupied Palestinian Territories. In it 1998 report the Committee stated that it was:

> deeply concerned that Israel continues to deny its responsibility to fully apply the Covenant in the occupied territories. In this regard, the Committee points to the long-standing presence of Israel in these territories, Israel's ambiguous attitude towards their future status, as well as the exercise of effective jurisdiction by Israeli security forces therein. In response to the arguments presented by the delegation, the Committee emphasizes that the applicability of rules of humanitarian law does not by itself impede the application of the Covenant or the accountability of the State under article 2, paragraph 1, for the actions of its authorities.[54]

The 2003 Report of John Dugard, the Special Rapporteur of the UN Commission on Human Rights on 'the situation of human rights in the Palestinian territories

[51] Report of the Human Rights Committee, UN GAOR, 46th Sess, Supp No 40, [652] UN Doc A/46/40 (1991).

[52] Walter Kälin, Report on the situation of human rights in Kuwait under Iraqi occupation, UN Doc E/CN.4/1992/26, [58–59] 16 January 1992, reprinted in W Kälin, *Human Rights in Times of Occupation: The Case of Kuwait* (n 34), 77, 86 The report notes that the Human Rights Committee in its General Comment No 15 'The Position of Aliens under the Covenant has stated that in 'general the rights set forth in the Covenant apply to everyone, irrespective of reciprocity, and irrespective of his or her nationality or statelessness.' CCPR/C/21/Rev.1, 27th Session, 11 April 1986, [1].

[53] 'Interim report on the situation of human rights in Afghanistan submitted by the Special Rapporteur of the Commission on Human Rights in accordance with General Assembly resolution 52/145 and Economic and Social Council decision 1998/267' General Assembly A/53/539 (26/10/1988); UN Commission on Human Rights, Special Rapporteur on the Situation of Human Rights in Afghanistan, Report, UN Doc E/CN.4/1987/22, 19 February 1987; UN Commission on Human Rights, Res, 1987/58, 11 March 1987.

[54] Concluding Observations of the Human Rights Committee: Israel. 18/08/98.
UN Doc CCPR/C/79/Add.93. [10] ; Commission on Human Rights, Report of the Fifth Special Session (17–19 October 2000) E/CN.4/S-5/5, 19 October 2000.

occupied by Israel since 1967' noted that the government of Israel still insists that:

its actions in the OPT [Occupied Palestinian Territories] are to be measured against the rules of international humanitarian law and not those of human rights law.'[55]

However, the Human Rights Committee is

unable to accept this argument and reaffirmed its determination to judge Israel's actions in terms of both legal regimes.'[56]

The Committee has also stated that obligations under the ICCPR are equally applicable to UN peacekeeping forces as to States engaged in unilateral actions; for example it has held that the ICCPR was applicable to UNOSOM II by virtue of the fact that it had de facto control over parts of Somalia. UNOSOM II was a UN commanded and run operation and whether or not such operations can qualify as occupation remains controversial: there was certainly no suggestion at the time that UNOSOM II was subject to the laws of occupation. Nevertheless in 1998, in its Concluding Observations on Belgium's Article 41 report, the Committee stated that it was:

concerned about the behaviour of Belgian soldiers in Somalia under the aegis of the United Nations Operation in Somalia (UNOSOM II), and acknowledges that the State party has recognized the applicability of the Covenant in this respect and opened 270 files for investigation. The Committee regrets that it has not received further information on the results of the investigations and adjudication of cases and requests the State party to submit this information.[57]

The Committee reiterated its concerns in 2004, in its Comments on Belgium's fourth periodic report, in which it expressed concern 'at the small number of convictions in criminal and disciplinary proceedings of military personnel suspected of human rights violations during the United Nations operation in Somalia.'[58] The Committee reiterated that:

The Covenant automatically applies when it [the State party] exercises power or effective control over a person outside its territory, regardless of the circumstances such power or effective control was obtained, such as forces constituting a national contingent assigned to an international peacekeeping force or peace support operation.

[55] 'Question of the Violation of Human Rights in the Occupied Arab Territories, including Palestine', Report of the Special Rapporteur of the Commission on Human Rights on the situation of human rights in the Palestinian territories occupied by Israel since 1967, submitted in accordance with Commission resolution 1993/2 A E/CN.4/2004/6, [2].

[56] Ibid. Since the government of Israel was unwilling to co-operate with the Special Rapporteur, he obtained his understanding of the Israeli position through attendance at Israel's presentation of its second periodic report (CCPR/C/ISR 2001/2) on its compliance with the ICCPR, before the Human Rights Committee.

[57] Concluding Observations of the Human Rights Committee: Belgium 19.11 1998, UN Doc CCPR/C/79/Add.99 [14].

[58] Concluding Observations of the Human Rights Committee: Belgium 12.08.2004 UN Doc CCPR/C/81/BEL [10].

The State party should respect the safeguards established by the Covenant, not only in its territory but also when it exercises its jurisdiction abroad, as for example in the case of peacekeeping missions or NATO military missions, and should train the members of such missions appropriately.[59]

In its 2001 concluding observations on the Netherlands report the Committee made it clear that Dutchbat's conduct at the time of the fall of Srebrenica came within the remit of the Committee's review. The Committee stated that it remained:

concerned that, six years after the alleged involvement of members of the State party's peacekeeping forces in the events surrounding the fall of Srebrenica, Bosnia and Herzegovina, in July 1995, the responsibility of the persons concerned has yet to be publicly and finally determined. The Committee considers that in respect of an event of such gravity it is of particular importance that issues relating to the State party's obligation to ensure the right to life be resolved in an expeditious and comprehensive manner (articles 2 and 6 of the Covenant).

The State party should complete its investigations as to the involvement of its armed forces in Srebrenica as soon as possible, publicize these findings widely and examine the conclusions to determine any appropriate criminal or disciplinary action.[60]

The Human Rights Committee in its General Comment No 31, of 29th March 2004 summed up the scope of extra-territorial jurisdiction of the ICCPR, stating that:

A State party must respect and ensure the rights laid down in the Covenant [ICCPR] to anyone within the power and effective control of that State party, even if not situated within the territory of that State party... This principle also applies to those within the power or effective control of the forces of a State party acting outside its territory, regardless of the circumstances in which such power or effective control was obtained, such as forces constituting a national contingent of a State party assigned to a national peace-keeping or peace-enforcement operation.[61]

The UN Committee against Torture has also observed that:

the Convention [against Torture and other Cruel, Inhuman or Degrading Treatment or Punishment] protections extend to all territories under the jurisdiction of a State party and considers that this principle includes all areas under the de facto effective control of the State party's authorities.[62]

[59] ibid [6].

[60] Concluding observations of the Human Rights Committee: Netherlands. 27/08/2001. CCPR/CO/72/NET 27 August 2001.

[61] General Comment No 31, 'Nature of the General Legal Obligation Imposed on States Parties to the Covenant' UN Doc CCPR/C/2/1/Rev.1/Add.13, 26 May 2004, [10]; The ECtHR, and the Inter-American Commission on Human Rights have adopted similar approaches: *Loizidou v Turkey*, (Merits) 15318/89 [1996] ECHR 70 (18 December 1996); *Cyprus v Turkey*, 25781/94 [2001] ECHR 331 (10 May 2001); Inter-American Commission on Human Rights, *Coard et Al v United States*, Report No 109/99, Case 10.951, September 29, 1999; Inter-American Commission on Human Rights, , *Alejandre and Others v Cuba*, Report No 86/89, Case 11.589, 29 September 1999.

[62] UN Committee against Torture, *Conclusions and Recommendations: United Kingdom of Great Britain and Northern Ireland—Dependent Territories*, CAT/C/CR/33/3, 10 December 2004.

In 2004, the International Court of Justice (ICJ), in its Advisory Opinion concerning the Legal Consequences of the Construction of a Wall in the Occupied Palestinian Territory (hereinafter Israeli Barrier) confirmed that all the human rights treaties to which Israel is party are applicable in the Occupied Palestinian Territories, (except to the extent that it formally derogates from them), as well as the human rights obligations that constitute customary law.[63] In December 2005 the ICJ held Uganda responsible for violations of both IHL and human rights law committed in the Democratic Republic of the Congo, in the Utari district, which was occupied by Ugandan forces. The Court held that in addition to IHL, the Ugandan forces were required to uphold all the human rights treaties to which their State is party.[64]

The European Court of Human Rights (ECtHR) has also affirmed the applicability of human rights to territory under the effective control of the State party. In the *Loizidou* case (which concerned the claims of a Greek Cypriot woman who had been forced to leave her house because of the Turkish occupation of northern Cyprus), the government of Turkey denied that it had jurisdiction over northern Cyprus arguing that responsibility for securing rights of the inhabitants lay with the Turkish Republic of Northern Cyprus (TRNC). The ECtHR rejected this argument stating that the responsibility of a Contracting Party was capable of being engaged 'when as a consequence of military action (lawful or unlawful) it exercised effective control of an area outside its national territory.'[65] Moreover the obligation to secure the Convention rights and freedoms was found to derive:

> from the fact of such control whether it was exercised directly, through the respondent State's armed forces, or through a subordinate local administration.[66]

It was not necessary to determine whether Turkey actually exercised detailed control over the policies and actions of the authorities of the 'TRNC':

> It is obvious from the large number of troops engaged in active duties in northern Cyprus... that her army exercises effective overall control over that part of the island. Such control, according to the relevant test and in the circumstances of the case, entails her responsibility for the policies and actions of the 'TRNC'... Those affected by such policies or actions therefore come within the 'jurisdiction' of Turkey for the purposes

[63] The Court advised that Israel's security barrier violated a number of provisions of the International Covenant on Civil and Political Rights, the International Covenant on Economic, Social and Cultural Rights and the Convention on the Rights of the Child; *Advisory Opinion concerning the Legal Consequences of the Construction of a Wall in Occupied Palestinian Territory* (ICJ July 9 2004) ILM 1009 (2004) <http://www.icj-cij.org>.

[64] The ICPPR, the African Charter on Human and Peoples Rights, the UN Convention on the Rights of the Child, and the Optional Protocol to the Convention on the Rights of the Child on the Involvement of Children in Armed Conflict: *Case Concerning Armed Activities on the Territory of the Congo: Democratic Republic of the Congo v Uganda* ICJ, 19 December 2005, [217].

[65] *Loizidou v Turkey* (n 61), [52].

[66] *Banković v Belgium and 16 Other Contracting States* (n 11), [70].

of Article 1 of the Convention. Her obligation to secure to the applicant the rights and freedoms set out in the Convention therefore extends to the northern part of Cyprus.[67]

Although the Court determined that Turkey had jurisdiction as a result of its military occupation, it did not discuss the relevant provisions of the Hague Regulations or the Geneva Conventions. Turkey was held to be responsible for securing the entire range of rights contained in the ECHR. Judge Bernhardt, joined by Judge Lopas Rocha in a strongly worded dissent, argued that Turkey could be held responsible for concrete acts done in northern Cyprus by Turkish troops or officials, but whilst the presence of Turkish troops and Turkey's support of the TRNC were important factors he felt:

unable to base a judgement of the European Court of Human Rights exclusively on the assumption that the Turkish presence is illegal and that Turkey is therefore responsible for more or less everything that happens in northern Cyprus.[68]

However, in a later case brought by Cyprus against Turkey, the Court stated unequivocally that:

Having effective control over northern Cyprus its [Turkey's] responsibility cannot be confined to the acts of its own soldiers or officials in northern Cyprus but must be engaged by virtue of the acts of the local administration which survives by virtue of Turkish military and other support. It follows that, in terms of Article 1 of the Convention, Turkey's 'jurisdiction' must be considered to extend to securing the entire range of substantive rights set out in the Convention and those additional Protocols which she has ratified, and that violations of those rights are imputable to Turkey.[69]

Nevertheless, in *Banković* (which concerned claims by relatives of those killed in the bombing of the Serbian television station by NATO forces during the Kosovo campaign), the ECtHR held the case inadmissible for lack of jurisdiction on the grounds (inter alia) that Convention 'is a multi-lateral treaty operating... in an essentially regional context and notably in the legal space (*espace juridique*) of the Contracting States.'[70] On the other hand in the subsequent *Issa* case (which concerned claims by a number of shepherdesses, living in Iraq, that their men had been unlawfully arrested, detained, tortured, and murdered by the Turkish army during the course of large-scale cross-border raid into northern Iraq between 19 March and 16 April 1995), the Court implied that the Convention is

[67] ibid [56].

[68] He commented that Mrs. Loizidou was not being prevented from accessing her property as a consequence of an individual act of Turkish troops directed against her property or her freedom of movement. It was the establishment of the borderline in 1974, now protected by forces under United Nations command, which made it impossible for Greek Cypriots to visit and to stay in their homes in the northern part of the island: *Loizidou v Turkey* (Merits) (n 61), Dissenting Opinion of Judge Bernhardt & Judge Lopas Rocha [1] [3].

[69] *Cyprus v Turkey* (n 61), [77]; Also *Djavit An v Turkey*, Judgment of February 20, 2003, App No 20652/192 [18–23].

[70] *Banković v Belgium and 16 Other Contracting States* (n 11), [80].

applicable beyond the regional limits of Europe if the contracting State is exercising de facto control over the territory. The Court observed that:

In their official statements on the conduct of military operations in northern Iraq at the relevant time, the Turkish authorities accepted that the area was under the authority of the Turkish State, and hence within its jurisdiction (see Government Statement. Subject: Military Operation in Northern Iraq. Permanent Mission of Turkey to the United Nations Office of the Press Counsellor, 20 March 1995).[71]

However, the Court did not think that this in itself was sufficient to render the Convention generally applicable:

notwithstanding the large number of troops involved in the aforementioned military operations, it does not appear that Turkey exercised effective overall control of the entire area of northern Iraq. This situation is therefore in contrast to the one which obtained in northern Cyprus in the *Loizidou v Turkey* and *Cyprus v Turkey* cases... In the latter cases, the Court found that the respondent Government's armed forces totalled more than 30,000 personnel (which is, admittedly, no less than the number alleged by the applicants in the instant case... but with the difference that the troops in northern Cyprus were present over a very much longer period of time) and were stationed throughout the whole of the territory of northern Cyprus. Moreover, that area was constantly patrolled and had check points on all main lines of communication between the northern and southern parts of the island.[72]

Nevertheless the Court did say that it:

does not exclude the possibility that, as a consequence of the military action, the respondent State could be considered to have exercised, temporarily, effective overall control of a particular portion of the territory of northern Iraq. Accordingly, if there is a sufficient factual basis for holding that, at the relevant time, the victims were within that specific area, it would follow logically that they were within the jurisdiction of Turkey (and not that of Iraq, which is not a Contracting State and clearly does not fall within the legal space (espace juridique) of the Contracting States (see the above-cited Bankovic decision, § 80).[73]

Some human rights treaties may also apply extra-territorially in those cases where individuals and property are brought within the jurisdiction of parties to a human rights treaty by the actions of State agents bringing them under the State's control, the most obvious example being kidnapping. In these cases it:

is the nexus between the person affected, whatever his nationality, and the perpetrator of the alleged violation which engages the possible responsibility of the State and not the place where the action takes place.[74]

[71] *Issa and others v Turkey*, 31821/96 [2004] ECHR 629 (16 November 2004) [63].
[72] ibid [75].
[73] ibid [74].
[74] F Hampson, 'Using International Human Rights Machinery to Enforce the International Law of Armed Conflicts' (1992) 31 *Revue de Droit Militaire et de Droit de la Guerre* 119, 122.

The principal justification for this category of jurisdiction is that articulated in *Delia Saldias de Lopez v Uruguay*, in which the Human Rights Committee held that it would be unconscionable to interpret the ICCPR in such a way as to permit a State party to perpetrate violations of the Covenant on the territory of another State that it could not perpetrate on its own territory.[75] The Committee took the same view in *Lilian Celiberti de Casariego v Uruguay*.[76]

Similar approaches have been taken by regional courts. In *Coard*,[77] the Inter-American Commission on Human Rights found persons detained by the United States, in October 1983, during the intervention in Grenada, had been carried out under conditions that did not ensure the full observance of the minimum safeguards required under the American Declaration on the Rights and Duties of Man. In *Cyprus v Turkey* the European Commission stated that:

> authorised agents of a State, including diplomatic or consular agents and armed forces, not only remain under its [the State's] jurisdiction when abroad but bring any other persons or property 'within the jurisdiction' of that State, to the extent that they exercise authority over such persons or property.[78]

The Commission adopted a similar approach in *Stocké v Germany*[79] and in *X and Y v Switzerland*.[80] In *Drozd and Janousek v France and Spain* and *Ilascu v Moldova and the Russian Federation*[81] the ECtHR virtually equated attribution of responsibility with jurisdiction, noting that:

> The term 'jurisdiction' is not limited to the national territory of the High Contracting Parties; their responsibility can be involved because of acts of their authorities producing effects outside their own territory.[82]

However, this category of jurisdiction was not endorsed by the ECtHR in *Banković*, at least in relation to acts of authorized agents of a State party producing effects outside of Europe. The Court stated that the ECHR 'was not designed to be applied throughout the world, even in respect of the conduct of Contracting States.'[83] However, in *Issa* the ECtHR, citing inter alia *Lopez* and *Coard*, stated that:

> Moreover, a State may also be held accountable for violation of the Convention rights and freedoms of persons who are in the territory of another State but who are found to

[75] *Delia Saldias de Lopez v Uruguay* (n 46), [12.3]

[76] *Lilian Celiberti de Casariego v Uruguay* (n 47), [10.3].

[77] *Coard et Al v United States*, Inter-American Commission on Human Rights (n 61).

[78] Apps Nos 6780/74 and 6950/75, 2 D & R 125, 136.

[79] Report of 12 October 1989, App No 1175/85, series A, Vol. 199, 24 [166].

[80] Apps. Nos. 7289/75 and 7349/76, 9 D & R 57, 71.

[81] *Drozd and Janousek v France and Spain*, 12747/87 [1992] ECHR 52 (26 June 1992), [91]; *Ilascu and others v Moldova and the Russian Federation*, 48787/99 [2004] ECHR 318 (8 July 2004).

[82] *Drozd and Janousek v France and Spain* (n 81); *Ilascu and others v Moldova and the Russian Federation* (n 81), [314]; *Öcalan v Turkey* Application No 46221/99 [2005] ECHR 282 (12 May 2005), [91].

[83] *Banković v Belgium and 16 Other Contracting States* (n 11), [47].

be under the former State's authority and control through its agents operating—whether lawfully or unlawfully—in the latter State (see, *mutatis mutandis, M v Denmark*, application no. 17392/90, Commission decision of 14 October 1992, DR 73, p. 193; *Illich Sanchez Ramirez v France*, application no. 28780/95, Commission decision of 24 June 1996, DR 86, p. 155; *Coard et al. v the United States*, the Inter-American Commission of Human Rights decision of 29 September 1999, Report No. 109/99, case No. 10.951, §§ 37, 39, 41 and 43; and the views adopted by the Human Rights Committee on 29 July 1981 in the cases of *Lopez Burgos v Uruguay* and *Celiberti de Casariego v Uruguay*, nos. 52/1979 and 56/1979, at §§ 12.3 and 10.3 respectively). Accountability in such situations stems from the fact that Article 1 of the Convention cannot be interpreted so as to allow a State party to perpetrate violations of the Convention on the territory of another State, which it could not perpetrate on its own territory (*ibid*.).[84]

The conflicting decisions in *Banković* and *Issa* were at issue in the *Al-Skeini* case, which concerned allegations that British forces serving in Iraq during the occupation of 2004 had violated the UK Human Rights Act, 1998. Lord Justice Rix and Justice Forbes of the UK High Court found the judgements in *Banković* and *Issa* difficult to reconcile commenting that:

it is difficult to understand what the jurisdictional difference is between deaths caused by ground troops in Iraq and deaths caused by aerial bombardment in Serbia. It is common ground that in *Issa* the Turkish troops did not have effective control of the area. The question was nevertheless whether Turkish troops exercised authority or control over the shepherds. Subject to the fact, which may possibly be important but was not stressed in *Issa*, that there the shepherds had been detained before they were shot and mutilated, it is difficult to see any principled difference between deaths caused by the extra-territorial military exercise by a state party *in the skies* of authority and control over civilians in another non-party state and deaths caused by the extra-territorial military exercise by a state party *on the ground* of authority and control over civilians in another non-party state.[85]

The Court concluded that the *Banković* admissibility decision of 2001 was a 'watershed' case in which:

the Court there went out of its way to analyse the exceptions in relatively limited ways, pointing in the context of the 'effective control of an area' exception to the importance of the vacuum and *espace juridique* doctrines, and otherwise making specific reference to embassies, consulates, vessels and aircraft.[86]

The dicta in the 2004 *Issa* case:

are inconsistent with *Bankovic* and the development of the Strasbourg jurisprudence in the years immediately before *Bankovic*. In a sense *Issa* seems to us to look back to an earlier period of the jurisprudence, which has subsequently made way for a more limited interpretation of article 1 jurisdiction. It may well be that there is more than one school of

[84] *Issa and others v Turkey* (n 71), [71].
[85] *The Queen on the application of Mazin Jumaa Gatteh Al-Skeini and others v Secretary of State for Defence* [2004] EWHC 2911 (Admin), [222].
[86] ibid [262].

thought at Strasbourg; and that there is an understandable concern that modern events in Iraq should not be put entirely beyond the scope of the Convention: but at present we would see the dominant school as that reflected in the judgment in *Bankovic* and it is to that school that we think we owe a duty under section 2(1)[87]

The High Court, Court of Appeal, and the House of Lords, followed *Banković* and held that, even during occupation, jurisdiction under the Human Rights Act does not extend to the acts of British forces in Iraq, except in cases such as Baha Mousa's, whose brutal maltreatment was perpetrated by British soldiers in a British prison.[88]

The Inter-American Commission on Human Rights has adopted a view closer to *Issa* than *Banković*. In *Alejandre and Others v Republic of Cuba*, which like *Banković* concerned the use of force in the air (the shooting down in international waters of light aircraft from the United States), the Inter-American Commission on Human Rights, citing *Cyprus v Turkey* stated that:

In analyzing the facts, the Commission finds that the victims died as a consequence of direct actions of agents of the Cuban State in *international air space*. The circumstance that the facts occurred outside the Cuban jurisdiction does not restrict nor limit the Commission's competent authority *ratione loci*, for, as has already been indicated, when agents of a State, whether they be military or civil, exercise power and authority over persons located outside the national territory, its obligation to respect human rights, in this case the rights recognized in the American Declaration, continues.[89]

Banković concerned potential liability under human rights law for the bombing of a building, an act that is not uncommon in warfare and is not in itself a breach of the laws of war. The lawfulness or otherwise of the bombing under IHL depends on whether the Belgrade television station was a legitimate military target and whether the principle of distinction was respected. These are not cut and dried issues and depend on the circumstances of the case. *Issa* concerned the torture, mutilation and murder of detained civilians. Baha Mousa's case also concerned torture and an unlawful death in custody. These acts are horrifically shocking and never lawful under any circumstances. Faced with similar horrific acts in a future case the ECtHR might well take an approach in line with *Issa*. Unfortunately soldiers, including peacekeepers, do commit abuses of human rights that can never be excused as errors of judgment or mistakes in the heat of battle. Whilst those who do so are in the minority, the problem is pervasive; most, if not all, militaries are affected, as are other international organizations, such as charities, that work in conflict situations. Some human rights abuses, such as rape, sexual abuse, extortion, and profiting from slavery, by their very nature, demonstrate the exercise of direct control over the victims. Such acts are

[87] ibid [265].

[88] Opinions of the Lords of Appeal for Judgment in the Cause *Al-Skeini and others v Secretary of State for Defence* [2007] UKHL 26.

[89] Inter-American Commission on Human Rights, Case 11.589, *Alejandre and Others v Cuba* (n 61), [25] (Emphasis original).

often only possible because of the vulnerability of the person to the greater power of the military force.

A third category of extra-territorial jurisdiction of human rights law is that based on an exception to the territorial principle in respect of certain areas or properties that are recognized and accepted as being under the jurisdiction of the State, wherever they are located, such as embassies. Whatever the future developments as regards the *espace juridique* of the ECHR as articulated in *Banković*, human rights treaties, including the ECHR, remain applicable in the category of cases that fall within this exception to the territorial limit of jurisdiction. In *Banković* the ECtHR noted that:

> the case-law of the Court demonstrates that its recognition of the exercise of extra-territorial jurisdiction by a Contracting State is exceptional: it has done so when the respondent State, through the effective control of the relevant territory and its inhabitants abroad as a consequence of military occupation or through the consent, invitation or acquiescence of the Government of that territory, exercises all or some of the public powers normally to be exercised by that Government.[90]

However:

> the Court notes that other recognised instances of the extra-territorial exercise of jurisdiction by a State include cases involving the activities of its diplomatic or consular agents abroad and on board craft and vessels registered in, or flying the flag of, that State. In these specific situations, customary international law and treaty provisions have recognised the extra-territorial exercise of jurisdiction by the relevant State.[91]

In the view of the UK High Court in the *Al-Skeini* case, a military prison falls within the specific exceptions recognized by customary international law and treaty provisions referred to in *Banković*:

> it is not at all straining the examples of extra-territorial jurisdiction discussed in the jurisprudence considered above to hold that a British military prison, operating in Iraq with the consent of the Iraqi sovereign authorities, and containing arrested suspects, falls within even a narrowly limited exception exemplified by embassies, consulates, vessels and aircraft, and in the case of *Hess v United Kingdom*, a prison.[92]

The Court of Appeal also held that the maltreatment of Baha Mousa was within the jurisdiction of the Human Rights Act but on the slightly different ground that 'Mr Mousa came within the control and authority of the UK from the time he was arrested at the hotel and thereby lost his freedom at the hands of British troops.'[93] This reasoning is more in line with the group of cases in which the ECHR has been held to be applicable where persons or property are brought

[90] *Banković v Belgium and 16 Other Contracting States* (n 11) [71].

[91] ibid [73].

[92] *The Queen on the application of Mazin Jumaa Gatteh Al-Skeini and others v Secretary of State for Defence* [2004] EWHC 2911 (Admin), [286–287].

[93] *The Queen on the application of Mazin Jumaa Gatteh Al-Skeini & others v Secretary of State for Defence* [2005] EWCA Civ 1609 21 December 2005, [108].

within the jurisdiction of a State by the actions of its agents on the basis that 'Article 1 of the Convention cannot be interpreted so as to allow a State party to perpetrate violations of the Convention on the territory of another State, which it could not perpetrate on its own territory.'[94]

3.1 The Extra-territorial Jurisdiction of Human Rights Treaties: Summary

In conclusion, it is well established that a State has obligations under human rights law where it is in control of territory outside its borders and also in a number of recognized exceptions to the territorial principle of jurisdiction (generally characterized by localized State control or authority), for example embassies and vessels flying the State's flag. Some human rights courts and monitoring bodies, including the former Human Rights Committee, have held that the actions of State agents may bring individual persons, within that State's jurisdiction, for example as a result of kidnap or detention.

The United States does not accept that human rights treaties are binding outside of its national borders but does accept that customary human rights law is binding on 'all its overseas operations.'[95] Moreover the United States Operational Law Handbook 2007 notes that:

> a number of existing and potential United States allies do not share our view on the restricted application of human rights treaties. Increasingly, States consider their human rights treaty obligations binding in all cases of State action. Expansion of the application of human rights treaties is evident in both United Nations treaties such as the International Covenant on Civil and Political Rights (ICCPR), as well as in regional human rights treaties such as the European Convention on Human Rights and the Inter-American human rights body's American Convention on Human Rights. Cases interpreting each of these regional treaties have confirmed their application beyond the borders of State parties. JAs [Judge Advocates] should therefore be aware that coalition armed forces may operate under treaty-based restrictions not applicable to United States Armed Forces.[96]

4. The Relationship between International Humanitarian Law and Human Rights Law

The potential applicability of international human rights law to peacekeepers and other forces deployed in situations of international armed conflict raises the question of the relationship between international humanitarian law and human

[94] *Issa and others v Turkey* (n 71), [71].

[95] United States Operational Law Handbook JA 422 (International and Operational Law Department The Judge Advocate General's Legal Center and School Charlottesville, Virginia), Chapter 3, II, [A].

[96] ibid ch 3, III, [J], footnotes omitted.

rights law since both may be applicable at the same time. A derogation from a human rights treaty on grounds of war does not in itself imply that human rights protections under human rights law may be displaced by equivalent provisions of IHL: the issue will depend on whether or not IHL is applicable and on the way in which the relationship between IHL and human rights law is interpreted. Conversely the absence of a derogation does not necessarily imply that protections under human rights law may not be effected by equivalent provisions of IHL since this becomes applicable whenever a State party is engaged in armed conflict, regardless of whether human rights law is, or is not, applicable. The nature of the relationship between concurrently applicable IHL and human rights law remains controversial and the extent to which one may be displaced by the other has not been clearly resolved.

Although IHL and human rights law can often be applied concurrently in respect of many protected rights, the scope of protection of certain rights, in particular the right to life, is markedly different under the two regimes and in these circumstances State parties, and troops, need to understand how the two regimes interact in order to have a clear idea of what their obligations are in respect of these rights. Since a war without killing is inconceivable, IHL permits attacks on combatants without restriction, so long as the rules of war regarding the manner in which attacks are conducted are complied with (for example rules designed to prohibit excessive infliction of unnecessary suffering such as those prohibiting the use of certain types of weapons). IHL also permits a certain amount of collateral damage, provided that any likely harm to civilians is proportionate to the military gain. By contrast, with the exception of the ECHR, international human rights conventions make no explicit provision for the taking of human life in combat or for acceptable levels of collateral damage.

The ICJ in its *Advisory Opinion concerning the Legality of the Threat of Use of Nuclear Weapons* suggested that in armed conflicts it may be necessary to interpret possible violations of human rights laws through the lens of IHL, as the *lex specialis* for armed conflict:

> the protection of the [International Covenant on Civil and Political Rights] does not cease in times of war... In principle the right not to be deprived on one's right to life also applies in hostilities. The test of what is an arbitrary deprivation of life, however, then falls to be determined by the applicable lex specialis, namely the law applicable in armed conflict which is designed to regulate the conduct of hostilities. Thus whether a particular loss of life, through the use of a certain weapon in warfare, is to be considered an arbitrary deprivation of life within the meaning of Article 6 of the Covenant, can only be decided by reference to the law applicable in armed conflict and not deduced from the terms of the Covenant itself.[97]

[97] *Advisory Opinion concerning the Legality of the Threat of Use of Nuclear Weapons* 1996 ICJ 226, 240 (June 24), [24–25].

The Court quoted this paragraph in its Advisory Opinion on the *Israeli Barrier*,[98] and went on to state that:

More generally the Court considers that the protection offered by human rights conventions does not cease in case of armed conflict, save through the effect of provisions for derogation of the kind to be found in Article 4 of the International Covenant on Civil and Political Rights. As regards the relationship between international humanitarian law and human rights, there are thus three possible situations: some rights may be exclusively matters of international humanitarian law; others may be exclusively matters of human rights law; yet others may be matters of both these branches of law. In order to answer the question put to it, the Court will have to take into consideration, both these branches of law, namely human rights law, and as *lex specialis* international humanitarian law.[99]

The treaty bodies of the inter-American human rights regime have taken a similar approach. In giving judgment in the *Tablada* case,[100] the Inter-American Commission on Human Rights stated that the American Convention on Human Rights and the 1949 Geneva Conventions 'share a common nucleus of non-derogable rights and a common purpose of protecting human life and dignity.'[101] However, although the human rights convention was formally applicable in times of armed conflict, it was not designed to regulate situations of war, therefore in order to reach a decision on whether human rights had been violated it might be necessary to consider the case through the *lex specialis* of IHL:

This is because the American Convention contains no rules that either define or distinguish civilians and other military targets, much less specify when a civilian can be lawfully attacked or when civilian casualties are a lawful consequence of military operations.[102]

Following this line of jurisprudence Peter Rowe has argued, citing the *Nuclear Weapons* case, that where certain rights are differently protected

98 *The Legal Consequences of the Construction of a Wall in Occupied Palestinian Territory* (n 63), [105]

99 ibid [106].

100 *Argentina*, Report No 55/97, Case No 11.137, approved by the Commission 18 Nov 1997; OEA/Ser.L/V/II.97, Doc 38 The case concerned the killing of 29 people, during an attack lasting 30 hours, by 42 armed civilians on an army barracks in Argentina in 1989.

101 ibid [158].

102 ibid [161] The Commission's approach was welcomed by many as offering a means by which violations of IHL could be adjudicated before civilian courts, but it also triggered criticism on the grounds that the Commission had no competence to apply IHL (L Zegveld, 'Remedies for victims of violations of international humanitarian law', International Review of the Red Cross No 851, 497, 516). The Inter-American Court of Human Rights in the *Las Palmeras* case and also in the *Valásquez* case acknowledged this lack of competence but approved the general approach of the Commission. In the latter case the Court went so far as to say that whilst it would be beyond the jurisdictional competence of both the Court and the Commission to declare a State to be internationally responsible for violations of IHL nevertheless 'it can observe that certain acts or omissions that violate human rights, pursuant to the treaties that they do have competence to apply, also violate other international instruments for the protection of the individual, such as the 1949 Geneva Conventions, in particular, common Article 3.' *Las Palmeras Case*, Inter-Am. Ct HR, (Ser C) No 90 (2001) Judgment of December 6, 2001, [32–34] and *Bámaca Velásquez Case*, Inter-Am Ct HR (Ser C) No 70 (2000) Judgment of November 25, 2000, [208].

under IHL and human rights law, the humanitarian law principles prevail in an armed conflict. Thus, although the ICCPR prohibits the arbitrary taking of life and this right is non-derogable, since IHL is the *lex specialis*, killing as a result of a lawful act of war is not arbitrary under the ICCPR and hence not a violation of the ICCPR.[103] Similarly, he argues that if a derogation notice is issued under the ECHR any killings that result from lawful acts of war will not violate the Convention.[104] However, recent cases of the ICJ[105] and of the ECtHR[106] appear to have taken a much more flexible approach to the applicability of human rights law with a greater leaning towards a 'convergence' based relationship between the two regimes than might be expected in the light of the *lex specialis* status of IHL. The case law suggests that it cannot be presumed that human rights provisions will be entirely displaced by comparable provisions of IHL in an armed conflict. Military exigencies and the principles of IHL may be taken into account in assessing compliance with human rights law but it is not simply a matter of replacing one criterion by another.

4.1 Developing Synthesis between the Two Regimes

The traditional view of the of the relationship between IHL and human rights law, as expressed by the ICRC, in its Commentary to the Additional Protocols of 1977, is that that IHL and human rights law are separate regimes, but they may apply concurrently.[107] IHL is triggered by the existence of 'armed conflict.' It does not apply where there is no armed conflict. Human rights law applies mainly in peacetime but it continues to apply in wartime except where a derogation is in place (and derogation is permissible only to the extent strictly necessary for the exigencies of the situation). Draper has suggested that:

> The essential nexus between the law of war and the regime of human rights has been made in theory, viz., that the former is essentially part of the latter. The law of war is a derogation from the normal regime of human rights.[108]

However, there remains considerable controversy over how the two regimes interreact. Draper accepts that human rights:

[103] P Rowe, *The Impact of Human Rights Law on Armed Forces* (n 11), 180, 134.

[104] ibid.

[105] *Advisory Opinion concerning the Legal Consequences of the Construction of a Wall in the Occupied Palestinian Territory*, ICJ (n 63); *Case concerning Armed Activities on the Territory of the Congo: Democratic Republic of the Congo v Uganda*, ICJ (n 64).

[106] *Isayeva, Yusupova, and Bazayeva v Russia*, 57947/00; 57948/00; 57949/00 [2005] ECHR 129 (24 February 2005).

[107] ICRC, *Commentary on the Additional Protocols of 8 June 1977 to the Geneva Conventions of 12 August 1949* (n 38), 1365 [4513].

[108] GIAD Draper, 'The Relationship Between the Human Rights Regime and the Law of Armed Conflict' (n 1), 206.

do not dissolve in time of war or public emergency affecting the life of the nation, but are subjected to a controlled and limited derogation from specific Human Rights to be justified to the extent of that emergency.[109]

However, he has also stated that:

The two regimes are not only distinct but are diametrically opposed. The confusion between the two was a heresy of the UN, brought about by political forces which achieved their purpose by the inclusion of struggles for self-determination within the law applicable to armed conflict.[110]

Likewise, Pictet, writing in 1975, argued that 'the two systems are complementary, and indeed they complement one another admirably, but they must remain distinct, if only for the sake of expediency.'[111] The reason he put forward was that the Geneva Conventions are universal and of a mandatory nature which 'is certainly not the case with human rights.'[112] In his view the close relationship between human rights and the State would compromise the effectiveness of IHL if the boundaries between the two regimes were to become blurred, because in 'case of war, only a neutral and non-political body [such as the ICRC] has any chance of access to the scene of hostilities and ensure protection for victims.'[113]

Professors Bothe, Partsch, and Solf, in their Commentary on the 1977 Protocols, have also argued that the two regimes complement and complete on another but their argument focuses more strongly on securing the highest standards of protection possible. In their view, where an IHL treaty and a human rights treaty are both applicable, States must apply whichever treaty provides the higher standard of protection in any particular case. Thus when Protocol II establishes a higher standard of protection than the ICCPR, the higher standard prevails, since IHL is *'lex specialis'* to the Covenant:

On the other hand, provisions of the Covenant which have not been reproduced in the Protocol which provide for a higher standard of protection than the Protocol should be regarded as applicable irrespective of the relative times at which the two instruments came into force for the respective State. It is a general rule for the application of concurrent instruments of Human Rights—and Part II 'Humane Treatment' [Protocol II] is such an instrument—that they complement and complete each other instead of forming a basis for limitations.[114]

[109] GIAD Draper, 'The Status of Combatants and the Question of Guerilla Warfare' (n 36), 218.

[110] GIAD Draper, 'Humanitarian Law and Human Rights', [1979] *Acta Juridica* 193, 205.

[111] J Pictet, *Le Droit Humanitaire des Victimes de la Guerre* (n 2), 15.

[112] ibid.

[113] ibid.

[114] M Bothe, K Partsch & W Solf, *New Rules for Victims of Armed Conflicts: Commentary on The Two 1977 Protocols Additional to the Geneva Conventions of 1949* (Martinus Nijhoff Publishers The Hague 1982), 636; also ICRC, *Commentary on the Additional Protocols of June 8, 1977 to Geneva Conventions of 1949* (n 38), 1340, [4429 & 4430].

However, it is very difficult to separate out the provisions of IHL into those that concern 'human rights,' and those that do not, particularly since the Additional Protocols are not intended to serve as stand alone instruments but as supplementary to the Geneva Conventions. Hence an approach that gives pre-eminence to whichever instrument provides the higher protection is likely to colour the way in which the whole regime of IHL is viewed and suggests that some integration of the two regimes is in the process of development.

A number of commentators have focused on the advantages to be gained by adopting a 'convergence' based approach. Walter Kälin, the UN Special Rapporteur on human rights in Kuwait following the Iraqi invasion in 1991, describes the convergence approach as:

> The application of both sets of norms (cumulatively whenever possible) as they reinforce each other; thus one should speak of a unified complex of HUMAN RIGHTS norms under different institutional umbrellas.[115]

In his report on Iraq's failure to observe human rights during its occupation of Kuwait, Kälin acknowledges the controversies surrounding the various approaches but seems to favour the convergence approach arguing that the 'cumulative application of humanitarian law and human rights guarantees' is both 'feasible' and 'is meaningful as it is capable of reinforcing the protection of individual' in a number of different ways.[116] Writing in 1987, Meron argued that:

> The convergence between humanitarian and human rights law is progressing rapidly. Although these systems of protection continue to have different institutional 'umbrellas'... a strict separation between the two is artificial and hinders efforts to maximize the effective protection of human rights.[117]

Aspects of a number of cases heard by international courts in the early part of the twenty first century appear to reflect a growing acceptance of some degree of convergence.[118] In addition the ICRC study on Customary International Law published in 2005,[119] has interpreted some analogous provisions of human rights law and IHL 'holistically' to such an extent that the separate origins of the two regimes have become blurred. Such an approach is likely to have a significant impact on the future development of IHL in two key areas: the use of force and the responsibilities of occupants.

[115] W Kälin, *Human Rights in Times of Occupation: The Case of Kuwait* (n 34), 26.

[116] ibid 27.

[117] T Meron, *Human Rights in Internal Strife: Their International Protection* (Grotius Publications Ltd Cambridge 1987), 28.

[118] *Case Concerning Armed Activities on the Territory of the Congo: Democratic Republic of the Congo v Uganda*, ICJ (n 64); *Isayeva, Yusupova, and Bazayeva v Russia*, ECHR (n 106).

[119] J-M Henckaerts and L Doswald-Beck, *Customary International Humanitarian Law* (n 42). The report is the result of 10 years of research in consultation with experts from different regions.

4.2 The Use of Force: *Isayeva, Yusopova & Bazayeva v Russia* and *Isayeva v Russia*

Two cases handed down by the ECtHR in February 2005, *Isayeva, Yusopova & Bazayeva v Russia* and *Isayeva v Russia*,[120] on violations of the ECHR in the course of security operations in Chechnya, also point to increasing acceptance of some degree of synthesis between IHL and international human rights law. Both cases concerned indiscriminate bombing by government forces in operations targeted against Chechen insurgents, resulting in the deaths of civilians and destruction of property. Russia has not derogated from the Convention in respect of Chechnya. In assessing compliance with Article 2 of the ECHR, which protects the right to life, the Court applied the same rules in *McCann* (which concerned a security operation mounted against three IRA activists believed to have been planning a terrorist attack), in *Ergi* (which concerned the shooting of a woman in her house during relatively low intensity conflict involving Turkish forces and the PKK, a Kurdish insurgent group), and the Chechnya cases. William Abresch comments that:

> the rules espoused by the ECtHR are not limited by any conflict intensity threshold: they form a single body of law that covers everything from confrontation with rioters and police officers to set-piece battles between rebel groups and national armies.[121]

These rules combine standard human rights law with certain principles analogous to some core IHL concepts. For example the ECtHR has relied on a principle similar to the humanitarian law principle of distinction in assessing the lawfulness of the use of force in security operations that fall short of full-scale 'armed conflict.' Thus a State's responsibilities under the ECHR may be engaged where its agents:

> fail to take all feasible precautions in the choice of means and methods of a security operation mounted against an opposing group with a view to avoiding and, in any event, minimising, incidental loss of civilian life.[122]

However, the Court has never said that it is applying IHL principles and has never clearly explained the basis for its use of them.[123] To a certain extent use of terms such as 'civilian' may simply reflect a common sense application of human rights principles, which would require that States should take care to ensure that

[120] *Isayeva, Yusupova, and Bazayeva v Russia*, ECHR (n 106); *Isayeva v Russia* 57950/00 [2005] ECHR 128 (24 February 2005).

[121] W Abresch, 'A Human Rights Law of Internal Armed Conflict: The European Court of Human Rights in Chechnya', '16 EJIL 4, 741, 742, 752.

[122] ECtHR, *Isayeva, Yusupova, and Bazayeva v Russia* (n 106), [176]; *Ergi v Turkey*, 23818/94 [1998] ECHR 59 (28 July 1998), [79].

[123] W Abresch, 'A Human Rights Law of Internal Armed Conflict: The European Court of Human Rights in Chechnya' (n 121), 746.

people who are not a danger to the State are not harmed as a result of a carelessly planned security operation.

The Chechnya cases differ from the earlier cases in that although the ECtHR applied the same principles as it had in *Ergi* and *McCann*, it also specifically addressed the relationship between human rights law and IHL in a manner that implied that the Court's decision would have been compatible with IHL if it had applied. The Russian government insists that there is no armed conflict taking place in the region. Nevertheless the description put to the Court in *Isayeva v Russia* of the operation by Major-General Barsukov, Deputy Commander of the Ministry of the Interior Troops in the Northern Caucasus, who was among the commanders of the operation, does not fit that of an ordinary peacetime law enforcement operation:

Some of the bandits... broke through our positions and reappeared in Lermontov-Yurt. We conducted a special operation there. But in planning and conducting this operation, we also blocked the nearby Shaami-Yurt. For two days we conducted a special operation there...

Their remaining forces were breaking through towards Katyr-Yurt. By that time it was also blocked. We let them enter Katyr-Yurt and conducted a special operation there with the forces of the 7th and the 12th special units. Again we met fierce resistance. The 7th unit sustained substantial casualties. We had to withdraw it... Again we used fire power—'Grad,' 'Uragan,' 'Buratino,'[124] artillery of the 47th regiment, cannons of the 46th regiment, mine-launchers. Fighter jets were also involved. But... the bandits broke through... and went towards the village of Gekhi-Chu...

Near Gekhi-Chu we were able to draw conclusions from the operation started in Alkhan-Kala. Over 150 bandits were detained, 548 dead bodies were seized. The rest the Chechens buried hastily in Alkhan-Kala... A large number of bodies were dumped or buried in shallow graves. In Shaami-Yurt and Katyr-Yurt we did not even take the bodies out, we did not have the resources to do that. Usually, after we had left, police units together with the forces of the Ministry of Justice came in... In the army we simply don't have enough trucks to take out so many bodies... According to our estimates, and this is supported by interception of radio communications, during this 'death raid' in the 'valley of death' (these are their expressions) they lost in total over one and a half thousand men.[125]

The Geneva Conventions 'apply to all cases of declared war or any other armed conflict between two or more High Contracting Parties, even if the state of war is

[124] 'Uragan' is a 16-round 220 mm multiple launch rocket system, firing two missiles per second, each missile fitted with high explosive fragmentation warhead, weight 280 kg, length 4.8 m and calibre 220 mm. It carries an explosive charge of 51.7 kg and is armed with a 100 kg warhead. TOS-1 'Buratino' is a thermobaric multiple launcher system, using 220 mm 'flame rocket', or a thermobaric warhead. The zone of assured destruction is 200 x 400 metres. When the warhead explodes, the combustible liquid inside is vaporized, creating an aerosol cloud which detonates when mixed with oxygen, first creating a high temperature cloud of flame followed by a crushing overpressure. It is also known as a 'vacuum bomb'.

[125] ECtHR, *Isayeva v Russia* (n 120), [111].

not recognized by one of them.'[126] Common Article 3, the only provision to apply in non-international armed conflict, sets an international standard, albeit a limited one, which brings the conflict out of the purely domestic criminal jurisdiction paradigm into one entailing the international responsibility of States. However, common Article 3 provides no guidelines at all for determining whether or not a situation of internal lawlessness has reached the level of non-international armed conflict. GI Draper has argued that the language used in common Article 3, which sets out 'as a minimum' certain basic standards of treatment to be afforded to protected persons 'in all circumstances,' is 'not consistent with a narrow application of the article.'[127] Nevertheless the reference in the article to the obligations of 'each Party to the conflict' implies that the groups fighting the government have some degree of organization that renders them capable of being considered a Party and capable of undertaking the obligations set out in the article.[128] The standards set out in common Article 3 are so basic that it does not require a high level of organization to be able to fulfil them but State practice has been to favour a narrow interpretation of the article. This is usually because of a reluctance to admit to the outside world that there is an armed conflict within the State's territory.[129] The Russian government's view of the situation in Chechnya is a prime example.

Protocol II applies to all cases of armed conflict not covered by Protocol I that take place in the territory of a High Contracting Party between its armed forces and dissident armed groups which, under responsible command, exercise such control over a part of its territory as to enable them to carry out sustained and concerted military operations and to implement the Protocol.[130] Reports indicate that 'the Chechen Republic of Ichkeria' operates under responsible command and exercises sufficient territorial control to carry out sustained military operations. During the period in which the operations with which these cases are concerned took place, the insurgents had control of the town of Grozny and from there they carried out attacks on Russian military outposts in groups of 15–20.[131] The insurgents certainly believe that there is an armed conflict to which Protocol II applies. The press page on the website of the 'Ministry of Foreign Affairs' for the 'Chechen Republic of Ichkeria,' states that Russia is 'clearly bound by its treaty obligations under IHL, in particular Article 3 common to the four Geneva Conventions of 1949 and Additional Protocol II of 1977.'[132]

[126] Common Article 2 of the Geneva Conventions (n 37).

[127] GIA Draper, 'The Geneva Conventions of 1949' (1965) 1 Receuil des Cours 59, 87.

[128] ibid 89

[129] ibid 87.

[130] 1977 Geneva Protocol Additional to the Geneva Conventions of 12 August 1949, and Relating to the Protection of Victims of International Armed Conflicts (Protocol II) 1125 *UNTS* (1979) 609–99, [1].

[131] W Abresch, 'A Human Rights Law of Internal Armed Conflict: The European Court of Human Rights in Chechnya' (n 121), 754.

[132] 'A Forgotten Conflict' Press Review 21/03/2005, Ministry of Foreign Affairs of the Chechen Republic of Ichkeria, <http://www.chechnya-mfa.info/print_press.php?func=detail&par=12765>.

The UN Commission on Human Rights also seems to have viewed the situation as an armed conflict. In its resolution on the 'Situation in the Republic of Chechnya of the Russian Federation,' adopted in 2000, the Commission states that:

> *Recalling* that the Russian Federation is a party to the International Covenant on Civil and Political Rights, the International Covenant on Economic, Social and Cultural Rights, the Convention against Torture and Other Cruel, Inhuman or Degrading Treatment or Punishment and other regional human rights instruments, such as the European Convention on Human Rights,
>
> *Recalling also* that the Russian Federation is a party to the Geneva Conventions of 12 August 1949 and Additional Protocol II thereto...
>
> *Underlining* the need to respect the principle of proportionality and to observe international human rights and humanitarian law in situations of conflict and in activities undertaken against terrorism...
>
> *Calls upon* the Government of the Russian Federation to establish urgently, according to recognized international standards, a national, broad-based and independent commission of inquiry to investigate promptly alleged violations of human rights and breaches of international humanitarian law committed in the Republic of Chechnya in order to establish the truth and identify those responsible, with a view to bringing them to justice and preventing impunity;
>
> *Requests* the Russian Federation to disseminate, and ensure that the military at all levels has a knowledge of, basic principles of human rights and international humanitarian law;...
>
> *Also urges* the Government of the Russian Federation to allow international humanitarian organizations, notably the Office of the United Nations High Commissioner for Refugees and the International Committee of the Red Cross, free and secure access to areas of internally displaced and war affected populations in the Republic of Chechnya and neighbouring republics, in accordance with international humanitarian law, and to facilitate their activities and the delivery of humanitarian aid to the victims in the region;[133]

The resolution's references to IHL treaties and to war affected populations clearly suggest that, in the Commission's view, there is an armed conflict, although its comments also suggest that, so far as the Commission is concerned, the same laws apply to 'situations of armed conflict' as to 'activities undertaken against terrorism.'[134]

[133] Commission on Human Rights resolution 2000/58 'Situation in the Republic of Chechnya of the Russian Federation'.

[134] Strictly speaking IHL does not apply outside of armed conflict. This has caused some problems in 'grey area' operations where it is difficult to determine whether or not there is an armed conflict. However the strict confinement of formal rules of IHL to armed conflict has been confirmed in the Convention on the Safety of UN and Associated Personnel (adopted 19 December 1994, entered into force 15 January 1999) 34 ILM (1995) and the Secretary-General's Bulletin on Observance by UN Forces of International Humanitarian Law (date of promulgation 6 August 1999, entered into force 12 August 1999) UN Doc ST/SGB/1999/13. However it is generally accepted that non-combatant forces deployed into conflict situations are bound to respect the

The ECtHR accepted that the situation in Chechnya called for 'exceptional measures' and that those measures 'could presumably include the deployment of army units equipped with combat weapons, including military aviation and artillery.'[135] Nevertheless since no martial law and no state of emergency had been declared in Chechnya, and no derogation has been made under Article 15 of the Convention, the Court stated that the operation had 'to be judged against a normal legal background.'[136]

Even though the Court and the defendant were in formal agreement that IHL did not apply since there was no armed conflict, an amicus brief was presented on behalf of the applicants by Rights International, a United States' based non-governmental organization, which stated that the 'norms of non-international armed conflict should be construed in conformity with international human rights law governing the right to life and to humane treatment.'[137] Moreover, the right to life and to humane treatment require that when force is used, it must be limited to that which would 'cause the least amount of foreseeable physical and mental suffering.'[138] Given that the ICJ, and the Inter-American Court of Human Rights, have taken the view that in cases of armed conflict IHL is *lex specialis* to other applicable law, it would not have been surprising had the argument formulated the relationship the other way round; that in an armed conflict human rights law must be construed in the light of IHL. The approach taken by Rights International is perhaps more understandable in the light of the fact that human rights law is well developed and applies all the time; whereas the provisions of IHL that apply in non-international armed conflict remain comparatively limited,[139] although Russia has ratified Protocol II Additional to the Geneva Conventions 1949 without reservation.[140]

The controversial implications of the amicus brief conclusions might have warranted some comment by the Court but none was made. The Court accepted that 'the situation that existed in Chechnya at the relevant time called for exceptional measures on behalf of the State in order to regain control over the Republic and to suppress the illegal armed insurgency.' Moreover '[t]hese measures could presumably include employment of military aviation equipped with heavy combat

principles and rules of IHL even where it is not formally applicable to them (though the Secretary General's Bulletin is not clear on the point): see ch 2. In addition the ECtHR has applied principles drawn from IHL in cases dealing with security operations outside of armed conflict eg *Ergi v Turkey* (n 122); *McCann v UK* (1995) 21 EHRR 97; *Isayeva, Yusupova, and Bazayeva v Russia* (n 106); *Isayeva v Russia* (n 120).

[135] ECtHR, *Isayeva v Russia* (n 120), [180].

[136] ibid [191].

[137] ibid [166].

[138] ECtHR, *Isayeva, Yusupova, and Bazayeva v Russia* (n 106), [166] citing *Güleç v Turkey* judgment of 27 July 1998, *Reports* 1998-IV.

[139] By contrast the law of international armed conflict is as extensive and detailed as human rights law.

[140] Signed 12.12.1977. Ratified 20.09.1989. <http://www.icrc.org>.

weapons' and 'if the planes were attacked by illegal armed groups, that could have justified use of lethal force, thus falling within paragraph 2 of Article 2.'[141] However:

Any use of force must be no more than 'absolutely necessary' for the achievement of one or more of the purposes set out in sub-paragraphs (a) to (c) [of Article 2(2)]. This term indicates that a stricter and more compelling test of necessity must be employed than that normally applicable when determining whether State action is 'necessary in a democratic society' under paragraphs 2 of Articles 8 to 11 of the Convention.[142] Consequently, the force used must be strictly proportionate to the achievement of the permitted aims.

...In the light of the importance of the protection afforded by Article 2, the Court must subject deprivations of life to the most careful scrutiny, taking into consideration not only the actions of State agents but also all the surrounding circumstances.

In particular, it is necessary to examine whether the operation was planned and controlled by the authorities so as to minimise, to the greatest extent possible, recourse to lethal force. The authorities must take appropriate care to ensure that any risk to life is minimised. The Court must also examine whether the authorities were not negligent in their choice of action[143]

Thus, even where Article 2(2) applies, the ECHR rules on the use of force require that care be taken to minimise any risk to life. There is no suggestion that had the Russian government acknowledged the existence of an armed conflict the Court might have come to a decision more favourable to it. It is possible that the Court would have reached the same decision in the case, even if an Article 15 derogation had been made: measures taken in derogation under Article 15 are limited to those that are strictly necessary in the exigencies of the situation. The Human Rights Committee, commenting on equivalent derogation provisions of the ICCPR, has stated that:

The mere fact that a permissible derogation from a specific provision may, of itself, be justified by the exigencies of the situation does not obviate the requirement that specific measures taken pursuant to the derogation must also be shown to be required by the exigencies of the situation. In practice this will ensure that no provision of the Covenant,

[141] ECtHR, *Isayeva, Yusupova, and Bazayeva v Russia* (n 106), [178] Article 2 of the ECHR, protects the right to life. It is not subject to limitations however Article 2(2) provides that deprivation of life shall not be regarded as inflicted in contravention of this article when it results from the use of force which is no more than absolutely necessary (a) in defence of any person from unlawful violence, (b) in order to effect a lawful arrest or to prevent the escape of a person lawfully detained, (c) in action lawfully taken for the purpose of quelling a riot or insurrection.

[142] Articles 8–11 protect the rights to respect for private and family life, freedom of thought, conscience and religion, freedom of expression, and freedom of assembly and association. The rights may be subject to limitations provided that these are in accordance with the law and necessary in a democratic society to achieve certain defined interests. These vary with each article but include national security, public safety, the economic well-being of the country, the prevention of disorder and crime, the protection of health and morals, and the protection of the rights and freedoms of others.

[143] ECtHR, *Isayeva, Yusupova, and Bazayeva v Russia* (n 106), [168–170]; *McCann v UK* (n 134), [194]; *Ergi v Turkey* (n 122) [79].

however validly derogated from, will be entirely inapplicable to the behaviour of the State party.[144]

Whilst a formal derogation on the grounds of armed conflict might grant the State more freedom with regard to the use of force than if no derogation had been declared, it would not necessarily mean that any killing as a result of a lawful act of war would also be lawful under the ECHR. Such killing must also be strictly necessary in the exigencies of the situation.[145]

Given that 'strict necessity' is a requirement of human rights law that is not used in the application of IHL at all, it is likely to be interpreted within the context of an overarching objective of human rights protection. The use of force under IHL is governed by the principles of proportionality[146] and distinction,[147] but the proportionality test of IHL is not a strict proportionality test and may give much greater leeway to military necessity than is commensurate with a human rights based determination of what is strictly necessary in the exigencies of the situation. Thus the ECHR requirement that any measures taken in derogation must be strictly necessary may shape the way that the relationship between human rights law and IHL is interpreted, even where a derogation is made.[148]

4.3 The Relationship between Occupation Law and International Human Rights Law

The key factor linking the applicability of human rights law to occupation is 'effective control,' a concept that is central to both occupation law and human rights law, triggering the coming into effect of the former and the potential extension of jurisdiction of the latter. However, the simultaneous application of two different regimes of law triggered by the same criterion raises issues as to what that criterion really means, and whether its interpretation under one regime should necessarily be synonymous with its interpretation under the other.

[144] UN Human Rights Committee, General Comment No 29, 'States of Emergency (Article 4)' CCPR/C/21/Rev.1/Add.11, 31 August 2001, [4].

[145] ECHR (n 9), Article 15.

[146] The principle of proportionality requires a commander to weigh the military advantage of targeting a military objective against the collateral damage likely to be caused to non-combatants. Some collateral damage is acceptable provided that it is not excessive in proportion to the direct and concrete military advantage to be gained. He principle is now codified in Article 51 of the 1977 Geneva Protocol Additional to the Geneva Conventions of 12 August 1949, and Relating to the Protection of Victims of International Armed Conflicts 1125 *UNTS* (1979) 3–608 (Protocol I).

[147] The principle of distinction requires combatants to distinguish between military objectives and the civilian population: parties to a conflict must direct their operations only against military objectives. This principle is now codified in Article 48 of Protocol I (n 146).

[148] The facts of the case suggest that the State took so little care to protect civilians that it might well have violated the principle of proportionality under IHL even without the need to construe it 'in conformity with international human rights law.'

4.3.1 The Al-Skeini Case

The House of Lords in rejecting the claim that jurisdiction under the ECHR extended to allegedly unlawful killings by British forces in Iraq, focused on the jurisprudence of the ECtHR and UK courts on extra-territorial jurisdiction. The relevance of the law of occupation was discussed in greater depth in the High Court. Lord Justice Brookes, in considering the applicability of The Human Rights Act 1998[149] to UK occupying forces in Iraq, argued that:

it is quite impossible to hold that the UK, although an occupying power for the purposes of the Hague Regulations and Geneva IV, was in effective control of Basra City for the purposes of ECHR jurisprudence at the material time. If it had been it would have been obliged, pursuant to the *Bankovic* judgement, to secure to everyone in Basrah City the rights and freedoms guaranteed by the ECHR. One has only to state the proposition to see how utterly unreal it is. The UK possessed no executive, legislative or judicial authority in Basrah City, other than the limited authority given its military forces... For the purposes of completeness, I should make it clear that I reject the arguments by the claimants to the effect that occupation for the purposes of the Hague Regulations must necessarily be equated with effective control of the occupied area for ECHR purposes.[150]

However, Lord Justice Sedley disagreed:

In respectful disagreement with what Brookes L.J. says in paragraph 124, I do not see why the presence or absence of civil power for effective control in international law should be tested by asking whether there is sufficient control to enforce the full range of [ECHR] Convention rights... What seems to me more material is the fact that as Brooke L.J. explains in his preceding paragraphs, the United Kingdom was an occupying power within the meaning of Article 42 of the Hague Regulations because the Basrah region was under the authority of its armed forces. Article 43 then makes it incumbent upon the UK, 'to take all the measures in [its] power to restore and ensure, *as far as possible*, public order and safety, while respecting, *unless absolutely prevented*, the laws in force in the country.'...

No doubt it is absurd to expect occupying forces in the near chaos of Iraq to enforce the right to marry vouchsafed by Article 12 or the equality guarantees vouchsafed by Article 14 [of the ECHR]. But I do not think effective control involves this... It does not make the occupying power the guarantor of all rights; nor therefore does it demand sufficient control for such purposes. What it does place upon the occupier is an obligation to do all it can.[151]

Lord Justice Brookes argument can be criticized on the grounds that there is a very strong emphasis in IHL on the protection of civilians, and to suggest that

[149] The act incorporates the major provisions of the European Convention on Human Rights and Fundamental freedoms into domestic law.

[150] *The Queen on the application of Mazin Jumaa Gatteh Al-Skeini and others v Secretary of State for Defence* [2005] EWCA Civ 1609 21 December 2005 [124–127]

[151] *The Queen on the application of Mazin Jumaa Gatteh Al-Skeini and others v Secretary of State for Defence* [2004] EWHC 2911 (Admin), [195–196].

the occupant has no obligation to comply with the international human rights standards set out in treaties to which it is party *in so far as it has the power to do so*, would seem to undermine the spirit of the Conventions. On the other hand Lord Sedley seems to be arguing that occupation law itself requires an occupant to apply international human rights standards. A more conservative approach would be to hold that the applicability of human rights law derives from the human rights regime and not from occupation law. It is not immediately clear how the Article 43 obligation to ensure 'public order and safety' encompasses an obligation to secure rights protected under human rights treaties unless those rights were already part of the existing local law.[152]

Greater support for Lord Sedley's argument might be found in the French text of the Hague Regulations (which is the only authoritative text):

> L'autorité du pouvoir légal ayant passé de fait entre les mains de l'occupant, celui-ci prendra toutes les mesures qui dépendent de lui en vue de rétablir et d'assurer, autant qu'il est possible, l'ordre et la vie publics en respectant, sauf empêchement absolu, les lois en vigueur dans le pays.[153]

Some commentators have interpreted *'l'ordre et la vie publics'* as encompassing more than simply law and order. It also entails 'qu'il s'agit des functions socials, des transactions ordinaires, qui constituent la vie des jours.'[154] It could be argued that an obligation to restore all those ordinary functions that constitute daily life, read in the light of human rights law development since the drafting of the Geneva Conventions, (in particular the now consistently held view of international courts and UN institutions that human rights law is applicable in armed conflict) encompasses a requirement that the occupant respect and ensure 'as far as possible' the international human rights standards protected by customary international law and those treaties to which it is a party. Such an approach would require a significant re-appraisal of the relevant provisions of the Hague Regulations and of Geneva Convention IV. The Hague Regulations were drafted in 1907, long before the principal international and regional human rights law treaties. By the time of the drafting of the Geneva Conventions in 1949, Article 43

[152] Under Article 43 of the Hague Regulations an occupant is required 'to restore and ensure as far as possible, public order and safety, while respecting unless absolutely prevented, the laws in force in the country.' Hague Regulations (n 29), Article 43.

[153] Hague Regulations (n 29), Article 43.

[154] The predecessors of Article 43 are Article 2 and 3 of the Declaration of Brussels 1874. At the Convention of Brussels Baron Lambermont stated that he thought 'la vie publics' should be interpreted as 'qu'il s'agit des functions socials, des transactions ordinaires, qui constituent la vie des jours.' The report comments that 'La commission interprète ce mot dans le même sens que M.le baron Lambermont.' Ministère des Affaires Étrangères, Actes de la Conférence de Bruxelles de 1874 (Paris 1874), 23 quoted in EH Schwenk, 54 Yale Law Journal 2, 393, 398; C Greenwood, 'The Administration of Occupied Territory in International Law' in E Playfair (ed), *International Law and the Administration of the Occupied Territories: Two Decades of Israeli Occupation of the West Bank* (Clarendon Press Oxford 1992) 241, 246; MJ Kelly 'Iraq and the Law of Occupation: New Tests for an Old Law', 6 Yearbook of International Humanitarian Law, 127, 147; M Sassòli, 'Legislation and Maintenance of Public Order and Civil Life by Occupying Powers' 16 EJIL 4, 661, 663.

was already recognized as constituting customary international law. None of the delegates to the *Diplomatic Conference of Geneva 1949* considered the Mexican delegate's proposal to include a reference to human rights standards in Article 64 of Geneva Convention IV important enough to make any comment on it worth recording, let alone adopt it.[155] Lord Sedley's interpretation of Article 43 was not discussed in the appeals to the Court of Appeal or the House of Lords. However, recent case law of the ICJ,[156] and to an extent the ICRC's study on Customary International Humanitarian Law, provide some support for a re-interpretation of Article 43.

4.3.2 'Fundamental Guarantees' under Customary International Humanitarian Law

The ICRC study on Customary International Humanitarian Law, states that it is a principle of customary law that human rights law 'applies at all times' although some human rights law treaties allow for certain derogations in a 'state of emergency,' but only to the extent strictly required by the exigencies of the situation.[157] An occupant in carrying out its duty to restore and ensure *'l'ordre et la vie publics,'* would be expected to comply with customary international law. However, as the ICRC study confirms, although obligations under human rights laws do not cease in armed conflict, the applicability of human rights law treaties to international armed conflict depends on whether there is jurisdiction. The ICRC notes that 'treaty bodies, and significant State practice, have interpreted this as meaning whenever a State as effective control.'[158] The study does not discuss how this criterion intersects with the law of occupation, which is also triggered by effective control.

In assessing the scope and meaning of customary rules of IHL, the ICRC study refers frequently to human rights law. Chapter 32 of the ICRC's study deals with 'Fundamental Guarantees,' which are described as 'overarching rules' that 'apply to all civilians in the power of a party to the conflict and who do not take direct part in hostilities.'[159] The study lists nine fundamental guarantees of customary IHL, together with a discussion of the State practice supporting the rule: each rule is supported by practice from human rights law as well as IHL.[160] Thus the study consistently relies on State practice with regard to human rights law to

[155] *Final Record of the Diplomatic Conference of Geneva 1949*, Vol. IIa, 670–2.

[156] *Case Concerning Armed Activities on the Territory of the Congo: Democratic Republic of the Congo v Uganda*, ICJ (n 64); *Isayeva, Yusupova, and Bazayeva v Russia*, ECHR (n 106).

[157] The report supports this conclusion with a considerable body of State practice, mainly in the form of UN resolutions, reports by the UN Commission on Human Rights and investigations conducted by the UN into human rights violations in armed conflicts in Liberia, Sierra Leone, the occupied Palestinian territories, Kuwait and Afghanistan: J-M Henckaerts and L Doswald-Beck, *Customary International Humanitarian Law* (n 42), 299–305.

[158] ibid 305.

[159] ibid.

[160] ibid 306–383.

support its conclusions as to rules of customary humanitarian law. The introduction to the chapter states that '[t]his was done, not for the purpose of providing an assessment of customary human rights law, but in order to support, strengthen and clarify analogous principles of humanitarian law.'[161] The introduction concludes by saying that:

> It is beyond the scope of this study to determine whether these guarantees apply equally outside armed conflict although collected practice appears to indicate that they do.[162]

On a semantic level it is quite difficult to appreciate how rules of customary humanitarian law intended for the protection of civilians that do not participate in hostilities, could be applicable where there is no armed conflict. However, on a practical level it is possible to see how such an approach could be relevant given that troops (especially those engaged in peace operations) are frequently deployed into situations where force is used but it does not reach the level of armed conflict, or where there is an armed conflict but the force is not party to it.

The ICRC's approach implies that certain customary rules of international law that are similar in both humanitarian law and human rights law have now developed to such an extent, that for many purposes, distinctions in their originating source are no longer significant. This does not resolve the problem of jurisdiction under human rights law but it does suggest that courts and monitoring institutions, when considering the implications of the customary law rule that human rights law remains applicable in armed conflict outside the State's territory where a State has effective control, may be likely to 'shortcut' the analysis of effective control criteria to the point where there is no distinction between effective control for occupation and effective control for human rights law purposes. If this approach is consistently adopted then for all practical purposes the Article 43 requirement that occupants observe and ensure all applicable human rights law (an obligation that can only be derived from the customary law status of the principle that human rights law remains applicable in armed conflict) will generally be taken to imply that the occupant must observe and ensure, so far as is possible, all the human rights treaties to which the occupying State is party, all the human rights treaties to which the occupied State is party, and customary human rights law—except to the extent of any measures that are taken pursuant to a declared derogation and that are strictly necessary in the exigencies of the situation. This would seem to be the approach taken by the ICJ, which has, in its two most recent decisions on occupation, the *Israeli Wall* opinion and the *Case Concerning Armed Activities on the Territory of the Congo* (hereinafter *Congo*) treated the status of occupation as in itself triggering jurisdiction under human rights laws to which the occupant is party.[163]

[161] ibid 299.

[162] ibid.

[163] *Advisory Opinion concerning the Legal Consequences of the Construction of a Wall in Occupied Palestinian Territory* (n 63); *Case concerning Armed Activities on the Territory of the Congo: Democratic*

4.3.3 The Case Concerning Armed Activities on the Territory of the Congo

In the *Congo* case the Court, having concluded on the basis of the evidence that Uganda was the occupying power in the district of Ituri at the relevant time, stated that:

> As such it was under an obligation, according to Article 43 of the Hague Regulations of 1907, to take all the measures in its power to restore, and ensure, as far as possible, public order and safety in the occupied area, while respecting, unless absolutely prevented, the laws in force in the DRC [Democratic Republic of the Congo]. This obligation comprised the duty to secure respect for the applicable rules of international human rights law and international humanitarian law, to protect the inhabitants of the occupied territory against acts of violence, and not to tolerate such violence by any third party.
>
> The Court having concluded that Uganda was an occupying Power in Ituri at the relevant time, finds that Uganda's responsibility is engaged both for any acts of its military that violated international obligations and for any lack of vigilance in preventing violations of human rights and international humanitarian law by other actors present in the occupied territory, including rebel groups acting on their own account.[164]

The Court then listed all the human rights and humanitarian law treaties that it considered applicable to Uganda as occupants.[165] The Hague Regulations were held to be applicable on the basis that they are customary law. The following treaties were then listed along with the dates of accession by both parties: the Geneva Conventions and Additional Protocol I, the ICCPR, the African Charter on Human and People's Rights, the Convention on the Rights of the Child and its Additional Protocol on the Involvement of Children in Armed Conflict. However, the significance of the fact that the occupied state, the DRC, was also

Republic of the Congo v Uganda (n 64); An Advisory Opinion is merely advisory and decisions of the ICJ are binding on the parties only. However both decisions and opinions are influential.

[164] *Case Concerning Armed Activities on the Territory of the Congo: Democratic Republic of the Congo v Uganda* (n 64),[178–179].

[165] In holding that jurisdiction extended to Uganda as occupants the Court cited paragraphs 107–113 of the Court's *Advisory Opinion concerning the Legal Consequences of the Construction of a Wall in Occupied Palestinian Territory* (n 63). The analysis in these paragraphs is fairly brief. On the ICCPR the Court cited the constant practice of the Human Rights Committee which 'has found the Covenant applicable where the State exercises its jurisdiction on foreign territory' and then referred to several reports by the Committee which conclude that the ICCPR is applicable in the occupied territories, citing 'the long standing presence' of Israel in the territories and 'the exercise of effective jurisdiction by Israeli security forces therein.' With regard to the ICESCR, which contains no provisions on jurisdiction, the Court cited the Committee's view 'that the State party's obligations under the Covenant apply to all territories under its effective control.' With regard to the Covenant on the Rights of the Child, the Court noted that Article 2 provides that 'State Parties shall respect and ensure the rights set forth... in the Convention to each child within their jurisdiction', hence '[t]hat Convention is therefore applicable in the Occupied Palestinian Territories.' The approach taken by the Court appears to have been that occupation necessarily encompasses jurisdiction under all human rights treaties to which the occupant is party. The effective control criterion articulated by the Human Rights Committee and the ECtHR is barely referred to, except in the case of the ICESCR and the reason for its inclusion there was presumably the absence of any reference to jurisdiction in the Convention.

party to these Conventions was not discussed at all. The mere listing of these treaties as applicable, without analysis, suggests that, in the Court's view, occupation constitutes jurisdiction for the purposes of human rights law.

The Court's finding that Article 43 requires occupants to apply the full range of rights under human rights law treaties to which it is a party (except where a derogation is in place, or where the treaty provides for the curtailing of a non-derogable right under certain circumstances and those circumstances are met) has important implications for the protection of civilians. The obligations of an occupant under human rights law are not limited to responsibility for violations committed by its own agents. However, the burden of a positive obligation must be a reasonable one. In *Osman v United Kingdom* the ECtHR stressed that where there is an allegation that the authorities have violated their positive obligation to protect the right to life it must be established:

> that the authorities knew or ought to have known at the time of the existence of a real and immediate risk to the life of an identified individual or individuals from the criminal acts of a third party and that they failed to take measures within the scope of their powers which, judged reasonably, might have been expected to avoid that risk.[166]

In the case of *Mahmout Kaya v Turkey*, the ECtHR reiterated that the duty to protect did not extend to the population as a whole:

> the positive obligation must be interpreted in a way which does not impose an impossible or disproportionate burden on the authorities. Accordingly, not every claimed risk to life can entail for the authorities a Convention requirement to take operational measures to prevent that risk from materialising. For a positive obligation to arise, it must be established that the authorities knew or ought to have known at the time of the existence of a real and immediate risk to the life of an identified individual or individuals from the criminal acts of a third party and that they failed to take measures within the scope of their powers which, judged reasonably, might have been expected to avoid that risk.[167]

However, in the *Congo* case, the ICJ, in analyzing the equivalent obligations under the ICCPR and other human rights treaties to which Uganda is party, adopted a much broader approach. The Court found by sixteen votes to one that Uganda had violated its obligations under human rights law and IHL both by direct acts 'as well as by its failure, as an occupying Power, to take measures to respect and ensure respect for human rights and IHL, in the Ituri district,'[168] on the grounds that Ugandan forces had failed to take action to put an end to violence that had resulted in some 100,000 deaths and the displacement of some 500,000 people in particular that 'UPDF [Uganda Peoples Defence Force] forces stood by during the killings and failed to protect the civilians.'[169] It would be

[166] *Osman v United Kingdom*, 23452/94 [1998] ECHR 101 (28 October 1998), [116].

[167] *Mahmout Kaya v Turkey*, 22535/93 [2000] ECHR 129 (28 March 2000), [86].

[168] *Case Concerning Armed Activities on the Territory of the Congo: Democratic Republic of the Congo v Uganda* (n 64), [345].

[169] ibid [209].

difficult to argue that those 100,000 deaths were all identified individuals known to be specifically at risk. The key factors in the Court's analysis seem to have been that Uganda was in occupation; atrocities were happening on a large scale; Ugandan forces did nothing about it; which was a violation of its obligations as an occupant to secure the human rights of the population.

5. Accountability for Human Rights Abuses

Although the *travaux préparatoires* to the ICCPR and the principal regional human rights treaties clearly show that the drafters intended human rights law to continue to be applicable in armed conflict, the scope of extra-territorial jurisdiction was considered limited. The drafters of the Geneva Conventions do not appear to have considered human rights law relevant to armed conflict. However, the applicability of human rights treaties is not determined by IHL. Moreover, in the late 1960s and the 1970s there was considerable pressure to improve the human rights protections of people caught up in conflict, which saw the start of a sustained expansion of the circumstances in which human rights law is recognized as applicable.

The ICRC, in its 2005 study on Customary International Humanitarian Law, states that it is now a principle of customary law that human rights law 'applies at all times' even in an armed conflict, provided that there is jurisdiction.[170] The case law of international and regional courts and treaty bodies now largely supports the view that a State has an obligation to respect and ensure international human rights laws where it is in control of territory even if that territory is outside its State borders; and also in a numbered of recognized exceptions to the territorial principle of jurisdiction, generally characterized by localized State control or authority, for example an embassy. Some human rights conventions, such as the ICCPR and the ACHR, and also the American Declaration on the Rights of Man, may also have extra-territorial effect where the actions of a State agent bring persons or property under their direct control. It is unclear whether this ground of jurisdiction applies to the ECHR: *Banković*, a Grand Chamber decision concerning the bombing of a television station, did not endorse this approach but the later *Issa* case, concerning the mutilation and murder of shepherds, suggests that jurisdiction may apply in these circumstances.

The decisions of the ICJ in its Advisory Opinion on the *Israeli Barrier* and its judgment in the *Congo* case; and judgments of the ECtHR in the Chechnya cases; suggest that obligations under human rights law are not easily displaced by military exigencies, or by IHL. There is also some indication that certain principles drawn from IHL, such as the principle of distinction, are to be regarded as

[170] J-M Henckaerts and L Doswald-Beck, *Customary International Humanitarian Law* (n 42), 299.

applicable in conflict situations that fall short of full scale 'armed conflict.' These developments suggest that the 'convergence' theory with regard to the relationship between IHL and international human rights law, articulated by commentators such as Theodor Meron and Walter Kälin, is gaining some ground.[171]

The 'convergence' approach is not without problems: Jean Pictet was particularly concerned that the two regimes should remain distinct on the grounds that too close a relationship with human rights law would risk the politicization of IHL and undermine the effectiveness of the ICRC as a monitoring body. However, since the 1990s troops have frequently found themselves engaged in operations in which it is difficult to determine whether or not there is an 'armed conflict' as such. An approach that emphasizes the continuing relevance of human rights law, and of some aspects of IHL, in conflict situations that do not formally amount to armed conflict, provides for a much more nuanced approach to the conduct of these types of operations. Kenneth Watkin, writing in the American Journal of International Law in 2004, has observed that:

> the nature and scale of violence in interstate conflict has had a distinct impact on how force is controlled under international humanitarian law. In contrast, the internal use of force is normally dealt with under a human rights paradigm. Notwithstanding these differences, both normative regimes may be brought into play simultaneously because of the nature of the violence that may be encountered during armed conflict. Such interface may occur during internal armed conflict and states of emergency, belligerent occupation, and global terrorism.
>
> ... the unique interface between these two normative frameworks that challenges the traditional idea that the use of force in armed conflict is governed exclusively by international humanitarian law ... the issue should not be the exclusive application of either framework but, rather, that appropriate principles should be applied to ensure that there are no gaps in humanitarian protection.[172]

These developments suggest that an approach that combines elements from both IHL and human rights law may provide a viable means of regulating the conduct of forces that might prove especially valuable in the context of complex military operations that have a multiplicity of objectives but also have a significant humanitarian component.

In general human rights treaties make no distinction, as regards their applicability, between positive obligations to protect human rights and prohibitions on abuse by a State party's own agents. The burden of positive obligations is limited to what is reasonable, but the criteria for what is reasonably expected in the context of serious abuses of human rights on a large-scale may be higher than in

[171] T Meron, *Human Rights in Internal Strife: Their International Protection* (n 117), 28; W Kälin, *Human Rights in Times of Occupation: The Case of Kuwait* (n 34), 26, 79; A Reinisch, 'Developing Human Rights and Humanitarian Law Accountability of the Security Council for the Imposition of Economic Sanctions', 95 AJIL, 851, 860.

[172] K Watkin, 'Controlling the Use of Force: A Role for Human Rights Norms in Contemporary Armed Conflict', 98 AJIL, 1, 1–2.

the case of a domestic murder. The ECtHR cases of *Osman v United Kingdom* and *Mahmout v Kaya*, in discussing the extent of positive obligations with regard to the right to life under the ECHR, have held that breach of the obligation to secure the right to life only arises where the authorities knew or ought to have known at the time of the existence of a real and immediate risk to the life of an identified individual or individuals from the criminal acts of a third party and that they failed to take measures within the scope of their powers which, judged reasonably, might have been expected to avoid that risk.[173] However, the ICJ in the *Congo* case held that Uganda was in violation of its obligations as an occupant under both IHL and human rights law for standing by during killings and failing to take action to protect the local population from violence that resulted in 100,000 deaths and the displacement of 500,000 people.[174]

The potential for positive obligations under human rights law has far reaching implications for troops, even where they are not in occupation of territory. For example, it seems at least plausible that military camps belonging to a State's forces would fall within the 'narrowly limited exception' to the territorial limits of jurisdiction recognized in *Banković* and exemplified by embassies, consulates, vessels, aircraft and prisons.[175] If that is the case, it could be argued that the conduct of Belgian troops immediately prior to the massacre in 1994 of 2000 Rwandans that had sought refuge at their camp at Kicukiro, should be assessed in the light of the human rights treaties to which Belgium is party. The ROE under which the force was operating stated that certain 'ethnically or politically motivated criminal acts' would 'morally and legally require UNAMIR (the UN Mission to Rwanda) to use all available means to halt them.'[176] Despite this, when the Belgian forces requested permission to withdraw from the camp they failed to inform their commanding officer of the presence of 2000 refugees in the camp and the fact that the Interhamwe were waiting outside with their machetes.[177]

Similarly it could be argued that the compliance of the Dutchbat contingent of the UN Protection Force in the 'evacuation' of the refugees sheltering in its military camp at Potocari prior to their massacre by Serb forces, should be assessed in the light of human rights treaties to which the Netherlands was party. In 2001 the Human Rights Committee expressed its concern at the Netherlands failure to include the events at Srebrenica in its Article 40 reports. The Committee stressed that the gravity of the crimes committed there placed a heavy responsibility on the State to examine issues relating to its obligation to ensure the right

[173] *Osman v United Kingdom* (n 166), [116] *Mahmout Kaya v Turkey* (n 167), [86].

[174] *Case Concerning Armed Activities on the Territory of the Congo: Democratic Republic of the Congo v Uganda* (n 64), [209], [345].

[175] *Banković v Belgium and 16 Other Contracting States* (n 11) [73]; *The Queen on the application of Mazin Jumaa Gatteh Al-Skeini and others v Secretary of State for Defence* [2004] EWHC 2911 (Admin), [286–287].

[176] *Report of the Independent Inquiry into the Actions of the United Nations during the 1994 Genocide in Rwanda* (United Nations New York 15th December 1999) 5.

[177] R Dallaire, *Shake Hands with the* Devil (Arrow Press London 2004), 290.

to life (under Articles 2 and 6 of the Covenant) in an expeditious and comprehensive manner and if appropriate take criminal or disciplinary action.[178] There is ample, though not unchallenged, evidence that Dutchbat 'knew or ought to have known at the time of the existence of a real and immediate risk' to the lives of the men in the camp,[179] and there are credible allegations that the force 'failed to take measures within the scope of their powers which, judged reasonably, might have been expected to avoid that risk.'[180] Corwin, the chief UN political officer in Bosnia, wrote in his diary on 12 July 1995:

> Not a single one of us believes that the Moslem population of Srebrenica will be safe. The pattern is all too familiar, and it is a pattern used by Croats and Moslems as well. The draft-age men will be separated from their families, then tortured, imprisoned, executed. Women will be raped. Mass graves will be hurriedly dug to hide the evidence.[181]

One Dutch soldier claims that he took photographs of Dutch troops assisting in the separation of the men from the women.[182] No derogations are permitted in respect of the right to life under any human rights treaty, with the exception of

[178] Concluding Observations of the Human Rights Committee: Netherlands 27/08/2001. CCPR/CO/72/NET 27 August 2001.

[179] P Corwin, *Dubious Mandate: A Memoir of the UN in Bosnia, Summer 1995* (Duke University Press Durham 1999), 212; General Assembly report A/54/549,15 November 1999, Report of the Secretary-General pursuant to General Assembly resolution 53/55, *The fall of Srebrenica*, [341–343]; The testimony of Major Franken in the Krstic trial confirms that the force knew that a massacre was about to take place: Major Franken's testimony, T. 2008–2009: *Krstic*, ICTY IT-98-33-T, Judgement (2/8/2001). However the 'Summary for the Press' of the report 'Srebrenica—a 'Safe' Area: Reconstruction, Background and Consequences of the Fall of a Safe Area', 10 April 2002 undertaken by the Netherlands Institute for War Documentation, states that 'Deputy Dutchbat commander Franken ... *could not* have suspected that this would lead to the mass slaughter of these and many other men who fell into the hands of the Bosnian Serbs during their flight to Tuzla.'[11] <http://www.srebrenica.nl/en/a_index.htm>.

[180] In *Mothers of Srebrenica Foundation et al v The State of the Netherlands and the United Nations*, the plaintiffs argued, inter alia, that Dutchbat's failure to take measures that might reasonably be expected of it to protect the inhabitants of the enclave; its failure to report war crimes although 'such reporting could have saved the lives of many'; its attitude towards the provision of air support; and the absence of a defence and evacuation plan, violated the plaintiffs right to life under Article 2 of the ECHR and Article 6 of the ICCPR. *Mothers of Srebrenica Foundation et al v The State of the Netherlands and the United Nations* LJN: BJD6796 *Rechtbank 's-Gravenhage*, 295247/ HA ZA 07–2973 Hearing 18 June 2008, Writ of Summons, [413–414] Judgment against the Netherlands is expected later in the year. The Court held that it had no jurisdiction to hear claims against the UN; The Court reached a similar conclusion in two other cases that were brought against the Netherlands on behalf of persons who were sheltering at the Potocari camp, at the time Srebrenica was overrun. Mustafic-Mujic, an electrician working for Dutchbat, was forced out of the camp and killed. Mr Nuhanovic, a translator for Dutchbat, survived, but his family were forced out and killed: *Rechtbank 's-Gravenhage, H. Nuhanovic / Staat der Nederlanden*, rolnummer 2006/1671; *Rechtbank 's-Gravenhage, M. Mustafic-Mujic, D. Mustafic en A. Mustafic / Staat der Nederlanden*, rolnummer 2006/1672. Hearing 16 June 2008. Decision 10.9.2008 LJN: BF0181, Rechtbank 's-Gravenhage , 265615 / HA ZA 06–1671.

[181] P Corwin, *Dubious Mandate: A Memoir of the UN in Bosnia, Summer 1995* (Duke University Press Durham 1999), 212.

[182] Major De Ruijter of the Dutch Military Intelligence Service took the film in for development but through some 'very bad luck' it was destroyed. However, the Dutch press noted that the leaked Ministry of Intelligence report stating that the film was 'destroyed' had been signed

the ECHR, which allows for derogation, to the extent strictly necessary in the exigencies of the situation, in respect of deaths arising from lawful acts of war.[183] The massacre at Srebrenica was not a lawful act of war.

However, recent case law of the ECtHR suggests that accountability for violations of the ECHR by UN forces lies with the Security Council alone and not international courts, and possibly not even domestic courts (although this may be different in States that have incorporated the Convention into their domestic law). The ECtHR in *Behrami and Behrami v France* and *Saramati v France, Germany and Norway*[184] refused to hear claims brought by civilians against the Kosovo Force (KFOR) for alleged human rights violations. *Behrami and Behrami* concerned the death of a young boy, and disfiguration and blinding of his brother, by landmines dropped by NATO; it was argued that KFOR knew that the mines were there but failed to defuse them, or to take any steps to close off the area. The case was brought against France because the incident occurred in the area run by French KFOR forces. *Saramati* concerned the detention of Mr Saramati by KFOR for over a year under the orders of a Norwegian KFOR commander, and subsequently a French one; he was then convicted of attempted murder but nine months later his conviction was quashed and the case sent for retrial.

The Court did not examine the issue of jurisdiction but denied admissibility in both cases on two grounds. The first was that KFOR was acting under 'lawfully delegated Chapter VII powers of the UNSC so that the impugned action was, in principle, "attributable" to the UN'[185] and not to troop contributing nations. The Court's second ground for declaring the case inadmissible was that the 'Convention cannot be interpreted in a manner which would subject the acts and omissions of Contracting Parties which are covered by UNSC Resolutions and occur prior to or in the course of such missions, to the scrutiny of the Court.'[186] To do so:

> would be to interfere with the fulfilment of the UN's key mission in this field, . . . with the effective conduct of its operations. It would also be tantamount to imposing conditions on the implementation of a UNSC Resolution which were not provided for in the text of the Resolution itself.[187]

The Court stated that 'the Convention has to be interpreted in the light of . . . two complementary provisions of the Charter, articles 25 and 103, as interpreted by the International Court of Justice.'[188] Under Article 25 the 'Member States of the United Nations agree to accept and carry out the decisions of the Security

on 25 July 1995: one day before the film was developed. 07/12/02 'Just Bad Luck Film Roll Was Destroyed' <http://www.nisnews.nl/dossiers/srebrenica/srebrenica.htm>.

[183] ECHR (n 9), Article 15.

[184] European Court of Human Rights *Behrami and Behrami v France* and *Saramati v France, Germany and Norway* Application nos. 71412/01 and 78166/01 2 May 2007, [71].

[185] ibid [138–141].

[186] ibid [149].

[187] ibid.

[188] ibid [147].

Council in accordance with the Charter. Article 103 of the Charter, provides that in 'the event of a conflict between the obligations of the Members of the United Nations under the present Charter and their obligations under any other international agreement, their obligations under the present Charter shall prevail.' The case has been followed in the subsequent admissibility decisions of *Dušan Berić and Others v Bosnia and Herzegovina*,[189] *Slavisa Gajic v Germany*[190] and *Kalinić and Bilbija v Bosnia and Herzegovina*.[191]

The relationship between the attribution issue and the immunity issue is not clear. Cases concerning domestic law enacted in order to incorporate a Security Council resolution probably do not attract complete immunity,[192] but it is not clear whether acts that are undertaken under the umbrella of a Chapter VII Security Council resolution but that are not attributable to the UN are always immune from the scrutiny of the Court. On the one hand the *Behrami* and *Saramati* decisions do suggest quite strongly that, as the Court's Annual report for 2007 notes, military 'operations carried out on behalf of the United Nations under Chapter VII of the Charter' have 'complete immunity from jurisdiction.'[193] The reason given by the ECtHR for according immunity to operations authorized by the UN is that even if contributions to the mission are voluntary, they are in the nature of a Charter obligation, or something very close to it, and hence take precedence over any other international obligations. Voluntary 'acts may not have amounted to obligations flowing from membership of the UN but they remained crucial to the effective fulfilment by the UNSC of its Chapter VII mandate and, consequently, by the UN of its imperative peace and security aim.'[194] In the view of the Court it is clear 'that ensuring respect for human rights represents an important contribution to achieving international peace' but:

> the fact remains that the UNSC has primary responsibility, as well as extensive means under Chapter VII, to fulfil this objective, notably through the use of coercive measures. The responsibility of the UNSC in this respect is unique and has evolved as a counterpart to the prohibition, now customary international law, on the unilateral use of force[195]

However, in response to arguments citing *Behrami* and *Saramati* put forward by the Council of Europe, the European Commission and the United Kingdom,

[189] European Court of Human Rights *Dušan Berić and Others v Bosnia and Herzegovina* Application nos. 36357/04, 36360/04, 38346/04, 41705/04, 45190/04, 45578/04, 45579/04, 45580/04, 91/05, 97/05, 100/05, 101/05, 1121/05, 1123/05, 1125/05, 1129/05, 1132/05, 1133/05, 1169/05, 1172/05, 1175/05, 1177/05, 1180/05, 1185/05, 20793/05 and 25496/05, 16 October 2007.

[190] European Court of Human Rights *Slavisa Gajic v Germany* Application no 31446/02, 28 August 2007.

[191] European Court of Human Rights *Kalinić and Bilbija v Bosnia and Herzegovina* Applications nos. 45541/04 and 16587/07, 13 May 2008.

[192] *Bosphorus Hava Yolları Turizm ve Ticaret Anonim Şirketi (Bosphorus Airways) v Ireland* [GC], no 45036/98, ECHR 2005-VI.

[193] European Court of Human Rights, Annual Report 2007, 6.

[194] European Court of Human Rights *Behrami and Behrami v France* and *Saramati v France, Germany and Norway* (n 184), [149].

[195] ibid [148].

in the *Kadi* case the Advocate General for the European Court of Justice[196] 'seriously doubt[ed] that the European Court of Human Rights limits its own jurisdiction' in such an absolute way.[197]

The *Behrami* and *Saramati* decisions and the subsequent cases *Dušan Berić and Others v Bosnia and Herzegovina, Slavisa Gajic v Germany*, and *Dragan Kalinić and Milorad Bilbija v Bosnia and Herzegovina* all heavily stress, in language that implies that the point was critical, that the impugned acts were attributable to the UN and not the States against which the cases were brought. This suggests that acts and omissions that are not attributable to the UN may not attract the same immunity, even if committed or omitted by forces mandated by a Security Council resolution. In the *Behrami* and *Saramati* decisions the Court stated that a 'key question' it had to determine was 'whether the Security Council retained ultimate authority and control so that operational command only was delegated'.[198] In the view of the Court the necessary donation of troops by willing troop contributing nations means that:

[196] *Kadi* concerned the freezing of the applicants' assets pursuant to a decision of the Sanctions Committee established under SC resolution 1267 (1999), which required the freezing of financial resources held by the Taliban abroad. The applicant argued that 'the Community institutions cannot abdicate their responsibility to respect his fundamental rights by taking refuge behind decisions adopted by the Security Council, especially since those decisions themselves fail to respect the right to a fair hearing.' Case T-315/01 *Kadi v Council and Commission* [2005] ECR II-3649, [149] The Court of First Instance held that 'it is not for the Court to review indirectly whether the Security Council's resolutions in question are themselves compatible with fundamental rights as protected by the Community legal order./Nor does it fall to the Court to verify that there has been no error of assessment of the facts and evidence relied on by the Security Council in support of the measures it has taken.... It must thus be concluded that... there is no judicial remedy available to the applicant, the Security Council not having thought it advisable to establish an independent international court responsible for ruling, in law and on the facts, in actions brought against individual decisions taken by the Sanctions Committee.' Ibid, [283–285] The case has been appealed to the European Court of Justice; Similar decisions: Case T-306/01 *Yusuf and Al Barakaat International Foundation v Council of the EU and Commission of the EC* [2005] 3 CMLR 49; Case T-49/04 *Faraj Hassan v Council and Commission* (12 July 2006) on appeal as Case C-399/06 *Hassan v Council and Commission* OJ 2004 C294/30; Case T-253/02 *Chafiq Ayadi v Council* [2006] ECR II-2139.

[197] Case C-402/05 P *Yassin Anbdullah Kadi v Council and Commission*, Opinion of Advocate General Poiares Maduro, 16 January 2008, [34–35], [38] citing *Bosphorus Hava Yolları Turizm ve Ticaret Anonim Şirketi (Bosphorus Airways) v Ireland* [GC], no 45036/98 and paragraph 151 of *Behrami and Saramati*, in which the ECtHR distinguished *Bosphorus*, the Advocate-General interpreted the position of the European Court of Human Rights 'to be that, where, pursuant to the rules of public international law, the impugned acts are attributable to the United Nations, the court has no jurisdiction *ratione personae*, since the United Nations are not a contracting party to the Convention. By contrast, when the authorities of a contracting State have taken procedural steps to implement a Security Council resolution in the domestic legal order, the measures thus taken are attributable to that State and therefore amenable to judicial review under the Convention' He concluded that given that there is no mechanism of judicial control by an independent tribunal at the level of the United Nations, the European Community cannot dispense with proper judicial review proceedings when implementing Security Council resolutions. The Advocate General's opinion is not binding on the Court.

[198] ibid [129], [133].

in practice, those TCNs [troop contributing nations] retain some authority over those troops (for reasons, *inter alia*, of safety, discipline and accountability) and certain obligations in their regard (material provision including uniforms and equipment). NATO's command of operational matters was not therefore intended to be exclusive, but the essential question was whether, despite such TCN involvement, it was 'effective'.[199]

Bearing this in mind it concluded that the issue of mines removal and detention were matters within the effective command of NATO rather than the troop contributing States. Since the Security Council retained ultimate authority and control over NATO the impugned actions were attributable to the UN:

even if the UN itself would accept that there is room for progress in co-operation and command structures between the UNSC, TCNs and contributing international organisations...the Court finds that the UNSC retained ultimate authority and control and that effective command of the relevant operational matters was retained by NATO.

In such circumstances, the Court observes that KFOR was exercising lawfully delegated Chapter VII powers of the UNSC so that the impugned action was, in principle, 'attributable' to the UN.[200]

In *Berić* the Court reiterated that the issue of attribution to the UN was 'key.' The case concerned a challenge to the High Representative's[201] dismissal of the applicants from office without compensation or right of appeal on the grounds that their 'overt and secret complicity of silence,' (among other things) had contributed to the failure to apprehend and deliver to just prosecution a number of persons indicted under Article 19 of the Statute of the ICTY. In July 2006 the Constitutional Court of Bosnia-Herzegovina had found dismissals on those terms unconstitutional but the High Representative had rendered the decision of no effect by declaring that he would view '[a]ny step taken by any institution or authority in Bosnia and Herzegovina in order to establish any domestic mechanism to review' his decisions, as an attempt to undermine the peace agreement. He stated that:

any proceeding instituted before any court in Bosnia and Herzegovina, which challenges or takes issue in any way whatsoever with one or more decisions of the High Representative, shall be declared inadmissible unless the High Representative expressly gives his prior consent.[202]

The applicants appealed to the ECtHR. The Court, in declaring the case inadmissable, stated that:

[199] ibid [138].

[200] ibid [138–141].

[201] Appointed, with the endorsement of Security Council resolution 1301, to oversee implementation of the Dayton Agreement (the Peace Agreement between the Republic of Bosnia and Herzegovina, the Republic of Croatia and the then Federal Republic of Yugoslavia, which came into force on 14 December 1995).

[202] The High Representative's decision of 23 March 2007, cited in *Dušan Berić and Others v Bosnia and Herzegovina* (n 189), [19].

Given that the UNSC had, as required, established a 'threat to international peace and security' within the meaning of Article 39 of the UN Charter, it had the power to authorise an international civil administration in Bosnia and Herzegovina and to delegate the implementation of that measure to specific member States, provided that it retained effective overall control... The key question, therefore, is whether the UNSC, in delegating its powers by UNSC Resolution 1031, retained effective overall control.

The High Representative argued that his office:

had been created by, and he derived his powers from, various international instruments, including legally binding UNSC resolutions, and that his actions could not engage the responsibility of any State. He added that the UNSC had consistently treated his office as an integral part of its efforts, under Chapter VII of the UN Charter, to restore and maintain peace in the region.[203]

The Court similarly concluded that the:

the High Representative was exercising lawfully delegated UNSC Chapter VII powers, so that the impugned action was, in principle, 'attributable' to the UN within the meaning of draft article 3 of the Draft Articles on the Responsibility of International Organisations.[204]

The Court noted that the measures complained of did not require any further procedural steps to be taken by the domestic authorities.[205]

Finally, in the very last paragraph, the Court considered 'whether Bosnia and Herzegovina could nevertheless be held responsible for the impugned acts,' and in answering this question quoted paragraphs 146–149 of the *Behrami* and *Saramati* decision, including the paragraph stating that:

Since operations established by UNSC Resolutions under Chapter VII of the UN Charter are fundamental to the mission of the UN to secure international peace and security and since they rely for their effectiveness on support from member states, the Convention cannot be interpreted in a manner which would subject the acts and omissions of Contracting Parties which are covered by UNSC Resolutions and occur prior to or in the course of such missions, to the scrutiny of the Court.[206]

The argument is couched in absolute terms but it is also clear that the context concerns whether a State could 'nevertheless' be held responsible for acts that the Court found were not legally attributable to it. The attribution analysis is fairly convoluted in most of these cases owing to the very complex command

[203] *Dušan Berić and Others v Bosnia and Herzegovina* (n189), [25].

[204] ibid [28]; Article 3 of the Draft Articles on the Responsibility of International Organisations provides that '(1) every internationally wrongful act of an international organization entails the international responsibility of the international organization, and (2) there is an internationally wrongful act of an international organization when conduct consisting of an action or omission: a. is attributable to the international organization under international law; and b. constitutes a breach of an international obligation of that international organization'.

[205] ibid [29].

[206] *Behrami and Behrami v France* and *Saramati v France, Germany and Norway* (n 184), [149].

and control issues involved, and it is possible that the immunity reasoning was intended to be read in conjunction with the attribution reasoning, rather than as a stand alone issue implying that all acts or omissions undertaken in the course of a mission mandated by the Security Council, even those that are clearly not attributable to the UN, are always inadmissible. This interpretation is supported by paragraph 121 of the *Berhami* and *Saramati* decisions in which the Court, in summarizing its position, stated that:

it has ascertained whether the impugned action of KFOR (detention in *Saramati*) and inaction of UNMIK (failure to de-mine in *Behrami*) could be attributed to the UN: in so doing, it has examined whether there was a Chapter VII framework for KFOR and UNMIK and, if so, whether their impugned action and omission could be attributed, in principle, to the UN...

In so doing, the Court has borne in mind that it is not its role to seek to define authoritatively the meaning of provisions of the UN Charter and other international instruments: it must nevertheless examine whether there was a plausible basis in such instruments for the matters impugned before it.[207]

The relative weights of the attribution and the immunity issues are not much clearer in the *Gajic* decision. The decision concerned a claim by Mr Slavisa Gajic, a citizen of the Republic of Serbia, that he was the owner of an apartment in Prizren, Kosovo, but fled during the 1999 bombing campaign. From 1999 to 2004 the apartment was used by the German KFOR contingent. Mr Gajic had unsuccessfully sought rent from German KFOR and subsequently sought compensation. The Federal Administrative Office of the German armed forces was suspicious of his claim because they had a number of similar claims relating to other apartments in the same building all of which relied on documents signed ostensibly by the same person but using a number of different signatures. The ECtHR stated that the application was premature because Mr Gajic was still awaiting a response to a claim for compensation from the domestic authorities. However, it did briefly reiterate its conclusions in the *Berhami* and *Saramati* decisions:

The Court recalls that, when the responsibility of contributing States for actions or inactions of KFOR is at issue, the question raised is less whether the respondent state exercised extra-territorial jurisdiction in Kosovo, but rather whether this Court is competent to examine under the Convention that State's contribution to the civil and security presences which exercised the relevant control of Kosovo (see *Behrami and Behrami v France and Saramati v France, Germany and Norway* (dec.), nos. 7412/01 and 78166/01, § 71, ECHR 2007-...).

The Court further reiterates that the actions or inactions of KFOR are, in principle, attributable to the UN and that the Court is incompetent *ratione personae* to review the acts of the respondent State carried out on behalf of the UN (see *Behrami and Behrami* and *Saramati*, cited above, §§ 144–152).[208]

[207] ibid [121–122].

[208] European Court of Human Rights *Slavisa Gajic v Germany*, (n 190) 5–6.

Again the attribution and the immunity issue appear to be inter-linked. One possibly important factor, briefly alluded to in the reference to the 'State's contribution to the civil and security presences which exercised the relevant control of Kosovo' is that all three cases concerned events that took place in the context of an international administration mandated by the UN. Thus the question of attribution could be considered to go beyond whether or not the specific acts could be traced to UN responsibility. The existence of an international administration might suggest that attribution in this context encompasses the broader responsibilities arising from the UN's quasi-governmental status as administrator for the whole territory. A similar point was pleaded by Hasan Nuhanovic and Mustafic-Mujic in the District Court of the Hague in their claims against the Netherlands and the UN for failing to protect their relatives, who were sheltering at the Dutchbat camp, from crimes against humanity at Srebrenica. They argued, unsuccessfully, that in contrast to *Berhami* and the other ECHR cases discussed above there was no international administration or international administrative authority in Bosnia-Herzegovina at the time of the Srebrenica genocide. Hence acts and omissions of Dutchbat would not interfere with any legislative or administrative powers of the UN (since it had none) and would not necessarily be attributable to the UN. Therefore it was not necessary for the purposes of Chapter VII of the Charter that Dutchbat's acts and omissions be immune from the Court's scrutiny.[209]

The issue was debated in the House of Lords in *Al Jedda*, which concerned a claim by a Briton, who has been held in administrative detention in Iraq for over three years, that his rights under Article 5 of the ECHR were being violated. The House of Lords in *Al-Skeini*, in finding that the maltreatment of Baha Mousa (also held in a British prison in Iraq), came within the jurisdiction of the Human Rights Act, did not discuss *Behrami* and *Saramati*, which was handed down six weeks prior to the judgment but after hearings had been held. Even had the time period been longer it is hard to see how maltreatment of a prisoner could ever be required under Chapter VII, or any other provision, of the Charter,[210] and it is difficult to imagine counsel for the UK presenting such an argument, notwithstanding the apparent absolute nature of the *Behrami* approach in relation to Chapter VII military operations. However, in *Al Jedda*, in which there was no suggestion that UK troops were involved in torture or murder, the Court held that, following the decision in *Behrami* and *Saramati*, the Chapter VII Security Council resolution authorizing the Multi-National Force (MNF) to 'take all

[209] Rechtbank 's-Gravenhage, H. Nuhanovic / Staat der Nederlanden, rolnummer 2006/1671; Rechtbank 's-Gravenhage, M. Mustafic-Mujic, D. Mustafic en A. Mustafic / Staat der Nederlanden, rolnummer 2006/1672 (I am very grateful to the applicants' solicitors Böhler Franken Koppe Wijngaarten for their assistance.) Decision 10.9.2008; the court rejected the applicants' claims on the basis that they related to responsibilities of the UN and the Court had no jurisdiction to hear claims against the UN: UN LJN: BF0181, Rechtbank 's-Gravenhage, 265615/HA ZA 06-1671.

[210] As noted by Baroness Hale: *R (on the application of Al-Jedda) (FC) (Appellant) v Secretary of State for Defence (Respondent)* [2007] UKHL 58, [123].

necessary measures to contribute to the maintenance of security and stability in Iraq' took precedence over Convention rights.[211] This was so regardless of the fact that the majority of the Court considered that the impugned actions of the UK forces deployed to Iraq were attributable to the UK, rather than to the UN.

The Court stated that there is a strong and 'persuasive body of academic opinion which would treat article 103 as applicable where conduct is authorised by the Security Council as where it is required':[212]

> Otherwise, the Charter would not reach its goal of allowing the SC to take the action it deems most appropriate to deal with threats to the peace–it would force the SC to act either by way of binding measures or by way of recommendations, but would not permit intermediate forms of action. This would deprive the SC of much of the flexibility it is supposed to enjoy. It seems therefore preferable to apply the rule of article 103 to all action under articles 41 and 42 and not only to mandatory measures.[213]

Lord Bingham of Cornwall, Baroness Hale of Richmond, Lord Carswell and Lord Brown of Eaton-under-Heywood held that any infringement of Convention rights must be kept to a minimum and be no greater than is necessary to carry out the State's obligation.[214] Baroness Hale held that Conventions rights are:

> qualified but not displaced. This is an important distinction, insufficiently explored in the all or nothing arguments with which we were presented. We can go no further than the UN has implicitly required us to go in restoring peace and security to a troubled land. The right is qualified only to the extent required or authorised by the resolution. What remains of it thereafter must be observed. This may have both substantive and procedural consequences.
>
> It is not clear to me how far UNSC resolution 1546 went when it authorised the MNF to 'take all necessary measures to contribute to the maintenance of security and stability in Iraq, in accordance with the 56 letters annexed to this resolution expressing, inter alia, the Iraqi request for the continued presence of the multinational force and setting out its tasks' (para 10). The 'broad range of tasks' were listed by Secretary of State Powell as including 'combat operations against members of these groups [seeking to influence Iraq's political future through violence], internment where this is necessary for imperative reasons of security, and the continued search for and securing of weapons that threaten Iraq's security'. At the same time, the Secretary of State made clear the commitment of the forces which made up the MNF to 'act consistently with their obligations under the law of armed conflict, including the Geneva Conventions'.

[211] *Al Jedda* concerned a claim by an Iraqi/UK national that his prolonged detention by UK forces in Iraq, without being charged and with no prospect of a trial in the foreseeable future, violated his rights under the ECHR: *R (on the application of Al-Jedda) (FC) (Appellant) v Secretary of State for Defence (Respondent)* (n 210).

[212] ibid [33] Lord Bingham.

[213] JA Frowein and N Krisch in Simma (ed), *The Charter of the United Nations: A Commentary* (2nd edn, 2002), 729 cited in *R (on the application of Al-Jedda) (FC) (Appellant) v Secretary of State for Defence (Respondent)* (n 210), [33].

[214] *R (on the application of Al-Jedda) (FC) (Appellant) v Secretary of State for Defence (Respondent)* (n 210), [39], [126], [136]; Lord Brown agreed with all that Lord Bingham said on the issue [156].

...We have been concerned at a more abstract level with attribution to or authorisation by the United Nations. We have devoted little attention to the precise scope of the authorisation. There must still be room for argument about what precisely is covered by the resolution and whether it applies on the facts of this case. Quite how that is to be done remains for decision in the other proceedings.[215]

Lord Rodger of Earlsferry was the only judge to hold that, because Mr Al Jedda's detention was pursuant to a Chapter VII resolution, the infringement of rights under Article 5 of the ECHR were not reviewable in the English courts at all. Rather:

Mr Al-Jedda must find his protection from arbitrary detention in the commitment, given by Mr Powell to the Security Council, that members of the MNF would at all times act consistently with their obligations under the law of armed conflict, including the Geneva Conventions. It is for the Security Council, exerting its ultimate authority and exercising its ultimate right of control, to ensure that this commitment is fulfilled.[216]

However:

The Security Council will always be concerned, of course, to avoid the danger that a force, though nominally acting on behalf of the Council, is truly just made up of the forces of member states pursuing their own ends by military means in contravention of both article 2(4) of the Charter and the ius contra bellum of modern international law. Hence the insertion into the Resolutions, first, of a clear mandate for the force, of an indication of the date when the mandate will expire, of a mechanism for reports to be made to the Council and, finally, of an indication that the Council will remain seised of the matter. Again, the need for all these matters to be spelled out will be well known to the experts who draft the Resolutions.[217]

Lord Rodger's confidence in the Security Council's willingness and ability to ensure the highest of motivations by States voting for resolutions, or contributing troops to UN missions, is probably misplaced. The UN is a highly politicized body and it would be impossible to exclude self-interest from the decision-making process. The desirability of clear mandates is well known but not so well implemented; consensus is often regarded as more important. David Pannick QC has argued that:

UN resolutions should be understood to oblige states to act in breach of international human rights standards, and so override the convention, only if this is made unequivocally clear in the text of the relevant resolutions. In the absence of such an express statement, a court should infer that the UN must have intended to promote, rather than

[215] ibid [126–129].

[216] ibid [113] Lord Rodger was also the only judge to hold that the impugned acts were attributable to the UN (although Lord Brown stated that he found Lord Rodger's reasoning sufficiently persuasive to cause him to doubt the correctness of his own conclusion and indicated that he might change his mind.) [105], [155].

[217] ibid [91].

frustrate, human rights norms, themselves a vital element of international law, and binding on the Security Council itself.[218]

The majority view in *Al Jedda* that any infringement of Convention rights must be kept to the minimum necessary seems close to this approach; but this view does not fit easily with the *Behrami* decision. In that case the dead and injured children's father was challenging a failure to take steps to prevent an area known to be full of landmines (laid by NATO, which forms the major part of KFOR) from being accessed by children (during a post conflict period in which KFOR and UNMIK had responsibility under resolution 1244 for security, including for mine-clearance). How could Member States' obligations under the Charter require them not to clear landmines nor investigate failure to do so? The District Court of the Hague in its interim judgement in *Mothers of Srebrenica Foundation et al v The State of the Netherlands and the United Nations*, a case brought by relatives of those killed at Srebrenica, interpreted *Behrami* and *Saramati* to mean that States 'cannot... be held liable for the actions of national troops they made available for international peace-keeping missions.'[219] The respondents in *Berhami* and *Saramati* argued that many States would be reluctant to contribute troops to UN operations if they thought there might be a risk of holding them accountable under human rights law.[220] The reluctance of contributing States to allow gross disregard for the welfare of the local community to be subject to the scrutiny of a human rights court, is hardly conducive to maintaining a good relationship with that community.

Although KFOR is immune from the scrutiny of local courts, and from that of the ECtHR, it is subject to UK domestic law by agreement; such agreements are standard practice in peacekeeping Status of Forces Agreements.[221] In *Bici and another v Ministry of Defence*,[222] the first successful high court damages claim by civilians injured by UK peacekeeping forces abroad, two Kosovan civilians won cases for negligence and trespass to the person. On July 2 1999, British soldiers shot at their car after the driver failed to obey instructions to stop. Two people were killed, and one of the applicants was shot in the jaw. An investigation by the Royal Military Police had cleared the soldiers of wrongdoing but Mr Justice Elias

[218] David Pannick, QC and Fellow of All Souls College, Oxford, 'In Basra as in Basildon—subject to the rule of law', The Times, 30 October 2007.

[219] *Mothers of Srebrenica Foundation et al v The State of the Netherlands and the United Nations* LJN: BJD6796 *Rechtbank 's-Gravenhage*,295247/ HA ZA 07–2973 Judgment in the incidental proceedings 10 July 2008, [5.16].

[220] European Court of Human Rights *Behrami and Behrami v France* and *Saramati v France, Germany and Norway* (n 184) *The German Government's written submissions*, [108].

[221] The ECHR is not part of the UK's domestic law, but under the Human Rights Act Convention rights can be enforced if they would be enforceable at Strasbourg. *R (on the application of Al-Jedda) (FC) (Appellant) v Secretary of State for Defence (Respondent)* [2007] UKHL 58, [51–56].

[222] *Bici and another v Ministry of Defence* [2004] All ER (D) 137 (Apr), [2004] EWHC 786 (QB).

dismissed arguments from the Ministry of Defence that the soldiers were acting in self-defence or that they were covered by 'combat immunity.' He rejected the self-defence argument because the civilians were shot at when their car was driving away from the soldiers and therefore they were not posing any threat to them. He recognized that 'very exceptionally'[223] the basic liberties of the citizen may have to give way to vital interests of state. When an attack is imminent, the citizen may be an unfortunate victim of the conflict, whether as a result of enemy action or friendly fire or precautionary action:

> However in relying upon the doctrine [of combat immunity], the defendants have to demonstrate that the defence would be available in similar circumstances if the events had taken place on British soil in relation to a British citizen. No special principles apply because the injured claimant is a citizen of a foreign state.[224]

Other than the embarrassment of possibly having to appear before an international body, is it that much more of a burden for contributing States to be held accountable for human rights violations, as for violations in tort?

One difference between liability under tort and under the ECHR is that under the ECHR evidence of a potentially unlawful killing requires the State to undertake an independent investigation.[225] Independent investigations are expensive and time-consuming; but the willingness to undertake them where there is sufficient evidence of deliberate abuse, or of negligence towards the local population, may contribute to the 'perceived legitimacy' of peacekeeping missions. In 2007, Human Rights Watch was highly critical of the UN's poor standard of investigation into alleged human rights abuses by peacekeepers in the DRC, which had been exposed both by Human Rights Watch and by the BBC.[226] Similarly in the Netherlands there was intense criticism of the inadequate 'in-house' investigation by the Department of Defence into allegations of serious abuses of the human rights of the Muslim population in Srebrenica.[227]

Some objections to UN accountability for human rights are similar to those raised in regard to the applicability of IHL to the UN, and have focused on the fact that the UN is not a party to any human rights treaties and since it is not a State it cannot become a party. Conversely it has been argued that a commitment to the promotion of human rights is contained in the Charter. Moreover, most of the major international human rights treaties have been drafted by UN committees. Nigel White argues that when administering territory the UN acts as 'the legal person of the state, while not losing its own legal personality as an IGO' thus 'while it is possible to argue that human rights law applies to the UN when acting

[223] ibid [90].

[224] ibid [90].

[225] *The Queen on the application of Mazin Jumaa Gatteh Al-Skeini and others v Secretary of State for Defence* [2004] EWHC 2911 (Admin).

[226] Human Rights Watch, Letter to Jean-Marie Guéhenno, UN Under-Secretary-General for Peacekeeping Operations, 23 July 2007.

[227] This is discussed in Chapter 2, at footnote 24 and in the accompanying text.

as an IGO, it clearly applies when in the ITA context as it is, in effect, acting as a state.'[228]

In contrast to the ECtHR, the Human Rights Committee has repeatedly affirmed its jurisdiction over UN forces; for example it has held that the ICCPR was applicable to Belgian forces deployed to UNOSOM II by virtue of the fact that they had de facto control over parts of Somalia[229] and also to Dutch forces deployed to UNPROFOR conduct at the time of the fall of Srebrenica.[230] The Committee confirmed the applicability of the Convention to peacekeepers in its General Comment No 31, of 29th March 2004 in which it stated that the Covenant was applicable to 'forces constituting a national contingent of a State party assigned to a national peace-keeping or peace-enforcement operation.'[231] The Committee has also stated that where the UN exercises executive power over territory it is directly bound by human rights law. Serbia argued, when it presented its 2006 Article 40 report, that it was not able to report on matters within Kosovo. The Committee then requested a report from the UN Mission in Kosovo (UNMIK), which reluctantly complied.[232] In its Concluding Observations the Committee made it clear that it considered that where the UN takes over the administration of a State, it is bound by the human rights treaties to which that State is a party:

The Committee notes that certain problems resulting from the role of UNMIK as an interim administration and, at the same time, a United Nations body whose staff members enjoy privileges and immunities, the gradual transfer of competencies from UNMIK to the Provisional Institutions of Self-Government (PISG), the existence of Serbian parallel court and administrative structures in some parts of Kosovo, and the uncertainty about the future status of Kosovo raise questions of accountability and impede the implementation of the Covenant in Kosovo. However, the Committee recalls general comment No. 26 (1977) on continuity of obligations which states that the rights guaranteed under the Covenant belong to the people living in the territory of a State party, and that once the people are accorded the protection of the rights under the Covenant, such protection devolves with territory and continues to belong to them, notwithstanding changes in the

[228] N White, 'Towards a Strategy for Human Rights Protection in Post-conflict Situations', in N White and D Klaasen (eds), *The UN, Human Rights and Post conflict Situations* Manchester University Press Manchester (2005), 463, 463.

[229] Concluding Observations of the Human Rights Committee: Belgium 19.11 1998, UN Doc CCPR/C/79/Add.99 [14]; Concluding Observations of the Human Rights Committee: Belgium 12.08.2004 UN Doc CCPR/C/81/BEL [10].

[230] Concluding observations of the Human Rights Committee: Netherlands. 27/08/2001. CCPR/CO/72/NET 27 August 2001.

[231] General Comment No 31, 'Nature of the General Legal Obligation Imposed on States Parties to the Covenant', UN Doc CCPR/C/2/1/Rev.1/Add.13, 26 May 2004, [10]; The ECtHR, and the Inter-American Commission on Human Rights have adopted similar approaches: *Loizidou v Turkey* (n 61); *Cyprus v Turkey* (n 61); Inter-American Commission on Human Rights, *Coard et Al v United States* (n 61); Inter-American Commission on Human Rights, *Alejandre and Others v Cuba*, Report No (n 61).

[232] Discussion with Walter Kälin, former Human Rights Committee member (Bern 1 September 2008).

administration of that territory. The protection and promotion of human rights is one of the main responsibilities conferred on UNMIK under Security Council resolution 1244 (1999). Moreover, as part of the applicable law in Kosovo and of the Constitutional Framework for the Provisional Institutions of Self-Government, the Covenant is binding on PISG. It follows that UNMIK, as well as PISG, or any future administration in Kosovo, are bound to respect and to ensure to all individuals within the territory of Kosovo and subject to their jurisdiction the rights recognized in the Covenant.[233]

6. Conclusion

Thus the jurisprudence of the ICJ and of regional human rights courts; the observations and comments of UN human rights committee bodies; and the statements of the ICRC; all support the view that human rights law is applicable during armed conflict and that jurisdiction may apply extra-territorially where a contracting party is in de facto control of an area and in certain recognized exceptions to the territorial principle of jurisdiction. Jurisdiction may also extend to situations where a State brings an individual under their control, typically by detaining them. The Human Rights Committee has held that the UN is bound by human rights law wherever it takes over the administration of territory. However, the ECtHR has made it clear that forces deployed pursuant to a Chapter VII Security Council resolution are immune from scrutiny in its Court. The UK House of Lords has taken a similar view with regard to British forces' liability under the ECHR (with the exception of cases involving maltreatment in British-run prisons). The ECHR is not part of British domestic law. In States that are monist, or that have incorporated human rights treaties into their domestic law, it is possible that UN forces may be held accountable under human rights law (including the ECHR) before domestic courts provided that the impugned act or omission is attributable to the State rather than the UN. The domestic law of the contributing State generally applies to UN forces through Status of Forces agreements. The Human Rights Committee does not exempt UN peacekeepers from its scrutiny. Peacekeepers deployed without a Security Council resolution may be held accountable for violations of their human rights obligations before international and domestic courts, including before the ECtHR.

One possible approach to minimizing differences in the degrees of accountability for human rights law violations between different contingents would be to insert an express requirement of compliance with UN human rights treaties and the human rights treaties to which the host State is party, in situations where contributing States would have jurisdiction, into all Status of Forces

[233] Consideration of Reports submitted by State Parties under Article 40 of the Covenant: Concluding Observations of the Human Rights Committee, Kosovo (Serbia) CCPR/C/UNK/CO/1 14 August 2006, [4].

Agreements between the UN and the host State and also into the Memoranda of Understanding between troop contributing States and the UN.[234] The lack of clarity regarding the UN's human rights obligations could also be reduced be means of protocols to the principle human rights treaties through which the UN would undertake to submit reports to the monitoring body in situations where it is exercising executive authority over territory, as has been the case in Kosovo and East Timor. Conceivably such an undertaking could include a right of individual petition.[235] Whilst the UN and many troop contributing States may be nervous of any such commitment, their concerns might mitigated by the benefits to the local population, and as a result to the perceived legitimacy of the mission, to the standing of the United Nations, and to the morale of troops. Soldiers are human; if they have to stand by and watch massacres, murders, mutilations and rapes, that experience will stay with them for the rest of their lives. Most soldiers would probably prefer to work for an organization that is efficient and takes its responsibilities towards the local community seriously. How is a soldier likely to feel when he hears that children have been blown up by his own force's (or an allied force's) landmines because no-one thought to clear or close the area? Sex with a girl who may have been trafficked might seem relatively harmless in such a context; but how is the local community supposed to feel about forces that leave landmines lying about and spend their time with trafficked girls?[236] The perceived legitimacy of the mission and the maintenance of the morale of troops are fundamental to the success of any mission, regardless of the nature of the mission's objective. It is indisputable that soldiers are frequently courageous and committed; it is likely that most would prefer to be part of a force that expects that of them.

Unfortunately it is also human nature to behave badly, or at the very least with a low commitment take it or leave it attitude, if that is what is expected of you. Since it is accepted that the 'the real or actual success' of peacekeeping missions 'is related to the human security of the local populace,'[237] a commitment

[234] R Murphy, *UN Peacekeeping in Lebanon, Somalia and Kosovo* (Cambridge University Press Cambridge 2007), 238.

[235] Suggestion made by Françoise Hampson in the course of a seminar on 'Recent Developments Regarding the Relationship between International Humanitarian Law and Human Rights Law' (Geneva Academy of International Humanitarian Law and Human Rights Geneva August 30, 2008).

[236] Amnesty International reported in 2004 that it was 'extremely concerned that the UN administration in Kosovo has effectively allowed the development of a flourishing industry dependent on the exploitation of trafficked women. Although the Kosovo sex-industry now services both local and international men, it is clear that it initially grew out of post-conflict militarization and the presence of a highly-paid international military and civilian community./The organization also considers that UNMIK—in failing to prosecute international personnel suspected of involvement in trafficking, or of knowingly using the services of trafficked women—has created a climate of impunity for abuses and violations against trafficked women': Amnesty International, 'So does that mean I have rights? Protecting the rights of women and girls trafficked for forced prostitution in Kosovo.' EUR700102004, 6 May 2004, ch 6.

[237] Ministry of Defence UK, Development, Concepts and Doctrine Centre, *Draft UK National Doctrine that will replace JWP 3–50 The Military Contribution to Peace Support Operations* (MOD Shrivenham 16 April 2008), [0113].

to protecting human security and human rights should be made a focal point of UN decision-making in relation to the deployment of troops and should be clearly provided for in all mandates. Respect for human rights and protection of human rights should be core aspects of peacekeepers' training and Member States should be held accountable for compliance. It hardly seems appropriate that States deploying forces unilaterally or through regional organizations, without Security Council authorization, should be bound by human rights law (if the impugned acts or omissions fall within the jurisdiction of the States involved) but that as soon as a Security Council mandate is obtained the force is effectively immune from scrutiny.

4

The Applicability of Occupation Law to Peacekeeping and other Multi-national Operations

1. Introduction

International law recognizes no relationship of a general nature between the inhabitants of territory in which a foreign military forces is deployed, and the State or organization that has deployed the force, although, as discussed in Chapters 2 and 3, the State or organization concerned may nevertheless have obligations towards the local population under IHL and international human rights law. However, where a State is in occupation of territory outside its own borders as a result of armed conflict, there is an extensive body of law governing the relationship between the occupant and the people of the occupied territory, focussed on Geneva Convention IV Relative to the Protection of Civilians in Time of War, 1949 (Geneva Convention IV).[1] This chapter explores the extent to which this body of occupation law applies to peacekeeping and other multi-national operations that differ from belligerent occupation as traditionally conceived.

There are many cases where multi-national forces have intervened in armed conflicts and have thus come into contact with the inhabitants of the territory in which the operation takes place and acquired some kind of administrative role akin to that of occupation. Some of these operations have been authorized by the UN: others have been carried out by States acting without UN authorization, although the States involved have usually argued that the action they have taken was nevertheless in support of, or was supported by, Security Council resolutions. In the latter cases the Security Council has, on several occasions, subsequently mandated the continuance of an operation that initially had no UN authorization.

[1] Regulations annexed to Hague Convention IV Respecting the Laws and Customs of War on Land, (Hague Regulations) (signed at The Hague, 18 Oct 1907, came into force 26 January 1910) UKTS 9 (1910) Cd. 5030; Geneva Convention IV Relative to the Protection of Civilians in Time of War, 75 UNTS 287 (adopted Geneva, 12 Aug 1949, came into force 21 October 1950); Protocol Additional to the Geneva Conventions of 12 August 1949, and relating to the Protection of Victims of International Armed Conflicts, 1977 (Protocol 1) (adopted 8 June 1977, entered into force 7 December 1978) 1125 UNTS 3.

International bodies have been hesitant to use the term 'occupation.' particularly where there has been a strong humanitarian component to the operation. This is partly because there are genuine differences between these operations and the kind of occupations to which Geneva Convention IV was intended to apply, and partly because of the negative connotations associated with occupation.

One key feature of administrations adopted under some form of international banner is their highly political character. International administrations have been forced to engage with political processes leading to the independence or autonomy of the territories concerned, or to a new or restored form of government, and meanwhile to make decisions relating to a whole range of matters that are normally the preserve of an indigenous government.[2] This engagement in political processes runs counter to the traditional approach to UN peace operations which always sought to maintain a neutral and impartial stance and to avoid as far as possible participation in political matters. It is also in tension with the basic premise of the law of occupation, which is that the occupant acquires only temporary authority over the territory,[3] and therefore its powers are limited to what is necessary for its effective administration, or the protection of the local population, or the security of the force.

2. The Laws of Occupation

The law pertaining to military occupation is set out in the Regulations annexed to Hague Convention IV Respecting the Laws and Customs of War on Land, 1907[4] (the Hague Regulations), and expanded upon in Geneva Convention IV Relative to the Protection of Civilians in Time of War, 1949[5] (Geneva Convention IV) and Protocol Additional to the Geneva Conventions of 12 August 1949, and relating to the Protection of Victims of International Armed Conflicts of 1977[6] (Protocol I).

2.1 The Applicability of Occupation Law

Article 42 of the Hague Regulations provides that:

> Territory is considered occupied when it is actually placed under the authority of the hostile army. The occupation extends only to the territory where such authority has been established and can be exercised.

[2] R Caplan, *International Governance of War-Torn Territories: Rule and Reconstruction* (Oxford University Press Oxford 2005), 2.

[3] E Benvenisti, *The International Law of Occupation: with a new preface by the author* (Princeton University Press Princeton 2004), 8; C Greenwood, 'The Administration of Occupied Territory in International Law' in E Playfair (ed), *International Law and the Administration of the Occupied Territories: Two Decades of Israeli Occupation of the West Bank* (Clarendon Press Oxford 1992), 241, 245.

[4] Hague Regulations (n 1). [5] Geneva Convention IV (n 1).

[6] Protocol 1 (n 1).

The provision is vague as to exactly what constitutes occupation. The purpose was to protect the sovereignty of the legitimate power by emphasising that occupation, howsoever achieved, does not confer sovereignty on the occupant.[7] There must be an identifiable foreign military command structure exercising authority in the territory,[8] but there is no necessity for a formal declaration that the territory is under occupation. The key determinant is the actual exercise of authority. The question is whether the invading forces have brought the area under their control 'to the extent that they can actually assume the responsibilities which attach to an occupying power,'[9] and this is treated as essentially a matter of fact.

Geneva Convention IV broadened the concept of occupation to include virtually all forms of non-treaty occupation.[10] Common Article 2 of the Geneva Conventions states that the Conventions shall apply:

> to all cases of declared war or any other armed conflict which may arise between two or more of the High Contracting Parties, even if the state of war is not recognised by one of them.

Article 2(2) states that:

> The Convention shall also apply to all cases of partial or total occupation of the territory of a High Contracting Party, even if the said occupation meets with no resistance.

Together paragraphs 1 and 2 of common Article 2 provide that the Geneva Conventions 1949 apply to virtually all occupations of one State party by the forces of another State. Paragraph 1 encompasses occupations taking place during hostilities, whether or not a state of war has been recognised. Paragraph 2 encompasses occupations taking place outside a state of war. It was intended to bring within the terms of the Convention occupations achieved without hostilities when the government of the occupied country considered that armed resistance was useless.[11] The reason for the occupation is irrelevant.[12] It is not necessary

[7] E Benvenisti, *The International Law of Occupation: with a new preface by the author* (n 3), 8.

[8] A Roberts, What is Military Occupation, BYIL 55 (1984), 249, 277.

[9] HP Gasser, 'Protection of the Civilian Population' in D Fleck (ed), *The Handbook of International Humanitarian Law* (3rd edn, Oxford University Press Oxford 1995), 243.

[10] MJ Kelly, *Restoring and Maintaining Order in Complex Peace Operations* (Kluwer The Hague 1999), 149; H McCoubrey and N White, *International Law and Armed Conflict* (Dartmouth Publishing Co. Ltd. Aldershot 1992), 282; A Roberts, What is Military Occupation (n 8), 253.

[11] J Pictet (ed), *The Geneva Conventions of 12 August 1949, Commentary, Geneva Convention IV* (ICRC Geneva 1958), 20.

[12] HP Gasser, 'Protection of the Civilian Population' in D Fleck (n 9), 243; The ICRC's legal team notes that 'for the applicability of the law of occupation, it makes no difference whether an occupation has received Security Council approval, what its aim is, or indeed whether it is called an "invasion", "liberation", "administration" or "occupation" ... it is solely the facts on the ground that determine its application.' ICRC, 'Occupation and international humanitarian law: questions and answers', 4. 08. 2004: <http://www.icrc.org/Web/Eng/siteeng0.nsf/html/634KFC>; D Thürer, ICRC Official Statement, 'Current challenges to the law of occupation', ICRC, 6th Bruges Colloquium, 20–21 October 2005: <http://www.icrc.org/Web/Eng/siteeng0.nsf/html/occupation-statement-211105>.

for a State to control the entirety of another State's territory for an occupation to exist.[13]

Any actual control by one State over the territory of another State brings with it the duty to respect some or all of the laws of occupation.[14] However, determining at what point an occupation has commenced or ceased is not always easy. The laws of occupation were intended to apply to stable situations rather than to areas that are still embattled,[15] but plainly 'stable' cannot have the same meaning in situations of armed conflict as it would in peacetime. In the *Ansar Prison* case[16] the Israeli Supreme Court, accepting that Article 43 of the Hague Regulations applied to the occupied territories, stated that:

> if the military force has taken control of the area in an effective and workable manner, then even though its presence in such an area is limited in time or its intention is to set up no more than a temporary military control, the situation thereby created is one to which the rules of warfare dealing with belligerent occupation apply...Allowing the former government to act does not alter the fact that the military force is maintaining an effective military control in the area.'[17]

The population of the West Bank has not disarmed but it also seems clear that, despite the violence of the *intifada*, Israeli forces have effective military control of the territory. UN General Assembly resolutions consistently refer to the Israeli presence in Gaza and the West Bank as an occupation.[18] The UK Manual of the Law of Armed Conflict states that:

> The fact that some of the inhabitants are in a state of rebellion, or that guerrillas or resistance fighters have occasional successes, does not render the occupation at an end. Even a temporarily successful rebellion in part of the area under occupation does not necessarily terminate the occupation so long as the occupying power takes steps to deal with the rebellion and re-establish its authority in the area or the area in question is surrounded and cut off.[19]

[13] ICRC, 'Occupation and international humanitarian law: questions and answers', 4. 08. 2004: <http://www.icrc.org/Web/Eng/siteeng0.nsf/html/634KFC>; D Thürer, ICRC Official Statement, 'Current challenges to the law of occupation' (n 12).

[14] A Roberts, 'What Is Military Occupation' (n 8), 250.

[15] HP Gasser, 'Protection of the Civilian Population' (n 9), 244; LC Green, *The Contemporary Law of Armed Conflict* (Manchester University Press Manchester 2000), 257.

[16] *Tzemel Adv. Et al v (a) Minister of Defence (b) Commander of the Ansar Camp* III HC 593/82 (*'Ansar Prison Case*). English translation cited in A Roberts 'What Is Military Occupation' (n 8), 286.

[17] *Ansar Prison Case* (n 16).

[18] Examples include A/RES/57/269 (2002); A/RES/57/127 (2002); A/RES/57/126 (2002); A/RES/57/125 (2002); A/RES/57/124 (2002).

[19] UK Ministry of Defence, *Manual of the Law of Armed Conflict (JSP 383)* (Oxford University Press Oxford 2004), [11.7.1]; WO UK, WO Code No 12333 *Manual of Military Law, Part III the Law of War on Land* (1958) [509] Adam Roberts states that 'in practice the status of occupation has not been viewed as being negated by the existence of violent opposition, especially when that opposition has not had full control of a portion of the state's territory.' A Roberts, 'The End of Occupation: Iraq 2004', 54 ICLQ 27, 34.

However, there are instances in which resistance to occupation is so widespread and persistent that it negates the status of occupation altogether. In the *Einsatzgruppen* case,[20] which concerned war crimes committed in the Soviet Union during the occupation by Nazi Germany, the tribunal held that occupation had ceased to exist at the relevant time because resistance had become so widespread that the invader, although still present in the territory, had lost capacity to exercise authority. The tribunal stated that:

> in many of the areas where the Einsatzgruppen operated, the so-called partisans had wrested considerable territory from the German occupant, and... military combat action of some dimensions was required to reoccupy those areas. In belligerent occupation the occupying power does not hold enemy territory by virtue of any legal right. On the contrary, it merely exercises a precarious and temporary actual control. This can be seen from Article 42 of the Hague Regulations which grants certain well limited rights to a military occupant only in enemy territory which is 'actually placed' under his control.[21]

This would suggest that resistance is merely an indicator of whether or not the occupant is effectively exercising authority. The guidelines set out in the UK Manual of the Law of Armed Conflict state that:

> Whether or not a rebel movement has successfully terminated an occupation is a question of fact and degree depending on, for example, the extent of the area controlled by the movement and the length of time involved, the intensity of operations, and the extent to which the movement is internationally recognized.[22]

These appear to be sound guidelines. But determining whether those criteria have been met is a matter of judgement and judgement is never non-political. The Geneva Conventions and Hague Regulations do not provide for the establishment of any body with the power to determine whether or not an occupation exists or has ceased to exist.[23] However, they do accord a special position to the ICRC that acknowledges its long established and internationally accepted role as a monitor of international humanitarian law compliance[24] and therefore the view of the ICRC carries exceptional weight.

[20] *USA v Otto Ohlendorf et al*, in *Trials of War Criminals* vol IV (1950).

[21] ibid 492–3. In this case the fact that occupation had ceased supported a conviction. The question of whether occupation had ceased as a result of loss of control was also raised in *USA v Wilhelm List et al*, in *Trials of War Criminals* vol XI (1950) 1243–4 and *In re Bauer and Others*: *United Nations War Crimes Commission, Law Reports of Trials of War Criminals* (1947–9), vol. 8, 18–19: A Roberts, 'What Is Military Occupation' (n 8), 260 n 37.

[22] UK Ministry of Defence *Manual of the Law of Armed Conflict* (n 19) [11.7.1].

[23] In the past, as in this case, it has frequently been the Security Council or General Assembly that has indicated whether or not a particular situation is an occupation. A Roberts, 'What Is Military Occupation' (n 8), 301.

[24] Geneva Convention IV (n 1), articles 10, 11; Protocol 1 (n 1) articles 5, 3; Common articles 9, 10 of Geneva Convention I for the Amelioration of the Condition of the Wounded and Sick in Armed Forces in the Field, 75 UNTS 31; Geneva Convention II for the Amelioration of the Condition of the Wounded, Sick and Shipwrecked Members of the Armed Forces at Sea, 75

Daniel Thürer, in an ICRC Official Statement on 'Current challenges to the law of occupation,' argues that there are two possible approaches to determining whether there is an occupation:

> [The] more restrictive approach, would be to say that a situation of occupation only exists once a party to a conflict is in a position to exercise the level of authority over enemy territory necessary to enable it to discharge *all* the obligations imposed by the law of occupation, i.e. that the invading power must be in a position to substitute its own authority for that of the government of the territory. This approach is suggested by a number of military manuals. For example the new British Military Manual[25]

The UK Manual of the Law of Armed Conflict, 2004 states that in order to determine whether a state of occupation exists, it is necessary to determine whether two conditions are satisfied:

1. that the former government has been rendered incapable of publicly exercising its authority in that area;
2. that the occupying power is in a position to substitute its own authority for that of the former government.[26]

The US Operational Law Handbook 2004 adopts similar criteria:

> [O]ccupation is a question of fact based on the invader's ability to render the invaded government incapable of exercising public authority. Simply put the occupation must be both actual and effective.[27]

The ICRC acknowledges that it adopts a 'pragmatic' approach to determining when Geneva Convention IV applies,[28] so as to afford the greatest protection to those who would benefit from the law's application:

> The aim of the ICRC's interventions is to ensure the protection of persons affected by an armed conflict, including occupation, in accordance with the law. In view of this, we adopted the possibly maximalist position that whenever—even in the so called-invasion phase—persons come within the power or control of a hostile army they should be ensured the protection of the Fourth Geneva Convention as a minimum.[29]

Adopting this 'maximalist' position the ICRC takes the view that:

> a situation of occupation exists whenever a party to a conflict is exercising some level of authority or control over territory belonging to the enemy. So, for example, advancing

UNTS 85; Geneva Convention III Relative to the Treatment of Prisoners of War, 75 UNTS 135 (all adopted Geneva, 12 Aug 1949, came into force 21 October 1950).

[25] D Thürer, ICRC Official Statement, 'Current challenges to the law of occupation' (n 12 above).

[26] UK Ministry of Defence, *Manual of the Law of Armed Conflict* (n 19), [11.3].

[27] *Operational Law Handbook 2004* JA 422, (The Judge Advocate's Legal Center and School, Charlottesville, Virginia 22903 <http://www.jagcnet.army.mil>), 28.

[28] D Thürer, ICRC Official Statement, 'Current challenges to the law of occupation' (n 12 above).

[29] ibid.

troops could be considered an occupation, and thus bound by the law of occupation during the invasion phase of hostilities.[30]

Jean Pictet puts forward a similar argument in the ICRC's 1958 'Commentary to the Fourth Geneva Convention' in his comments on Article 6, which provides that the Convention 'shall apply from the outset of any conflict or occupation mentioned in Article 2.' Pictet argues that:

> [b]y using the words 'from the outset' the authors of the Convention wished to show that it became applicable as soon as the first acts of violence were committed, even if the armed struggle did not continue... The Convention should be applied as soon as troops are in foreign territory and in contact with the civilian population there... In all cases of occupation, whether carried out by force or without meeting any resistance, the Convention becomes applicable to individuals i.e. to the protected persons, as they fall into the hands of the Occupying Power.
>
> It follows from this that the word 'occupation' as used in the Article [Article 2] has a wider meaning than it has in Article 42 of the Regulations annexed to the Fourth Hague Convention of 1907. So far as individuals are concerned, the application of the Fourth Geneva Convention does not depend upon the existence of a state of occupation within the meaning of the Article 42 referred to above. The relations between the civilian population of a territory and troops advancing into that territory, whether fighting or not, are governed by the Convention. There is no intermediate period between what might be termed the invasion phase and the inauguration of a stable regime of occupation. Even a patrol which penetrates into enemy territory without any intention of staying there must respect the Conventions in its dealings with the civilians it meets... The same thing is true of raids made into enemy territory or on his coasts...
>
> Some of the Convention's provisions become applicable immediately, such as those in Article 136, which concerns the setting up of an Official Information Bureau. Others—Articles 52, 55, 56, and even some of the provisions of Articles 59 to 62, for example—presuppose the presence of the occupation for a fairly long period. However, all the provisions relating to the rights enjoyed by protected persons or to the treatment which must be given to them become applicable forthwith whatever the duration of the occupation.[31]

The difference between the 'maximalist' approach of the ICRC and the more restrictive approach adopted in the *UK Manual on the Law of Armed Conflict* and the US *Operational Law Handbook*, is not as great as might first appear. The ICRC's objective is to ensure that there is no gap between the invasion phase and the commencement of occupation during which civilians falling into the hands of foreign forces find themselves without legal protection. Occupation law is not a discrete body of law: many of the provisions in Geneva Convention IV on the protection of civilians apply not only during occupation but in all circumstances in which the Conventions are applicable, for example Part II, which is concerned

[30] ibid.

[31] J Pictet (ed), *The Geneva Conventions of 12 August 1949, Commentary, IV Geneva Convention* (n 11), 60.

with the 'General Protection of Populations against Certain Consequences of War.'[32] To the extent that the invading force exercises any administrative authority or undertakes any similar activity that would normally be the preserve of the sovereign, it will be bound by the relevant rules and principles of the law of occupation, however transient the period of control.[33] The obligations on an occupying power that deal with conduct towards protected persons are set out in unequivocal terms; however obligations dealing with matters such as restoring law and order, providing food and medical supplies, and maintaining public health and hygiene standards, are ones that the occupying power must 'ensure as far as possible'[34] or to 'the fullest extent of the means available to it.'[35] Moreover, as Adam Roberts has observed 'to a large extent the nexus of rights and duties' that make up the law on occupation 'is a body of minimum rules, which any power should be able to follow at any time.'[36]

The Eritrea Ethiopia Claims Commission,[37] in determining the applicability of occupation law to villages and towns on the front line, control of which moved back and forth during the course of the armed conflict of 1998–2000, has adopted an approach that is based on the *de facto* exercise of authority in accordance with Article 42 of the Hague Regulations, but which is also in line with the ICRC's 'maximalist' position. The Commission has stated that:

> clearly an area where combat is ongoing and the attacking forces have not yet established control cannot normally be occupied within the meaning of the Geneva Conventions 1949. On the other hand, where combat is not occurring in an area controlled even for just a few days by the armed forces of a hostile Power, the Commission believes that the legal rules applicable to occupied territory should apply.[38]

However, the Commission has also recognized that:

> not all of the obligations of Section III of Part III of Geneva Convention IV (the section that deals with occupied territories) can reasonably be applied to an armed force anticipating combat and present in an area for only a few days. Nevertheless, a State is obligated by the remainder of that Convention and by customary humanitarian law to take appropriate measures to protect enemy civilians and civilian property within the areas under the control of its armed forces.[39]

[32] Geneva Convention IV (n 1), Art 13; A Roberts, What is Military Occupation (n 8), 250; H McCoubrey and N White, *International Law and Armed Conflict* (n 10) 282.

[33] H McCoubrey and N White, *International Law and Armed Conflict* (n 10) 282.

[34] Hague Regulations (n 1), Article 43.

[35] Geneva Convention IV (n 1), Articles 55 and 56.

[36] A Roberts, What is Military Occupation (n 8), 304.

[37] The Commission was established to determine compensation for breaches of international law committed by both parties from 1998–2000 during the course of the armed conflict between them.

[38] Partial Award, Central Front, Eritrea's Claims 2, 4, 6, 7, 8, 22 between the State of Eritrea and the Federal Republic of Ethiopia, Eritrea Ethiopia Claims Commission, The Hague April 28 2004, [57].

[39] Partial Award, Western Front, Aerial Bombardment and Related Claims, Eritrea's Claims 1,3, 5, 9–13, 14, 21, 25 and 26, between the State of Eritrea and the Federal Republic of Ethiopia, Eritrea Ethiopia Claims Commission, The Hague, December 19 2005, [27].

The approach of the Commission reflects the ICRC's objective in maximizing the protection of civilians whilst at the same time recognizing that an armed force that is still engaged in combat operations cannot undertake all the duties of an occupant. However, where a force is in control of territory, even if it is only for a few days, it must comply, in so far as it is possible to do so, with the laws of occupation. These laws are sufficiently flexible to allow the occupant to take measures that are necessary for its military operations or security needs[40] whilst at the same time respecting the provisions enacted for the protection of civilians (for example the prohibition on deportations).[41]

2.2 Responsibilities of the Occupying Power

Article 43 of the Hague Regulations functions as 'a sort of mini-constitution for the occupation administration; its general guidelines permeate any prescriptive measure or other acts taken by the occupant.'[42] It provides that:

> The authority of the legitimate power having in fact passed into the hands of the occupant, the latter shall take all measures in his power to restore and ensure as far as possible, public order and safety, while respecting unless absolutely prevented, the laws in force in the country.

The phrase used in place of 'public order and safety' in the French text, which is the authoritative text, is *'l'ordre et la vie publics.'* Many commentators regard this as encompassing not only 'public order and safety' narrowly construed but also the whole social, commercial and economic life of the country.[43] However, the primary objective of the Hague Regulations was to preserve the sovereign rights of the ousted government: the occupant was expected to ensure that, as far as possible, ordinary life in the territory carried on as normal until an agreement could be reached that would facilitate the return of the sovereign.[44]

Art 55 of the Hague Regulations provides that in respect of public buildings, real estate, forests and agricultural estates, the occupying power 'shall be regarded as administrator and usufructor' of these properties.[45] Thus the occupant has a responsibility to prevent waste. Profits may be used to pay the occupant's local

[40] Geneva Convention IV (n 1) art 64.

[41] Geneva Convention IV (n 1) art 49.

[42] E Benvenisti, *The International Law of Occupation: with a new preface by the author* (n 3), 9.

[43] EH Schwenk, 'Legislative Power of the Military Occupant under Article 43, Hague Regulations', 54 Yale Law Journal 2, 393, 398; C Greenwood, 'The Administration of Occupied Territory in International Law' in E Playfair (ed), *International Law and the Administration of the Occupied Territories: Two Decades of Israeli Occupation of the West Bank* (n 3), 246; MJ Kelly, 'Iraq and the Law of Occupation: New Tests for an Old Law', 6 Yearbook of International Humanitarian Law, 127, 147; M Sassòli, 'Legislation and Maintenance of Public Order and Civil Life by Occupying Powers', 16 EJIL 4, 661, 663.

[44] E Benvenisti, *The International Law of Occupation: with a new preface by the author* (n 3), 28.

[45] Hague Convention IV (n 1), 55. There is no mention of mineral resources.

administration costs, but not to enrich the occupying State. The UK Manual of the Law of Armed Conflict states that:

> Land and buildings that belong to the state but are essentially civilian in character such as public buildings, land, forests, parks, farms, and coal mines, may not be damaged or destroyed unless that is imperatively necessitated by military operations. The occupying power is the administrator, user, and in a sense, guardian of the property. It must not waste, neglect or abusively exploit these assets so as to decrease their value.[46]

The occupying power may sell crops, cut and sell timber and work mines but cutting or mining must not exceed what is necessary or usual.[47]

Whilst Article 43 remains the 'cornerstone' of occupation law,[48] it has been supplemented by the extensive provisions on occupation in Geneva Convention IV,[49] which is primarily concerned with the protection of civilians. Geneva Convention IV has been described as:

> a bill of rights with a catalogue of fundamental rights which, immediately upon occupation and without any further actions on the part of those affected, becomes applicable to the occupied territories.[50]

Torture, inhuman and degrading treatment, deportation, slave labour, reprisals, collective punishments against the civilian population, wholesale seizure of property, and compulsion to do military work for the occupant are prohibited.[51] In addition, the occupant has duties relating to the provision of education; the supply of foodstuffs and medical supplies to the civilian population; the maintenance of medical and hospital facilities; the distribution of books and articles required for religious needs; and the facilitation of relief efforts where necessary.[52]

In addition to obligations under the Hague Regulations and the Geneva Conventions, the occupant may have obligations under human rights law that would require it, in so far as it is possible to do so, to respect and secure all the

[46] UK Ministry of Defence, *Manual of the Law of Armed Conflict* (n 19), [11.86].

[47] ibid.

[48] E Benvenisti, *The International Law of Occupation: with a new preface by the author* (n 3), 9.

[49] Geneva Convention IV (n 1), art 54; The provisions relating to occupation in Geneva Convention IV and Protocol 1, have not abrogated the Hague Regulations, 'so that the powers of an occupant are now defined by customary law and these three documents.' LC Green, *The Contemporary Law of Armed Conflict* (2nd edn, Manchester University Press Manchester 2004), 257.

[50] HP Gasser, 'Protection of the Civilian Population' (n 9), 242; In general the protections of the Geneva Conventions do not extend to nationals of a State that is not party to the Convention or to nationals of a neutral State or of a co-belligerent State if that State has normal diplomatic representation in the occupying State. However the protections contained in Part II of Geneva Convention IV (Articles 13–34) cover the whole of the populations of the countries in conflict. In addition, Article 75 of Protocol 1 requires the occupying power to maintain a minimum standard of human rights in the treatment of all persons including those persons who do not qualify as protected persons under Geneva Convention IV: Geneva Convention IV (n 1) Articles, 4, 13; Protocol 1 (n 1), Art 75; J Pictet (ed), *The Geneva Conventions of 12 August 1949, Commentary, IV Geneva Convention* (n 11), 46, 118.

[51] Geneva Convention IV (n 1), Articles 32, 33, 40, 49, 51, 95, 97.

[52] ibid, Articles 50, 55, 56, 58(2), 59–62.

human rights protected under the human rights treaties to which it is party, or that constitute customary international law, in those territories over which it exercises effective control (except to the extent that it has formally derogated from them).[53] The International Court of Justice (ICJ), in its *Advisory Opinion concerning the Legal Consequences of the Construction of a Wall in the Occupied Palestinian Territory* and in its judgment in the *Case concerning Armed Activities on the Territory of the Congo* implied that the obligation to secure human rights is an integral component of occupation law.[54]

2.2.1 Respect for Local Law

Article 43 requires the occupant to respect 'unless absolutely prevented, the laws in force in the country.' This obligation:

> refers not only to laws in the strict sense of the word, but also to the constitution, decrees, ordinances, court precedents...as well as administrative regulations and executive orders, provided that the norms in question are general and abstract.[55]

It is permissible to suspend the functioning of political organs of the central government and also some constitutional guarantees such as those related to the political process but the restrictions on these rights should be limited to the duration of the occupation, unless the changes are necessary to enable the full implementation of obligations under the Convention or other rules of international humanitarian law or human rights law.[56] The ICRC recognizes that some institutional changes 'might be considered necessary or even an improvement'.[57] However, the flexibility to make improvements to the institutional framework is not an open-ended freedom allowing the occupant to introduce whatever institutional changes it thinks best since this would be incompatible with the principle that the occupant acquires temporary authority, not sovereignty, over the occupied territory,[58] and therefore has a role akin to that of a 'trustee.'[59]

[53] Discussed in Chapter 3.

[54] *Advisory Opinion concerning the Legal Consequences of the Construction of a Wall in Occupied Palestinian Territory*, ICJ, July 9 2004, ILM 1009 (2004); *Case concerning Armed Activities on the Territory of the Congo: Democratic Republic of the Congo v Uganda*, ICJ, 19 December 2005; discussed in Chapter 3.

[55] M Sassòli, 'Legislation and Maintenance of Public Order and Civil Life by Occupying Powers' (n 43), 668; E Benvenisti, *The International Law of Occupation: with a new preface by the author* (n 3) 17, 19.

[56] C Greenwood, 'The Administration of Occupied Territory in International Law' (n 3), 245.

[57] Commentary to Article 47 of Geneva Convention IV, which prohibits the occupant from making any changes to the institutions or government of the territory, or from making any agreement with the authorities of the occupied territory, that would deprive protected persons of the benefits of the Convention: J Pictet (ed), *The Geneva Conventions of 12 August 1949, Commentary, Geneva Convention IV* (n 11), 274.

[58] C Greenwood, 'The Administration of Occupied Territory in International Law' (n 3), 245.

[59] Adam Roberts argues that 'the idea of trusteeship is implicit in all occupation law...The Hague Regulations and the 1949 Geneva Convention IV can be interpreted as putting the occupant in a quasi-trustee role.': A Roberts, 'What is Military Occupation' (n 8), 295; E Benvenisti,

Today the trusteeship implicit in the concept of occupation is as much for the people as the ousted government. Article 64 of Geneva Convention IV, which supplements but does not displace Article 43 of the Hague Regulations, not only allows, but by implication requires, changes to the laws in force where this is necessary to implement the occupant's humanitarian obligations under the Convention. Article 64(1) of Geneva Convention IV provides that:

The penal laws of the occupied territory shall remain in force, with the exception that they may be repealed or suspended by the occupying power in cases where they constitute a threat to its security or an obstacle to the application of the present Convention. Subject to the latter consideration and to the necessity for ensuring the effective administration of justice, the tribunals of the occupied territory shall continue to function in respect of all offences covered by the said laws.

Article 64(2) provides that:

The Occupying Power may, however, subject the population of the occupied territory to provisions which are essential to enable the Occupying Power to fulfil its obligations under the present Convention, to maintain the orderly government of the territory and to ensure the security of the Occupying Power, of the members and property of the occupying forces or administration, and likewise of the establishments and lines of communication between them.

The ICRC takes the view that Article 64(2) expresses in 'a more precise and detailed form' the terms 'unless absolutely prevented' contained in Article 43 of the Hague Regulations and that this implies that modifications are permitted to any types of law, not just penal laws.[60] Moreover the occupant may introduce provisions essential to implementing any aspect of applicable international humanitarian law not just Geneva Convention IV 'since IHL cannot possibly require specific conduct from an occupying power and also prohibit it to legislate for that purpose.'[61] Similarly if the occupant is obligated to uphold certain international human rights standards under human rights law and the local law is not in compliance, it must be able to legislate in order to carry out those obligations.[62]

The International Law of Occupation: with a new preface by the author (n 3) 6; However Christopher Greenwood observes that the concept of trusteeship implicit in occupation, is 'far more rudimentary' than any concept of trusteeship founded upon law. Occupation law 'endeavors to strike a balance between the military interests of the occupant, the humanitarian protection of the population, and the preservation, pending a final settlement, of certain interests of the displaced power, rather than requiring the occupant to act as a disinterested administrator.' C Greenwood, 'The Administration of Occupied Territory in International Law' (n 3), 241, 251.

[60] J Pictet (ed), *The Geneva Conventions of 12 August 1949. Commentary* (n 11), 335 Benvenisti, after analysing the *travaux préparatoires*, observes that 'it is not a mere coincidence that the adjective penal is missing.' E Benvenisti, *The International Law of Occupation: with a new preface by the author* (n 3), 101.

[61] M Sassòli, 'Legislation and Maintenance of Public Order and Civil Life by Occupying Powers' (n 43), 675–677.

[62] ibid 676.

Article 43 of the Hague Regulations, read together with Article 64 of Geneva Convention IV, prohibits any changes to the laws in force except where these are necessary in order to restore the functioning of the State, or to implement obligations under IHL or human rights law, or for the security of the occupying force. Since any changes made to legislation, must be *necessary* for one of these purposes it can be strongly argued that any changes that are made must be undertaken conservatively and carried out in a manner that stays as close as possible to the local cultural, legal and economic traditions.[63] Feilchenfeld, writing in 1942 and reflecting the politics of the day, comments that:

> It would seem that an occupant has no right to transform a liberal into a communistic or fascist economy, except in so far as military or public order needs should require individual changes.[64]

Communism and fascism are no longer the dominant concerns but the core argument remains valid: a State cannot transform another State into one that supports its aims and ideals, except in so far as the changes are necessary in order to provide for rights protected by international law. However, the obligation to ensure *'l'ordre et la vie publics,'* encompasses such a wide spectrum of activity that occupants have tended to regard it as justification for virtually full discretionary powers.[65]

3. The Laws of Occupation and UN Military Operations

The Hague Regulations and Geneva Conventions make no provision for occupation by multi-national forces. However, States contributing troops to UN operations have an obligation to ensure their troops comply with IHL.[66] One of the basic principles of IHL is that it applies to all parties engaged in armed conflict irrespective of the lawfulness or moral validity of the conflict. The distinction between *jus in bello* and *jus ad bellum* renders the objectives, motives and legitimacy of the intervention irrelevant to the question of the applicability of IHL.

[63] For example an occupant may change law to ensure a fair trial but cannot introduce an adversarial criminal procedure if the legal system of the occupied State uses an inquisitorial system: it can only introduce such changes as are absolutely necessary to provide for a fair trial: M Sassòli, 'Legislation and Maintenance of Public Order and Civil Life by Occupying Powers' (n 43), 677.

[64] EH Feilchenfeld, *The International Economic law of Belligerent Occupation* (William S Hein & Co Inc Buffalo 2000 reprint of 1942 edition), 90

[65] E Benvenisti, *The International Law of Occupation: with a new preface by the author* (n 3), 12 McCoubrey and White comment that 'it is clear that in many cases occupying powers have far exceeded their very limited 'legislative' capacities.' H McCoubrey and N White, *International Law and Armed Conflict* (n 10), 284.

[66] Forces engaged in a UN operation remain bound by the rules of IHL to which they would be bound if they were acting independently of the UN. The contributing State is responsible for ensuring compliance: A Roberts and R Guelff, *Documents on the Laws of War* (3rd edn, Oxford University Press Oxford 2000) 723.

Thus it can be argued that UN authorization does not affect the applicability of occupation law.[67] But prior to the UN mandated post-conflict occupation of Iraq, under which the Multi-National Force (MNF) are required to comply with the laws of occupation, there was considerable reluctance to hold that the laws of occupation apply to UN operations. Resolution 1483 of 22 May 2003 made plain that occupation law was applicable to the MNF at least up until the 'transfer of sovereignty' in June 2004. But the resolution also mandated objectives (and wide powers to achieve them) going far beyond what has been expected of occupants in the past, with no guidance as to how achieving those objectives should be reconciled with the requirements of occupation law. Resolution 1483 was specific to the situation in Iraq and is not determinative as to whether occupation law applies to UN forces generally and if so whether its applicability extends to UN-run operations or only those that are UN mandated. But if occupation law is applicable to some UN authorized operations but not others, that distinction must be based on legal criteria, and factual differences relevant to the applicability of the legal criteria.

The debate on the extent to which the UN is bound by IHL has been ongoing for many years but it has been primarily directed towards ensuring accountability for misconduct by troops. Occupation law encompasses much broader obligations, including many positive duties towards the local population. Statements by the UN do not support the view that the UN itself (as distinct from contributing States) is bound by occupation law. Under the UN Model Agreement between the United Nations and Member States Contributing Personnel and Equipment to United Nations Peacekeeping Operations (1991), the UN undertakes to 'observe and respect the principles and spirit of the general international conventions applicable to the conduct of military personnel.'[68] The wording suggests that the agreement is primarily concerned with the conduct of troops.[69] The commitment to respect the 'principles and rules of the laws of war' is also now routinely inserted into Status of Forces Agreements.[70] But again the undertaking is concerned with the conduct of personnel, rather than general responsibilities under IHL. In 1999

[67] M Sassòli, *Article 43 of the Hague Regulations and Peace Operations in the Twenty-First Century* (Background Paper for Informal High-Level Expert Meeting on Current Challenges to International Humanitarian Law, Cambridge 25–27 June 2004), 1, 16; Benvenisti defines occupation 'as the effective control of a power (be it one or more states or an international organization, such as the United Nations) over a territory to which that power has no sovereign title, without the volition of the sovereign of that territory.' E Benvenisti, *The International Law of Occupation: with a new preface by the author* (n 3), 4.

[68] UN Doc A/46/185 of 23 May 1991 [28].

[69] A Roberts and R Guelff, *Documents on the Laws of War* (n 66), 723.

[70] If possible the UN tries to conclude a Status of Forces Agreement between itself and States in which peacekeeping forces are to be deployed. From 1993 such agreements included the obligation to respect the 'principles and spirit' of the laws of armed conflict but 'spirit' has now been replaced by 'rules.' PC Szasz, 'UN Forces and International Humanitarian Law' in MN Schmitt (ed), *International Law across the Spectrum of Conflict, Essays in Honour of Professor LC Green on the Occasion of His Eightieth Birthday* (US Naval War College Newport 2000) 507, 516; A Roberts and R Guelff, *Documents on the Laws of War* (n 66), 625.

the Secretary-General promulgated a Bulletin on the Observance by UN forces of International Humanitarian Law,[71] which provides that the:

fundamental principles and rules of international humanitarian law are applicable to UN forces when in situations of armed conflict they are actively engaged therein as combatants, to the extent and for the duration of their engagement.[72]

As in the previous undertakings the Bulletin focuses on the conduct of forces.[73] Even if it were interpreted to include all the relevant rules of IHL there would still be situations that are not covered by the Bulletin. The Secretary-General's Bulletin limits the UN's obligations under IHL to 'situations of armed conflict' in which UN forces are 'actively engaged therein as combatants, to the extent and for the duration of their engagement.'[74] Thus the Bulletin, even if it does encompass occupation law, does not appear to encompass occupations arising in the circumstances set out in Article 2(2) of the Geneva Conventions, which deals with occupations arising outside of armed conflict. The problem is exacerbated by the difficulty of determining the threshold at which IHL applies to UN forces.[75] Troops may be exercising considerable force and exercising considerable authority over territory and yet the contributing States may consider that it is not armed conflict.[76]

[71] Secretary-General's Bulletin on Observance by UN Forces of International Humanitarian Law, (date of promulgation 6 August 1999, entered into force 12 August 1999) UN Doc ST/SGB/1999/13 Since the Bulletin is an internal document of the UN it is binding on UN troops but does not in itself create direct legal obligations for States: Report of Experts Meeting on Multi-National Operations, 11–12 December 2003 (ICRC Geneva), 2.

[72] Secretary-General's Bulletin on Observance by UN Forces of International Humanitarian Law (n 71).

[73] However Daphna Shraga comments that '[w]ith the promulgation of the Secretary-General's Bulletin on the Observance by UN Forces of Internationl Humanitarian Law, the applicability to UN operations of the entire body of international humanitarian law, of which the laws of occupation are a part, was officially recognized.' D Shraga, Military Occupation and UN Transitional Administrations—The Analogy and Its Limitations in MG Koehen (ed), *Promoting Justice, Human Righst and Conflict Resolution through International Law* (Liber Amicorum Lucius Caflisch Leiden 2007), 479.

[74] ibid.

[75] The Secretary-General's Bulletin is careful to limit the application of IHL to combatants in order to avoid conflict with the Convention on the Safety of UN and Associated Personnel (adopted 19 December 1994, entered into force 15 January 1999) 34 ILM (1995) 482–93. The Convention protects non-combatant UN personnel by making attacks against them an international crime, but UN forces engaged as combatants are subject to IHL (which does permit attacks). However there must be a threshold level of force separating situations in which the Convention on the Safety of UN and Associated Personnel applies and that in which IHL applies. This means that there is potentially a gap in the situations under which IHL applies to UN forces because UN forces may be engaged in some level of force and yet not be engaged as combatants: A Roberts and R Guelff, *Documents on the Laws of War* (n 66), 625.

[76] For example during the Unified Task Force (UNITAF) operation in Somalia, despite the deaths of thirty United States soldiers and the wounding of nearly two hundred, and many hundreds more Somali casualties, the United States argued that there had yet to be an event in Somalia 'that makes it clear to everyone that this is combat, not peacekeeping': S Turley, 'Keeping the Peace: Do the Laws of War Apply?' (1994) 73 Texas Law Review, 139, 163.

A further problem arises in the context of UN-run 'occupations' established after the surrender of the enemy. It is generally agreed that Geneva Convention IV is applicable to post-surrender occupations.[77] Under Article 6 of the Geneva Conventions the laws of occupation continue to apply for one year after hostilities have ceased and the most important provisions continue to apply for as long as the occupation continues.[78] Protocol 1 has abrogated the one-year limitation: parties to the Protocol are bound by all the provisions until 'the termination of the occupation.'[79] However, if 'the duration of their engagement' mentioned in the Secretary-General's Bulletin refers to the duration in which they are engaged as combatants, UN forces would not be bound by international humanitarian law once hostilities had ceased. It is arguable that if UN forces engaged in armed conflict become de facto occupants then the relevant laws of occupation should continue to apply so long as they continue to be in the position of an occupant. However, this is not reflected in the Bulletin, which makes no mention of the laws of occupation.

3.1 Do the Laws of Occupation Constitute Customary Law?

There is some dispute as to the applicability of customary law to UN forces. Some commentators argue that the fact that the UN denies that it is de jure subject to IHL:

> raises some doubts as to whether the IHL rules that are customary between States, are also customary in armed conflicts involving international organizations.[80]

However, a significant body of opinion holds that most customary IHL does apply to UN forces.[81]

[77] Adam Roberts, 'What is Military Occupation' (n 8), 270.

[78] Geneva Convention IV (n 1), Article 6. The reason for the one-year limitation was that 'if the Occupying Power is victorious, the occupation may last more than one year, but as hostilities have ceased, stringent measures against the civilian population will no longer be justified.' J Pictet (ed) *The Geneva Conventions of 12 August 1949, Commentary, Geneva Convention IV* (n 11), 62–63. Article 6 does not say when the Convention will cease to apply in the case of occupation arising outside of armed conflict where there has been no resistance. 'This omission appears to be deliberate and must be taken to mean that the Convention will be fully applicable in such cases, so long as the occupation lasts.' ibid, 63.

[79] Protocol 1 (n 1), Article 3(b).

[80] M Sassòli, 'Legislation and Maintenance of Public Order and Civil Life by Occupying Powers' (n 43), 687.

[81] A Roberts, 'What is Military Occupation' (n 8), 289–91; Y Dinstein, 'War, Aggression and Self-Defence' (3rd edn, Cambridge University Press Cambridge 2001), 146; DW Bowett, *United Nations Forces: A Legal Study of United Nations Practice* (Steven & Sons London 1964), 484–516; D Shraga and R Zacklin, 'The Applicability of International Humanitarian Law to United Nations Peace-Keeping Operations: Conceptual, Legal and Practical Issues' in U Palwankar (ed), *International Committee of the Red Cross Symposium on Humanitarian Action and Peacekeeping Operations* (ICRC Geneva 1994), 44; Judge Lauterpacht in a decision of the ICJ has stated that peremptory norms are binding on the UN and that even Security Council resolutions cannot derogate from them: *Case Concerning Application of the Convention on the Prevention and Punishment*

One problem in determining whether provisions of IHL constitute customary international law is that the actual practice of belligerents is not easy to identify particularly as it often consists of omissions.[82] The ICTY Appeals Court has observed that it is difficult to pinpoint the actual behaviour of troops in the field because access to operations is normally refused to independent observers. Parties to the conflict do not give out information or 'what is worse, often recourse is had to misinformation.'[83] Moreover the conventions on IHL came about precisely because the international community found the actual practice of belligerents unacceptable.[84] Because the norms of IHL enjoy strong moral support, judges, non-governmental organizations and academics are often prepared to accept a 'rather large gap between practice and the norms concerned without questioning their binding character.'[85] Given the humanitarian nature of the conventions this approach is relatively uncontroversial as regards the prohibition of serious violations of IHL by members of one's own forces but much more controversial when it comes to asserting positive obligations requiring the occupant to administer the territory and to do so in a manner that ensures the basic well being of the inhabitants, particularly if the obligation extends to preventing violations of IHL by others.[86]

Nevertheless drawing on statements made by the International Court of Justice,[87] several major international tribunals,[88] and ten years of research by the ICRC culminating in the publication in March 2005 of an extensive and detailed report on customary rules of IHL, it is possible to draw some conclusions

of the Crime of Genocide (Bosnia and Herzegovina v Yugoslavia) Provisional Measures, Order of 13 September 1993 Separate Opinion of Judge Lauterpacht [1993] ICJ Rep. 325, 440–441 [100–102].

[82] M Sassòli and A Bouvier (eds), *How Does Law Protect in War? Cases, Documents and Teaching Materials on Contemporary Practice in International Humanitarian Law* (ICRC Geneva 1999) 108.

[83] ICTY *Prosecutor v Dusko Tadic (Jurisdiction)* No IT-94-1-AR72, [99].

[84] M Sassòli and A Bouvier (eds), *How Does Law Protect in War? Cases, Documents and Teaching Materials on Contemporary Practice in International Humanitarian Law* (n 81), 109.

[85] T Meron, 'The Humanization of Humanitarian Law' (2000) 94 AJIL 239, 244.

[86] R Wiener and F Ni Aolain, 'Beyond the Laws of War: Peacekeeping in Search of a Legal Framework' (1996) 27 Columbia Human Rights Law Review 293, 309.

[87] *Military and Paramilitary Activities in and against Nicaragua (Nicar v US)*, Merits, 1986 ICJ Rep 14, 114, [218–20] (June 27).

[88] *United States v von Leeb 'The High Command Case'* Trials of War Criminals Vol XI 462, 533–35 (1948); ICTY *Prosecutor v Dusko Tadic (Jurisdiction)* (n 83), [126] The Appeals Chamber held that many (but not all) principles and rules previously considered applicable only in international armed conflict are now applicable in internal armed conflicts, but that '(i) only a number of rules and principles governing international armed conflicts have gradually been extended to apply to internal conflicts; and (ii) this extension has not taken place in the form of a full and mechanical transplant of those rules to internal conflicts; rather, the general essence of those rules, and not the detailed regulation they may contain, has become applicable to internal conflicts.' Because it is difficult to pinpoint the actual behaviour of troops in the field the Court recommended that in order to determine 'what principles and rules of customary law have emerged in the international community for the purpose of regulating civil strife', States should rely primarily on official State pronouncements, military manuals, and judicial decisions, and not on actual State practice: ibid, [99].

as to the extent to which occupation law may be considered customary law.[89] It is generally agreed that the provisions on occupation in the Hague Regulations constitute customary international law[90] as do a great many of the substantive provisions contained in Geneva Convention IV.[91] The Secretary-General in his Report on the setting up of the International Criminal Tribunal for the former Yugoslavia (ICTY) referred to the Geneva Conventions, the Hague Convention and the Charter of the International Military Tribunal of 8 August 1945 as 'part of conventional international law which has beyond doubt become part of international customary law.'[92] While there is no dispute over the truth of this in general terms, when it comes to the details the matter seems not to be so clear-cut. It is unlikely that all the provisions of the Geneva Conventions constitute customary law. For example article 72 of Geneva Convention III[93] entitling prisoners of war to receive scientific equipment is almost certainly not (since POWs never do receive such equipment). Although the customary law rules set out in the ICRC report on customary IHL include many drawn from Geneva Convention IV, encompassing a wide range of general fundamental guarantees regarding the treatment of civilians in all circumstances, as well as more specific rules dealing with the sick, wounded and persons deprived of their liberty, none of the rules set out in the report deal with broad based duties such as the duty of an occupant to establish an administration, maintain law and order, and ensure that other parties to the conflict in the area under their control comply with international norms of IHL and human rights law.

Even if it is accepted that the UN is bound by customary international law,[94] and that occupation law constitutes customary law, the UN would only be bound

[89] J-M Henckaerts and L Doswald-Beck, *Customary International Humanitarian Law* (Cambridge University Press Cambridge 2005). The report is the result of 10 years of research in consultation with experts from different regions.

[90] The International Military Tribunal in Nuremberg, The Trial of Major War Criminals 65 (1947) cited in E Benvenisti, *The International Law of Occupation: with a new preface by the author* (n 3), 96.

[91] A great many of the provisions contained in Geneva Convention IV are likely to be part of customary law including the right of protected persons to enjoy respect for their persons, honour, family rights, religious convictions and practices, (Article 27); the prohibition of physical and moral coercion to obtain information from protected persons (Article 31); the prohibition on collective penalties, pillage and reprisals (Article 33); the prohibition on deportations (Article 49); the prohibition on compelling persons to serve in the occupant's armed force (Article 51); the prohibition on destruction of property unless required by military necessity (Article 53): T Meron, *Human Rights and Humanitarian Norms as Customary Law* (Clarendon Press Oxford 1989), 46–47; David Kretzmer, *The Occupation of Justice* (State University of New York Press Albany 2002) 43; MJ Kelly, *Restoring and Maintaining Order in Complex Peace Operations* (n 10), 157–159.

[92] Report of the Secretary-General Pursuant to Paragraph 2 of Security Council Resolution 808, UN SCOR, 48th Sess, UN Doc S/25704.

[93] Geneva Convention III Relative to the Treatment of Prisoners of War (n 24).

[94] In the *Cumaraswamy* case the ICJ affirmed the potential responsibility of the United Nations under general international law for the conduct of its organs and agents: *Advisory Opinion concerning Difference Relating to Immunity from Legal Process of a Special Rapporteur of the Commission on Human Rights*, ICJ, 29 April 1999; Peacekeeping is not mentioned in the Charter but in its *Certain Expenses* Advisory Opinion, the ICJ held that the UN Security Council and General Assembly are

if the situation closely parallels that to which the laws of occupation would apply to States. It is one thing to assert that certain rules apply in occupation; it requires a different set of rules to determine whether or not there is an occupation. The ICRC report on customary IHL sets out many rules that are binding on all occupying powers by virtue of their customary law nature, but the report does not define 'occupying power' or 'occupied territory.' UN exercise of control over territory bears some similarities with occupations by States, but there are also important differences.

The remainder of this chapter analyses some of the problems that have arisen in specific operations undertaken by multi-national forces in respect of whose activities the laws of occupation were, or may have been, applicable, focusing in particular on the interventions in Somalia, Iraq and Kosovo.

4. The Extent to which the Laws of Occupation were Applicable to Somalia

The issue of whether the laws of occupation applied to UN forces first came to prominence in the context of UN operations in Somalia in the early 1990s. Resolution 794, adopted under Chapter VII, mandated the Unified Task Force (UNITAF) to use 'all necessary means to establish as soon as possible a secure environment for humanitarian relief operations in Somalia.' However, whilst the UN Secretariat wanted a stronger approach that would encompass disarmament of Somali factions;[95] since the mission's objective was humanitarian the US did not want to appear to be intervening in the State's internal affairs, particularly since Somalis traditionally carry arms.[96] This difference in understanding of the mandate led to different approaches to the applicability of occupation law. The legal advisor to the Australian forces in UNITAF considered that the laws of occupation applied de jure to its UN operation in Somalia,[97] because UNITAF was the sole organized entity capable of exercising authority in the areas it occupied.[98] But UNITAF command believed that reference to occupation was

competent to establish peacekeeping operations: *Advisory Opinion concerning Certain Expenses of the United Nations*, ICJ Reports, 1962, 151, 165, 177; D Akande, 'International Organizations' in MD Evans (ed), *International Law* (Oxford University Press Oxford 2003), 282; C Gray, 'The Use of Force and the International Legal Order' in MD Evans (ed), *International Law* (Oxford University Press Oxford 2002), 598, 611.

[95] RG Patman, 'Disarming Somalia: The Contrasting Fortunes of United States and Australian Peacekeepers During United Nations Intervention 1992–1993' 96 African Affairs, 509, 512.

[96] ibid.

[97] MJ Kelly, *Restoring and Maintaining Order in Complex Peace Operations* (n 10), 17.

[98] ibid 29; Kelly states that by mid-January 1993 'the force had the capacity to exert a measure of control over this territory [the regions south of the Galguduud Province] and assume many of the prerogatives of the sovereign, and in fact did so in a broad variety of areas', for example it took control of Mogadishu airport and setting up an Airspace Control Authority for Somalia (1 February 1993); ibid, 16–17.

inappropriate since the operation was a humanitarian one. The US emphatically rejected the view that occupation law was applicable stating that:

> there was concern over the responsibilities that might flow from acknowledging the application of the law in the context of the extremely minimalist approach dictating the shape of the mission.[99]

Thus the laws of occupation were applied in the area of Somalia under the control of Australian forces but not in the US and French sectors.[100] Pursuant to its obligation to maintain law and order under the laws of occupation, the Australian contingent at Baidoa re-established the local police force and legal system, and re-opened the local courts and jails.[101] By contrast, very little action was taken by UNITAF at the national level to re-establish a Somali police force or judiciary.[102]

Kelly argues that had the US accepted that the laws of occupation were applicable, much of the chaos and confusion that led both to the lack of respect for IHL on the part of some UN troops and the lack of respect shown towards peacekeeping forces by local factions could have been significantly reduced.[103] He argues that Australia's decision to apply the laws of occupation gave the Australian contingent a body of laws from which to draw guidelines and standards that enabled them to tackle the security problems endemic to a collapsed State much more effectively than was the case in other sectors.[104] The Security Council resolutions establishing UNITAF and establishing the UN operations under the command of the Secretary-General (UNOSOMs I and II) provided authorization for the deployment of troops and for some specific objectives. But they did not provide a clear framework for dealing with the problems troops were likely to encounter in a collapsed State such as the handling of detainees, and how to deal with crime in the absence of any functioning judicial system:

> The Security Council Resolutions in fact posed more questions than they answered. Something more was clearly needed and this is where the laws of occupation could have provided the standard against which the force measured the legitimacy of its actions and the steps that ought to have been taken.[105]

[99] ibid 17.

[100] MV Bhatia, *War and Intervention: Issues for Contemporary Peace Operations* (Kumarian Press Inc. Bloomfield 2003), 98; MJ Kelly, *Restoring and Maintaining Order in Complex Peace Operations* (n 10), 17.

[101] T Findlay, *The Use of Force in Peace Operations* (Oxford University Press Oxford 2002) 177.

[102] S Chesterman, *You, The People: United Nations Transitional Administration and State-Building* (Oxford University Press Oxford 2004), 115; Increased attacks on US Marines did eventually prompt some attempts to establish a local police force in Mogadishu in February 1993: RG Patman, 'Disarming Somalia: The Contrasting Fortunes of United States and Australian Peacekeepers During United Nations Intervention 1992–1993' (n 95), 517.

[103] MJ Kelly, *Restoring and Maintaining Order in Complex Peace Operations* (n 10), 31.

[104] ibid 63.

[105] ibid 70.

Kelly argues that it was virtually impossible to maintain law and order without adopting some of the rights and duties of an occupant. In his view the failure of the UN to effectively support the reconstruction of the police force and the refusal to take any measures at all to establish an efficacious justice administration was 'an abrogation of the obligations of international law.'[106] He points out that there was no reference in either the Security Council resolutions or in the operation's Rules of Engagement, as to what the overall legal framework governing relations with the community was to be.[107] Since there was no government with which to negotiate there was also no Status of Forces Agreement or Memorandum of Understanding.[108] In Kelly's view some of the violence perpetrated against Somalis can be attributed to frustration felt by troops who were unable to do anything about constant but relatively minor offences against them, such as theft. The torture and beating to death of a Somali caught within the perimeter of a Canadian contingent:

> was only the most severe of what was not an uncommon practice of administering some form of physical punishment to those caught stealing or breaching perimeters as a means of discouraging further attempts and seeing some 'justice' done.[109]

Some commentators have noted that the approach taken in the Australian sector was a great deal more successful than that of contingents operating in other sectors and, moreover, that the societal benefits of the Australian approach continue to be apparent long after the peace operations' withdrawal.[110] Bhatia argues that the Australians succeeded in restoring local security because they had a legal framework in which to carry out that task and because they put a great deal of effort into working with the local population through pro-active political-military programmes.[111] In his view, the fact that the Australians undertook 'a fully fledged civil affairs programme, which it regarded as essential for restoring security in its area,' whereas the US 'view[ed] such efforts as mission creep,' was crucial to the success of the Australian operation.[112] Findlay considers that, whilst comparisons are a little unfair given that the Australians were based in Baidoa, a backwater compared with Mogadishu, there is an element of truth in Bhatia's argument.[113] Patman comments that:

[106] ibid 28. Kelly cites as an example the arrest of faction leader Omar Jess (there was evidence that he was responsible for the massacre of a large number of civilians) and subsequent release because there was no procedure for dealing with him. No tribunals were convened to deal with such offences 'due specifically to uncertainty over the legal basis for the exercise of such jurisdiction and the reluctance to acknowledge the laws of occupation.' ibid, 24.

[107] ibid 21. [108] ibid. [109] ibid 29.

[110] MV Bhatia, *War and Intervention: Issues for Contemporary Peace Operations* (n 100), 98; T Findlay, *The Use of Force in Peace Operations* (n 101), 177; RG Patman, 'Disarming Somalia: The Contrasting Fortunes of United States and Australian Peacekeepers During United Nations Intervention 1992–1993' (n 95), 519, 526.

[111] MV Bhatia, *War and Intervention: Issues for Contemporary Peace Operations* (n 100), 98.

[112] ibid.

[113] T Findlay, *The Use of Force in Peace Operations* (n 101), 177.

Even allowing for differences in development, population size and clan composition between Mogadishu and Baidoa, a comparison of the disarmament efforts of the two cities is illuminating. At the beginning of the UN's humanitarian intervention, both places were full of the sounds of death and destruction. However by the time UNITAF was replaced by UNOSOM II in May 1993, the security situation in the two locations had markedly diverged. Mogadishu saw a somewhat marginal improvement while Baidoa underwent a positive transformation.

... The Australians arrived in Baidoa with a well-defined game plan... Because Somalia was a heavily armed 'failed state' with no effective civil authority, the Australians took the view there was no sovereignty to offend. In placing themselves above the belligerents, the Australians not only sought to maintain a ceasefire in Baidoa through forcible disarmament, but also to re-establish a law and order structure as part of a wider social reconstruction effort.[114]

The legal advisor to the Australians viewed the applicability of occupation law as an integral part of that game plan. It gave the force a legal framework governing its relationship with the local population within which it could undertake administrative and policing tasks.

UNITAF was replaced by UNOSOM II, which had one of the most extensive mandates ever undertaken by a UN force. It was the first peace enforcement operation explicitly authorized under Chapter VII of the Charter that was both organized and commanded by the UN,[115] and for the short duration of the operation, UNOSOM II was the de facto government in Somalia.[116] The force was given a Chapter VII mandate to undertake a wide range of tasks that included ensuring compliance with peace agreements to which the factions had agreed and taking appropriate action against any faction that threatened violence; maintaining control of the heavy weapons of organized factions which were to be brought under international control pending their destruction; seizing small arms of unauthorized armed elements; securing all ports, airports and lines of communication; protecting personnel and equipment of the UN, ICRC, NGOS and other agencies:

and to take such forceful action as may be required to neutralize armed elements that attack, or threaten to attack, such facilities and personnel, pending the establishment of a new Somali police force which can assume this responsibility.[117]

The resolution also provided for a wide-ranging agenda of other tasks to be undertaken (but not under Chapter VII) that included assistance in re-establishing local and national police forces and offering:

[114] RG Patman, 'Disarming Somalia: The Contrasting Fortunes of United States and Australian Peacekeepers During United Nations Intervention 1992–1993' (n 95), 526–7.

[115] *The United Nations and Somalia* (UN Department of Public Information New York 1996), 40.

[116] S Chesterman, *You, The People: United Nations Transitional Administration and State-Building* (n 102), 85, 107.

[117] S/RES 814 26 March 1993.

assistance to help the people of Somalia to promote and advance political reconciliation, through broad participation by all sectors of Somali society, and the re-establishment of the of national and regional institutions and civil administration in the entire country.

The US Permanent Representative in New York, Madeline Albright, interpreted the resolution as providing for 'an unprecedented enterprise aimed at nothing less than the restoration of an entire country as a proud, functioning and valuable member of the community of nations.'[118]

Arguably UNOSOM's extensive mandate, in a country where there was no government outside the will of local war lords, put it in the position of an occupant.[119]

The Human Rights Committee held that the International Convention on Civil and Political Rights was applicable to UNOSOM II by virtue of the fact that it exercised de facto control over Somalia,[120] but it did not suggest that the laws of occupation might have been applicable. However, in 2004 the *Commission of Inquiry Established pursuant to SC Res. 885 (1993) to Investigate Armed Attacks on UNOSOM II Personnel which Led to Casualties among Them*, published a report which stated that:

The finding that a country is without a government... has such far reaching legal and political consequences that careful criteria for invoking it are required. If the United Nations operates in a country that it has thus characterized, it necessarily has to bear responsibility for at least some of the basic state concerns traditionally appertaining to a government and that could invariably raise the spectre of a United Nations trusteeship or neo colonialism.[121]

5. The Applicability of the Laws of Occupation to Iraq

The invasion and subsequent occupation of Iraq in 2003 brought about a change in perceptions regarding the relevance of occupation law to multi-national forces that has implications for peace support forces, including those acting under a UN mandate. The drafters of the UK's most recent military manual on the Laws of Armed Conflict had initially considered omitting any section on the laws of occupation as irrelevant to UK forces in the modern world.[122] It was only

[118] S/PV.31888, cited in *The United Nations and Somalia* (n 115), 44.

[119] Michael Kelly, 'UN, security and human rights: achieving a willing balance' in *The UN, Human Rights and Post Conflict Situations*, eds Nigel White and Dirk Glassen (Manchester University Press Manchester 2005), 121, 129.

[120] UN Doc CCPR/C/79/Add.99 [14]; UN Doc CCPR/C/81/BEL [10].

[121] Report of the *Commission of Inquiry Established pursuant to SC Res. 885 (1993) to Investigate Armed Attacks on UNOSOM II Personnel which Led to Casualties among Them*, established on 24 November 1993, Report issued 31 May 1994, Annex 5, UN Doc S/1994/653, [251] ; Michael Kelly, 'UN, security and human rights: achieving a willing balance' in *The UN, Human Rights and Post Conflict Situations*, eds Nigel White and Dirk Glassen (n 119), 131.

[122] Dr Stephen Haines, Chairman of the Editorial Board, UK Ministry of Defence Manual of the Law of Armed Conflict, speaking at a conference on 'UK Perspectives on the Laws of Armed Conflict', 30 June–2 July 2004, St Anthony's College, Oxford.

the highly controversial nature of the invasion of Iraq and the failure to obtain Security Council authorization[123] that triggered an insistence on explicit recognition of the applicability of the laws of occupation.[124] However, occupation law had been relevant to multi-national operations in Iraq since 1991.

5.1 Operation Provide Comfort

Operation Provide Comfort was a short-term intervention into northern Iraq in 1991 to protect Kurds from attacks perpetrated by the Baghdad government. Its purpose was to establish 'safe havens' so that refugees caught on the mountains on the borders of Turkey (to which they were refused entry) and dying of exposure, could return home. The operation was not authorized by the Security Council but the intervening States argued that it was 'consistent with' and 'in support' of Security Council resolutions.[125] The intervening States were reluctant to use the word occupation,[126] partly because of its negative connotations but also because of the possible legal obligations such an acknowledgement might entail. But it clearly had the elements of an occupation.[127] Coalition forces were present in comparatively large numbers and exercised control over the area to the complete exclusion of the Baghdad administration.[128] Saddam Hussein protested strongly but did not resist militarily.[129] No concessions were made to mitigate his anger: following his invasion of Kuwait he had no international support and following his defeat in that war he was not in a position to oppose the intervening forces militarily.[130] The New York Times quoted US officials as saying that the designation of 'informal safe havens' reflected 'a compromise intended to

[123] The earlier interventions were not authorized by the UN either but there was little protest from UN Member States.

[124] S/RES 1483 22 May 2003. Resolution 1483 of May 2003 mandated the continued presence of the Multi-National Force (MNF) but also confirmed the status of the US and UK as occupiers thereby making it clear that occupation and UN authorization are not mutually incompatible.

[125] In particular S/RES/688, 5 April 1991; Press Conference of President Bush 17 April 1991 cited in E Coltran, 'The Establishment of A Safe Haven for the Kurds in Iraq' in N Al-Naiumi and R Meese (eds), *International Issues Arising under the United Nations Decade of International Law* (Martinus Nijhoff Publishers The Hague 1995) 855, 867; *Keesing's Record of World Events,* Vol 37 (1991) 38127; Statement of French Foreign Ministry 2/9/1996 cited in N Krisch, 'Unilateral Enforcement of the Collective Will', Max Planck UN Year Book 3 (1999) 59, 76.

[126] E Benvenisti, *The International Law of Occupation: with a new preface by the author* (n 3), 181; H McCoubrey and N White, *International Law and Armed Conflict* (n 10), 281.

[127] ibid.

[128] For three months soldiers from the United States, Great Britain, France, Netherlands, Spain, Italy and Austria, occupied 10,000 square kilometres of Iraqi territory. At the height of the operation there were 20,000 troops there. Iraqi forces were not permitted to enter the protected zone: H Cook, *The Safe Haven in Iraq: International Responsibility for Iraqi Kurdistan* (Human Rights Centre, University of Essex Colchester 1995) 46.

[129] P Malanczuk, 'The Kurdish Crisis and Allied Intervention in the Aftermath of the Second Gulf War', 2 EJIL 2, 114, 120.

[130] ibid 120.

side-step problems of international law and regional sensitivities about the nature and future of the area.'[131]

Although there has been some criticism of the motives of the coalition States,[132] there is little doubt that the multi-national operation achieved notable success in providing protection to the Kurdish refugees. Troops were able to assist their return, and ensure the distribution of humanitarian aid, such as food, shelter, access to water, and medical supplies and treatment.[133] Some 450,000 Kurds were encouraged and assisted to come down from the mountains to the protected zone. Despite the highly questionable legal basis for the intervention, most criticisms centre not on the occupation itself but on the manner of its ending.

5.2 The No Fly Zones

In July 1991, the last 3000 soldiers of the coalition forces withdrew.[134] Prior to their departure, the coalition States declared a No Fly Zone barring flights of Iraqi military aircraft above the 36th parallel in northern Iraq. About 5000 troops remained stationed in Turkey, ready to intervene in Iraq if necessary.[135] These troops left on the 10 October 1991 but some American, British and French aircraft remained at the Turkish base of Incirlik.[136] Use of the airbase was subject to approval every six months by the Turkish Parliament. In August 1992 the coalition States declared a No Fly Zone covering Iraqi territory below the 32nd parallel in southern Iraq. In 1996, the southern No Fly Zone was extended up to the 33rd parallel.[137] The No Fly Zone was presented as a humanitarian operation necessary to provide protection for the inhabitants after the intervening forces

[131] *Bush Sees Accord on 'Safe Havens' for Kurds in Iraq*, NY Times, April 12, 1991, at A1; E Benvenisti, *The International Law of Occupation: with a new preface by the author* (n 3), 181.

[132] Bill Frelick has argued that Operation Provide Comfort was 'as much to shore up US alliances with friendly governments as to assist refugees... Turkey the good ally, was essentially let off the hook with the creation of a "safe haven" inside Iraq. The needs of the refugees were a considerably lower priority than the need to cement political alliances.': B Frelick, 'The False Promise of Operation Provide Comfort: Protecting Refugees or Protecting State Power' Middle East Report, No 176, Iraq in the Aftermath (May–June 1992) 22, 25.

[133] Philip Alston writes that in 'practical terms neither the desirability, nor the effectiveness of the allied initiative can, at least in retrospect, be convincingly challenged': P Alston, 'The Security Council and Human Rights: Lessons to be Learned from the Iraq-Kuwait Crisis and its Aftermath', 13 Australian Yearbook of International Law, 107, 151; Major General R Ross, 'Some Early Lessons From Operation Haven' [Winter 1991] Royal United Service Institute Journal, 19, 21.

[134] Christine Gray suggests that they left '[o]nce the issue of the Kurds had ceased to interest the world's media': C Gray, 'After the Ceasefire: Iraq, The Security Council and the Use of Force', 65 British Yearbook of International Law 135, 163.

[135] P Malanzczuk, 'The Kurdish Crisis and Allied Intervention in the Aftermath of the Second Gulf War' (n 129), 123.

[136] ibid.

[137] France did not participate in the extended no-fly zone and in 1997 it withdrew from participation in the northern no-fly zone alleging a lack of humanitarian character in the operation. In 1998 it also withdrew from the southern no-fly zone: N Krisch, 'Unilateral Enforcement of the Collective Will' (n 125), 74.

left. The small UN Guards contingent that replaced the coalition forces provided a visible UN presence but did not provide direct protection to the Kurdish people. Most were armed security guards rather than professional trained military troops.[138] They carried only light arms supplied by the Iraqi authorities.[139] They were supposed to be deployed anywhere in Iraq in connection with the humanitarian programme but in practice they were not permitted into certain areas, particularly in the south.[140] The States that operated the No Fly Zones (the USA, the UK and until 1997, France), argued that although not strictly 'authorized' by the Security Council the zones were 'based' on UN resolutions. The Defence Secretary of the United Kingdom stated that the zones:

> were set up in support of UN Security Council Resolution 688 to bring protection to the Kurds in the north and the Shia in the south, and as long as that need remains, we will continue to enforce the no-fly zones.[141]

Similar statements were made by the US Department of Defence.[142] However, other statements by US officials indicated that the justification for the No Fly Zones also encompassed the containment of Iraq and the reduction of its military capability.[143]

It is clear that the laws of occupation were applicable to the safe havens during the three months that coalition forces were present in large numbers in the country.[144] The position after the forces left when the coalition had control of the skies through the No Fly Zones, but not of the ground, is much less clear. Helena Cook has suggested that during the period in which the No Fly Zones operated, although the coalition forces no longer exercised authority for day-to-day administration they may have 'remain[ed] responsible for areas such as defence and security in the area.'[145] Writing in 1995, she said that 'to the extent that the coalition forces are still in occupation and have displaced the Iraqi Government, leaving a vacuum in Iraqi Kurdistan' the coalition powers may still be under an obligation to ensure the protection of the population.[146] She suggested that the coalition may have had a responsibility to ensure that the UN aid programme could meet the population's essential food and medical needs

[138] Major General R Ross, 'Some Early Lessons From Operation Haven' (n 133), 46.

[139] ibid.

[140] ibid.

[141] UK Ministry of Defence, Press Release 334/98 of 30 December 1998; N Krisch, 'Unilateral Enforcement of the Collective Will' (n 125), 75.

[142] US Department of Defense, News Briefing, 5 January 1999; N Krisch, 'Unilateral Enforcement of the Collective Will' (n 125), 75.

[143] N Krisch, 'Unilateral Enforcement of the Collective Will' (n 125), 75, citing remarks by the US President 28 December 1998.

[144] E Benvenisti, *The International Law of Occupation: with a new preface by the author* (n 3), 181; H McCoubrey and N White, *International Law and Armed Conflict* (n 10), 281.

[145] H Cook, *The Safe Haven in Iraq: International Responsibility for Iraqi Kurdistan* (n 128), 158.

[146] ibid.

and also a responsibility for the maintenance of security.[147] But to what extent could the coalition be regarded as 'still in occupation' after their forces left? There is nothing in the Hague Regulations or Geneva Conventions that requires an occupant to remain and once it is no longer in occupation the laws of occupation cease to apply to it.[148] The fact that the force retains control of the air after its forces have left does not necessarily imply that occupation law remains applicable. Helena Cook's approach reflects the reality of the power relationships but although the No Fly Zones gave the coalition a certain amount of control over the area it was not the kind of control envisaged by the Hague Regulations and Geneva Conventions. Article 42 of the Hague Regulations provides that territory is 'considered occupied when it is actually placed under the authority of the hostile army.' Although the Geneva Conventions expanded the concept to include occupations occurring outside of an armed conflict, it was still envisaged that control would be exercised through the actual presence of forces.[149]

The guidelines set out in the UK Manual of the Law of Armed Conflict, 2004 suggest that in order for an occupation to exist it must be shown that the former government has been rendered incapable of publicly exercising its authority in that area and that the occupant is in a position to substitute its own authority for that of the former government.[150] The No Fly Zones did render the former government incapable of exercising some of it sovereign powers, in particular defence of the territory from attacks by other States. Whether or not the former government was capable of exercising powers of local administration is not clear, since it chose not to. In the same month that the alliance forces left, Iraq withdrew all of its civil administration from northern Iraq and imposed a punitive economic embargo on the area that extended to medical supplies, foodstuffs, petrol and heating oil.[151] The Iraqi Kurdistan Front (an alliance of KDP and PUK) took over the running of public services. In July 1992 an elected Council of Ministers took over responsibility for local self-government.[152]

[147] ibid.

[148] G von Glahn, *The Occupation of Enemy Territory...A Commentary on the Law and Practice of Belligerent Occupation* (University of Minnesota Press Minneapolis 1957), 29; However under Article 6 of Geneva Convention IV 'protected persons' whose release or reestablishment may take place after the Convention has ceased to be applicable 'shall meanwhile continue to benefit from the present Convention.' The purpose of this was to ensure protection continued in the interim period after the Convention ceased to be applicable but before the 'protected persons' were in a position to be able 'to resume a normal existence.' J Pictet (ed), *The Geneva Conventions of 12 August 1949. Commentary IV Geneva Convention* (n 11), Article 6, [4].

[149] Hans Peter Gasser writes that 'Supremacy in the air alone does not fulfil the requirements of actual occupation.' HP Gasser, 'Protection of the Civilian Population' in D Fleck (ed), *The Handbook of International Humanitarian Law* (n 9), 243.

[150] UK Ministry of Defence, *Manual of the Law of Armed Conflict* (n 19), [11.3].

[151] H Cook, *The Safe Haven in Iraq: International Responsibility for Iraqi Kurdistan* (n 128), 51.

[152] The Baghdad government did not withdraw from all the towns in the No Fly Zone. For example Mosul was within the No Fly Zone but remained under government control. On the other hand Sulaimaniyya, one of the largest cities in the region, was under Kurdish control but outside the No Fly Zone.

In the opinion of Lieutenant Colonel Schmitt, Staff Judge Advocate for Operation Northern Watch, 'a no-fly zone is a de facto aerial occupation of sovereign airspace.'[153] However, he did not think occupation law applied:

> It should be noted, however, that the concept of aerial occupation is not a legal one. In traditional humanitarian law, occupation is a term of art for physical control by one belligerent over land territory of another (or of a State occupied against its will, but without resistance). When an occupation occurs, rights and duties arise as between the occupying power and individuals located in the occupied area. An aerial occupation, by contrast, is simply a de facto, vice de jure, status in which limits are placed on a State's use of its own airspace.[154]

Schmitt's terminology is confusing. Rights and duties arise as a consequence of de facto occupation hence the contrasting of a de facto occupation with one in which 'rights and duties arise as between the occupying power and the individual,' is untenable. However, whilst IHL recognizes the possibility of an occupation limited to a particular geographical area within a State it makes no provision for an occupation limited in scope. To apply occupation law to States that control the air but not the ground would have implications that would be strongly resisted by many States. Similar questions over the responsibilities that should accompany control of air space were raised in *Banković v Belgium and 16 Other Contracting States*. The case concerned the application of the European Convention on Human Rights and Fundamental Freedoms. The applicants argued that NATO had effective control over the airspace in Kosovo and were responsible for securing certain Convention rights within the area of the airspace. The claim was rejected.[155]

The situation in Iraq differed from *Banković* in so far as the No Fly Zones concerned a reduction of control following a period that indisputably constituted occupation, whereas NATO forces had never been in occupation of the ground in Kosovo. Article 6 of Geneva Convention IV provides that key provisions shall remain in force for as long as the occupation continues.[156] But these provisions still envisage the occupant exercising authority on the ground. For example Article 27 deals with respect for protected persons, and for their honour, family rights and religious convictions, and states that women shall be protected from attacks on their honour, including rape and enforced prostitution.[157] Article 52 prohibits measures aimed at creating unemployment or at restricting the opportunities offered to workers in order to induce them to work for the occupant.[158]

[153] Lieutenant Colonel M Schmitt, 'Clipped Wings: Effective and Legal No-fly Zone Rules of Engagement' (1998) 20 Loyola of Los Angeles International & Comparative Law Journal, 727, 729.

[154] ibid n 6.

[155] *Banković v Belgium and 16 Other Contracting States* European Court of Human Rights (52207/99) (2001), [75–76].

[156] Geneva Convention IV (n 1), art 6.

[157] ibid art 27.

[158] ibid art 52.

However, it could be argued that when it withdrew its forces but retained control of the air, the coalition did not end its occupation but merely gave up some of its rights in the occupied territory. Whether or not the coalition powers could be considered to still be in occupation would depend on whether their control of the air was sufficient to render them in effective control of the territory. There is some precedent for occupying powers giving up their rights but remaining in overall control. On 28 September 1995, the Palestinian Liberation Organization (PLO) and Israel entered into the Israeli-Palestinian Interim Agreement on the West Bank and Gaza Strip, known as Oslo II.[159] Oslo II set up a complex geographical framework for limited Palestinian self-rule. It divided the West Bank into three areas (A, B, and C). The Palestinian Council assumed all civil powers and responsibilities in Areas A and B. It also assumed limited 'civil powers and responsibilities not relating to territory' in Area C. The Palestinian Council was responsible for internal security and public order in Area A. In Area B, the Palestinian Council had responsibility for public order, but Israel retained overriding responsibility for internal security. Israel retained all security and public order responsibilities in Area C but it was planned that the Israeli responsibility for internal security would eventually be transferred to the Palestinian police. Thus the occupant retained responsibility for external security in all three areas but the Palestinian Council had extensive responsibilities relating to civilian administration, public order and internal security. The control exercised by the coalition over northern Iraq was considerably less than that exercised by Israel in the West Bank; but on the other hand they were the only powers capable of exercising authority and control over matters outside the domestic arena.

5.2.1 Security and Human Rights Protection in the No Fly Zones

Control of the air space put the US and UK in a position where it could exercise control over some important aspects affecting the lives of the inhabitants such as security. By setting up the No Fly Zones, the coalition States prevented the Iraqi government from exercising military control over its territory. However, the extent to which they themselves took control of the protected area, was limited.[160] Both Turkey and Iran carried out military raids in northern Iraq but the No Fly Zones prevented the Iraqi authorities from taking any action.[161]

[159] Israeli-Palestinian Interim Agreement on the West Bank and the Gaza Strip, Sept. 28, 1995, Isr.-PLO, Ch. 5, art. XXXI, P 5, 36 ILM 551 (1997).

[160] The southern No Fly Zone did little to deter human rights abuses against the population. Large-scale military attacks and massive human rights violations by Iraqi agents continued in the southern areas: H Cook, *The Safe Haven in Iraq: International Responsibility for Iraqi Kurdistan* (n 128), 48.

[161] Human Rights Watch, 'Iraq and Iraqi Kurdistan: Human Rights Developments' World Report (2001), 7 <http:www.hrw.org>. However, during the Iran–Iraq War Turkish forces had twice crossed the border to attack Kurdish insurgents, with Iraqi permission: L Freedman and D Boren, '"Safe Havens" for Kurds in Post-War Iraq' in NS Rodley (ed), *To Loose the Bounds of Wickedness: International Intervention in Defence of Human Rights* (Brassey's London 1992) 43, 49.

In 1995, citing the activities of Turkish Kurd guerrillas in Iraq, Turkey sent in 35,000 troops.[162] Thousands of people were displaced and the head of the UN contingent in Iraq reported that UN guards were prevented by Turkish troops from visiting Kurdish villages to carry out their normal patrols.[163] One writer comments that the US gave the Turkish incursion its 'tacit endorsement.'[164] Others go further and argue that the management of the crisis in 1991 'was shaped from the start by the government in Ankara' which wanted to avoid any boost to Kurdish plans for separatism.[165] The coalition relied on permission from Turkey to operate from its base at Incirluk. It is alleged that serious human rights violations were committed in the course of these raids.[166] The States controlling the No Fly Zone did not take any steps to protect the inhabitants from these attacks.[167] Quite the reverse, in 1999 the Turkish and US militaries established separate air lanes so that US aircraft patrolling the No Fly Zone would not cross paths with Turkish planes bombing alleged Kurdish terrorist bases.[168] A spokesman for coalition forces in the region, Major Michael McKinney of the US army, said the forces were there to protect the Kurds from Iraq, not from Turkey.[169]

Although the coalition took no action against Turkish incursions, in 1996 when Iraqi troops intervened in fighting between the two largest Kurdish groups (giving their support to one faction) the US and UK reacted with missile strikes. However, even though the Kurds are based in the north, the retaliatory strikes were against targets in southern Iraq. The coalition also extended the southern No Fly Zone up to the 33rd parallel to reduce Iraq's military capability.[170] Michael Byers questions:

> with regard to humanitarian intervention, what weight should be accorded to the 1996 decision to strike at targets in southern rather than northern Iraq in response to renewed persecution of the Kurds?[171]

Lieutenant Colonel Schmitt, Staff Judge Advocate for Operation Northern Watch wrote that:

[162] K Landgren, 'Safety Zones and International Protection: A Dark Grey Area', 7 International Journal of Refugee Law 3, 436, 443.

[163] ibid.

[164] ibid.

[165] L Freedman and D Boren, '"Safe havens" for Kurds in post-war Iraq' (n 161), 44.

[166] In one case brought before the European Court of Human Rights villagers alleged that a number of shepherds were detained, tortured, mutilated and murdered by Turkish soldiers. The ECtHR held that there was insufficient proof that Turkish forces were responsible: *Issa and others v Turkey* App No 31821/96 Judgment 16 November 2004, [63].

[167] H Cook, *The Safe Haven in Iraq: International Responsibility for Iraqi Kurdistan* (n 128), 50.

[168] TE Ricks, 'Containing Iraq: A Forgotten War' *Washington Post* (October 25, 2000).

[169] L Freedman and D Boren, '"Safe Havens" for Kurds in Post-War Iraq' (n 161), 79.

[170] N Krisch, 'Unilateral Enforcement of the Collective Will' (n 125), 74.

[171] M Byers, 'The Shifting Foundations of International Law: A Decade of Forceful Measures Against Iraq', 13 EJIL 1, 21, 34.

the specter of Kurds turning to the Iraqis for assistance caused many to rethink the viability of the operation. Soon thereafter, the humanitarian element of the mission was terminated, the French pulled out, and Provide Comfort was renamed Northern Watch.[172]

One of the worrying aspects of humanitarian interventions (particularly if they are unauthorized and without any readily recognized rules for regulating them) is the possibility that 'the humanitarian element of the mission' can be terminated by the intervening States, without giving any explanation (or even acknowledgement of this change) to the local population or to institutions of the international community.

Although the humanitarian element was terminated in 1996, 'the rhetoric surrounding the zones still reiterate[d] the formulas used to justify them since 1991.'[173] A number of commentators have suggested that the history of the zones displays 'a considerable gap between publicly declared purposes and real intentions.'[174] There were further missile strikes over the years, and these increased significantly after December 1998 (in response to increased Iraqi activity in the No Fly Zones).[175] In 1999 alone the US and the UK used almost two thousand bombs and cruise missiles on Iraq.[176] Iraq alleged hundreds of civilian deaths and injuries as a result of bombing by alliance forces and that view has been supported, at least partially, by humanitarian organizations.[177] The UK and the US expressed regret for any civilian deaths but insisted that the bombing was necessary in order take out Iraqi missile defence systems that threatened alliance aircraft and that all attacks were proportionate and in accordance with IHL.[178] The No Fly Zones remained in place until coalition forces invaded Iraq in March 2003.

[172] Lieutenant Colonel M Schmitt, 'Clipped Wings: Effective and Legal No-fly Zone Rules of Engagement' (n 153), 736.

[173] S Graham-Brown, 'No Fly Zones: Rhetoric and Real Intentions', *MERIP* (February 20 2001) <http://www.merip.org/mero/mero022001.html>.

[174] ibid.

[175] At the same time as the bombings increased, the 1998 Iraq Liberation Act required the USA administration to identify Iraqi opposition groups working for democracy and to give them $97 million in financial aid and arms: C Gray, 'From Unity to Polarization: International Law and the Use of Force against Iraq', 13 EJIL 1, 1, n 45; Over the next five years, the CIA disbursed approximately $20 million annually to Iraqi opponents of the Hussein regime: RJ Smith and DB Ottaway, 'Anti-Saddam Operation Cost CIA $ 100 million', *Washington Post* (Sept. 15, 1996); GE Bisharat, 'American Presence Abroad, US Foreign Policy and Its Implications for Gender, Race and Justice: Facing Tyranny with Justice: Alternatives to War in the Confrontation with Iraq', 7 The Journal of Gender, Race & Justice, 1, 32.

It has been suggested in some newspapers that some of the bombing that took place in 2000 was carried out more for domestic policy reasons than because of the situation in Iraq: 'Operation Desert Prick' *The New Republic* (30 September 1996) 7; K Bennoune, 'Sovereignty vs. Suffering? Re-Examining Sovereignty and Human Rights Through the Lens of Iraq', 13 EJIL 1, 243, 258.

[176] MV Bhatia, *War and Intervention: Issues for Contemporary Peace Operations* (n 100), 9.

[177] Amnesty International, 'Iraq' in *Annual Report* 2000, 2 >http:www.amnesty.org>; Amnesty International, 'Iraq: People come first' <http://web.amnesty.org/pages/irq-index-eng>; Human Rights Watch, 'Human Rights Development' *World Report* 2000, 2 <http://www.hrw.org>; TE Ricks, 'Containing Iraq: A Forgotten War', *Washington Post* (October 25, 2000).

[178] M Byers, 'The Shifting Foundations of International Law: A Decade of Forceful Measures Against Iraq', 13 EJIL 1, 21, 29, n 37.

5.3 The 2003 Intervention and Subsequent Occupation

The primary reason given by the US and UK for going to war in March 2003 was an allegation that Iraq possessed weapons of mass destruction which presented a threat to international peace and security. However, the case for war was strongly bolstered by the fact that Saddam Hussein was a notorious tyrant, and human rights abuses under his rule were widespread and serious. No weapons of mass destruction have since been found and as a result humanitarian concerns have retrospectively become the main case for the war.[179]

President Bush officially announced the end of 'major combat operations' on the 1 May 2003.[180] On 6 May, President Bush named Paul Bremer, former head of the Counter-Terrorism Department at the United States State Department, as the Administrator of the Coalition Provisional Authority (CPA). The basis for the establishment of the CPA is not very clear.[181] The US Congressional Research Service has commented that:

> The lack of an authoritative and unambiguous statement about how this organization was established, by whom, and under what authority leaves open many questions, particularly in the areas of oversight and accountability.[182]

On 8 May 2003, the permanent representatives of the United Kingdom and the United States sent a letter to the president of the Security Council pledging to:

> strictly abide by their obligations under international law, including those relating to the essential humanitarian needs of the people of Iraq.[183]

The letter did not refer to occupation but it made clear their intention to undertake transformation of the political situation in order to enable the Iraqi people to determine their own political future:

> The United States, the United Kingdom and Coalition partners are facilitating the establishment of representative institutions of government, and providing for the responsible

[179] JM Welsh, 'Conclusion: Humanitarian Intervention after 11 September' in JM Welsh (ed), *Humanitarian Intervention and International Relations* (Oxford University Press Oxford 2004) 176, 183; The Independent, A Grice and B Russell, 'Now Blair cites regime change as basis for war. So was it legal?' (July 15, 2004) 5.

[180] Press Release, Office of the Press Secretary, President Bush Announces Major Combat Operations in Iraq Have Ended (May 1, 2003), <http://www.whitehouse.gov/news/releases/2003/05/iraq/200305 01–15.html>.

[181] SD Murphy, 'Contemporary Practice of the United States Relating to International Law: Coalition Laws and Transition Arrangements During Occupation of Iraq' (2004) 98 AJIL, 601, 601.

[182] Congressional Research Service, The Coalition Provisional Authority (CPA): Origin, Characteristics and Institutional Authorities (CRS Order Code RL32370, 2004), available at <http://www.fas.org/man/crs/RL32370.pdf>.

[183] Letter from the Permanent representatives of the UK and the US (Jeremy Greenstock and John G. Negroponte) addressed to the President of the Security Council, UN Doc S/2003/538 of May 8, 2003. Available at <http://www.globalpolicy.org/security/issues/iraq/document/2003/0608usukletter.htm>.

administration of the Iraqi financial sector, for humanitarian relief, for economic reconstruction, for the transparent operation and repair of Iraq's infra-structure and natural resources, and for the progressive transfer of administrative responsibilities to such representative institutions of government, as appropriate. Our goal is to transfer responsibility for administration to representative Iraqi authorities as early as possible.[184]

On 16 May 2003 the first CPA regulation set out the powers of the CPA. These included the temporary exercise of government powers to 'provide for the effective administration of Iraq during the period of transitional administration.'[185] The goal of the CPA was to restore security and stability, create conditions in which the Iraqi people can freely determine their political future, and facilitate economic recovery and reconstruction.[186] The US granted the CPA exclusive executive, legislative, and judicial authority over Iraq.[187] All CPA regulations or orders had to be approved by the Administrator, Paul Bremer.[188]

On 22 May 2003 the Security Council adopted Resolution 1483 in which it resolved that the UN should play:

a vital role in humanitarian relief, the reconstruction of Iraq, and the restoration and establishment of national and local institutions for representative governance.

The resolution noted the letter of 8 May 2003 from the Permanent Representatives of the US and the UK to the President of the Security Council. The resolution went further than that letter noting:

the specific authorities, responsibilities, and obligations under applicable international law of these states as occupying powers

The resolution then called upon 'all concerned to comply fully with their obligations under international law including in particular the Geneva Conventions of 1949 and the Hague Regulations of 1907.'[189] However, the Security Council also set out a number of goals that the occupants should aim to achieve that went far beyond what is normally required under occupation law. One commentator has described Resolution 1483, as 'a study in deliberate ambiguity' that might possibly become the latest example of 'hegemonic international law.'[190] There is certainly no suggestion that failure to comply with relevant obligations under international humanitarian law may result in the occupying powers being held to

[184] ibid.

[185] Coalition Provisional Authority Regulation Number 1, CPA/REG/16 May 2003/01, <http://www.cpa-iraq.org/regulations/REG1.pdf>.

[186] ibid. [187] ibid. [188] ibid.

[189] The preamble to Resolution 1483 of May 2003 confirmed that the US and UK were occupying powers in Iraq but it also stated that 'other States that are not occupying powers are working now or in the future may work under the Authority [Coalition Provisional Authority].' However in paragraph 5 the Security Council calls upon 'all concerned to comply with their obligations under international law including in particular the Geneva Conventions of 1949 and the Hague Regulations of 1907.' which suggests that the 'other States that are not occupying powers' (presumably 'all concerned' includes these) are under an obligation to comply with the laws of occupation.

[190] JE Alvarez, 'Hegemonic International Law Revisited', (2003) 97 AJIL, 873, 883.

account: no reference is made for example to the International Committee of the Red Cross which could have been designated to undertake a monitoring task and to report on matters such as the number of civilian deaths, as well as compliance with humanitarian law.[191] The ambivalence in the resolution probably reflects the sharp political differences within the Security Council with regard to the intervention in Iraq, alongside recognition that restoration of peace and security would require the involvement of the UN.[192]

Resolution 1483 provided for a Special Representative for Iraq to work with the CPA and international agencies in undertaking a wide range of tasks. These included, among other things, humanitarian and reconstruction assistance; promoting the return of refugees and displaced persons; advancing efforts to restore and establish national and local institutions for representative governance; facilitating the reconstruction of key infrastructure; promoting economic reconstruction and sustainable development; and encouraging international efforts to promote legal and judicial reform.[193] The resolution does not state how the Special Representative, the Authority and the various agencies are to work together other than that they must co-ordinate. Since the same resolution referred to the US and the UK as occupying powers and stated that they must comply with their obligations as occupants under the Hague Regulations and Geneva Conventions, it must be assumed that the additional tasks listed above were not intended to replace responsibilities under occupation law, but to supplement them. These wider tasks are not necessarily incompatible with occupation law. Article 43 of the Hague Regulations which requires occupants to restore *'la vie publics'* has been interpreted as extending beyond maintaining law and order and requiring restoration and maintenance of the commercial and economic life of the country.[194] But Resolution 1483 did not make clear the relation between the objectives concerning the transformation of the Iraqi administration, infrastructure,

[191] Resolutions 1483 of 22 May 2003 and 1546 8 June 2004 establish the International Advisory and Monitoring Board but its task is limited to ensuring that the Development Fund for Iraq is used in a transparent and equitable manner and ensuring that all proceeds of export sales of petroleum, petroleum products and natural gas from Iraq are deposited into the Development Fund for Iraq in accordance with the provisions of resolution 1546: <http://www.iamb.info/tor.htm>.

[192] The US and the UK argue that the 2003 intervention was authorized by the Security Council: US Operational Law Handbook 2004 (International and Operational Law Department, The Judge Advocate General's Legal Center and School <http://www.jagcnet.army.mil>), 3. But the Secretary-General has stated that in his view the intervention was illegal: Interview with BBC 16 September 2004: 'The United Nations Secretary-General Kofi Annan has told the BBC the US-led invasion of Iraq was an illegal act that contravened the UN Charter.' <http://news.bbc.co.uk/2/hi/middle_east/3661134.stm>. It is a view shared by many leading legal academics: 'War would be Illegal' Letter to the Guardian, 7 March 2003.

[193] S/RES 1483, 22 May 2003, [8].

[194] EH Schwenk, 'Legislative Power of the Military Occupant under Article 43, Hague Regulations' (n 43), 398; C Greenwood, 'The Administration of Occupied Territory in International Law' (n 3), 246; MJ Kelly, 'Iraq and the Law of Occupation: New Tests for an Old Law' (n 43), 147; M Sassòli 'Legislation and Maintenance of Public Order and Civil Life by Occupying Powers' (n 43), 663.

economy, and judicial system—and the existing body of law on occupations. For example it gave no guidelines on how occupation law might shape the way in which the transformation tasks were to be undertaken.[195]

A number of CPA orders not only go far beyond what would be permitted under occupation law but also go further than was strictly necessary to carry out the tasks set out by the Security Council in its resolutions. CPA Order No. 39 provides that:

> *Acting* in a manner consistent with the Report of the Secretary General to the Security Council of July 17, 2003, concerning the need for the development of Iraq and its transition from a non-transparent centrally planned economy to a market economy characterized by sustainable economic growth through the establishment of a dynamic private sector, and the need to enact institutional and legal reforms to give it effect.
>
> ...A foreign investor shall be entitled to make foreign investments in Iraq on terms no less favorable than those applicable to an Iraqi investor, unless otherwise provided herein.
>
> ...No legal text that impedes the operation of this Order shall hold and all investors, foreign and Iraqi, shall be treated equally under the law, except as otherwise specifically provided in this Order.[196]

Section 7(2) provides that a foreign investor may transfer abroad without delay all funds associated with its foreign investment. Resolution 1483 gives the Special Representative in Iraq, working in co-ordination with the Authority and international organizations, the task of 'promoting economic reconstruction and the conditions for sustainable development.' But this very general provision does not justify such extensive changes to existing law. Orders promoting investment in Iraqi companies might have served the long-term interests of the Iraqi economy better. Under CPA Order No 17:

> The MNF [Multi-National Force], Sending States and Contractors shall be exempt from general sales taxes, Value Added Tax (VAT), and any similar taxes in respect of all local purchases for official use or for the performance of Contracts in Iraq. With respect to equipment, provisions, supplies, fuel, materials and other goods and services obtained locally by the MNF, Sending States or Contractors for the official and exclusive use of the MNF or Sending States or for the performance of Contracts in Iraq, appropriate administrative arrangements shall be made for the remission or return of any excise or tax paid as part of the price. In making purchases on the local market, the MNF, Sending States and Contractors shall, on the basis of observations made and information provided by the Government in that respect, avoid any adverse effect on the local economy.[197]

[195] A Roberts, 'The End of Occupation: Iraq 2004' (n 19) 36. Resolution 1511 of 16 October 2003 reiterated the framework of occupation set out in Resolution 1483 again with no explanation of the relationship between the transformative tasks and existing obligations under occupation law.

[196] CPA Order No 39 'Foreign Investment' issued by L. Paul Bremer, Administrator, CPA, Baghdad, 19 September 2003, amended December 2003. <http://www.cpa-iraq.org>.

[197] CPA/ORD/27 June 2004/17Coalition Provisional Order No 17 (Revised) Status of the Coalition Provisional Authority, MNF-Iraq, Certain Missions and Personnel in Iraq, [10.1].

What exactly the duty to 'avoid any adverse effect on the local economy' entails, and how it is to be monitored (other than by 'observations' and 'information provided by the Government') is unclear.[198] In addition, Contractors and International Consultants were accorded exemption from taxes in Iraq on their earnings[199] and were also declared exempt from Iraqi legal processes.[200] CPA Order No. 17 was revised on 27 June 2004 so as to continue to be in force after the 'hand-over' to the Iraqi Interim government on June 28, on which day the occupation was officially declared to be at an end.

5.4 The Transfer of Sovereignty on 28 June 2004

The controversy over the extent to which coalition forces are bound by the laws of occupation in Iraq was not resolved by the official declaration of an end to that occupation on the 28 June 2004. Resolution 1546 of 8 June 2004 stated that it was 'looking forward' to the ending of the occupation with the 'transfer of sovereignty' to the Iraqi Interim government. But the 'transfer of sovereignty' that subsequently took place on the 28 June 2004 is a somewhat peculiar concept. The CPA was an occupant not a sovereign power and therefore did not have any sovereignty to transfer.[201] Iraq's continuing sovereignty had been explicitly confirmed in several Security Council resolutions dealing with the occupation: 1483 of 22 June 2003, 1511 of 16 October 2003 as well as 1546 of 8 June 2004. Even after the 'transfer,' the sovereign powers of the Iraqi interim government remain constrained.[202] Firstly, its powers were constrained by its reliance on the military and economic support of the former occupants, and the fact that it could only exercise very limited control over the MNF. But its sovereign powers were also constrained by Resolution 1546 itself, which prohibited it from 'taking any actions affecting Iraq's destiny beyond the limited interim period.' Effectively what took place was the transfer of some powers of occupancy from an occupant to a government that had powers similar to an occupant, whilst at the same time making arrangements for full resumption of sovereignty in due course.

[198] That the intervention forces in Iraq failed to give sufficient attention to the obligations that would arise once they took control of it, is tellingly illustrated by an anecdote told by Andy Bearpark, former Deputy Head of the CPA, who said that he came across a draft US Department of Defence document which stated that the only currencies that could be used in Iraq during the period of occupation were the US Dollar and the German Reichsmark: 'The Economics of State Building: the CPA in Iraq', Speaker: Simon Gray, Discussant: Andy Bearpark, St Antony's College, Oxford, 21 February 2005.

(Presumably those responsible for the drafting of this extraordinary ruling had simply rehashed documents used in the post World War II occupation of Germany.)

[199] CPA/ORD/27 June 2004/17 Coalition Provisional Order No 17 (Revised) Status of the Coalition Provisional Authority, MNF-Iraq, Certain Missions and Personnel in Iraq, [10.2].

[200] ibid [4.2–4.3].

[201] A Roberts, 'The End of Occupation: Iraq 2004' (n 19), 41.

[202] ibid 42.

5.5 The Applicability of Occupation Law to the MNF during the Period of the Interim Government

Although the initial intervention was not authorized by the UN the continued presence of the MNF was mandated by Resolution 1546. Resolution 1546 recognized that the continued presence of the MNF was at the request of the Prime Minister of the Interim Government of Iraq and recognized the importance of the consent of the 'sovereign government' of Iraq to the presence of the MNF and of the close co-operation between the MNF and that government.[203] In most cases when foreign forces are present at the request of the government of a State, their presence is governed by agreements between the host State and the States that have contributed forces, rather than IHL. However, Resolution 1546 also noted the commitment of all the forces contributing to the MNF to 'act in accordance with international law, including obligations under international humanitarian law' which suggests that IHL remained applicable despite the fact the interim government had given its consent to the operation.[204] IHL applies to all armed conflict. Colin Powell's letter annexed to Resolution 1546 states that the tasks of the MNF include 'combat operations.' The subsequent operations in Fallujah in 2004 and Operation Iron Gate and Iron Fist in October and November 2005 clearly support the view that the MNF continues to be engaged in armed conflict.[205]

The continued involvement of the MNF in armed conflict, together with the explicit confirmation of the applicability of IHL in Resolution 1546 leaves little doubt that IHL continued to be applicable, albeit in novel circumstances. But was the applicable law that of international or non-international armed conflict? The provisions applicable in non-international armed conflict are considerably less extensive than those applicable in international armed conflict. The ICTY in the *Tadic* case held that, with the development of customary IHL, many of the rules that previously applied only in international armed conflict may now be applicable in non-international armed conflict. However, not all of these rules have been extended to apply in non-international armed conflict and moreover this extension has not taken place in the form of a full and mechanical transplant of those rules to internal conflicts, but rather the general essence of those rules.[206]

[203] S/RES 1546, June 8, 2004, [9].

[204] ibid.

[205] These operations involved a high degree of force, and have resulted in large numbers of deaths: 'City of Ghosts' *Guardian* (11.1.2005); <http://www.bbcnews.co.uk>: Deaths rise in US Iraqi offensive 5.10.2005; 'Many dead' in US strike in Iraq 31.10.2005 The Pentagon has admitted that white phosphorus and thermobaric fuel-air explosives were used against insurgents and civilians in Fallujah. Both are known to cause devastating and indiscriminate harm. Their use must be carefully controlled so as to accord with IHL and they should not be used outside of armed conflict: DP Fidler 'The Use of White Phosphorus Munitions by US Military Forces in Iraq', ASIL Insight, 6 December 2005 <http:www.asil.org/insights.htm>.

[206] ICTY *Prosecutor v Dusko Tadic (Jurisdiction)* No IT-94-1-AR72, [126].

Hence the question of whether the applicable law is that of international armed conflict or of non-international armed conflict remains critical. The ICRC has determined that the conflict in Iraq has been non-international since 28 June 2004, with the establishment of the Interim Government of Iraq.[207] Daniel Thürer, in his ICRC Official Statement on 'Current challenges to the law of occupation' argues that the recognition of the Interim Government by the Security Council granted it legitimacy to act for Iraq and thus its consent to the MNF carrying out operations on its soil ended the occupation and rendered the conflict non-international.[208] The ICRC's approach to this issue is controversial. A State has the power to consent to the presence of foreign forces in its territory and clearly such an invitation differentiates their presence from that of invading forces. On the other hand, little attention has been paid to assessing criteria for determining the legal consequences of a new authority's capability to consent to the continued deployment, and engagement in combat, of the foreign forces that assisted in bringing that authority to power. Adam Roberts has suggested that the presence of large numbers of non-Iraqi troops and non-Iraqi terrorist groups indicate that the applicable law was that of international armed conflict.[209]

By virtue of common Article 2 (2) of the Geneva Conventions, occupation triggers the applicability of the law of international armed conflict. The extent of the control exercised by the US over Fallujah[210] suggests that occupation law was still an appropriate frame of reference, despite the formal ending of the occupation.[211] Nevertheless, where the government has consented to the presence of the 'occupant,' occupation law is not normally applicable. However, Article 47 of Geneva Convention IV[212] states that protected persons cannot be deprived of the benefits of the Convention by any change introduced as a result of the occupation of a territory; or as a result of changes to the institutions or government of the territory; nor by any agreement concluded between the authorities of the occupied territories and the occupying power. This provision was included because of the danger of the occupant putting pressure on the legitimate authority to conclude agreements prejudicial to protected persons.[213] This implies that an occupation that began as a result of military intervention can only be ended by agreement with a

[207] ICRC 'Iraq post 28 June 2004: protecting persons deprived of freedom remains a priority' 9 August 2004 <http://www.icrc.org/web/eng/siteeng0.nsf/html/63KKJ8>.

[208] D Thürer, ICRC Official Statement, 'Current challenges to the law of occupation' (n 12 above).

[209] A Roberts, 'The End of Occupation: Iraq 2004' (n 19), 46.

[210] The operation to remove insurgents and destroy their power base in Fallujah lasted some weeks during which time most of the city was destroyed and many civilians died: 'City of Ghosts' *Guardian* (11.1. 2005); Refugees have since been permitted to return but only if they obtain an Identity Card from the US military. A curfew was imposed: anyone who moved inside the city after 6pm was to be shot on sight by the US military.

[211] E Benvenisti, *The International Law of Occupation: with a new preface by the author* (n 3), xv.

[212] Geneva Convention IV (n 1), Art 47

[213] J Pictet (ed), *The Geneva Conventions of 12 August 1949, Commentary, Geneva Convention IV* (n 11), 275.

government that is genuinely chosen by the people (for example at an election).[214] This suggests that occupation law remained applicable to the coalition at least up until the elections held in 2005.[215] Article 6 of Geneva Convention IV provides that the application of the Convention shall cease one year after the close of military operations but:

The Occupying Power shall be bound, for the duration of the occupation, to the extent that such Power exercises the functions of government in such territory, by the provisions of the following Articles of the present Convention: 1 to 12, 27, 29 to 34, 47, 49, 51, 53, 59, 61 to 77, 143.[216]

This covers most of the important provisions.

5.6 The Significance of the Government's Consent after the Elections

Elections were held in February 2005 and therefore although the MNF is still present in Iraq, it is there at the 'invitation' of a government chosen by the people. IHL does not normally apply to forces that are invited into a country by the legitimate government.[217] This approach can create practical difficulties: for example an operation may take place in a number of territories some of which have consented and others have not, which creates problems for consistent administration. But the fact that problems can arise as a result of applying a legal principle is not in itself a sufficient reason to depart from it.[218] Sassòli has observed that 'in the Westphalian system, the consent of a State is a factor which carries significant legal consequences.'[219] Therefore it cannot be simply set aside on the grounds that real power remains with the former occupants. (The Iraqi government exercises no control over MNF operations.) But on the other hand the elected government's

[214] M Sassòli, *Article 43 of the Hague Regulations and Peace Operations in the Twenty-First Century* (n 67), 10.

[215] The ICRC takes a different view. Following Security Council Resolution 1546 the ICRC determined that 'As stated in the resolution [SC Resolution 1546], the presence and the military operations of the Multinational Forces in Iraq are based on the consent of the Interim Government of Iraq. The ICRC therefore no longer considers the situation in Iraq to be that of an international armed conflict between the US-led coalition and the state of Iraq and covered by the Geneva Conventions of 1949 in their entirety. The current hostilities in Iraq between armed fighters on one hand opposing the Multinational Force (MNF-I) and/or the newly established authorities on the other, amount to a non-international armed conflict. This means that all parties including MNF-I are bound by Article 3 common to the four Geneva Conventions, and by customary rules applicable to non-international armed conflicts.' 'Iraq post 28 June 2004: protecting persons deprived of freedom remains a priority' 9 August 2004 <http://www.icrc.org/web/eng/siteeng0.nsf/html/63KKJ8> Accessed 10 October 2008.

[216] Geneva Convention IV (n 1), Article 6.

[217] A Roberts, 'What is Military Occupation' (n 8), 291; M Sassòli 'Legislation and Maintenance of Public Order and Civil Life by Occupying Powers' (n 43), 689.

[218] M Sassòli, 'Legislation and Maintenance of Public Order and Civil Life by Occupying Powers' (n 43), 690.

[219] ibid 20.

heavy dependence on the MNF and the fact that the MNF is clearly still involved in combat operations should not be ignored.[220]

The effect of consent in relation to occupation is more complex than merely obtaining agreement to the deployment of forces. When the Soviet Union argued that the presence of its forces in Afghanistan during the 1980s was with the consent of the Afghan government many commentators questioned whether the consent was genuine. On 4 April 1980 a treaty 'on the terms of the temporary stay on Afghan territory of the limited Soviet military contingent' was signed. The text was never published and was not submitted to the UN.[221] Benvenisti observes that:

> Under the authority of the responsive Afghan government, long-term Soviet domination was sought through measures that included not only financial investments to the infra-structure, but also acculturation projects, such as indoctrination by Soviet personnel... [and] instruction in Russian[222]

A number of commentators took the view that since the Afghan government's invitation was clearly a 'mere fabrication,' the Soviet Union was an occupant under IHL.[223] It would be going too far to argue that the Iraqi government's consent to the presence of the MNF was a fabrication. Nevertheless, it is a circumscribed consent; the extreme difficulties that have arisen in trying to reach mutually acceptable terms for a Status of Forces Agreement (SOFA) between Iraq and the United States to replace the current arrangements when the MNF-I Security Council mandate expires at the end of 2008, and the resistance of the United States to certain Iraqi demands (such as the loss of foreign security

[220] Compare the sharply critical response of the majority of UN Member States to the Vietnamese invasion of Kampuchea in 1978 and the removal of the Pol Pot regime (whose appalling human rights record included large scale mass killings). In the Security Council meetings of 11–15 January 1979 most States argued that no matter how badly a government treated its people no State had the right to forcibly remove it: S/PV. 2109 and S/PV. 2110. Following the Vietnamese intervention a Vietnamese backed insurgent group, the United Front for National Salvation of Kampuchea, published a programme which included the overthrow of the Pol Pot regime, the holding of general elections and the adoption of a constitution. In 1981 the pro-Vietnamese Kampuchean People's Revolutionary Party won elections to the National Assembly. The UN refused to recognise this new government and Pol Pot's delegate continued to represent the State until 1990, but with little support from within Kampuchea. Vietnam withdrew its forces in 1989 in response to international political pressure, a US-backed economic boycott of Kampuchea, and a cut-off of aid from the Soviet Union. The Paris Peace Accords of 1991 led to the establishment of the State of Cambodia and a UN Transitional Authority Commission supported by 22,000 troops. The new State's delegate was then accepted as the rightful representative at the UN in place of Pol Pot's delegate.

[221] E Benvenisti, *The International Law of Occupation: with a new preface by the author* (n 3), 161.

[222] ibid 162.

[223] E Benvenisti, *The International Law of Occupation: with a new preface by the author* (n 3), 163; WM Reisman and J Silk, 'Which Law Applies to the Afghan Conflict', 82 AJIL, 459; But Hans Peter Gasser argued that the Afghan government's consent to the presence of Soviet troops 'may have put an end to the conflict.' HP Gasser, 'Internationalized Non-International Armed Conflicts: Case Studies of Afghanistan, Kampuchea, and Lebanon' (1983) 33 American University Law Review, 145, 151.

companies' immunity from prosecution from crimes committed under Iraqi law) suggest that the terms on which the Iraqi government initially agreed to the presence of the multinational force were not truly voluntary.[224]

The principal test for the applicability of the laws of occupation is de facto control: formal declarations announcing the commencement or cessation of occupation are of less importance.[225] The ICTY said, in the Tadic case, that Geneva Convention IV:

> does not make its applicability dependent on formal bonds and purely legal relations... Article 4 [of that Convention] intends to look to the substance of relations, not to their legal characterisation as such.[226]

Adam Roberts suggests that:

> One might hazard as a fair rule of thumb that every time the forces of a country are in control of foreign territory, and find themselves face to face with the inhabitants, some or all of the provisions on the law on occupations are applicable.[227]

Even if occupation law is not strictly applicable de jure, the Iraqi government's consent to the presence of the MNF is sufficiently lacking in independence for the principles of the laws of occupation to be considered relevant as a useful framework.

5.7 Overall Assessment of the Applicability of the Laws of Occupation to Interventions in Iraq

The invasion in 2003 was not initially authorized by the UN but the Security Council subsequently mandated the MNF's continued presence and affirmed the status of the US and UK as occupants. After the 'transfer of sovereignty' in June 2004 the MNF continued to exercise authority comparable to that of an occupant which was particularly noticeable in operations such as the one conducted in Fallujah in November of that year. Although the MNF had formally 'transferred sovereignty' it was to a government that had been established by the occupants

[224] 'Iraqi PM seeks changes to pact on US forces presence in the country' *Irish Times*, 27 October 2008; M Chulov 'Shias stage protests against Iraq-Us pact' Guardian 22 November 2008; There is evidence to suggest that the relationship between the MNF and local government officials in some areas is, or has been, quite poor. For example on 19 September 2005, in Basra, a number of British tanks smashed through the walls of Basra's central jail and freed two UK soldiers arrested earlier in the day. The incident led to a riot in the town in which British tanks were set ablaze by Iraqi civilians. A Basra judge subsequently issued an arrest warrant for the two soldiers. UK Defence Secretary John Reid commented that 'British forces remain subject to British jurisdiction' and that 'Even if such a warrant was issued, it would therefore be of no legal effect.': 'British forces break soldiers out of Basra jail', 19.10.05 <http://www.timesonline.uk>; Basra warrant for two UK soldiers 25.9.05 <http://www.bbc.co.uk/news>.

[225] A Roberts, 'The End of Occupation: Iraq 2004' (n 19), 47.

[226] ICTY, *Prosecutor v Dusko Tadic* (IT-94-1-A), 15 July 1999, [168].

[227] A Roberts, 'What Is Military Occupation' (n 8), 250.

without democratic elections and therefore arguably occupation law remained applicable, despite the formal declaration that the occupation ceased on the 28 June, the date of the hand-over. The status of the MNF after the elections is more difficult to determine. The consent of the elected government would normally vitiate the applicability of the laws of occupation. Whether the laws of occupation can be considered applicable in the context of a circumscribed consent where the former occupants continue to carry out major military operations without consultation with the government, is debateable. De facto control is normally considered the key factor in determining whether the laws of occupation apply, not formal statements declaring when they apply or cease to apply: but the consent of a State to an operation is a legally significant factor that cannot simply be swept away as irrelevant. Part of the problem has been that occupation law has been generally ignored (both in Iraq and elsewhere) even when grounds for its applicability were clear. Thus in Iraq the question of the applicability of the laws of occupation to Operation Provide Comfort was avoided, as was the question of what legal regime applied to the No Fly Zones. Similarly the question of how the laws of occupation were to be reconciled with facilitating regime change or what the legal status of the MNF after the elections should be, were never raised. It was all grey area law from beginning to end, confronted by very real and pressing human need.

6. The Laws of Occupation and UN-run Administrations

One of the less dramatic consequences of the invasion and occupation of Iraq was a revival of interest in occupation law that had previously been limited to discussion of Israel's obligations in the Occupied Palestinian Territories. Operation Provide Comfort fulfilled the criteria for occupation but this was played down at the time. Even after the intervention in 2003, although occupation law was explicitly stated to be applicable, Resolution 1483 gives no guidance on how these obligations are to be reconciled with the objectives set out in the resolution and wide powers given to the MNF. It is therefore questionable what real weight the obligations under occupation law carry in the context of such a broad mandate. However, occupation law certainly featured large on the academic radar in 2004 and raised further questions. If occupation law applied to the UN authorized occupation in Iraq, does it apply to other UN authorized administrations? Does it apply to administrations directly responsible to the UN? For example, is it applicable to the transitional administration in Kosovo, (which is still 'sovereign' despite Kosovo's declaration of independence in March 2008)?

6.1 The Transitional Administration in Kosovo

Like the interventions in Iraq, the bombing campaign in Kosovo was undertaken without UN authorization but the UN subsequently became involved in the administration of the territories after the former governments had been defeated by multi-national forces and forced to flee. Nigel White has commented that:

The interventions in northern Iraq in 1991 and Kosovo in 1999 appear to be context-breaking actions, aimed at creating a new right to take military action in support of Security Council resolutions. In those two cases the justification given by the states using military force was to protect human rights, principally the right to life, the violation of which had been recognized by the Security Council. A further instance of military action being taken to enforce Security Council resolutions is the bombing of Iraq that has occurred since the cease-fire embodied in Resolution 687 of 1991,... in December 1998 and regularly thereafter, the purpose being to enforce compliance with the disarmament provisions of that resolution.[228]

To that list could now be added the intervention in Iraq in 2003, though in that case the need to protect human rights was presented as a secondary objective, the first being the need to neutralize the threat posed by the weapons of mass destruction that Saddam Hussein was alleged to have acquired.

The Independent International Commission on Kosovo,[229] which examined the legality of the NATO bombing campaign, concluded that, although there were many flaws in the way in which the campaign was conducted, it was a legitimate undertaking because of the seriousness of the humanitarian catastrophe and the failure of the Security Council to respond effectively. However:

the intervention was legitimate, but not legal, given existing international law. It was legitimate because it was unavoidable: diplomatic options had been exhausted, and two sides were bent on a conflict which threatened to wreak humanitarian catastrophe and generate instability through the Balkan peninsula. The intervention needs to be seen within a clear understanding of what is likely to have happened had intervention not taken place: Kosovo would still be under Serbian rule, and in the middle of a bloody civil war. Many people would still be dying and flows of refugees would be destabilizing neighbouring countries.[230]

The conclusions of the Committee lend weight to the view that the criteria for intervention in Kosovo in 1999 were compelling, despite strong criticism of the nature of the bombing campaign.[231] The invasion of Iraq in 2003 has not garnered

[228] ND White, 'The Legality of Bombing in the Name of Humanity', 5 Journal of Conflict and Security Law 1, 27.

[229] The Independent International Commission on Kosovo *The Kosovo Report* (Oxford University Press Oxford 2000).

[230] ibid 289.

[231] Not all commentators agree that the intervention was necessary or appropriate. David Chandler comments that the 'use of available facts to challenge the case for war, found relatively little support or media space in this climate of consensus... It seemed the facts on the ground mattered less to the Western advocates of intervention than the principle that a stand must be made on the side of the human rights cause.' D Chandler, *From Kosovo to Kabul: Human Rights and International Intervention* (Pluto Press London 2004), 15.

similar support.[232] But there is no plausible basis for holding that different laws apply to legitimate but illegal operations, as to illegal operations in which there is much less agreement as to their legitimacy. If occupation law applies in Iraq but not in Kosovo it must be because the situations are legally or factually different in ways that are pertinent to the issue.

In Iraq, the UN mandated the presence of the MNF after the defeat of Saddam Hussein. In Kosovo, the UN itself took responsibility for the administration after the defeat of the Serb government, although NATO still exercises considerable authority in Kosovo independently of the UN administration there. Resolution 1244 mandates a post-conflict administration to be run jointly by the 'UN Interim Administration Mission' (UNMIK) with responsibility for administration of the territory and the Kosovo Force (KFOR), an international force 'with substantial North Atlantic Treaty participation' deployed 'under unified command and control'[233] with responsibility for security in the province.

Under Resolution 1244 Serbia[234] still retains sovereignty over Kosovo. Although the United States, the European Union, and many other States have recognized Kosovo's status as a State following its declaration of independence on 17 February 2008, the UN has not done so, largely because of the objections of Russia. Kosovo's parliament approved a new constitution on the 9 April 2008, which came into force on the 15 June 2008. Serbia has said that the declaration of independence represents a forceful and unilateral secession of a part of the territory of Serbia, and does not produce any legal effect either in Serbia or in the international legal order.[235] The EU is planning to deploy 'a rule of law mission within the framework provided by resolution 1244'.[236] However, KFOR is to remain in Kosovo on the basis of UN Security Resolution 1244, until the Security Council decides otherwise. In his report of the 28 March 2008 Secretary-General Ban Ki Moon affirmed that UNMIK will continue to exercise its authority in the area but '[p]ending Security Council guidance, there might be a need for UNMIK to adjust its operational deployment to deal with developments and changes on the ground in a manner consistent with resolution 1244.'[237]

UNMIK is tasked with providing 'an interim administration for Kosovo under which the people of Kosovo can enjoy substantial autonomy within the Federal Republic of Yugoslavia'[238] Among other things UNMIK was tasked with overseeing the development of provisional institutions for democratic and autonomous

[232] R Caplan, *International Governance of War-Torn Territories: Rule and Reconstruction* (n 1), 11.

[233] S/RES 1244, 10 June 1999, Annex 2, [4].

[234] On the 21 May 2006 Montenegro voted by a majority of 56% to 44% to split with Serbia and establish a new independent State. The referendum attracted a turnout of almost 90%: I Traynor 'Monetengro vote finally seals death of Yugoslavia' *The Guardian* (22 May 2006).

[235] Report of the Secretary-General on the United Nations Interim Administration Mission in Kosovo S/2008/11 28 March 2008, [6].

[236] ibid [5].

[237] ibid [32].

[238] S/RES 1244 (n 233), [10].

self-government; reconstructing key infrastructure and other economic reconstruction; supporting humanitarian and disaster relief aid; maintaining civil law and order; protecting and promoting human rights; and assuring the safe and unimpeded return home of all refugees and displaced persons.[239] KFOR was tasked with:

a) Deterring hostilities, maintaining and where necessary enforcing a cease-fire, ensuring the withdrawal and preventing the return into Kosovo of Federal and Republic military, para-military and police forces.
b) Demilitarizing the KLA [Kosovo Liberation Army] and other armed Kosovan military groups.
c) Establishing a secure environment in which refugees and displaced persons can return home in safety, the international civilian presence can operate, a transitional administration can be established and humanitarian aid can be delivered.
d) Ensuring public safety and order until the international civilian presence can take responsibility for this task.
e) Supervising de-mining until the international civilian presence can, as appropriate, take over responsibility for this task.
f) Supporting as appropriate and co-ordinating closely with the work of the international civilian presence.
g) Conducting border-monitoring duties as required.
h) Ensuring the protection and freedom of movement of itself, the international civilian presence, and other international organizations.[240]

The UNMIK/KFOR administration has been described as:

> a unique operation in which the international community formally withdrew central authority in part of the territory and in its place established, de facto as well as de jure, a protectorate by taking over the administration, albeit for an interim period, pending a definitive settlement of the status of Kosovo.[241]

The fact that Serbia retained sovereignty over the province meant that for a long time no serious plans were made for the development of an independent Kosovo or to clarify its long term status. The lack of progress on the issue of the final status of the province, along with economic stagnation, fuelled resentment amongst the Kosovar Albanian community.[242] The uncertainties regarding sovereign status also prevented the province from being able to give the guarantees necessary to receive funding from the International Monetary Fund and resulted in difficulties

[239] ibid [11] The various tasks to be undertaken were broken up into four 'pillars' and assigned to the UN, the OSCE, the UNHCR and the EU.

[240] ibid [9].

[241] D Leurdijk and D Zandee, *Kosovo: From Crisis to Crisis* (Ashgate Burlington 2001), 105–6.

[242] Gareth Evans, co-chair of the ICISS and president of the International Crisis Group warned in January 2005, that 'time is running out' for Kosovo 'The political capital of the UN mission in Kosovo is all but exhausted. Reintroduction of violence into the equation has raised the very real possibility the process may be decided by brute force rather than peaceful negotiation.' International Crisis Group, 'Kosovo—Working towards Final Status', Europe Report No 161, 24 January 2005, 1–2.

concerning the ownership of companies and property, which have hindered economic development.[243] By 2005 it was recognized that Kosovo's unsettled status could not be maintained for too much longer,[244] and on 24 October 2005 the UN Security Council authorized the Secretary-General to appoint former Finnish President Martti Ahtisaari as special envoy to start a political process to determine Kosovo's future status. Since the declaration of independence there have been outbreaks of violence and attacks against KFOR in Mitrovica; some parts of northern Kosovo currently operate parallel structures in defiance of both UNMIK and the provisional government. On the 11 May 2008 Serbia extended the vote in its national elections to the Serbian enclaves in Kosovo; an act that was condemned by the Secretary-General's Special Representative to Kosovo on the basis that:

> The Serbian authorities conducted these elections in the full knowledge that they were acting in defiance of UNMIK's exclusive mandate to authorize elections in Kosovo under UN Security Council resolution 1244.[245]

The difficulties relating to status have been compounded by the ad hoc approach to the administration of the territory and the lack of an external framework against which to monitor and assess progress and provide for accountability. UNMIK has been heavily censured for its autocratic nature; the absence of substantive checks; and failure to control widespread abuse of human rights.[246] The Secretary General's Report of July 12, 1999, which sets out the authority and competencies of UNMIK requires it to be guided by internationally recognized human rights standards as the basis for the exercise of its authority.[247] But

[243] International Crisis Group, 'Collapse in Kosovo', Europe Report 115, 22 April 2004, 3.

[244] The Secretary-General's Special Representative Soren Jessen-Peterson has observed 'there's a limit to how long you can keep a place in limbo.' International Crisis Group, 'Kosovo—Working towards Final Status' (n 242), 3.

[245] 'Statement regarding Serbian 'local elections" held today in Kosovo' UNMIK/PR/1732 Sunday, 11 May 2008.

[246] Amnesty International Reports: Federal Republic of Yugoslavia (Kosovo), 'Setting the Standard? UNMIK and KFOR's Response to Violence in Mitrovica', Al Index EUR 70/013/2000; 'Criminal justice system still on trial Al Index EUR 70/063/2000 22 November 2000; Amnesty International protests the unlawful detention of Afrim Zequiri Al Index EUR 70/004/2001 21 February 2001; Serbia and Montenegro (Kosovo/Kosova) 'Minority Communities: Fundamental Rights Denied' AL Index 70/011/2003 1 April 2003 and Serbia and Montenegro (Kosovo/Kosova) 'Prisoners in Our Own Homes' AI Index EUR 70/010/02003 29 April 2003; D Marshall and S Inglis, 'The Disempowerment of Human Rights-Based Justice in the United Nations Mission in Kosovo', 16 Harvard Human Rights Journal, 95, 132.

[247] Report of the Secretary-General on the United Nations Interim Administration Mission in Kosovo, 12 July 1999, UN Doc S/1999/779, [38]; UNMIK Regulation 1999/24 states that in exercising their functions, all persons undertaking public duties or holding public office in Kosovo shall observe internationally recognized human rights as reflected in the Universal Declaration of Human Rights, The European Convention on Human Rights and Fundamental Freedoms; the International Covenant on Civil and Political Rights; the International covenant on Economic, Social and Cultural Rights; the Convention on all Forms of Racial Discrimination; the Convention on the Elimination of all Forms of Discrimination against Women; the Convention Against

because all legislative and executive power is located in one body, the limited mechanisms in place to ensure that these standards are adhered to have not been effective. UNMIK and KFOR personnel are immune from arrest or detention or local jurisdiction in respect of any civil or criminal act committed by them in Kosovo.[248] There is an ombudsman for Kosovo but he cannot hear complaints regarding KFOR.[249] His 2001–2002 report was sharply critical of both UNMIK and KFOR:

> Since the establishment of the United Nations regime in Kosovo, UNMIK has both perpetuated and created obstacles to the full protection of human rights, issuing Regulations granting themselves and the international military presence (KFOR) total immunity from legal process in Kosovo, removing decision-making authority over important civil rights from the courts and placing it in administrative bodies under the direct control of UNMIK, and pursuing similar courses of action that serve to eliminate or severely restrict the rights of individuals from Kosovo. The applicable law is often unclear, with UNMIK Regulations and subsidiary legal acts declared as the supreme law of the land, prevailing over any domestic laws in force. Whatever law a court in Kosovo may apply is of little importance, however, as UNMIK will choose whether or not to permit the execution of any resulting judgment.[250]

The ombudsman goes on to contrast the situation in Kosovo with the situation in Serbia, commenting that:

> Since the 2000 elections, the Federal Republic of Yugoslavia has moved towards greater participation in the international human rights regime, accepting ever increasing levels of external monitoring and control. In 2001, it accepted the right of individual petition to the Human Rights Committee, which reviews complaints under the International Covenant on Civil and Political Rights. Within the next year, it will become a member of

Torture and other Cruel, Inhuman or Degrading Treatment; the International Convention on the Rights of the Child.

[248] UNMIK Regulation No 2000/47 On the Status, Privileges and Immunities of KFOR and UNMIK and their Personnel in Kosovo, 18 August 2000, sections 2, 3.

[249] From 2000 to 2005, the Ombudsperson Institution was led by an International Ombudsperson and two local deputies. The International Ombudsperson left in December 2005 and Hilmi Jashari, a Kosovo Albanian, was appointed Acting Ombudsperson. Since February 2006, the Assembly of Kosovo has had authority to appoint a local Ombudsperson in accordance with UNMIK Regulation No 2006/6 on the Ombudsperson Institution in Kosovo. Under this regulation, the Ombudsperson Institution retains its mandate to investigate complaints against local authorities or other bodies of Kosovo's Provisional Institutions of Self-Government, but is not competent to investigate complaints against UNMIK. Following promulgation of UNMIK Regulation No 2006/12 on the Establishment of the Human Rights Advisory Panel, the Human Rights Advisory Panel (HRAP) has jurisdiction to examine complaints of persons or groups claiming to be a victim of a violation of human rights by UNMIK after all other available remedies have been exhausted. HRAP's jurisdiction covers 'alleged violations of human rights that had occurred not earlier than 23 April 2005 or arising from facts which occurred prior to this date where these facts give rise to a continuing violation of human rights.' 'Ombudsperson Institution Helps to Ensure Protection of Human Rights' UNMIK/PR/1719 Wednesday, 9 January 2008.

[250] Ombudsman Institution in Kosovo, *Second Annual Report*, 2001–2002, 1.

the Council of Europe and thus, within the foreseeable future, be subject to the jurisdiction of the European Court of Human Rights.

People from Kosovo can gain little, if any, benefit from these or other similar positive developments, as it is the Federal Republic of Yugoslavia that will be bound by these new human rights obligations, and not the United Nations Mission in Kosovo or the local governmental authorities in Kosovo, neither of which can become a party to international human rights instruments or become subject to the external controls of human rights treaty bodies or judicial mechanisms. It is ironic that the United Nations, the self-proclaimed champion of human rights in the world, has by its own actions placed the people of Kosovo under UN control, thereby removing them from the protection of the international human rights regime that formed the justification for UN engagement in Kosovo in the first place.[251]

The failure of the UNMIK/NATO administration to prevent attacks against Serbs and its failure, at least in the early years, to ensure that the criminal justice system operated impartially and effectively have been widely documented.[252] This is despite the fact that the potential risks to the Serb minority were apparent even before the bombing campaign began, since a significant proportion of the killings and other human rights abuses documented in the period prior to the NATO intervention were attacks against Serbs and Serb sympathisers.[253] There have been suggestions that KFOR's inability to control the reprisals that followed the 1999 intervention was to some extent the result of deliberate policy. Tim Judah, a journalist, witnessed Kosovar Albanians destroying a Serbian Orthodox priest's house in Vučitrn, smashing religious pictures and carrying away everything from sofas to church candles, whilst two French soldiers from

[251] ibid 5; On the 23 March 2006 the Special Representative of the Secretary-General established a Human Rights Advisory Panel with power to examine complaints from any persons claiming to be a victim of a violation by UNMIK of their human rights that occurred not earlier than 23 April 2005 or arising from facts that occurred before this date where the facts give rise to a continuing violation. The findings of the Advisory Panel, which may include recommendations, are to be of an advisory nature: UNMIK/REG/2006/12, 23 March 2006.

[252] William O'Neill writes that Albanian judges openly admitted that they applied different standards—if not entirely different laws—to Serbian defendants. He also notes 'the undue depth of deference accorded by some UNMIK officials to the local power structure dominated by Albanian hard-liners and a lack of understanding about how ethnic bias affected the judiciary.' W O'Neill, *Kosovo: An Unfinished Peace* (Lynne Rienner Publishers Boulder 2002) 84, 89; D Marshall and S Inglis, 'Human Rights in Transition: The Disempowerment of Human Rights-Based Justice in the United Nations Mission in Kosovo' (n 246), 120–124; Amnesty International Reports, above (n 246).

[253] *The Prosecutor v Ramush Haradinaj, Idriz Balaj, Lahi Brahimaj* Case No IT-04-84-I Indictment, 4 March 2005. The indictment of Ramush Haradinaj, former leader of the KLA and currently Prime Minister of Kosovo, by the ICTY, states that from 24 March 1998, KLA forces under the command of Haradinaj began a systematic campaign to take control over a number of villages and drive Serbs out of their homes by targeting individuals for abduction, mistreatment and murder; Human Rights Watch documented abuses against Serbs as well as Kosovars in the period leading up to the NATO intervention: 'Legal Standards and the Kosovo Conflict' Appendix B to the Report 'A Week of Terror in Drenica: Human Rights Violations in Kosovo' <http://www.hrw.org/hrw/reports/1999/kosovo/Obrinje6–08.htm#P1158_187851>.

KFOR 'looked on amiably.'[254] Meanwhile up the road a house that belonged to a Gypsy was set on fire. Judah spoke to the local French commander of KFOR who happened to be passing in his jeep, and was told that '[t]he orders are to let them plunder.'[255] The Independent International Commission on Kosovo, in its 2001 follow up to the Kosovo Report, commented that 'KFOR has proved itself both unable and unwilling to stop continuing violence against ethnic minorities.'[256] Another report, published in the summer of 1999, is unreservedly condemnatory of the UN's response to the ethnic cleansing of non-Albanians:

For all practical purposes, Kosovo has been ethnically cleansed by the KLA and other Albanians AFTER the international community arrived. This is neither regretted nor condemned in the report. [Report of the UN Secretary-General on the UN Mission in Kosovo S/1999/987 of September 16 1999]

... there is not a word about Albanian atrocities, war criminals or any hesitation on the part of the West to co-operate with individuals, groups and institutions who is likely to have caused this exodus. Neither does it regret that Albanians are intimidated by KLA and forced out of their temporary houses upon return, or punished for not wanting to join KLA.[257]

In 2002, Michael Steiner, Special Representative of the Secretary-General at the time, set out a policy to deal with the need to improve human rights, which subsequently became known as 'Standards before Status.'[258] Under this policy the future political status of Kosovo depended on the extent to which the situation on the ground in Kosovo accorded with a future independent State in which all people:

regardless of ethnic background, race or religion, are free to live, work, and travel without fear, hostility and danger, and there is tolerance, justice and peace for everyone.[259]

In 2002, the same year as the Standards before Status policy was adopted, the first long-term prison sentences were handed down to former KLA members.

[254] T Judah, *Kosovo: War and Revenge* (2nd edn, Yale University Press New Haven CT 2002), p. xviii.

[255] ibid.

[256] Independent International Commission on Kosovo, *Follow up to the Kosovo Report: Why Conditional Independence?* (2001), 19 <http://www.kosovocommission.org>.

[257] Transnational Foundation, 'Misleading UN Report on Kosovo', 3 October 1999 (Emphasis original) <http://www.jacksonprogressive.com/issues/kosovo/misleadingunreport.html>.

[258] Michael Steiner, April 25 2002, <http://www.undp.or.jp/hotspots_e/kosovo.hdr2.html>. The 'Standards before Status' policy has been criticized on the grounds that initially the interim administration merely set a standards of respect for human rights as the required benchmark for independence negotiations but did little to ensure that these goals were met: Kai Eide 'The Situation in Kosovo' 15 July 2004, [29] <http://www.kosovo.com/news/archive/2004/August-17/1.html>. Eide's report was produced at the request of the Secretary-General; International Crisis Group, 'Kosovo—Working towards Final Status' (n 242), 2–3.

[259] Joint Statement of the Contact Group on Kosovo, 20 April 2004 <http://www.state.gov/p/eur/rls/or/37535.htm>. The Contact Group was established in 1994 to co-ordinate the key States interested in the Balkans. It consists of the United States, United Kingdom, France, Germany, Italy and the Russian federation.

Since then 'many Kosovar Albanians have come to believe that the KLA heritage is being delegitimised by the peacekeeping mission.'[260] This suggests that whilst NATO forces were welcomed at the beginning because they were seen as allies in the Kosovar Albanians' war for independence, once UNMIK and KFOR began to adopt a more neutral stance that welcome began to turn to resentment.

Problems came to a head in March 2004 when Serb civilians were murdered, Serb women brutally beaten and Serb homes burnt, in a wave of violence carried out by ethnic Albanians. Human Rights Watch believes that KFOR and UNMIK failed 'catastrophically' in their mandate to protect minority communities:

> In Svinjare, French KFOR troops failed to come to the assistance of the Serbs even though their main base was just a few hundred metres away—in fact, the ethnic Albanian crowd had walked right past the base on its way to burning the village. French troops similarly failed to respond to the rioting in Vucitrn, which is located between two major bases. In Prizren, German KFOR troops failed to deploy to protect the Serb population and the many historic Serb Orthodox churches, despite calls for assistance from their UNMIK international police counterparts, who later accused German KFOR commanders of cowardice. In Kosovo Polje, UNMIK and KFOR were nowhere to be seen as Albanian crowds methodically burnt Serb homes. The village of Belo Polje, rebuilt on the outskirts of Pec to house returning Serbs, was burnt to the ground even though it was adjacent to the main Italian KFOR base.[261]

The shock created by these attacks and the potential for complete breakdown that they reveal triggered renewed efforts to achieve the Standards set out in the 2002 plan. In 2005 UNMIK published a Standards Implementation Plan in order to drive forward this goal.[262] But up until this point, despite the fact that abuses of the human rights of Serbs had been ongoing ever since UNMIK/KFOR took control of the province and before, the UN/NATO administration had been under the impression that things in Kosovo were going pretty well. General Brännström, the commander of KFOR's Swedish contingent, commented 'it is rather embarrassing that we could be this naïve.'[263]

The naïvety observed by General Brännström with regard to the violence against the Serbs, may stem in part from the shift in NATO's role. During the bombing campaign the Serbs were the enemy. The International Commission on Intervention and State Sovereignty has argued:

> the responsibility to protect is fundamentally a principle designed to respond to threats to human life, and not a tool for achieving political goals such as greater political autonomy,

[260] International Crisis Group, 'Collapse in Kosovo', Report No 155, 22 April 2004, 8.

[261] Human Rights Watch, 'Failure to Protect: Anti-Minority Violence in Kosovo, March 2004' (July 2004, Vol. 16 No 6 (D)), 2.

[262] 'Standards Implementation Plan' Published Pristina 10 December 2003. Endorsed by the Security Council 12 December 2003. <http:www.unmikonline.org>.

[263] A Brännström, 'Swedish KFOR General Warns About Total Ethnic Cleansing of Serbs' translated from Swedish Daily Dagens Nyheter of May 3, 2004 <http://www.transnational.org/features/2004/Cleansing_serbs.html>.

self-determination, or independence for particular groups within the country (though these may well be related to the underlying issues that prompted the military intervention.) The intervention itself should not become the basis for further separatist claims.[264]

But, as the ICISS itself acknowledges, separatist claims may well be related to the underlying issues that prompted the military intervention. The bombing campaign in Kosovo, although targeted at preventing abuses, was clearly understood both by the intervening States and the Kosovar Albanians to be supportive of Kosovar claims to independence. The peace agreements that ended the NATO bombing campaign left resolution of the final status of Kosovo to a later date but nevertheless the success of the NATO campaign forced Serb forces to withdraw leaving no one to represent Serb interests:

Just about every aspect of the Serb government also decided that it wasn't prudent to stay in Kosovo under the new circumstances, for whatever reason. So the whole structure went; there was no political structure left, no administrative structure, the public utilities were falling apart, power, water, the hospitals, telephones, all of that. Most of this infrastructure had been operated by Serbs and they also decided to go. In this vacuum the UCK [Kosovo Liberation Army] began to behave rather like the victorious party which they think they were, and getting themselves into positions of influence and power.[265]

6.2 Do the Laws of Occupation Apply to UNMIK and KFOR?

Under Resolution 1244 Serbia remained formally sovereign but UNMIK was tasked with overseeing the development of provisional institutions for democratic and autonomous self-government and facilitating a political process designed to determine Kosovo's future political status—a task difficult to reconcile with the Security Council's affirmation of Serbian sovereignty. Up until February 2008, when Kosovo unilaterally declared its independence, the province was governed by a transitional administration, run jointly by the UN (together with other international organizations) and a NATO-led security force that has almost unfettered authority in the province.[266] The administration was established following the military defeat of Serb forces by NATO forces acting without UN authorization. It was neither democratically legitimate nor accountable.[267] Although independence has been declared the State remains dependent on the international administration, which is still in place. The situation bears some close parallels with military occupation.[268] Were the laws of occupation applicable? Are they still?

[264] International Commission on Intervention and State Sovereignty (ICISS), *The Responsibility to Protect* (Ottawa International Development Research Centre 2001), [5.23].

[265] Lieutenant General M Jackson, 'KFOR: The Inside Story' [February 2000] Royal United Services Institute Journal, 13, 16.

[266] D Marshall and S Inglis, 'Human Rights in Transition: The Disempowerment of Human Rights-Based Justice in the United Nations Mission in Kosovo' (n 246), 112.

[267] S Chesterman, *You, The People: United Nations Transitional Administration and State-Building* (n 102), 132–134, 226.

[268] Benvenisti argues that Security Council resolutions 1244 of 19 June 1999 and 1272 of 25 October 1999, establishing the UN Mission in Kosovo (UNMIK) and the United Nations

The provisions on occupation in the Geneva Conventions were drafted broadly so as to try and encompass all situations where there was a de facto occupation and this includes post-surrender occupations.[269] Clearly in a post-surrender occupation the consent of the vanquished party is circumscribed and therefore occupation law would normally apply to the de facto government, at least until a democratically elected government has taken over. Chesterman, writing in 2004, argued that, despite delegation of some responsibilities, UNMIK 'govern[s] through military occupation.'[270] It took three years for UNMIK to get around to publishing its Regulations in Albanian and Serbian as well as in English, which rendered them inaccessible to the majority of the population.[271]

A Constitutional Framework for Self-Government was adopted in May 2001 but the text that was finally adopted had not been agreed to by any of the local participants.[272] Kosovar Albanians had wanted to include a reference to the 'will of the people' but because of the impasse regarding resolution of the problem of final status, UNMIK officials were 'in the odd position of having to resist'[273] these demands, and therefore in the final text references to the will of the people are carefully circumscribed.[274] Dr Javier Solana, the EU High Representative for the Common Foreign and Security Policy, commented that 'I am aware that no community in Kosovo is fully satisfied with the constitutional framework, but the text is a very fair compromise.'[275] However, 'a very fair compromise,' whatever the merits of the framework and regardless of whether or not it is the best deal

Transitional Administration in East Timor (UNTAET) 'created trusteeships toward the indigenous communities and ousted governments, trusteeships of the kind the law of occupation is designed to address.' E Benvenisti, *The International Law of Occupation: with a new preface by the author* (n 3), xvii.

[269] Adam Roberts, 'What is Military Occupation' (n 8), 270.

[270] S Chesterman, *You, The People: United Nations Transitional Administration and State-Building* (n 102), 239.

[271] Ombudsman Institution in Kosovo, *Second Annual Report*, 2001–2002, 2

[272] Independent International Commission on Kosovo, *Follow up to the Kosovo Report: Why Conditional Independence?* (n 256), 20; S Chesterman, 'Kosovo in Limbo; State Building and Substantial Autonomy' (International Peace Academy Report, August 2001), 6–7; S Chesterman, *You, The People: United Nations Transitional Administration and State-Building* (n 102), 132–134, 226;.

[273] S Chesterman, *You, The People: United Nations Transitional Administration and State-Building* (n 102), 133; S Chesterman, 'Kosovo in Limbo; State Building and Substantial Autonomy' (n 272), 8.

[274] For example the preamble to the Constitutional framework states that 'within the limits defined by UNSCR 1244(1999), responsibilities will be transferred to Provisional Institutions of Self-Government which shall work constructively towards ensuring conditions for a peaceful and normal life for all inhabitants of Kosovo, with a view to facilitating the determination of Kosovo's future status through a process at an appropriate future stage which shall, in accordance with UNSCR 1244(1999), take full account of all relevant factors including the will of the people.' Constitutional Framework for Provisional Self-Government, UNMIK/REG/2001/9–15 (May 2001). <http://www.unmikonline.org/constframework.htm>.

[275] Dr Javier Solana, EU High Representative for the CFSP, welcomes the promulgation of the Constitutional Framework for Interim Self-Government in Kosovo, Brussels, 16 May 2001.

that can be achieved in the circumstances, does not constitute democratic legitimacy if it is imposed by an international administration, even if the subsequent elections agreeing to the imposed compromise do give it some form of legitimacy. The Independent International Commission on Kosovo argued that the terms of the Constitutional Framework would mean that Kosovo would remain under an 'indefinite protectorate'[276] and that:

> Instead of the substantial autonomy promised the Kosovars under Resolution 1244, they will instead get very limited autonomy. They will have the illusion of self rule rather than the reality. A pervasive distrust of the administrative and political capacity of the population seems to underlie the constitutional provisions.[277]

The fact that considerable authority was delegated to democratically elected institutions and that some authority was exercised in defiance of UNMIK/KFOR would not necessarily preclude the application of the laws of occupation provided that UNMIK/KFOR retained overall control.[278] As the Israeli Supreme Court stated in the *Ansar Prison* case '[a]llowing the former government to act does not alter the fact that the military force is maintaining an effective military control in the area.'[279] However, the Geneva Conventions never envisaged an occupation by the UN. Unlike Resolution 1483, which specifically requires the major contributors to the MNF in Iraq to comply with the rules applicable to

<http://ue.eu.int/cms3_applications/applications/solana/details.asp?cmsid=246&BID=109&DocID=66458&insite=1>.

276 Independent International Commission on Kosovo, *Follow up to the Kosovo Report: Why Conditional Independence?* (n 256), 23

277 ibid 20 The Commission argued that effective supervision of 'conditional independence' would require a continuing international presence with special responsibility for borders and minorities but that it could 'see no convincing reason why the Kosovo government should not have control over customs, judiciary, police, public, state and socially owned property, railways and transport, civil aviation, the housing and property directorate, commercial property, municipal boundaries, the regulation of firearms,—indeed the whole range of powers reserved to the SRSG under Ch. 8.1 sections a–z, and 8.2, as well as the undefined residual powers allocated to the SRSG under Chapter 12 [of the Constitutional Framework]. If there is no good reason why these powers should not be exercised by the Kosovo government the Commission predicts that a struggle will ensue to acquire them.' ibid, 25.

The International Crisis Group took a more positive view of the Constitutional Framework and subsequent elections for an Assembly in November 2001, commenting that 'whatever its limitations, the Assembly will provide a new and significant forum from which local leaders, with the legitimacy of a democratic mandate, will be able to challenge UNMIK in ways which are as yet unclear.' However the report went on to say that '[i] n any event, the newly elected officials will be unlikely to accept for long the straightjacket imposed by the unelected international administration.' International Crisis Group, 'Kosovo Landmark Election', Balkans Report No 120, 21 November 2001, Executive Summary, i–ii.

278 KLA former members are influential in the Provisional Institutions of Self-Government and the Kosovo Protection Corps consists largely of demobilised KLA members. In addition, in several Serb areas parallel institutions of local government have been set up that effectively operate independently of official Kosovar institutions.

279 *Tzemel Adv. Et al v (a) Minister of Defence (b) Commander of the Ansar Camp* III HC 593/82 (*'Ansar Prison Case*). English translation cited in A Roberts 'What Is Military Occupation' (n 8), 286.

occupants under the Geneva Conventions,[280] Resolution 1244 said nothing at all about the laws of occupation or the larger body of general IHL. This indicates that the Security Council did not consider occupation law applicable to Kosovo and did not consider it necessary to address the issue. However, the International Commission on Kosovo, in its *Follow up to the Kosovo Report*, argued that '[g] reater efforts should have been taken from the inception of the occupation to protect civilians in Kosovo, and to establish the Rule of Law,'[281] comments that imply that the Commission views the UN/NATO administration as an occupation. Referring to the framework of contextual principles that should govern humanitarian intervention that it had proposed in the *Kosovo Report*,[282] the Commission recommended that, taking into account lessons learned from the transitional administration in Kosovo, a new provision emphasizing the importance of providing protection to minorities should be added to Principle 9 so that it should now read:

There must be even stricter adherence to the laws of war and international humanitarian law than in standard military operations. This applies to all aspects of military occupation, including post-cease-fire occupation, and imposes a particular duty on occupying forces and their administrative counterparts to give the highest protection of threatened segments of the civilian population, including the prevention of acts of revenge and retribution.[283]

KFOR is not commanded and controlled by the UN and it is not subject to the authority of the Secretary-General or his Special Representative. It is unclear to what extent KFOR is bound by UNMIK regulations. Regulation 2000/47, 'On the Status, Privileges and Immunities of KFOR and UNMIK and their Personnel in Kosovo' states that KFOR shall respect applicable law and regulations in so far as they do not conflict with the fulfilment of their mandate under Resolution 1244.[284] But there is no indication of how broadly or narrowly that is to be construed. Moreover although an ombudsman was appointed to

[280] Coalition forces invaded and occupied Iraq before acquiring a Security Council mandate endorsing their continued presence. KFOR ground forces did not enter and occupy Kosovo until mandated to do so by Security Council resolution 1244 in June 1999. But this seems a very thin ground for different application of IHL. In both cases a coalition of States intervened militarily in another State without the authorization of the Security Council and only after the former government was defeated did the Security Council mandate the continued presence of forces.

[281] Independent International Commission on Kosovo, *Follow up to the Kosovo Report: Why Conditional Independence?* (n 256), 37.

[282] *Kosovo Report* (n 229), 193–195.

[283] The Commission emphasized that 'even in the context of a humanitarian intervention backed by UN authority, there exists an international duty to comply with these guidelines.' Independent International Commission on Kosovo, *Follow up to the Kosovo Report: Why Conditional Independence?* (n 256), 36 (Emphasis original).

[284] UNMIK/REG/2000/47 (On the Status, Privileges and Immunities of KFOR and UNMIK and Their Personnel in Kosovo), 18 Aug. 2000; D Marshall and S Inglis, 'Human Rights in Transition: The Disempowerment of Human Rights-Based Justice in the United Nations Mission in Kosovo' (n 246), 110.

receive and investigate complaints from any person alleging abuses of authority by UNMIK, or by other institutions, KFOR is exempt from the ombudsman's jurisdiction. There have been a number of reports of human rights violations by KFOR soldiers and criticism of the fact that there is no human rights oversight of the actions of KFOR.[285] The dominating presence of the international community over the nine years since the 1999 intervention has been instrumental in creating and perpetuating a parallel economy in which corruption and human rights abuses are endemic, particularly those of women. Amnesty International, reporting on Kosovo in 2004, stated that it was:.

> extremely concerned that the UN administration in Kosovo has effectively allowed the development of a flourishing industry dependent on the exploitation of trafficked women. Although the Kosovo sex-industry now services both local and international men, it is clear that it initially grew out of post-conflict militarization and the presence of a highly-paid international military and civilian community.
>
> The organization also considers that UNMIK—in failing to prosecute international personnel suspected of involvement in trafficking, or of knowingly using the services of trafficked women—has created a climate of impunity for abuses and violations against trafficked women.[286]

In October 2000, UNMIK Police established a specialized Unit, the 'Trafficking and Prostitution Investigation Unit' and on 12 January 2001 UNMIK promulgated a regulation providing for the 'Prosecution and punishment of perpetrators of the crime of trafficking in persons and related criminal acts, and the assistance and protection of victims of trafficking and related criminal acts.' Under this regulation any person who uses or procures the sexual services of a person with the knowledge that that person is a victim of trafficking in persons commits a criminal act and shall be liable upon conviction to a penalty of up to 5 years imprisonment. This could extend up to 10 years imprisonment where the victim is under the age of 18 years. However, UNMIK and KFOR personnel, and

[285] D Marshall and S Inglis, 'Human Rights in Transition: The Disempowerment of Human Rights-Based Justice in the United Nations Mission in Kosovo' (n 246), 112, 96, 103; Amnesty International, 'Kosovo: KFOR and UNMIK fail to uphold human rights standards in Mitrovica' Amnesty International news Release, 13 March 2000, AI Index: EUR 70/14/00.

[286] Amnesty International, 'So does that mean I have rights? Protecting the rights of women and girls trafficked for forced prostitution in Kosovo.' EUR700102004, 6 May 2004, ch 6; However UNMIK has commented that 'Unfortunately, the focus in public presentation of the report on instances from 1999–2000, and the situation that prevailed in the immediate post-conflict environment, have created a misleading impression in some quarters that the same situation continues today. Certain general allegations made in Amnesty International's Press Release on the launch of the report, such as the statements that 'the international community is responsible for the growth of a sex-industry based on the abuse of trafficked women' and that 'UNMIK, KFOR and PISG have failed to protect and respect the human rights of these women', are at variance with the more detailed findings of Amnesty International contained in its report and are certainly not borne out by the facts on the ground today. Accordingly, UNMIK has conveyed these concerns in a letter addressed to Amnesty International.' UNMIK Combating Human Trafficking in Kosovo: Strategy and Commitment May 2004, 28.

contractors working for UNMIK and KFOR, are immune from prosecution.[287] In 2006 Amnesty International commented that in 'scant few cases has immunity from prosecution granted to UN personnel and members of the NATO-led Kosovo Force (KFOR) been lifted to allow criminal investigations into human rights violations, including the trafficking of women and girls for the purposes of forced prostitution.'[288] In addition to its poor record on tackling women's rights the international administration has also failed repeatedly to protect the population from ethnically motivated attacks.[289] Amnesty International reportd that KFOR itself has used excessive force in attacks against minority communities and has tortured members of minority communities.[290] Violations of applicable international human rights law or IHL committed by KFOR are subject to the jurisdiction of the force's respective sending States only.[291] Marshall and Inglis comment that '[p]ractically speaking, KFOR has boundless and unfettered authority in Kosovo.'[292]

In these circumstances, given that the presence of KFOR (a NATO-dominated force) is a consequence of the military defeat of the former government by NATO and not the result of any democratic process, and bearing in mind that KFOR is not UN commanded or controlled, the laws of occupation should be considered applicable to it, at least to the extent that it exercises authority comparable to that of a de facto government but independently of UNMIK. But in practice it would be difficult to hold that occupation law applies to KFOR if it does not apply to UNMIK, since although KFOR has extensive powers and is not subject to the authority of the Secretary-General or to oversight by any local agency such as an ombudsman, it operates in association with UNMIK which also exercises extensive governmental powers.

Whether the laws of occupation applied to UNMIK, being UN commanded, is more difficult to determine. The applicability of occupation law is not limited to situations of armed conflict. The Geneva Conventions apply to 'to all cases of partial or total occupation of the territory of a High Contracting Party, even if the said occupation meets with no resistance'[293] and the most important provisions of Geneva Convention IV continue for as long as the occupation exists.[294] However, all of the documents published by the UN that deal with the

[287] UNMIK Regulation 2000/47, *On the status, privileges and immunities of KFOR and UNMIK and their personnel in Kosovo*, 18 August 2000. The immunity of KFOR personnel can be waived by the head of their battalion.

[288] Amnesty International, 'The UN in Kosovo—A Legacy of Impunity.' EUR 700152006, 8 November 2006, 1 (and 3).

[289] ibid 7–8.

[290] ibid 9–10.

[291] R Caplan, *International Governance of War-Torn Territories: Rule and Reconstruction* (n 2), 209.

[292] D Marshall and S Inglis, 'Human Rights in Transition: The Disempowerment of Human Rights-Based Justice in the United Nations Mission in Kosovo' (n 246), 112.

[293] Common Article 2(2).

[294] Article 6.

applicability of IHL relate primarily to the conduct of forces and are specifically limited to situations of armed conflict in which the troops are engaged as combatants. Thus they would appear not to encompass occupations outside of armed conflict.[295] There is no continuing armed conflict in Kosovo. Nevertheless many of the IHL provisions on occupation constitute customary law and therefore are likely to be binding on a UN-run administration provided that the factual circumstances are sufficiently similar to those that would trigger the applicability of occupation law to States.

A number of commentators have argued that the administration of territory by the UN raises completely different issues to that of belligerent occupation. Sylvain Vité argues that international administrations are juridically distinct from belligerent occupations because the administration 'dans ce contexte sert un intérêt général, celui de la communauté internationale, et a spécifiquement pour objectif de protéger les populations locales.' Conversely 'l'occupation répond à un intérêt particulier, celui de l'Etat occupant.'[296] Similarly Daphna Shraga comments that:

> whereas the essence of an occupant-occupied relationship is that of conflict of interest, that which characterizes a United Nations 'administration' of a territory is co-operation between the force and the local population.[297]

In the same vein she notes that:

> the laws of occupation strike a balance between the rights of the inhabitants to protection and humane treatment and the security needs of the Occupying forces. The UN Administration, on the other hand, has no interest of its own other than to facilitate a transition to another administration or form of governance, and in so doing act solely for and on behalf of the population of the administered territory.[298]

There is some persuasive force to these arguments but they fail to take into account both the complexities of the local population's response to a UN administration and the deeply political nature of Security Council decision-making. Co-operation between UN forces and the local population cannot be taken for granted and similarly it is an oversimplification to suggest that the UN administration will always have no interests of its own. The Security Council in mandating a UN administration acts in the interests of maintaining international peace and security, as those interests are perceived by its Member States, particularly

[295] Discussed above in the text accompanying footnotes 68 to 79.

[296] S Vité, 'L'applicabilité du droit international de l'occupation militaire aux activités des organisations internationales' (2004) International Review of the Red Cross 853, 17, 25.

[297] D Shraga, 'The UN as an actor bound by international humanitarian law' in L Condorelli, AM La Rosa, S Scherrer (eds), *Les Nations Unies et le droit international humanitaire, Actes du Colloque international à l'occasion du cinquantiè anniversaire des Nations Unies, Genè 19, 20 et 21 Octobre 1995* (Pedone Paris 1996) 317, 328.

[298] D Shraga, Military Occupation and UN Transitional Administrations—The Analogy and Its Limitations in MG Koehen (ed), *Promoting Justice, Human Righst and Conflict Resolution through International Law* (Liber Amicorum Lucius Caflisch Leiden 2007), 479, 496.

the Permanent Five. The inhabitants of the administered territory may be only marginally concerned with wider matters of international peace and security (and may not share the view of the Permanent Five on these matters) but they may have very strong feelings and beliefs regarding nationality, territorial claims, religious affiliation, clan affiliation and relationships with neighbouring States, among other things. They may have a different perspective, or many different perspectives, to the UN on all of these issues and may not always regard the UN as an impartial representative of their interests.

The arguments put forward by Vité and Shraga are in many respects very similar to arguments put forward by a number of commentators that the laws of occupation are inappropriate in the context of situations such as Iraq where there has been a regime change following the defeat of an autocratic ruler with an appalling human rights record. David Scheffer writing in the American Journal of International Law in 2004 argued that:

> In most cases, modern multilateral military interventions, particularly Security Council-authorized missions that are followed by prolonged and widely supported multilateral occupations aimed at transforming societies, will require a far more pragmatic body of rules and procedures than occupation law currently affords.[299]

Scheffer argues that the dominant premise of occupation law has been that regulation is required for the military occupation of foreign territory but that these rules are not designed to achieve its transformation.[300] This is true. But how is it possible to reconcile the principle of respect for State sovereignty if humanitarian intervention is permitted to go beyond preventing human rights abuses and take on State transformation? Is it possible to objectively distinguish between a 'legitimate' transformation and one that is 'illegitimate?' The effectiveness of a Security Council mandate as a distinguishing factor is weak in the face of 'context-breaking actions' taken in support of Security Council resolutions but where the UN mandate is only granted after the intervention.

US objections to the restrictiveness of occupation law are nothing new. At the Diplomatic Conference held in Geneva in 1949 to draft the Geneva Conventions the US representative proposed that Article 55 of the working draft (which became Article 64 of the final draft)[301] should be deleted and replaced with:

[299] DJ Scheffer, 'Agora: Future Implication of the Iraq Conflict: Beyond Occupation Law' (2004) 97 AJIL, 842, 844.

[300] ibid 849.

[301] Article 55 of the Draft Convention for the Protection of Civilians in Time of War , which was approved by the XVIIth International Red Cross Conference at Stockholm in August 1948, and provided the basis for discussion at the Diplomatic Conference, read: 'The penal laws of the occupied territory shall remain in force and the tribunals thereof shall continue to function in respect of all offences covered by the said laws./ The Occupying Power may however, subject the population of the occupied territory to provisions intended to secure the security of members and property of the forces or administration of the occupying forces and likewise of the establishment used by the said forces and administration.' *Final Record of the Diplomatic Conference of Geneva 1949*, Vol. I, 122.

Until changed by the Occupying Power the penal laws of the occupied territory shall remain in force and the tribunals thereof continue to function in respect of the offences covered by the said laws.[302]

The US delegate explained that the amendment was prompted by the experience of the American authorities in Germany where they had to deal with a whole series of laws based on Nazi ideology that were 'incompatible with a legal system worthy of the name.'[303] But the representative for Monaco argued that:

The reasons given in support of the proposal were satisfactory in the particular case quoted, but would not hold as a general rule.

What would be the position in the opposite case, that of an invader other than a democratic power who exercises that right? Under the United States amendment the invader could change the penal legislation of the occupied territory. The Committee should think very carefully before amending the wording of the Convention in the way suggested.[304]

[302] *Final Record of the Diplomatic Conference of Geneva 1949*, Volume III, 139 [294]; The delegate for the Union of Soviet Socialist Republics also proposed an amendment to add the words 'except in cases where this constitutes a menace to the security of the Occupying Power' to the first paragraph. These proposed amendments became the subject of some debate on 18 and 19 May 1949. Mr Morosov, the delegate for the USSR said that the proposed US amendment would grant the Occupying Power an absolute right to modify penal legislation, a right which 'greatly exceeded the limited right laid down in the Hague Regulations, as well as in the Stockholm text.' Mrs Manole, the delegate for Rumania said that the US amendment 'changed the whole sense of Article 55.' Mr de Alba, the delegate for Mexico, noting that '[the principal aim of the Convention was the protection of the civilian population' and that it was 'important, therefore, to adopt provisions which would not constitute a retrogression by comparison with those laid down at the Hague', proposed that '[i]n order to take account of the legitimate concern expressed by the United States Delegation' wording should be adopted 'to the effect that the Occupying Power could only modify the legislation of an occupied territory if the legislation in question violated the principles of the "Universal Declaration of the Rights of Man."' Mr Day, the delegate for the UK, suggested that there should be a provision to cover cases where local courts were unable to function. He suggested that this might be achieved by adding the words 'without prejudice to the effective administration of justice' to the first paragraph of Article 55 and adding into the second paragraph words to the effect that the Occupying Power had the right to take such legislative measures as might be necessary to secure the application of the Convention and the proper administration of the territory. On 28 May the UK proposed an amendment to delete Article 55 and substitute it with 'The penal laws of the occupied territory shall remain in force unless they contravene the principles of this Convention or endanger the security of the Occupying Power. Subsequent to the same consideration, and to the necessity for securing effective dispensation of justice, the tribunals of the occupied territory shall continue to function in respect of all offences covered by the said laws./ The Occupying Power may subject the population of the occupied territory to provisions which are essential to ensure the application of this Convention and the orderly government of the territory, and to provisions intended to assure the security of the members of the forces of the Occupying Power, and likewise of the establishments used by the said forces and administration.' Article 55 was referred to the drafting committee. The text approved by the majority of the drafting committee and submitted to the delegates for adoption was 'in accordance with the spirit of the amendments submitted by the United Kingdom and the Soviet Delegations.' The text submitted by the minority took into account only the amendment proposed by the USSR. The text of the majority was adopted by 20 votes to 8. *Final Record of the Diplomatic Conference of Geneva 1949*, Vol. IIa, 670–2, 771; Vol. III, 139–140.

[303] ibid Volume IIa, 670.

[304] ibid.

The representative of Norway thought that the United States amendment would 'represent a retrogressive step of considerable importance in relation to existing international law.'[305] The delegates for Romania, Mexico, and the Union of Soviet Socialist Republics also voiced strong objections.[306]

The observations of the delegates to the Diplomatic Conference regarding the US proposal (which was not supported by any of them) remain pertinent today despite perceived changes in the nature of armed conflict and the conduct of military operations. Carte blanche for an occupying power to change legislation as it thinks fit would be a disturbing development even in the context of a transitional administration established following the removal of a regime with an appalling human rights record, and even when operating under a UN mandate. Even in the context of a UN supported intervention it is unlikely that outside forces would be willing to intervene in humanitarian crises primarily on the basis of the urgent needs of threatened peoples.[307] Although self-interest and moral imperative may conjoin and result in a greater willingness to see action on behalf of vulnerable people through to a successful conclusion, they are rarely, if ever, likely to be synonymous. Admittedly the status of occupancy draws attention to the fact that the occupants are foreigners imposing their administration on the occupied State, for a limited time. This creates difficulties in the context of UN control of territory because it is not desirable that the UN be viewed as a hostile power. On the other hand for UN forces to be reminded that they are foreigners in someone else's land may not be such a bad thing. There is a tendency when an administration is imposed for the benefit of the population to assume that its values are universal values agreed by everyone and to gloss over the rights and interests of those people that don't fit into the plan. As Michael Reisman has pointed out, whereas humanitarian intervention is short term and directed towards stopping human rights violations, regime change, although premised on past human rights violations, is future-oriented. It is conducted to change the structure and/or personnel of a government and whilst:

> It is easy to conclude that a regime is wicked and violent. It is difficult and indeed culturally arrogant to determine what sort of contextually workable regime should replace it.[308]

The primary motivation for the intervention in Kosovo was humanitarian but it took the form of a heavy bombing campaign that had the effect of giving support to insurgent groups seeking secession. As Richard Caplan notes:

[305] ibid 671.

[306] ibid 671–2; See note 292.

[307] A Roberts, 'The So-Called 'Right' of Humanitarian Intervention', 3 Yearbook of International Humanitarian Law, 3, 41.

[308] M Reisman, 'The Manley O. Hudson Lecture: Why Regime Change is (Almost Always) a Bad Idea' (2004) 98 AJIL, 516, 522.

from the standpoint of the unwilling 'host'—for instance, Serbia in the case of Kosovo—there may be little difference between a NATO backed administration and a foreign military occupation.'[309]

Stephen Ratner argues that:

the analogy between administration by international organizations and occupation by states... retains much traction. Both missions can resemble each other in the eyes of those living in the occupied or administered territory and face much the same challenges or acceptability, both within the territory and by actors outside it.[310]

But Caplan argues that, notwithstanding the viewpoint of the 'unwilling host,' UN administrations and military occupations are not sufficiently similar to warrant the applicability of occupation law:

military occupation entails the occupation of sovereign territory by a state or group of states acting jointly and without the authorization of the United Nations or a similar body, as with the Allied-occupation of Germany and Japan after the Second-World War and the US-led occupation of Iraq following the defeat of Saddam Hussein in March 2003. By contrast an international administration is under the control of, and answerable to, an international body, whether it is the United Nations or an ad hoc organization, such as the Peace Implementing Council (PIC) in the case of BiH [Bosnia-Herzegovina], which will have authorized or sanctioned its establishment. An international administration is thus subject to constraints that an occupying power can more easily elude.[311]

Caplan's distinction is valid in so far as that it is probably the case that territories governed by administrations answerable directly to an international body such as the UN are less likely to be exposed to economic and political exploitation. However, occupation law is concerned not only with preventing exploitation but also with taking on positive responsibilities towards the welfare of the local population. Transitional administrations, whether UN-run or not, generally operate in the context of a democratic vacuum in that the governing authorities have not been elected and do not represent the local population. The Kosovo Report concluded that the intervention was legitimate because it was necessary to prevent a humanitarian crisis, nevertheless the political consequences of the intervention should not be glossed over. The intervention provided support to the Kosovo Liberation Army. The UN/NATO run administration appointed after the defeat of the Serbs not only failed to make efforts to ensure the protection of the Serbian population, it failed to even properly consider how to protect their rights. As the International Commission on Kosovo observed KFOR was 'both unable and unwilling to stop continuing violence against ethnic minorities,'[312]

[309] R Caplan, *International Governance of War-Torn Territories: Rule and Reconstruction* (n 2), 3.

[310] S Ratner, 'Foreign Occupation and International Administration: The Challenges of Convergence', 16 EJIL 4, 695, 697.

[311] R Caplan, *International Governance of War-Torn Territories: Rule and Reconstruction* (n 2), 4.

[312] Independent International Commission on Kosovo, *Follow up to the Kosovo Report: Why Conditional Independence?* (n 256), 19.

a view supported by Amnesty International reports[313] and the observations of journalists.[314] Both during the bombing campaign and in the establishment of the subsequent administration, the US and its allies focused on the behaviour of political leaders and governments seeming to assume that once these oppressive agencies were dealt with peaceable and democratic governance would (after some initial teething problems) follow. The ombudsman for Kosovo noted that:

> the situation of members of minority communities inside and outside of Kosovo is a highly politicised issue. All sides envision these people as objects of political debate, rather than subjects of law, an approach that is incompatible with human rights. This politicised approach has led to the establishment of contradictory policies that obstruct not only the realisation of the political agenda but the capacity of the individuals affected to realise their rights.[315]

Paragraph 46 of the Secretary-General's progress report to the Security Council in August 1999 comments that:

> The international community must make it clear to extremists that it cannot and will not tolerate ethnically motivated violence and murders. It must also make it clear to the Kosovo leadership that they must make far greater efforts to restrain and redirect the emotions unleashed by the conflict. The international community must also redouble its own efforts to create a secure environment, especially for Kosovo's vulnerable minorities.[316]

But nowhere in the report is there any condemnation of the attacks nor any reference to the fact such attacks constitute gross violations of international human rights law and may constitute crimes against humanity, nor any comment on the need to hold the perpetrators of these acts to account. Although subsequent reports, particularly after March 2004, are much stronger in their condemnation of human rights violations, condemnatory comments in the early reports are muted in relation to the scale of the problem, though the reports themselves indicate that the scale of the problem was huge.

Observers on the ground, such as NGOs and journalists, have reported what appears to have been fairly widespread tolerance of reprisals and revenge attacks against Serbs and other minorities in the period following the bombing campaign. The Secretary-General's August 1999 report refers several times to the 'international community' but does not refer to the responsibilities of UNMIK and KFOR. The Security Council represents the 'international community,' or at any rate UN Member States, and therefore generalized exhortatory language seeking support for dealing with these attacks may be the most appropriate for reports addressed to it. The emphasis on security is also appropriate given that the primary task of the Council is the maintenance of international peace and

[313] Amnesty International Reports, above (n 246).

[314] T Judah, *Kosovo: War and Revenge* (n 254) p. xviii.

[315] Ombudsman Institution in Kosovo, *Second Annual Report*, 2001–2002, 4.

[316] Report of the UN Secretary-General on the UN Mission in Kosovo S/1999/987 of August 16, 1999.

security. But ethnically motivated violence is not solely a security issue: it is also a rule of law issue. The 'international community' may have responsibilities of some sort towards Kosovo but since the 'international community' is a largely rhetorical entity these are of limited significance in dealing with rule of law issues. The 'international community' has no direct legal powers in the province: UNMIK and KFOR do. The Security Council is a political institution (with extensive enforcement powers) but UNMIK/KFOR is a de facto government: it has legal as well as political responsibilities. Section 11(j) of Resolution 1244 states that, 'the main responsibilities of the international civil presence will include... protecting and promoting human rights.'

Neither the Secretary-General nor the Security Council have commented on the widespread and critical reports of human rights abuses (in particular unlawful detentions)[317] perpetrated by KFOR and to a lesser extent UNMIK. The criticisms of KFOR and UNMIK have been made not only be non-governmental organizations such as Amnesty International but also by the Commissioner for Human Rights for the Council of Europe, the UN Human Right's Commission's Special Representative for Bosnia and Yugoslavia, the Organization for Security and Co-operation in Europe and the Ombudsman for Kosovo.[318] Considerations normally considered fundamental to the maintenance of the rule of law are notably lacking in the UNMIK/KFOR administration. Sergio Vieira de Mello, who was for a time administrator of UNMIK and was subsequently administrator of the UN Transitional Administration in East Timor,[319] observed that:

> The UN administrator is nominated by the Secretary-General with little or no consultation with those who are to be administered... There is no separation of the legislative or judicial from the executive authority... The question remains open how the UN can exercise fair governance with absolute powers.'[320]

[317] The OSCE in its 2003 review of the criminal justice system in Kosovo commented that the 'OSCE has consistently held the view that, under the circumstances existing in Kosovo, KFOR detentions are both illegal and unjustified: there is no longer a state of emergency in Kosovo and during the past four years great progress has been made in redeveloping the criminal justice system. Criminal incidents that were previously of military concern can now be satisfactorily dealt with in civil, as opposed to military, criminal proceedings.' OSCE Mission in Kosovo: Review of the Criminal Justice System (March 2002–April 2003), 33, available at <http://www.osce.org/kosovo>.

[318] *Kosovo: The Human Rights Situation and Fate of Persons Displaced in their Homes: Report by Mr. Alvaro Gil-Robles*, 16 October 2002, CoE Doc CommDH (2002) 11; *Situation of Human Rights in Parts of South Eastern Europe: report of the special representative of the Commission on Human Rights on the Situation of Human Rights in Bosnia and the Federal Republic of Yugoslavia, Jose Cutileira*, 8 January 2002, UN Doc E.CN. 4/2002/41; OSCE Mission in Kosovo: Review of the Criminal Justice System (March 2002–April 2003) (n 317); Ombudsman Institution in Kosovo, *Second Annual Report*, 2001–2002 and *Special Report No 3* 29 June 2001 available at <http://www.ombudspersonkosovo.org>; S Ratner, 'Foreign Occupation and International Administration: The Challenges of Convergence' (n 310), 714.

[319] He was later tragically killed in the explosion in the UN building in Iraq on 19 August 2003.

[320] Sergio Vieira de Mello, 'How Not to Run a Country: Lessons for the UN from Kosovo and East Timor' Unpublished manuscript 2000, cited in J Beauvais, 'Benevolent Despotism: A Critique

Some progress towards accountability for human rights has now been made; since 2006 the Human Rights Committee received its first ever report from a UN mandated administration on its compliance with the ICCPR in the administered territory.[321] However, the Committee, which published its concluding observations on UNMIK in August 2006, noted a number of areas of continuing concern. The Committee stated that 'the Human Rights Advisory Panel established under UNMIK Regulation 2006/12 to receive and examine complaints against UNMIK lacks the necessary independence and authority' and recommended that UNMIK 'reconsider arrangements for the authoritative human rights review of acts and omissions by UNMIK.'[322] The Committee was also concerned, among other things, at the failure to investigate war crimes and crimes against humanity and the low priority given to tracing missing and disappeared persons; the detention of persons on the directive of KFOR commanders with no opportunity for them to be 'brought before a judge promptly and without access to an independent judicial body to determine the lawfulness of their detention'; the 'persistence of male-dominated attitudes within Kosovar society,' together with high levels of domestic violence, high levels of trafficking of women and low levels of prosecution; the widespread discrimination against minorities; the 'restricted freedom of movement and access to essential services, such as judicial remedies, health care and education, and personal documents, of minority communities living in microenclaves' and the low number of minority returns and the inability of returning displaced persons to recover their property.[323]

7. Overall Assessment of the Laws of Occupation to UN Administrations

The question of whether the laws of occupation are formally applicable to UN operations is a matter of debate. On the one hand the Security Council made it clear in the aftermath of the invasion of Iraq that the laws of occupation may be applicable to operations that are UN mandated.[324] But it is not clear what the

of UN State Building in East Timor' (2001) NYU Journal of International Law and Politics 33, 1101, 1101 and in D Marshall and S Inglis, 'The Disempowerment of Human Rights-Based Justice in the United Nations Mission in Kosovo' (n 246), 96.

[321] In its 2004 concluding observations on Serbia's Article 40 report the Human Rights Committee recommended that UNMIK should also submit a report on Kosovo, which it subsequently did.

[322] Consideration of Reports submitted by State Parties under Article 40 of the Covenant: Concluding Observations of the Human Rights Committee, Kosovo (Serbia) CCPR/C/UNK/CO/1 14 August 2006, [10].

[323] ibid [11–22].

[324] Benvenisti argues that Resolution 1483 'revives the neutral connotation' of occupation, which 'is a temporary measure for re-establishing order and civil life after the end of hostilities, benefiting also, if not primarily, the civilian population. As such occupation does not amount to

position is with regard to UN-run operations. UN-run operations may be no more democratically legitimate and no more accountable to the population than those that are merely UN mandated. However, UN statements on the applicability of IHL to its forces are directed towards accountability for misconduct by troops and limited to situations of armed conflict in which troops are engaged as combatants. To the extent that the laws of occupation constitute customary law they may be binding on UN forces anyway, but only if the situation is sufficiently comparable to that in which the laws of occupation would be applicable to States. There is disagreement as to whether a UN-run operation can ever be considered comparable to a military occupation.

Adam Roberts argues that when UN forces find themselves in the de facto role of an occupant most, or all, customary and conventional laws of war apply.[325] The International Commission on Kosovo appears to have viewed the UNMIK/KFOR administration there as an occupation and in its follow up to the Kosovo report it argued in favour of adopting principles emphasizing the need for compliance with IHL, including all aspects of military occupation;[326] but a number of commentators have argued that UN administrations raise completely different issues to that of military occupation because unlike military occupations there is no hostile relationship between the administration and the population. However, these arguments bear some similarities to arguments put forward that the laws of occupation should not be considered applicable to operations (whether UN-run or not) whose objective is social transformation following the removal of a tyrannical governing regime. The Security Council made it clear in Resolution 1483 that such operations may be bound by occupation law, although the same resolution gave such extensive additional powers to the occupants that one critic has described it as 'a study in deliberate ambiguity,' possibly the latest example of 'hegemonic international law.'[327]

Caplan has argued that international administrations differ from military occupations in that the former are answerable to an international body, such as the UN, and are therefore subject to constraints that an occupying power can more easily elude.[328] On the other hand there has been strong criticism of UNMIK/KFOR on the grounds that it failed in its duty to establish the rule of law and to protect minorities.[329] It has also been censured for its lack of

unlawful alien domination that entitles the local population to struggle against it.' E Benvenisti *The International Law of Occupation: with a new preface by the author* (n 3) xi.

[325] A Roberts, 'What is Military Occupation' (n 8), 290.

[326] The Commission emphasized that 'even in the context of a humanitarian intervention backed by UN authority, there exists an international duty to comply with these guidelines.' Independent International Commission on Kosovo, *Follow up to the Kosovo Report: Why Conditional Independence?* (n 256), 36–37.

[327] JE Alvarez, 'Hegemonic International Law Revisited' (n 190), 883.

[328] R Caplan, *International Governance of War-Torn Territories: Rule and Reconstruction* (n 2), 4.

[329] Independent International Commission on Kosovo, *Follow up to the Kosovo Report: Why Conditional Independence?* (n 256), 37.

accountability;[330] a colonial style arrogance subsumed beneath institutions created to grant the illusion of self-rule;[331] and 'the comic hypocrisy of pursuing an objective of democracy through symbolically dictatorial powers.'[332] Chesterman argues that the fact that powers are exercised benevolently does not deprive them of their authoritarian character and that:

> it is both inaccurate and counter-productive to assert that transitional administration depends upon the consent or 'ownership' of local populations. It is inaccurate because if genuine local control were possible then a transitional administration would not be necessary. It is counter-productive because insincere claims of local ownership lead to frustration and suspicion on the part of local actors.[333]

He adds that failure to acknowledge the 'colonial' nature of transitional administrations:

> leads to a measure of doublethink on the part of administering authorities. In particular not acknowledging the interests at stake in the creation of transitional administrations sometimes gives rise to dubious claims of altruism on the part of international actors. Meanwhile, disingenuous assertions that local 'ownership' is central to the success of an operation ignore the political circumstances that required international administration at the outset.[334]

Arguably a legal regime that places greater emphasis on the political and economic development of the territory might be more appropriate to UN administrations such as Kosovo than occupation law. But what alternatives are there? The ICISS suggests, in the section of its report dealing with UN administrations and 'the responsibility to rebuild', that:

> useful guidelines for the behaviour of intervening authorities' during intervention and in the follow-up period might be found in a constructive adaptation of Chapter XII of the UN Charter.[335]

Chapter XII of the UN Charter deals with the International Trusteeship System, which was primarily intended for the administration of former colonies in the

[330] Sergio Vieira de Mello, 'How Not to Run a Country: Lessons for the UN from Kosovo and East Timor' (n 320); S Chesterman, *You, The People: United Nations Transitional Administration and State-Building* (n 102), 132–134, 226; Independent International Commission on Kosovo, *Follow up to the Kosovo Report: Why Conditional Independence?* (n 256), 20.

[331] Independent international Commission on Kosovo, *Follow up to the Kosovo Report: Why Conditional Independence?* (n 256), 20.

[332] MV Bhatia, *War and Intervention: Issues for Contemporary Peace Operations* (n 100), 87; W O'Neill, *Kosovo: An Unfinished Peace* (n 252) 84, 89; D Marshall and S Inglis, 'Human Rights in Transition: The Disempowerment of Human Rights-Based Justice in the United Nations Mission in Kosovo' (n 246), 120–124; Amnesty International Reports: Serbia and Montenegro (Kosovo/Kosova) 'Minority Communities: Fundamental Rights Denied' and 'Prisoners in Our Own Homes' (n 246).

[333] S Chesterman, *You, The People: United Nations Transitional Administration and State-Building* (n 102), 239.

[334] ibid 47.

[335] ICISS, *The Responsibility to Protect* (n 264), 43.

transition to independence. Article 76 lists among the basic objectives of the system; furthering international peace and security; promoting the economic, social and educational advancement of the people of the territory in question; encouraging respect for human rights; ensuring the equal treatment of all peoples in the UN in social, economic and commercial matters; and ensuring equal treatment in the administration of justice.[336] The trusteeship system was overseen by a Trusteeship Council. The Council's powers were limited but it was responsible for receiving reports from the administering State and making periodic visits. It was also able to receive petitions from inhabitants of the administered State. Chesterman comments that:

The limited powers [of the Trusteeship Council] to formulate questionnaires and consider reports, to accept petitions from inhabitants, and to undertake periodic visits represented a greater level of accountability (at least in principle) than was available to the populations of Bosnia, Kosovo, or East Timor in the 1990s.[337]

The International Trusteeship System has another important advantage in situations such as Kosovo in that it specifically allows for progress towards independence. However, in practice there is little likelihood that the Charter provisions on trusteeship could be revived. Article 78 of the UN Charter prohibits applying the trusteeship system to members of the UN, therefore a revival of the system would entail a Charter amendment and it is unlikely that there would be sufficient support for such a move.[338] Attempts to resurrect the trusteeship system would probably be construed as providing a mechanism for interference in internal affairs and limiting the right to self-determination. Hence they are unlikely to be supported by States that have only relatively recently emerged from colonial rule.[339]

It might be possible to set up a new body similar in function to the Trusteeship Council to supervise international administrations. But this would imply, as the Panel on United Nations Peace Operations noted in the Brahimi report, the probability that the UN would be asked to engage in more and more of these operations, something it is not keen to do.[340] Chesterman argues that simply improving clarity could in itself mitigate many of the problems that have beset international administrations. He argues in favour of making clarity a priority in three key areas: the strategic objectives of the mission; the relationship between

[336] Charter of the United Nations (Adopted San Francisco 26 June 1945, came into force 24 October 1945) <http://www.un.org/law/>, art 76; Richard Caplan argues that by the mid-1990s the 'exceptional authority' being exercised by UN and other multi-lateral bodies in Eastern Slavonia, Bosnia-Herzegovina, Kosovo and East Timor constituted a form of international trusteeship in all but name: R Caplan, *International Governance of War-Torn Territories: Rule and Reconstruction* (n 2), 2.

[337] S Chesterman, *You, The People: United Nations Transitional Administration and State-Building* (n 102), 45.

[338] ibid 47.

[339] ICISS, *The Responsibility to Protect* (n 264), 43.

[340] Report of the Panel on United Nations Peace Operations (Brahimi report) A/55/305—S/2000/809 August 21 2000, [78].

international and local actors and how this will change over time; the extent of the commitment required by international actors in order to achieve the objectives that warrant the establishment of the administration.[341] Unfortunately the highly political nature of the Security Council is not conducive to encouraging clarity. Since it is such a useful political tool I see little likelihood of Security Council members choosing to abandon the practice of drafting agreements in deliberately opaque terms where to do so would enable a consensus to be reached. Without some formal arrangement as to what approach the UN should take to the running of administrations, and without the creation of a system of monitoring and appeals, it is likely to make the same kind of mistakes it has made in the past. Given that UN administrations may be in place for a long time and that human rights may be at stake, this is unacceptable. As the Panel on United Nations Peace Operations noted in the Brahimi report, if the UN does not prepare in advance for the possibility of undertaking transitional administrations and make institutional arrangements, it will find itself responding to future comparable situations in the same ad hoc fashion it has adopted in the past, and 'do badly if it is once again flung into the breach.'[342]

In December 2005 the Security Council and General Assembly adopted resolutions establishing a Peace Building Commission,[343] to act as an intergovernmental advisory body to 'marshal resources and advise on and propose integrated strategies for post-conflict peace-building and recovery.'[344] The Peacebuilding Commission will be an advisory subsidiary organ of the General Assembly and the Security Council. The Secretary-General welcomed the establishment of the Commission saying that:

> The work of the United Nations to build peace has intensified in recent years as the complexity and scope of post-conflict challenges have increased. We have worked to provide humanitarian assistance and to better link emergency aid to longer-term reconstruction and recovery efforts. In East Timor and Kosovo, we have even had to assume responsibilities normally undertaken by Governments...

[341] S Chesterman, *You, The People: United Nations Transitional Administration and State-Building* (n 102), 240.

[342] ibid R Caplan, *International Governance of War-Torn Territories: Rule and Reconstruction* (n 2), 249.

[343] S/RES/1645 20 December 2005; A/RES/60/1 24 October 2005.

[344] A/RES/60/1 24 October 2005, [98]; The concept of a Peacebuilding Commission was first introduced in the report published in 2004 by the Secretary-General's High Level Panel on Threats, Challenges and Change 'A More Secure World: Our Shared Responsibility' (A/59/565 >www.un.org//secureworld>). The Secretary-General subsequently proposed the establishment of a Peacebuilding Commission in his report of March 2005, 'In larger freedom: towards development, security and human rights for all' (A/59/2005). At the World Summit in October 2005, the UN Member States, at a plenary meeting of the General Assembly, agreed to establish a Peacebuilding Commission, and agreed that it should begin its work no later than 31 December 2005 (A/RES/60/1 24 October 2005 [97–105]). On 20 December 2005 the Security Council adopted a resolution establishing a Peacebuilding Commission (S/RES/1645, 20 December 2005) On the same day the General Assembly adopted a resolution endorsing the establishment of the Commission (S/RES/60/180, 66th Plenary Meeting, 20 December 2005).

> Yet, till now, a critical institutional gap persisted. For while many parts of the United Nations have been involved in the peacebuilding process, the system has lacked a dedicated entity to oversee the process, ensure its coherence, or sustain it through the long haul. This resulted in fractured peacebuilding operations, with no single forum for all the relevant actors to come together, share information, and develop a common strategy. Too often, a fragile peace has been allowed to crumble into renewed conflict.
>
> Today's General Assembly resolution goes a long way towards bridging this gap.[345]

The establishment of the Commission is an important step forward in recognizing the need for a greater focus on the rebuilding of a State after an armed conflict or military intervention. Given sufficient resources and an appropriate mandate the Peace Building Commission could carry out monitoring activities and provide for an appeals system in post-conflict administration. In an Explanatory Note on the establishment of the Peacebuilding Commission the Secretary-General commented that 'As part of the overall process, I believe it would be valuable if there were regular, independent evaluation of peacebuilding activities.'[346] However, whilst some general progress evaluation might be possible there is little likelihood that Member States would agree to give the Peacebuilding Commission power to monitor the activities of troops and their administrative counter-parts engaged in post-conflict administration. During the process leading to the establishment of the Commission there was considerable tension over the location of the Commission within the UN organization, partly stimulated by concerns over the extent to which the permanent members of the Security Council should be able to exercise a controlling influence, which suggests that the major powers would not be supportive of the creation of institutional mechanisms with the authority to oversee the exercise of military and administrative power in post-conflict operations.

8. Conclusion

There has been a general tendency for occupants (whether or not acting under the authority of the UN) to wish to avoid the restrictions and negative connotations of occupation law. Hence it is comparatively rare for occupying powers to acknowledge their status.[347] Difficulties are exacerbated by the fact that in 'grey area' operations where the level of control is partial and may change during the

[345] SG/SM/10277, GA/10440, 20 December 2005 <http://www.un.org/News/Press/docs/2005/sgsm10277.doc.htm>.

[346] Explanatory Note of the Secretary General: Peacebuilding Commission, 'In larger freedom: towards development, security and human rights for all.' (A/59/2005), Addendum 2, [35].

Initially transmitted by the Secretary-general to the President of the General Assembly on April 19, 2005: <http://www.globalpolicy.org/reform/initiatives/annan/2005/0417peacebuilding.htm>.

[347] E Benvenisti, *The International Law of Occupation: with a new preface by the author* (n 3), 181; H McCoubrey and N White, *International Law and Armed Conflict* (n 10), 281.

course of the operation it may be impossible to apply occupation law: but at the same time the sovereign may no longer be in control, leaving a vacuum. Problems can also arise when neither the force nor local authorities have full control over the area. Who is then responsible for securing public order and safety and the fundamental rights of the inhabitants? In a volatile situation what criteria determine whether or not sufficient authority is being exercised to constitute occupation? What is the position of former occupants that continue to remain in the territory at the request of a newly elected government but are entirely outside the control of that government and are still engaged in armed conflict? These difficulties give rise to uncertainty as to when and if occupation law applies and as to what legal regime governs the relationship between the troops and the local population.

Operation Provide Comfort was one of the earliest interventions to have been clearly premised on humanitarian needs. It was not authorized by the Security Council but UN Member States voiced no serious objections to it at the time. Its success in providing relief to the Kurds and reducing flows of refugees were viewed as positive signals for the future development of humanitarian intervention. Commenting on its effects, the former Secretary-General Boutros Boutros-Ghali wrote:

> While respect for the fundamental sovereignty and integrity of the state remains central, it is undeniable that the centuries old doctrine of absolute and exclusive sovereignty no longer stands, and was in fact never so absolute as it was conceived in theory.[348]

Operation Provide Comfort temporarily resolved pressing human needs and even those States that reject humanitarian intervention were reluctant to criticize action that saved so many lives. At the time, Malcolm Shaw wrote that the intervention by the coalition was welcome because to do nothing would be 'criminal.'[349] But he warned that 'one thing is clear and that is the need to create immediately a comprehensive and viable legal framework for this operation and the future.'[350] He recommended the adoption of a Security Council resolution authorizing the use of all necessary measures to protect the Kurds and the proclamation of a temporary 'United Nations humanitarian zone.' He suggested that the Secretary-General initiate discussions leading to an internationally guaranteed local autonomy for the Kurds and acknowledging the territorial integrity of Iraq but providing for the protection of the human rights and minority rights of the Kurdish people.[351] The safe havens he warned could provide only very temporary relief and 'to raise unrealistic expectations that simply cannot be fulfilled would be irresponsible and dangerous.'[352]

[348] B Boutros-Ghali, 'Empowering the United Nations' (Winter 1992/3) 71 Foreign Affairs 5, 89, 98–99.

[349] M Shaw, 'Safe havens and the prospect of a permanent solution in Iraq' Letter: *Independent* (London 18 April 1991).

[350] ibid. [351] ibid. [352] ibid.

There was a logical rationale for the continuing presence of coalition control in the form of No Fly Zones so as to prevent an immediate return to the abusive situation that had prevailed before. However, the southern No Fly Zone provided no human rights protection at all and the northern No Fly Zone only provided protection against Iraqi abuses, not from attacks by other States. Helena Cook has suggested that it might be argued that when the former occupants departed leaving only the No Fly Zones they delegated their responsibility for defence and security of the territory to the UN.[353] However, the UN never exercised authority over the territory: it did not authorize the No Fly Zones or the safe havens. However, Rosalyn Higgins has also raised the question of the potential responsibility of the United Nations. She asks:

> What of the acts of certain western States, among the original coalition, who later patrolled no-fly zones, asserting such action to be 'based on' the UN resolutions which called for humanitarian support without in terms authorizing such acts? What are the implications, for the attribution of responsibility, of the silence of the United Nations in the face of such action? Did the UN thereby take responsibility for what the States concerned said had anyway been implicitly authorized by it?[354]

The uncertain legal status of the various interventions in Iraq since 1991 and the lack of clarity regarding objectives has contributed to the long-term instability of Iraq. Unfortunately, many of the human rights abuses reportedly perpetrated against Iraqi civilians in 2004, were committed not by the former dictator Saddam Hussein, but by coalition forces. Whilst the primary responsibility for these abuses lies with the forces involved and their governments, the UN itself must take some responsibility because it failed to create a viable legal framework for the intervention in Iraq at an early stage: instead it stepped aside for over 10 years.

In 1984 Adam Roberts recommended that the UN adopt a resolution affirming that the laws of occupation apply to all situations where a military force exercises authority over territory outside its accepted international frontiers.[355] This might go some way towards improving accountability since occupation law is a well-established sector of IHL, for the most part codified in the Hague Regulations and Geneva Conventions, and thus all troops should be familiar with it. As Sassòli observes occupation law offers a pre-existing normative framework adequate for the maintenance of civil life and public order, that can be applied immediately as soon as an international administration starts and so 'avoids 'a la carte' solutions adopted by the international presence, which are arbitrary (because they are not

[353] H Cook, *The Safe Haven in Iraq: International Responsibility for Iraqi Kurdistan* (n 128), 158.

[354] R Higgins, 'The Responsibility of State Members for Defaults of International Organizations: Continuing the Dialogue' in S Schlemmer-Schulte & Ko-Yung Tung eds, *Liber Americorum Ibrahim Shihata* (Kluwer Law International The Hague 2001) 440, 446.

[355] A Roberts, 'What Is Military Occupation' (n 8), 303.

ruled by a normative framework) or at least perceived as arbitrary.'[356] Because the rules of occupation are well known it should be possible to apply the principles of occupation law by analogy even if there is dispute as to whether the facts fit occupation law criteria. The comparative success of Australian troops engaged in the UNITAF operation in Somalia suggests that the Australian decision to comply with the laws of occupation, even though the situation was not that of a traditional occupation, had major benefits.

An acknowledgement that the intervening States must operate within a regime that requires them to strive as far as possible to respect local law, whilst doing all that it can to secure public order and safety and the fundamental rights of the inhabitants, might go some way towards countering resistance to developing a formal doctrine of humanitarian intervention. Much of that opposition is grounded in the fear that humanitarian intervention may be used as a cover for more self-interested interventions.[357] This fear is present even when intervention is authorized by the Security Council, for as Hans Morgenthau observed as long ago as 1953 '[t]here is no such thing as the policy of an organization, international or domestic, apart from the policy of its most influential member.'[358] The problem may be exacerbated if, as some commentators predict, a trend in which the UN is looked to 'solely in terms of post-intervention administration'[359] continues, and its role in the shaping and authorizing of the use of force is thus marginalized. Chesterman has commented that Security Council action in the area of post-conflict administration has 'been characterized by reaction and improvisation' and that this, together with the highly sensitive nature of these operations, particularly the Kosovo conflict, 'has hampered efforts to develop best practices for such operations or plan for future contingencies.[360]

However, if the UN is likely to be involved in future multi-national administrations (whether through an authorizing mandate or by directly undertaking them) it needs to make further institutional arrangements. The Geneva Conventions envisaged that the belligerent parties could request a Protecting Power (a State that is a neutral party to a conflict) to protect the interests of

[356] M Sassòli, 'Legislation and Maintenance of Public Order and Civil Life by Occupying Powers' (n 43), 691.

[357] A Roberts, 'The So-Called 'Right' of Humanitarian Intervention' (n 307), 4; The Independent International Commission on Kosovo noted that 'in many countries of the world there is a much stronger commitment to the protection of their sovereignty than in the West. Given the dual history of colonialism and the Cold War, there is widespread concern about Western interventionism. The growing global power of NATO creates a feeling of vulnerability in other parts of the world, especially in a case such as Kosovo where NATO claims a right to bypass the United Nations Security Council': The Independent International Commission on Kosovo *The Kosovo Report* (n 229), 11.

[358] HJ Morgenthau, 'Political Limitations of the United Nations' in GA Lipsky (ed), *Law and Politics in the World Community* (University of California Press Berkeley 1953) 143, 150.

[359] MV Bhatia, *War and Intervention: Issues for Contemporary Peace Operations* (n 100), 27.

[360] S Chesterman, *You, The People: United Nations Transitional Administration and State-Building* (n 102), 51.

warring States' nationals, 'protected persons' and those detained in an armed conflict. The Conventions also provide that humanitarian organizations such as the ICRC may assume the functions performed by Protecting Powers.[361] It might be possible to create a mechanism for monitoring the situation in occupied territories through developing the role of Protecting Powers but it would be difficult to apply in the context of multi-national operations. The ICRC, with its long established and internationally accepted special position as monitor of IHL, would be able to carry out this task in so far as compliance with IHL is concerned: but administrations involving multi-national actors generally entail much more complex political engagement than is common in belligerent occupation by States. The UN should consider adopting rules specifically tailored for international administrations, incorporating some of the principles of trusteeship. These could include an obligation to work towards establishing a democratically legitimate government and maintaining economic development, with regular time-based assessment procedures to assess what progress is being made in these areas.

Securing the political consensus need to create an institutional body and rules governing international administrations may be difficult. In the meantime Professor Roberts's recommendation that the UN adopt a resolution affirming that the laws of occupation applies to all situations where a military force exercises authority over territory outside its accepted international frontiers,[362] would reduce controversy regarding its applicability to situations that were not envisaged at the time of the drafting of the Geneva Conventions. This would go some way to improving accountability and ensuring that any exercise of authority by foreign military forces is conducted within a standardized legal framework rather than the ad hoc approach that has characterized post-conflict administration of territory to date. Use of the term occupation may create political difficulties for forces seeking to present their role positively both to the local population and to other States, and seeking to emphasize that they are acting on behalf of the local population: but if there was no coercive element to the exercise of authority by outside actors there would be little need for their presence at all. Blurring of the military and political realities in order to garner local and international support is in the long run counter-productive, since false assertions of local ownership fuel resentment and make it more difficult to assess the true state of progress in the territory. A reluctance to acknowledge the coercive aspects of control may also encourage the adoption of a politicized approach to minority groups and with it the turning of a blind eye to human rights abuses. The principal purpose of occupation law is to provide a means of regulating the temporary exercise of authority over territory and to provide rules governing

[361] Geneva Convention I (n 24), articles 9, 10; Protocol 1 (n 1), articles 5, 3.
[362] A Roberts, 'What Is Military Occupation' (n 8), 303.

the occupant's relationship with the local population. Geneva Convention IV provides:

a bill of rights with a catalogue of fundamental rights which, immediately upon occupation and without any further actions on the part of those affected, becomes applicable to the occupied territories.[363]

In this respect it can serve a valuable function regardless of the nature of the authority mandating the occupant's presence.

Accountability would be further enhanced if the UN were to formally recognize the applicability of international human rights standards to all UN activities[364] and to accept the oversight of human rights monitoring bodies, such as the Human Rights Council, particularly where it is undertaking the administration of territory. There are no comparable oversight mechanisms for ensuring compliance with IHL; a combination of respect for local ownership and the protection of civilians and other 'protected persons,'[365] which are central to the concept of occupation, together with accountability for human rights compliance, would require occupants, and administrations undertaking roles akin to occupation, to give protection and human rights a much higher priority than is currently the case. However, there may be stiff opposition to a UN commitment to be formally bound by Human Rights law as it would be likely to result in the entrenchment of a new standard for compliance with human rights norms in all military occupations. Some States, among them the United States and Israel, do not accept that the ICCPR is applicable extra-territorially or in armed conflict.

Nevertheless, a UN resolution affirming that the laws of occupation, and core human rights norms, apply to all situations where a military force exercises authority over territory would not only clarify the circumstances in which these laws apply, it would also require that they be incorporated into military training, and into military doctrine for peace operations. The adoption of contextual principles governing humanitarian intervention encompassing a requirement of strict adherence to IHL, including the laws of occupation, as recommended by the International Commission on Kosovo, but with an added emphasis on the 'particular duty on occupying forces and their administrative counterparts to give the highest protection of threatened segments of the civilian population'[366] could usefully complement a UN resolution on the applicability of occupation law, by strengthening the obligation to protect vulnerable groups. Multi-national

[363] HP Gasser, 'Protection of the Civilian Population' (n 9), 242.

[364] Nigel White has argued that 'there is a pressing need for a formal recognition by the UN's political organs of the applicability of human rights standards': N White, 'Towards a Strategy for Human Rights Protection in Post-conflict Situations', in N White and D Klaasen (eds), *The UN, Human Rights and Post conflict Situations* (Manchester University Press Manchester) 2005, 463, 463.

[365] Article 4, Geneva Convention IV.

[366] Independent International Commission on Kosovo, *Follow up to the Kosovo Report: Why Conditional Independence?* (n 256), 36–37; *Kosovo Report* (n 229), 193–195.

military interventions frequently cite prevention of human rights abuses as a secondary objective even in operations where this is not the primary objective. Therefore the International Commission's proposed contextual principles could be considered applicable to a wider range of operations than would normally be encompassed by the term humanitarian intervention.

The laws of occupation are not a miracle cure. They do not provide for institutional mechanisms to carry out visits or hear petitions. But they do provide a measure of accountability since they constitute a well-established legal regime (comprising extensive rights, obligations and legal powers in relation to the exercise of authority over territory and the people of that territory) and public pressure is likely to ensure a degree of respect for it. However, they are not a substitute for the political engagement necessary to resolve issues regarding the democratic legitimacy of the de facto government and of any permanent government that should follow.

5

Implications for Peacekeepers and Other Multi-National Forces

1. Introduction

The need for clarification on the extent of the obligations of military forces to provide civilian protection has been a priority concern since at least the early 1990s when forces engaged in peace operations found themselves faced with egregious violations of human rights committed on a large scale, such as genocide and ethnic cleansing. The relevant international rules and principles governing peacekeepers' responsibilities include international humanitarian law, international human rights law, the UN Charter and the mission's mandate, which is of key importance and has standing in international law. The legal obligations of peacekeepers are distinct from those of their States and of the international organizations on whose behalf they act. In a situation involving armed conflict, troops' obligations come within the *ius in bello*, whereas the deploying State's obligations vis a vis the 'host State' fall within the *ius ad bellum*; however, the two cannot be kept entirely separate because troops are agents of their State and if they use force without the consent of the host State, that State's government is likely to allege a breach of its sovereignty and of Articles 2(4) and 2(7) of the Charter.[1]

The Charter provides for enforcement action under Chapter VII where there is a threat to international peace and security. Peacekeeping is not provided for at all, but was traditionally conceived as belonging to Chapter VI and a half, as it falls somewhere between traditional methods of resolving disputes peacefully such as negotiation and mediation (outlined in Chapter VI), and forceful action (provided for in Chapter VII).[2] In recent years national and regional

[1] 'All Members shall refrain in their international relations from the threat or use of force against the territorial integrity or political independence of any state, or in any other manner inconsistent with the Purposes of the United Nations.' and 'Nothing contained in the present Charter shall authorize the United Nations to intervene in matters which are essentially within the domestic jurisdiction of any state or shall require the Members to submit such matters to settlement under the present Charter; but this principle shall not prejudice the application of enforcement measures under Chapter VII.'

[2] A definition coined by Dag Hammarskjöld: United Nations Information Service '60 Years United Nations Peacekeeping' May 2008 <http://www.unis.unvienna.org/pdf/60years_peacekeeping.pdf> Accessed 6 June 2008.

peace support operations doctrines have tended to move away from the practice of focusing attention on Charter-based categorizations of missions and instead emphasize that 'all operations can be approached fundamentally in the same manner... because peacekeepers must expect to perform a wide range of potentially simultaneous activities across the whole spectrum of conflict from conflict prevention before a crisis to major combat.'[3] The UK's 2004 Peace Support Operations Doctrine commented that:

> Earlier PSO doctrine suggested distinct boundaries between phases of PSO and tended to create the impression that forces could be deployed under a mandate, for a particular period, prepared and equipped to deal solely with the demands of a particular task, such as Peacekeeping. In practice, this led to grave errors, most notably in Srebrenica, where peacekeeping forces were unable to respond to the escalation of violence and tension. More alarmingly, some nations and security coalitions have assumed, with scant appreciation of the risk, that a force of limited capability, trained and authorized to conduct only specific operations, can have full utility in the inherently volatile context of PSO. Experience has shown that campaigns do not progress in a linear manner.[4]

As the UN Department of Peacekeeping Operations Best Practices Unit observes in its 2008 Guidelines '[p]eace operations are rarely limited to one type of activity whether United Nations-led or conducted by non-United Nations actors.'[5] This is likely to remain true even if explicitly designed 'responsibility to protect' operations are added to the cornucopia of the various types of peace operations that are available to be deployed.

Traditional approaches to the applicability of human rights and humanitarian laws held that human rights law applies predominantly in peacetime; the laws of war applied during armed conflict. The laws of war fell into two categories: the very extensive body of laws that apply to an international armed conflict and the much more limited body of laws that applies to a non-international armed conflict occurring within the territory of a single State. But the nature of armed conflict has changed radically. In addition to the two traditional categories of armed conflict there now exists the possibility of a conflict between a State and a non-State actor that is not confined to a single territory or region but takes place in the international arena. This situation was not anticipated at the time the Geneva Conventions were drafted and so they do not address it. Similarly they do not address the possibility of a conflict between two non-State actors operating from different States. Likewise the position of peacekeeping forces

[3] Ministry of Defence, Development, Concepts and Doctrine Centre, *Draft UK National Doctrine that will replace JWP 3–50 The Military Contribution to Peace Support Operations* (MOD Shrivenham, 16 April 2008), [0003].

[4] UK Ministry of Defence, Joint Warfare Publication (JWP) 3.50 *The Military Contribution to Peace Support Operations* (2nd edn, The Joint Doctrine and Concepts Centre Shrivenham 2004), [238].

[5] United Nations Peacekeeping Operations, Principles and Guidelines (Department of Peacekeeping Operations Best Practices Unit New York 2008), 18.

remains controversial: they are not parties to the conflict, but may nevertheless be engaged in very robust action or may exercise considerable control over territory outside their own borders. The approach originally taken was that IHL applies to all forces engaged as combatants, which at least in the early days of peacekeeping would generally have excluded peacekeepers. The Secretary-General's Bulletin of 1999 on the Observance by UN forces of International Humanitarian Law,[6] which is an internal document that is binding on forces under UN command but does not create direct legal obligations for States,[7] provides that the 'fundamental principles and rules' of IHL are applicable to UN forces 'when in situations of armed conflict they are actively engaged therein as combatants, to the extent and for the duration of their engagement'; but there must be some threshold level of force to be crossed before troops will be regarded as being engaged in armed conflict. However, even when not engaged in combat peacekeepers have always been expected to respect the principles and spirit, and latterly rules of IHL.[8] More recently the ICRC has stated that all actors in an armed conflict are bound by IHL, whether they are combatants or not, including civilians, private military companies and peacekeepers.[9]

Engaging in armed conflict even for purely humanitarian purposes inevitably increases security risks for the participating States. Increased security risks may lead some States to condone violations of human rights by their own forces in order to get information about threats to their own or their State's security. One worrying development is the tendency by some States to exploit potential gaps in the protections provided to both civilians and combatants under international law, rather than seeking to close the gap by applying relevant analogous principles.[10] In contrast, and possibly partially in response, there has been a growing tendency on the part of international courts and treaty monitoring bodies to view IHL and international human rights law holistically allowing a synthesis between the two regimes that facilitates an overarching emphasis on human

[6] Secretary-General's Bulletin on Observance by UN Forces of International Humanitarian Law (date of promulgation 6 August 1999, entered into force 12 August 1999) UN Doc ST/SGB/1999/13.

[7] Report of Experts Meeting on Multi-National Operations, 11–12 December 2003 (ICRC Geneva), 2.

[8] A Roberts and R Guelff, *Documents on the Laws of War* (3rd edn, Oxford University Press Oxford 2000), 625.

[9] FAQ 'International humanitarian law and private military/security companies' <http://www.icrc.org/Web/eng/siteeng0.nsf/html/pmc-fac-230506>; *The Prosecutor v Jean Paul Akayesu* Case no ICTR 94-4-A Judgment, I June 2001, [443–444].

[10] For example the reluctance of the US administration to grant the prisoners held at Guantanamo Bay the protections of the Geneva Conventions or to recognize the applicability of human rights law to international armed conflict or military occupation: *Hamdan v Rumsfeld*, Secretary of Defense et al, Supreme Court of the United States, No 05–184, Argued March 28, 2006. Decided June 29, 2006; MJ Dennis (Office of the Legal Adviser, US Department of State), 'Application of Human Rights Treaties Extraterritorially in Times of Armed Conflict and Military Occupation', 99 AJIL 1, 119, 141.

rights protection.[11] It is now widely accepted that international human rights law remains applicable to certain situations arising in armed conflict and military occupation. The ICRC states that this is a rule of customary international law.[12] Thus forces will remain bound by the human rights treaties to which their State is party whenever they are engaged in armed conflict within their own State, and also when engaged in armed conflict outside their own State, provided that jurisdiction under the relevant treaty extends extra-territorially in the particular circumstances. The increased emphasis on human rights protection, together with the expansion of the jurisdictional scope of human rights treaties, is likely to have a significant transformative effect on the principles of IHL creating a heavier weighting in favour of humanitarian values. The case law of the ECtHR in the Chechnya cases[13] and of the ICJ in its *Advisory Opinion on the Legal Consequences of the Construction of a Wall in Occupied Palestinian Territory* and in the *Case Concerning Armed Activities on the Territory of the Congo*, suggest that obligations under human rights law are not easily displaced. This would imply that commanders and their advisors may be required to construe the principles of IHL within a broader overarching framework that seeks to maximize the protection of human rights in all circumstances.

2. Developments in Response to Egregious Violations of Human Rights in the 1990s

Serious criticism of peacekeepers' attitudes towards the local populations of the areas in which they were deployed began to be voiced in relation to operations in Somalia and Cambodia. The problems came to a head most dramatically in the mid-1990s with the mass killings in Rwanda, and the UN's inadequate response despite warnings going back at least a year from the UN Special Rapporteur and human rights organizations,[14] and despite efforts of the force commander Romeo

[11] W Kälin, *Human Rights in Times of Occupation: The Case of Kuwait* (Law Books of Europe Berne 1994), 79; J-M Henckaerts and L Doswald-Beck, *Customary International Humanitarian Law* (Cambridge University Press Cambridge 2005), 300–305; *The Legal Consequences of the Construction of a Wall in Occupied Palestinian Territory*, Advisory Opinion (ICJ July 9 2004) ILM 1009 (2004) and the *Case Concerning Armed Activities on the Territory of the Congo: Democratic Republic of the Congo v Uganda* ICJ, 19 December 2005; *Isayeva, Yusupova, and Bazayeva v Russia* Applications nos. 57947/00,57948/00 and 57949/00, [2005] ECHR 129 (24 February 2005); and *Isayeva v Russia* Application no 57950/00, European Court of Human Rights, [2005] ECHR 128 (24 February 2005) Final Judgment 6 July 2005.

[12] J-M Henckaerts and L Doswald-Beck, *Customary International Humanitarian Law* (n 11), 299.

[13] *Isayeva, Yusupova, and Bazayeva v Russia* Applications nos. 57947/00,57948/00 and 57949/00, [2005] ECHR 129 (n 11); and *Isayeva v Russia* Application no 57950/00 (n 11)

[14] Report of the Independent Inquiry into the Actions of the United Nations during the 1994 Genocide in Rwanda (New York United Nations, 15 December 1999), 3.

Dallaire to take proactive action in response to information regarding weapons caches to be used to kill Tutsis.[15]

A year later UN forces were also unprepared for dealing with the atrocities committed against civilians in Bosnia-Herzegovina despite numerous resolutions condemning the ethnic cleansing,[16] an appeal in June 1993 from the World Conference on Human Rights to the Security Council to take measures to end the 'genocide' in Bosnia-Herzegovina,[17] a report by a UN Commission of Experts in 1994 detailing grave breaches of the Geneva Conventions in the former Yugoslavia,[18] and two strongly worded interim resolutions of the International Court of Justice.[19] As a consequence of an ill-drafted mandate,[20] poor communications,[21] poor hasty training,[22] and insufficient troop numbers[23] the inaptly named UN Protection Force (UNPROFOR), which undertook many peacekeeping tasks including providing humanitarian assistance, but did not protect; found itself impotent in the face of 'scenes from hell, written on the darkest pages of human history.'[24]

Whilst the UN was initially slow to examine its own failings in response to the atrocities in Rwanda and Srebrenica, when Kofi Annan became Secretary-General he initiated a much more robust approach to the UN's role in preventing crimes against humanity and war crimes. He commissioned two high level inquiries: the Independent Inquiry into the Actions of the United Nations during the 1994 Genocide in Rwanda and a UN inquiry to *The Fall of Srebrenica* undertaken pursuant to General Assembly Resolution 53/55, both of which published their findings in 1999.[25] In March 2000 he convened a Panel on United Nations Peace

[15] ibid 12; R Dallaire, *Shake Hands with the Devil* (Arrow Press London 2004), 167; United Nations, Lessons Learned Unit, Department of Peacekeeping Operations, *Comprehensive Report on Lessons Learned from the United Nations Assistance Mission for Rwanda (UNAMIR) October 1993–April 1996* (December 1996), 10.

[16] SC Res 779, 6 October 1992; SC Res 780, 6 October 1992; SC Res 787, 16 November 1992.

[17] A/CONF.157/24 (Part I), ch IV.

[18] Commission of Experts Final Report S/1994/1674.

[19] Application of the Convention of the Prevention and Punishment of the Crime of Genocide (Bosnia and Herzegovina v Serbia and Montenegro) Order of 3 April 1993 and Order of 13 September 1993.

[20] See ch 1, s 4.5 The United Nations Protection Force (UNPROFOR) at the Fall of Srebrenica; Netherlands Institute for War Documentation *Srebrenica 'A Safe Area': Reconstruction, Background, Consequences and Analyzes of the Fall of a Safe Area* (2002) pt II, ch 6, s 2 'Struggling with the UNPROFOR mandate in Bosnia' and ch 8, s 9 'Dutchbat's problems: what should be done and how should it be done?'

[21] Netherlands Institute for War Documentation *Srebrenica 'A Safe Area': Reconstruction, Background, Consequences and Analyzes of the Fall of a Safe Area'*, (2002) pt II, ch 1, s 4 'Standing Operating procedures and Rules of Engagement'.

[22] ibid pt II, ch 5, s 6 'The Dutchbat training' and ch 8, s 4 'Conclusion: was the training deficient?'.

[23] Report of the Secretary-General pursuant to General Assembly Resolution 53/55: *The Fall of Srebrenica* UN Doc A/54/549, 15 November 1999, [226–238].

[24] Press release issued by the International Tribunal for the Former Yugoslavia (cc/PIO/026-E), The Hague, 16 November 1995.

[25] Report of the Independent Inquiry into the Actions of the United Nations during the 1994 Genocide in Rwanda (n 14) <http://www.un.org/News/ossg/rwanda_report.htm>; Report of the Secretary-General pursuant to General Assembly Resolution 53/55: *The Fall of Srebrenica* (n 23).

Operations to assess the effectiveness of peacekeeping missions and to make recommendations for change. The Panel supported 'the desire on the part of the Secretary-General to extend additional protection to civilians in armed conflicts' and agreed that 'the actions of the Security Council to give United Nations peacekeepers explicit authority to protect civilians in conflict situations are positive developments.'[26] The report went further and asserted that:

Indeed, peacekeepers—troops or police—who witness violence against civilians should be presumed to be authorized to stop it, within their means, in support of basic United Nations principles and, as stated in the report of the Independent Inquiry on Rwanda, consistent with 'the perception and the expectation of protection created by [an operation's] very presence'.[27]

However, the Panel was:

concerned about the credibility and achievability of a blanket mandate in this area... The potentially large mismatch between desired objective and resources available to meet it raises the prospect of continuing disappointment with United Nations follow-through in this area. If an operation is given a mandate to protect civilians, therefore, it also must be given the specific resources needed to carry out that mandate.'[28]

Since the publication of this report considerable efforts have been made by national defence departments to improve the their forces' protection of civilians in armed conflict but considerable practical difficulties, as well as differences of opinion as regards a force's legal obligations, remain.

3. The Implications of the Collective Responsibility to Protect

The concerns and debates that emerged from the Srebrenica[29] and Rwanda reports,[30] and from NATO's bombing campaign in Kosovo in 1999 (which was undertaken in the context of concerns over widespread human rights abuses), led to the emergence of a new doctrine on the responsibilities of States with regard to serious and widespread abuses of human rights. The concept of the collective 'responsibility to protect' was developed by the International Commission on Intervention and State Sovereignty (ICISS) as a means of changing arguments about humanitarian intervention from questions relating to the rights of States to intervene (an approach regarded warily by many States as threatening

[26] UN General Assembly and Security Council, *Report of the Panel on United Nations Peace Operations*, A/55/305-S/2000/809, 21 August 2000, [62].

[27] ibid.

[28] ibid [63].

[29] Report of the Secretary-General pursuant to General Assembly Resolution 53/55: *The Fall of Srebrenica* (n 23).

[30] Report of the Independent Inquiry into the Actions of the United Nations during the 1994 Genocide in Rwanda (n 14) <http://www.un.org/News/ossg/rwanda_report.htm>.

to their sovereignty) to questions about the human security responsibilities of States—first and foremost vis-à-vis their own subjects. The 'responsibility to protect' is primarily a responsibility of States, and of the international organizations through which they co-operate: it is not a responsibility that entails direct obligations for peacekeepers. However, a logical consequence of changing the focus of humanitarian intervention from State's rights to their collective responsibilities, is that the responsibilities of States cannot stop at a decision to intervene militarily (if this is deemed necessary) but must include a preparedness to make the intervention effective: they have a responsibility to ensure that the forces they deploy to provide protection have an appropriate mandate, resources and training to enable them to do so. Louise Arbour has argued that the 'responsibility to protect,' in conjunction with the Genocide Convention, may entail legal liability for States, particularly the Permanent Five, that fail to use their 'tools of authority' to stop genocide; even more so when they exercise or threaten use of a veto that 'would block action that is deemed necessary by other members to avert genocide, or crimes against humanity.'[31]

UN Member States' responsibilities under the 'responsibility to protect' are distinct from the civilian protection obligations of individual soldiers under international humanitarian law and human rights law. These do not flow from the 'responsibility to protect.' However, through the expectations of the local and the international community, as well as of the forces themselves, the collective 'responsibility to protect' has added two elements (at least) to the already existing debate on civilian protection by peacekeepers and other multi-national forces.

The first concerns operations specifically undertaken pursuant to the 'responsibility to protect.' Gareth Evans, a member of the International Crisis Group and co-director of the ICISS, argues that:

> a crucial practical operational issue is to address the question, up until now almost completely neglected by the world's militaries, of developing detailed concepts of these R2P/civilian protection operations... It's not just a matter of force configuration, but of developing new doctrine, and new kind of rules of engagement, and new kinds of training.[32]

Victoria Holt, in a contribution to a 2006 report by the Humanitarian Protection Group on *Trends and Issues in Military and Humanitarian Relations*, observes that:

> [e]ven as reference to civilian protection is used in debates on the purpose of the AU mission in Darfur, and the possible contributions of military support from non-African countries, these discussions seem disconnected from considerations of how forces in

[31] L Arbour, 'The responsibility to protect as a duty of care in international law and practice' Review of International Studies (2008), 34, 445, 453.

[32] G Evans, 'Making Idealism Realistic: The Responsibility to Protect as a New Global Security Norm' Address to launch Stanford MA Program in International Policy Studies, Stanford University, 7 February 2007 <http://www.crisisgroup.org>.

Africa, the UK and most states are trained and prepared to act, even in peace and stability operations, and how that would apply in Darfur.[33]

The second element is the added weight that the 'collective international responsibility to protect' gives to civilian protection issues in operations that are not explicitly designated as 'responsibility to protect' operations. The borders between a 'responsibility to protect' operation and a peacekeeping operation with protection elements are not as distinct as some advocates of the 'responsibility to protect' suggest. Any collective decision to intervene, since it must be authorized by some organization representing the intervening States (preferably by the UN), is at its root a political one. States contributing to UN operations have a variety of reasons for doing so and are answerable to their electorates at home. In order to reach consensus Council members may (and frequently do) adopt resolutions couched in ambiguous terms that are open to a variety of interpretations.[34] Whilst it is unrealistic to expect States to undertake interventions on humanitarian grounds unless it would also serve other objectives (and possibly undesirable because the political will necessary to sustain the mission may be absent), a lack of clarity with regard to the extent of the force's obligations towards the local population is likely to damage the force's relationship with the local community.[35] Ultimately it may jeopardize the success of the operation and even the force's own security.[36] The ICISS notes that:

> Many interventions were triggered throughout the 1990s by an imperative to 'do something.' And this lack of strategic vision is usually disastrous.[37]

These problems are as likely to arise in UN peacekeeping operations conducted with the consent of the government of the host State, or in UN-authorized uses of force under national or alliance control, as in interventions without consent or UN authorization, since one of the principal sources of tension lies in the gap between the expectation that protection will be provided (an expectation that may be shared by troops as well as the population) and the international

[33] VK Holt, 'The military and civilian protection: developing roles and capacities' in 'Trends and Issues in Military and Humanitarian Relations' (eds) V Wheeler and A Harmer, Humanitarian Protection Group Report, March 2006, 53, 66.

[34] Report of the Secretary-General pursuant to General Assembly Resolution 53/55: *The Fall of Srebrenica*, UN Doc A/54/549, 15 November 1999, [43]; Y Akashi 'The Use of Force in a United Nations Peace-Keeping Operation: Lessons Learnt from the Safe Areas Mandate', 19 Fordham International Law Journal, 312, 315–316; AT Arulanatham, 'Restructured Safe Havens: A Proposal for Reform of the Refugee Protection System', 22 HRQ 1, 20, 22.

[35] Netherlands Institute for War Documentation *Srebrenica 'A Safe Area': Reconstruction, Background, Consequences and Analyzes of the Fall of a Safe Area'* (2002) pt II, ch 8, s 13 'Peacekeeper Stress'; UK Ministry of Defence, Joint Warfare Publication (JWP) 3.50 *The Military Contribution to Peace Support Operation* (n 4), [560].

[36] UK Ministry of Defence, Joint Warfare Publication (JWP) 3.50 *The Military Contribution to Peace Support Operation* (n 4), [560].

[37] International Commission on Intervention and State Sovereignty (ICISS), *The Responsibility to Protect: Supplementary Volume* (Ottawa International Development Research Centre 2001), 182.

community's commitment to providing that protection. Resolution 1674, in affirming Article 139 of the World Summit Outcome Document, commits the Security Council 'to take collective action, in a timely and decisive manner' and 'in accordance with the Charter' should 'peaceful means be inadequate and national authorities are manifestly failing to protect their populations from genocide, war crimes, ethnic cleansing and crimes against humanity.'[38] This commitment increases the pressure on the Council to consider some sort of response to genocide, ethnic cleansing, crimes against humanity and war crimes; but it cannot take away the political element that underlies any Security Council decision. If the State abusing or tolerating the abuse of its inhabitants happens to have powerful allies, or a geography or military capability that makes intervention without its consent an unworkable proposition, an explicitly designed 'responsibility to protect' intervention is unlikely to take place. However, constant international pressure in response to conscience-shocking events may force the State concerned to accept a peacekeeping force, albeit with a constrained mandate. A peacekeeping force deployed in those circumstances is likely to be faced with human rights abuses similar to those faced by troops deployed in an explicitly designed 'responsibility to protect' intervention and it will need to know what its protection obligations are.

Moreover, some time before the concept of the 'responsibility to protect' had been developed, the ICRC and other commentators argued that Article 1 of the Geneva Conventions creates, at the very least, an 'obligation for governments to consider seriously whether there is something they might do'[39] in respect of violations of the Conventions by other parties. All States are High Contracting Parties to the Geneva Conventions. The ICRC in its 'position statement' on humanitarian intervention, issued prior to the publication of the ICISS report but in language reflective of obligations to protect, rather than rights to intervene, stated that:

> Under Article 1 common to the Geneva Conventions, there is an individual and collective obligation to 'respect and ensure respect for' international humanitarian law. If grave violations of that law are committed, the States are obliged to take action jointly or separately, in co-operation with the United Nations and in accordance with the UN Charter.[40]

[38] A/RES/6/1, 24 October 2005, [139]; S/RES/1674, 28 April 2006, [4].

[39] Yves Sandoz, in an interview with Fritz Kalshoven: F Kalshoven, 'The Undertaking to Respect and Ensure Respect in All Circumstances: From Tiny Seed to Ripening Fruit' (1999) 2 Yearbook of International Humanitarian Law 3, 61; *Military and Paramilitary Activities in and against Nicaragua (Nicaragua v United States of America)*, Merits, Judgment, ICJ Reports (1986), 14, [220]; L Boisson de Chazournes and L Condorelli, 'Common Article 1 of the Geneva Conventions revisited: protecting collective interests' [2000] International Review of the Red Cross 837, 67, 85–86.

[40] A Ryniker, 'The ICRC's Position on Humanitarian Intervention' (2001) 83 International Review of the Red Cross 482, 527, 530 (citing in support Article 89 of Protocol I additional to the Geneva Conventions); The International Court of Justice in its *Advisory Opinion concerning the*

The ICRC has an unparalleled status as the leading interpreter of international humanitarian law. Their view, which is shared by many other commentators, that Article 1 carries third party obligations for States, regardless of whether or not they are involved in the conflict,[41] must surely have a normative impact on peacekeepers' expectations of themselves (especially since the Conventions are binding not only on State parties but also on individual soldiers) as well as on the expectations of both the local and international community, particularly given that there is now so much emphasis on the role of peacekeepers in providing protection.

Unless otherwise provided for in the mandate peacekeepers may only use force in self-defence. However, the UN's interpretation of self-defence has expanded from its original concept, which allowed only for the right 'of the individual soldier in the force to defend his person and his weapons after he had been subjected to an attack upon him or them,'[42] to a much broader concept encompassing 'defence of the mission';[43] but States have different views on what degree of force is permissible in '(self)-defence of the mission.'[44] Thus different contingents contributing to a multi-national mission may have different rules on the extent to which force is permissible in situations that go beyond defence of itself. The most effective means of resolving this problem is through the adoption of clear mandates; but the need to obtain a consensus in order to adopt any resolution at all sometimes results in wording that is deliberately vague. Since 1999 it has been

Legal Consequences of the Construction of a Wall in the Occupied Palestinian Territory' also affirmed that Article 1 entails third party obligations, stating that *Advisory Opinion concerning the Legal Consequences of the Construction of a Wall in the Occupied Palestinian Territory*, ICJ, 9 July 2004, [158].

[41] *The Legal Consequences of the Construction of a Wall in the Occupied Palestinian Territory*, ICJ, Advisory Opinion, 9 July 2004, [158]; Official Statement by ICRC President Dr Jacob Kellenberger, 'The Two Additional Protocols to the Geneva Conventions: 25 years later—challenges and prospects', 26th Round Table, San Remo, 5/9/2002; Under Rule 144 of the Rules of Customary International Humanitarian Law compiled by the ICRC, States 'must exert their influence, to the degree possible, to stop violations of international humanitarian law': J-M Henckaerts and L Doswald-Beck, *Customary International Humanitarian Law* (n 11), Volume 1, 509 <http://www.icrc.org/Web/Eng/siteeng0.nsf/iwpList74/EFC5A1C8D8D8DD70B9C1256C3600>; L Boisson de Chazournes and L Condorelli, 'Common Article 1 of the Geneva Conventions revisited: protecting collective interests' 837 International Review of the Red Cross, 67, 70; HP Gasser, 'Ensuring Respect for the Geneva Conventions and Protocols: the Role of Third States and the United Nations' in H Fox and MA Meyer (eds), *Armed Conflict and the New Law: Volume II 'Effecting Compliance'* (The British Institute of International and Comparative Law London 1993) 16, 24–25; U Palwankar, 'Measures available to States for fulfilling their obligation to ensure respect for international humanitarian law', 298 International Review of the Red Cross, 9, 10; K Sachariev, '"States" entitlement to take action to enforce humanitarian law', 270 International Review of the Red Cross, 177, 186.

[42] GIAD Draper, 'The Legal Limitations Upon the Employment of Weapons by the United Nations Force in the Congo' (1963) 12 International and Comparative Law Quarterly 387, 401.

[43] United Nations, Report of the Secretary-General on the implementation of Security Council resolution 340 (1973), UN document S/11052/Rev.1, 27 October 1973.

[44] Report by the Secretary-Generals' High Level Panel on Threats, Challenges and Change *'A More Secure World: Our Shared Responsibility'* <http://www.un.org//secureworld>, [213]; Use of Force Concept for EU-led Military Crisis Management Operations EUMC DOC/CCD 02-14-06-OPS 16/2001 Final Draft (27/09/2002), Annex A 19.

standard practice, in both UN peacekeeping operations and those mandated by a regional organization, to authorize protection of civilians under imminent threat in the vicinity of the force, within force capabilities and without prejudice to the responsibilities of the government of the State in which the mission is deployed. This phraseology, or a similar variant, is consistently used; but rarely expanded upon. The requirement that peacekeeping forces should constrain their actions so as not to prejudice the responsibilities of the government of the host State is a political necessity since the Security Council has no authority under the UN Charter to override the internal affairs of a State (except where these constitute a threat to international peace and security); but this opaque wording is not helpful to force commanders or to soldiers suddenly faced with egregious violations of human rights. The difficulties are particularly acute where the human rights violations taking place cross over from the kind of abuses inherent in all armed conflict, to those identified by the ICISS[45] as being such as might trigger the collective 'responsibility to protect': principally genocide, crimes against humanity and war crimes committed on a large scale entailing massive loss of lives.[46]

Even where agreement can be reached on the degree of force that the mission is permitted to use, spelling out the protection obligations of peacekeepers may create problems for achieving the objective of upholding human rights and humanitarian norms. States may be unwilling to take on the responsibility to protect at all if they fear that they may be held culpable for a failure to fulfil certain obligations. In 2000, London-based lawyer Geoffrey Robinson and former South Australian State-prosecutor Michael Hourigan, planned to sue the UN for alleged complicity in the Rwandan genocide, acting for two Rwandan women whose families were among the victims.[47] The women said that the UN soldiers who were assigned to protect them either ran away or handed their families over to the Hutu militia to be killed.[48] One of the women said that the UN soldiers who were supposed to protect her and her family were drinking and socializing with the Hutus while she and her children were being tortured.[49] Kofi Annan

[45] And subsequently endorsed by the General Assembly and Security Council: A/RES 60/1 24 October 2005; S/RES 1674 28 April 2006; Security Council Report, 'Update Report No 7, Protection of Civilians in Armed Conflict', 20 April 2006; UN General Assembly, *A More Secure World: Our Shared Responsibility, Report of the Secretary-General's High-level Panel on Threats, Challenges and Change*, A/59/565, 2 December 2004, 66, [203]; UN General Assembly, *In Larger Freedom: Toward Development, Security and Human Rights for All, Report of the Secretary-General*, A/59/2005, 21 March 2005, [135].

[46] A/RES 60/1 24 October 2005; The ICISS proposed a threshold criteria for triggering the collective responsibility to protect where there is 'large scale loss of life, actual or apprehended, with genocidal intent or not, which is the product either of deliberate state action, or state neglect or inability to act, or a failed state situation; or large scale 'ethnic cleansing', actual or apprehended, whether carried out by killing, forced expulsion, acts of terror or rape.' ICISS, *The Responsibility to Protect* (n 37), xii.

[47] <http://www.reliefweb.int/w/rwb.nsf/0/0140bb8c46674d7dc1256864004d344c?OpenDocument>.

[48] ibid.

[49] ibid.

argued that, not only did the UN have nothing to answer for, but also, 'if we allowed our peacekeepers to be brought to courts and tried over matters like this, that would be the end of peacekeeping.'[50] On the other hand lack of clarity and accountability regarding the obligations of troops may affect the morale of troops[51] and contribute to serious psychological stress;[52] damage the reputation of the UN and contributing States;[53] and undermine the relationship with the local population leading potentially to increased violence and opposition to the force,[54] as happened with certain UNPROFOR units in Bosnia.

4. Occupation and Situations Akin to Occupation

Where forces are in occupation of territory an extensive body of law, comprising both rights and obligations, governs the relationship with the local population. An occupant's obligations include restoring *'l'ordre et la vie publics,'* which would include making efforts to protect the population from genocide, crimes against humanity and war crimes. Human rights law is applicable where forces are

[50] M Riley, 'UN To Seek Immunity on Rwanda' *Sydney Herald* (January 14, 2000) <http://www.globalpolicy.org/security/issues/rwanda/suit.htm>, The US is not a party to the Rome Statute, but it is concerned that it will nevertheless become the target of malicious prosecutions, for alleged violations of international law, committed on the territory of a State that is a party to the statute. At the insistence of the US, the Security Council, acting under Chapter VII of the UN Charter, adopted Resolution 1422 (2002), which requests 'that the ICC, if a case arises involving current or former officials or personnel from a contributing State not a Party to the Rome Statute over acts or omissions relating to a United Nations established or authorised operation, shall for a twelve month period starting 1 July 2002 not commence or proceed with investigation or prosecution of any such case, unless the Security Council decide otherwise.' The request was renewed for a further 12-months period in 2003. S/RES/1502 (2003). It was not renewed in 2004, but this was due largely to the negative publicity concerning human rights abuses in the Abu Ghraib detention centre in Iraq and the need to secure UN support for restoring order in the aftermath of the intervention there in 2003.

[51] Netherlands Institute for War Documentation, *Srebrenica 'A Safe Area': Reconstruction, Background, Consequences and Analyzes of the Fall of a Safe Area* (2002) pt II, ch 8, s 13 'Peacekeeper Stress'; Interview with Lt. Col. Philip Wilkinson OBE 25.03.04; J Sloboda, J Kemp and C Abbot, 'Putting People First' Oxford Research Group, July 5 2004 <http://www.oxfordresearchgroup.org.uk/publications/briefings/puttingpeoplefirst.htm>.

[52] Netherlands Institute for War Documentation, *Srebrenica 'A Safe Area': Reconstruction, Background, Consequences and Analyzes of the Fall of a Safe Area* (2002) pt II, ch 8, s 13 'Peacekeeper Stress'.

[53] The UN is currently investigating allegations that, during joint operations with DRC [Democratic Republic of the Congo] forces, the UN Mission in the Democratic Republic of the Congo (MONUC) repeatedly stood aside and watched as DRC forces killed civilians and torched their huts in a series of attacks against villages in the Ituri district (Guardian 'UN accused over Congo village massacre.' 18.6.06; Channel 4 'Unreported World—The UN's Dirty War' 23.6.06). MONUC is authorized to use all necessary means to ensure the protection of civilians: S/RES 1565(1 Oct 2004); S/RES 1592 (30 March 2005); S/RES 1635 (28 October 2005); S/RES 1649 (21 December 2005).

[54] Ministry of Defence UK, Development, Concepts and Doctrine Centre, *Draft UK National Doctrine that will replace JWP 3–50 The Military Contribution to Peace Support Operations* (n 3) [0226].

in effective control of territory but the criteria for determining when a force is in occupation, or in effective control of territory, are not entirely clear and may not be consistent under IHL and human rights law. The UK courts in the *Al Skeini* case held that occupation does not necessarily give the occupying force sufficient control to secure the wide range of protections provided by the ECHR.[55] Decisions of the ICJ suggest that occupants are required to uphold, in the areas that they occupy, the human rights treaties to which they are party, as well as the human rights treaties to which the occupied State is party, and customary human rights law.[56] However, the question of whether occupation law is applicable to UN forces is controversial. Adam Roberts has made a strong case for the view that at least some of the rules of international law regarding occupation apply 'whenever the armed forces of a country are in control of foreign territory, and find themselves face to face with the inhabitants.'[57] Benvenisti argues that occupation:

> can be defined as the effective control of a power (be it one or more States or an international organization, such as the United Nations) over a territory to which that power has no sovereign title, without the volition of the sovereign territory.[58]

Resolution 1483 on Iraq[59] indicates that occupation law is applicable to an occupation that has some degree of recognition from the UN Security Council. However, it remains a matter of debate as to whether occupation law is applicable to UN-run 'occupations,' as distinct from those that are recognized by the UN but are not under its command and control. The UN is not a party to the Geneva Conventions, which are presently open to ratification by 'Powers,' that is, 'States.' Although the UN has accepted that IHL is applicable to UN forces when engaged in combat, the Secretary-General's Bulletin[60] says nothing about the applicability of occupation law. It is possible that many of the rules on occupation are applicable to the UN on the basis that they constitute customary international law but only if the administration of territory by the UN is considered sufficiently similar to an occupation by a State, and there are differing views as to whether this can ever be so.[61]

[55] Opinions of the Lords of Appeal for Judgment in the Cause *Al-Skeini and others v Secretary of State for Defence* [2007] UKHL 26.

[56] *Case Concerning Armed Activities on the Territory of the Congo: Democratic Republic of the Congo v Uganda* (n 11), [178–179]; *The Legal Consequences of the Construction of a Wall in Occupied Palestinian Territory*, Advisory Opinion (n 11) [107–113].

[57] A Roberts, What is Military Occupation, BYIL 55 (1984), 249, 250; C Greenwood, 'The Administration of Occupied Territory in International Law' in E Playfair (ed) *International Law and the Administration of the Occupied Territories: Two Decades of Israeli Occupation of the West Bank* (Clarendon Press Oxford 1992) 241, 241.

[58] E Benvenisti, *The International Law of Occupation: with a new preface by the author* (Princeton University Press Princeton 2004), 4.

[59] S/RES 1483, 22 May 2003.

[60] Secretary-General's Bulletin on Observance by UN Forces of International Humanitarian Law (date of promulgation 6 August 1999, entered into force 12 August 1999) UN Doc ST/SGB/1999/13.

[61] See Chapter 4.

Even if occupation law does not apply de jure, to apply it de facto could have many benefits, since occupation law provides a flexible comprehensive regime of law governing the relationship between the administrators and the population.[62] However, if the UN is likely to be involved in transitional administrations in the future it will need to adopt a regulating framework that is specifically tailored to the task. The principal rules of occupation law were drafted at a time when it was assumed that the occupation would be relatively short and that the ousted government would return. Transitional administrations may be in place a long time and often the ousted government will not be returning and therefore arrangements may have to be made to prepare for the transfer of authority to a new government representative of the people. Moreover, provisions for monitoring compliance with IHL are limited and rely in the main on the ICRC. The ICRC can play a crucial role in ensuring compliance with IHL but it is not ideally suited to monitoring the other wide-ranging, complex, and often politically sensitive tasks undertaken by UN transitional administrations. Occupation law does not refer to human rights at all, hence, although respect for human rights is intrinsic to restoring *'l'ordre et la vie publics,'* occupation law provides no monitoring mechanisms to establish compliance; nor any means by which members of the local population can bring a complaint. The absence of procedures for monitoring the compliance with human rights norms of KFOR, which arguably has had 'boundless and unfettered authority in Kosovo'[63] has been sharply criticized by the Ombudsman and others.[64] A number of cases alleging violations by KFOR of the ECHR have been brought to the ECtHR but all have been held inadmissible on the grounds that that 'operations carried out on behalf of the United Nations under Chapter VII of the Charter' have 'complete immunity from jurisdiction.'[65]

[62] D Shraga, Military Occupation and UN Transitional Administrations—The Analogy and its Limitations in MG Koehen (ed) *Promoting Justice, Human Rights and Conflict Resolution through International Law* (Liber Amicorum Lucius Caflisch Leiden 2007), 479.

[63] D Marshall and S Inglis, 'Human Rights in Transition: The Disempowerment of Human Rights-Based Justice in the United Nations Mission in Kosovo', 16 Harvard Human Rights Journal, 95, 112.

[64] Ombudsman Institution in Kosovo, *Second Annual Report*, 2001–2002, 1; Amnesty International, 'Kosovo: KFOR and UNMIK fail to uphold human rights standards in Mitrovica' Amnesty International news Release, 13 March 2000, AI Index: EUR 70/14/00; *Kosovo: The Human Rights Situation and Fate of Persons Displaced in their Homes: Report by Mr. Alvaro Gil-Robles*, 16 October 2002, CoE Doc CommDH (2002) 11; *Situation of Human Rights in Parts of South Eastern Europe: report of the special representative of the Commission on Human Rights on the Situation of Human Rights in Bosnia and the Federal Republic of Yugoslavia, Jose Cutileira*, 8 January 2002, UN Doc E.CN. 4/2002/41; OSCE Mission in Kosovo: Review of the Criminal Justice System (March 2002–April 2003) available at <http://www.osce.org/kosovo>.

[65] European Court of Human Rights, Annual Report 2007, 6; European Court of Human Rights *Behrami and Behrami v France* and *Saramati v France, Germany and Norway* Application nos. 71412/01 and 78166/01 2 May 2007; *Dušan Berić and Others v Bosnia and Herzegovina* Application nos. 36357/04, 36360/04, 38346/04, 41705/04, 45190/04, 45578/04, 45579/04, 45580/04, 91/05, 97/05, 100/05, 101/05, 1121/05, 1123/05, 1125/05, 1129/05, 1132/05, 1133/05, 1169/05, 1172/05, 1175/05, 1177/05, 1180/05, 1185/05, 20793/05 and 25496/05 16 October 2007.

In his comments on the plans to establish a Peacebuilding Commission the former Secretary-General, Kofi Annan, suggested periodical reviews of the progress of post-conflict administrations towards medium-term recovery goals:

At planned intervals (roughly two to four months after the establishment of an operation and then on a quarterly or semi-annual basis), the Peacebuilding Commission (in country-specific format) should meet to review progress towards medium-term recovery goals, especially in the areas of developing public institutions and laying the foundation for economic recovery. Carefully planned meetings of this type, drawing on information and analysis of the UN mission, country team and World Bank offices, could provide an opportunity to identify gaps in progress, areas where greater concentration of effort is required, funding gaps, and the like. Such meetings should not duplicate normal consultative group or similar in-country or country-based donor mechanisms, but should focus on critical links between the ongoing process of stabilization at the military/political level and the underlying process of recovery at the economic/financial/institutional level.[66]

Although this recommendation falls far short of the monitoring requirement necessary to incorporate rule of law principles into transitional administrations it would at least mean frequent reviews of the situation and provide a forum within which to highlight concerns.

Kofi Annan in his 2004 report to the Security Council on the Rule of Law and Transitional Justice in Conflict and Post-Conflict Societies said that:

The 'rule of law' is a concept at the very heart of the Organization's mission. It refers to a principle of governance in which all persons, institutions and entities, public and private, including the State itself are accountable to laws that are publicly promulgated, equally enforced and independently adjudicated, and which are consistent with international human rights norms and standards. It requires as well, measures to ensure adherence to the principles of supremacy of law, equality before the law, accountability before the law, fairness in the application of the law, separation of powers, participation in decision-making, legal certainty, avoidance of arbitrariness and procedural and legal transparency.[67]

In the concluding paragraph of his report he stated that he intends to instruct the Executive Committee on Peace and Security to propose concrete action on the matters discussed in the report and to give consideration to ensuring that rule of law and transitional justice considerations are integrated in the UN's strategic and operational planning of peace operations.[68] In order for the UN to be able to comply with rule of law principles an institutional body specifically tasked with dealing with multi-national administrations and capable of hearing petitions or

[66] Explanatory Note of the Secretary General: Peacebuilding Commission, 'In larger freedom: towards development, security and human rights for all.' (A/59/2005), Addendum 2, [12].

[67] Report of the Secretary-General on the Rule of Law and Transitional Justice in Conflict and Post-Conflict Societies S/2004/616 23 August 2004, [5–6].

[68] ibid [65].

appeals from the population of the administered territory is essential. This body should be set up so as to monitor both UN-run administrations and those that are UN mandated but run by particular Member States. It could be modelled along the lines of the Trusteeship Council. Alternatively the Security Council could establish a committee to monitor multi-national administrations, perhaps linked to the Peacebuilding Commission.[69] But whatever form the institution takes, if the UN Secretariat anticipates that UN involvement in future administrations is likely to occur then 'a dedicated and distinct responsibility centre for those tasks must be created somewhere within the United Nations system.'[70]

5. Peacekeepers' General Responsibility to Protect

Where forces are not in occupation (and do not exercise comparable executive or administrative authority over territory) there is no comprehensive body of law governing the force's relationship with the local community but the mission may have specific obligations under IHL or human rights law, in addition to those set out in the mandate. The draft UK national peace support operations doctrine that is to replace *JWP 3–50 The Military Contribution to Peace Support Operations* distinguishes between peacekeepers' general responsibility to protect and mission responsibility to protect. Mission responsibility to protect arises in operations with 'a primary specified task of responsibility for the physical protection of civilians.'[71] 'For this, military success depends upon: a clear mandate and mission; willingness of TCN [Troop Contributing Nations] to actively participate; and robust authority and capacity to act.'[72] By contrast, peacekeepers' general responsibility to protect arises in all missions since '[a]ll PS themed operations contain general elements of expectation and responsibility for the military to protect civilians.'[73] General areas of protection responsibility that concern peacekeeping forces fall into three broad categories: preventing attacks and abuse by their own troops; protecting people in their care from attacks and abuses by third-parties; and protecting the local population from attacks and abuses.

5.1 Preventing Abuse by Peacekeepers

It hardly needs stating that peacekeepers have a responsibility not to abuse people. Unfortunately, although NGOs have made efforts to publicise the problem and

[69] S Chesterman, *You, The People: United Nations Transitional Administration and State-Building* (Oxford University Press Oxford 2004), 152.

[70] Report of the Panel on United Nations Peace Operations (Brahimi report) A/55/305—S/2000/809 August 21 2000, [78].

[71] Ministry of Defence, Development, Concepts and Doctrine Centre, *Draft UK National Doctrine that will replace JWP 3–50 The Military Contribution to Peace Support Operations* (n 3), [3A24].

[72] ibid. [73] ibid [3A23].

States and international organizations have made efforts to combat it, abuse of both civilians and combatants continues to be widespread: the vulnerability of local populations is exploited by peacekeepers to obtain money, goods, and sex. There is now no dispute that abuse of civilians is a breach of peacekeepers' obligations under IHL. The exculpation by military courts in Canada and Italy of peacekeepers' misconduct in Somalia in the early 1990s, on the grounds that IHL is not applicable to non-combatant peacekeepers, was widely criticized at the time;[74] it is unlikely that today any court would come up with such an argument. Likewise Siekmann's argument, put forward in 1998, that misconduct by peacekeepers at Srebrenica 'can, notwithstanding moral and ethical considerations, stand the test of legal criticism,' on the grounds that since Dutchbat was a UN peacekeeping force that was not engaged in combat, IHL did not apply to it;[75] would not be accepted today. Although the Secretary-General's Bulletin of 1999[76] fails to clarify critical questions regarding the applicability of IHL to non-combatant peacekeepers, the UN's long-standing commitment to respect the principles and spirit of IHL in all circumstances; the decision of the ICTR in *Akayesu* regarding the applicability of IHL to civilians;[77] the UN's acknowledgment that IHL applies to civilian private military companies;[78] and the ICRC's current stance, which holds that IHL is applicable to all actors in an armed conflict, including civilians; strongly support the view that under IHL peacekeepers are bound at all times not to abuse civilians. Common Article 3 of the Geneva Conventions and Article 75 of Additional Protocol I, which prohibit the most egregious abuses and provide for core human rights protections, including a minimum standard of treatment for detainees and rights to a fair trial, (and which also form part of customary IHL), apply in all types of armed conflict, including some not envisaged at the time of the drafting of the Geneva Conventions, such as those between a non-State actor and a foreign or international force. At the very minimum these would be applicable to peacekeepers whatever the nature of the conflict.

[74] *Commission of Inquiry into the Deployment of Canadian Forces to Somalia*, <http://www.dnd.ca/somalia/somaliae.htm>; Judgment of the Belgian Military Court regarding violations of IHL committed in Somalia and Rwanda Nr 54 AR 1997, 20 November 1997; Journal des Tribunaux 24 April 1998, 286–289 (French language): Comment by M Cogen (1998) 1 Yearbook of International Humanitarian Law, 415–416; F Mégret and F Hoffman, 'The UN as a Human Rights Violator? Some reflections on the United Nations Changing Human Rights Responsibilities', 25 Human Rights Quarterly, 314, 327.

[75] RCR Siekmann, 'The Fall of Srebrenica and the Attitude of Dutchbat from an International Legal Perspective', 1 Yearbook of International Humanitarian Law, 301, 312.

[76] Secretary-General's Bulletin on Observance by UN Forces of International Humanitarian Law (date of promulgation 6 August 1999, entered into force 12 August 1999) UN Doc ST/SGB/1999/13.

[77] *The Prosecutor v Jean Paul Akayesu* Case no ICTR 94-4-1 Judgment, 22 September 1998, [443–444].

[78] FAQ 'International humanitarian law and private military/security companies' <http://www.icrc.org/Web/eng/siteeng0.nsf/html/pmc-fac-230506>.

It is also possible that troops would have responsibilities under the international human rights law treaties to which their State, or the host-State, is party. If the abuse occurred on a board a ship flying the flag of the force's State, or in one of its prisons, or within the confines of its own camp, then jurisdiction under human rights law will almost certainly extend to the situation, if the State is party to a relevant treaty.[79] Outside of these recognized exceptions to the territorial limits of jurisdiction, human rights treaties are generally only applicable to territories, or to persons, over which the State has effective control. The leading case on the extra-territorial jurisdiction of the ICCPR is *Delia Saldas de Lopez v Uruguay*.[80] The Human Rights Committee noted that Article 2 of the ICCPR places an obligation upon a State party to respect and ensure rights 'to all individuals within its territory and subject to its jurisdiction'; but stated that this does not imply that the State party concerned cannot be held accountable for violations of rights under the Covenant which its agents commit on the territory of another State, whether with the acquiescence of the Government of that State or in opposition to it.[81] Citing Article 5(1) of the Covenant,[82] the Committee held that it would be unconscionable to interpret the responsibility under Article 2 of the Covenant in such a way as to permit a State party to perpetrate violations of the Covenant on the territory of another State that it could not perpetrate on its own territory.[83] In its General Comment No 31, of 29th March 2004 the Committee stated that:

A State party must respect and ensure the rights laid down in the Covenant [ICCPR] to anyone within the power and effective control of that State party, even if not situated within the territory of that State party... This principle also applies to those within the power or effective control of the forces of a State party acting outside its territory, regardless of the circumstances in which such power or effective control was obtained, such as forces constituting a national contingent of a State party assigned to a national peacekeeping or peace-enforcement operation.[84]

[79] Discussed in Chapter 3 in the section on 'The Extra-territorial Jurisdiction of Human Rights Treaties'.

[80] *Delia Saldias de Lopez v Uruguay*, United Nations Human Rights Committee, Communication No 52/1979 (29 July 1981) UN Doc CCPR/C/OP/1 at 88 (1984); Sergio Ruben Lopez Burgos had been detained by the Uruguyan authorities for four months in December 1974. No charges were brought. In May 1975 he moved to Argentina. He was then kidnapped in Buenos Aires by Uruguyan security forces (aided by Argentine para-militaries) and held for two weeks in a secret location. Witnesses arrested with him stated that he was beaten and tortured. He was then taken to Uruguay, held for several months, tortured and forced to sign false statements.

[81] *Delia Saldias de Lopez v Uruguay* (n 80), [12.3].

[82] 'Nothing in the present Covenant may be interpreted as implying for any State, group or person any right to engage in any activity or perform any act aimed at the destruction of any of the rights and freedoms recognized herein or at their limitation to a greater extent than is provided for in the present Covenant'.

[83] *Delia Saldias de Lopez v Uruguay*, (n 80), [12.3].

[84] General Comment No 31, 'Nature of the General Legal Obligation Imposed on States Parties to the Covenant', UN DocCCPR/C/2/1/Rev.1/Add.13, 26 May 2004, [10]; The ECtHR, and the Inter-American Commission on Human Rights have adopted similar approaches: *Loizidou v Turkey*, (Merits) 15318/89 [1996] ECHR 70 (18 December 1996); *Cyprus v Turkey*, 25781/94 [2001] ECHR 331 (10 May 2001); Inter-American Commission on Human Rights,

In the *Coard* case[85] the Inter-American Commission on Human Rights found that the detention of the petitioners during the first few days of the United States' military intervention in Grenada, on October 25 1983, had been carried out under conditions that violated Article I, XVII and XXV of the American Declaration on the Rights and Duties of Man:

> Given that individual rights inhere simply by virtue of a person's humanity, each American State is obliged to uphold the protected rights of any persons subject to its jurisdiction. While this most commonly refers to persons within a state's territory, it may, under given circumstances, refer to conduct within an extra-territorial locus where the person concerned is present in the territory of one state, but subject to the control of another state—usually through the acts of the latter's agents abroad. In principle the inquiry turns not on the presumed victims' nationality or presence within a geographic area, but on whether, under the specific circumstances, the State observed the rights of a person subject to its authority and control.[86]

The scope of extra-territorial jurisdiction under the ECHR is not entirely clear. Prior to the *Banković* case the ECtHR repeatedly affirmed that the Convention applies extra-territorially if the Contracting party has effective control over the territory or over the victim.[87] In the *Banković* case the Court stated that the ECHR 'was not designed to be applied throughout the world, even in respect of the conduct of Contracting States':[88] jurisdiction is primarily territorial but may extend to territory in Europe under the effective control of the State. The UK High Court held that the ECHR was not applicable to possible negligent killing of civilians in Iraq in shooting incidents, but did apply to maltreatment by British forces of prisoners in a British prison in Iraq.[89] The *Issa* case, which concerned torture, mutilation and murder of Iraqi civilians, suggests that the ECHR may be applicable outside of Europe where the contracting State is exercising de facto

Coard et Al v United States, Report No 109/99, Case 10.951, September 29, 1999; Inter-American Commission on Human Rights, *Alejandre and Others v Cuba*, Report No 86/89, Case 11.589, 29 September 1999; In 1995 the Committee, in its observations on the US Article 40 report, rejected the view of the US government that the ICCPR lacked extra-territorial reach in all circumstances. It went on to say that such a view is 'contrary to the consistent interpretation of the Committee on this subject that, in special circumstances, persons may fall under the subject matter of a State Party even when outside that State territory: UN Doc CCPR/C/79/Add 50 (1995) [19].

[85] *Coard et Al v United States*, Inter-American Commission on Human Rights, Case 10.951, Report No 109/99 September 29, 1999

[86] ibid [38].

[87] Leading cases: *Loizidou v Turkey*, (Merits) 15318/89 [1996] ECHR 70 (18 December 1996); *Cyprus v Turkey*, 25781/94 [2001] ECHR 331 (10 May 2001).

[88] European Court of Human Rights *Banković v Belgium and 16 Other Contracting States* (52207/99) (2001), [47].

[89] *The Queen on the application of Mazin Jumaa Gatteh Al-Skeini and others v Secretary of State for Defence* [2004] EWHC 2911 (Admin); *The Queen on the application of Mazin Jumaa Gatteh Al-Skeini & others v Secretary of State for Defence* [2005] EWCA Civ 1609 21 December 2005; Opinions of the Lords of Appeal for Judgment in the Cause *Al-Skeini and others v Secretary of State for Defence* [2007] UKHL 26.

control over the territory, or over persons.[90] The ECtHR stated that 'Article 1 of the Convention cannot be interpreted so as to allow a State party to perpetrate violations of the Convention on the territory of another State, which it could not perpetrate on its own territory.'[91] However, the ECtHR has stated in a number of cases that military operations that are authorized by the Security Council under Chapter VII are immune from its scrutiny.[92] All of the cases to date have concerned acts and omissions of forces operating in territory that is under UN administration; however, the Court has not cited this as a reason for its refusal to review the force's conduct. In all cases the Court has held that the impugned acts were attributable to the UN, not the contributing State; but it has also stated that if it were to review UN forces' compliance with the ECHR it would 'be tantamount to imposing conditions on the implementation of a UNSC Resolution which were not provided for in the text of the Resolution itself.'[93] Arguably the implementation of all Security Council resolutions must comply with certain international law norms that are not specified in the text of the resolution itself (at a minimum those relating to State sovereignty, and peremptory norms of human rights law and humanitarian law); unless the resolution specifically provides otherwise. Nevertheless, the ECtHR might well take a similar view of peacekeeping operations deployed under the traditional 'Chapter VI and a half,' since peacekeeping is not provided for at all in the Charter but it has become core to the UN's mission of maintaining international peace and security. Unfortunately it is well known that some peacekeepers abuse their power and commit acts such as torture, rape, and gross exploitation that are incontrovertibly unacceptable. It is obvious that misconduct by troops, particularly when it involves serious abuses of the rights of the local population, will undermine the 'perceived legitimacy' or 'campaign authority' of the mission.[94] The explicit inclusion in Status of Forces Agreements with the host State, and in Memoranda of Understanding between the UN and troop contributing States, of a commitment to comply with relevant human rights law treaties would be a positive way of addressing this problem[95]

[90] *Issa and others v Turkey*, 31821/96 [2004] ECHR 629 (16 November 2004).

[91] ibid [71].

[92] European Court of Human Rights *Behrami and Behrami v France* and *Saramati v France, Germany and Norway* Application nos. 71412/01 and 78166/01 2 May 2007; *Dušan Berić and Others v Bosnia and Herzegovina* Application nos. 36357/04, 36360/04, 38346/04, 41705/04, 45190/04, 45578/04, 45579/04, 45580/04, 91/05, 97/05, 100/05, 101/05, 1121/05, 1123/05, 1125/05, 1129/05, 1132/05, 1133/05, 1169/05, 1172/05, 1175/05, 1177/05, 1180/05, 1185/05, 20793/05 and 25496/0516 October 2007; *Slavisa Gajic v Germany* Application no 31446/02 28 August 2007.

[93] European Court of Human Rights *Behrami and Behrami v France* and *Saramati v France, Germany and Norway* Application nos. 71412/01 and 78166/01 (n 92), [149].

[94] Ministry of Defence UK, Development, Concepts and Doctrine Centre, *Draft UK National Doctrine that will replace JWP 3–50 The Military Contribution to Peace Support Operations* (n 3) [0226]; UK Ministry of Defence, Joint Warfare Publication (JWP) 3.50 *The Military Contribution to Peace Support Operations* (n 4), [306].

[95] R Murphy, *UN Peacekeeping in Lebanon, Somalia and Kosovo* (Cambridge University Press Cambridge 2007), 238.

that would require conscious commitment by the mission and the UN Secretariat, but would enhance respect for the force and the UN from the local and international community, and possibly from the mission personnel themselves.

5.2 Protection of Civilians in the Care of the Force

Both IHL and human rights law require peacekeeping forces to protect from direct attack people that are in their immediate care, in so far as they are capable of doing so; and to take reasonable precautions, where feasible, to prevent attacks where these are clearly foreseeable. Common Article 1 of the Geneva Conventions requires the High Contracting parties 'to ensure' respect for the Conventions. Whilst valid arguments may be made that this provision was not originally intended to encompass the acts of third parties against civilians outside the care of the force, the ICRC's Commentaries on the Conventions make clear that even in the early days of their existence the Conventions were intended to 'ensure' a high level of respect for their provisions at all levels of the contracting State's legislative, administrative, and military systems. As the Commentary to the Fourth Convention states, the motive of the Convention is a 'lofty one... universally recognized as an imperative call of civilization:

> The Contracting Parties do not merely undertake to respect the Convention, but also to *ensure respect* for it. The wording may seem redundant. When a state contracts an engagement, the engagement extends to all those over whom it has authority, as well as to the representatives of its authority; and it is under an obligation to issue the necessary orders. The use in all four Conventions of the words 'and to ensure respect for' was however deliberate: they were intended to emphasize the responsibility of the Contracting Parties... It would not be enough for example for a state to give orders or directions to a few civilian or military authorities, leaving it to them to arrange as they please for their detailed execution. It is for the state to supervise the orders it gives. Furthermore if it is to fulfil the solemn undertaking it has given, the state must of necessity prepare in advance, that is to say in peacetime, the legal material or other means of ensuring the faithful enforcement of the Convention when the occasion arises.[96]

Moreover:

> The proper working system of protection provide by the Convention demands in fact that that the contracting Parties should not be content merely to apply its provisions themselves, but should do everything in their power to ensure that the humanitarian principles underlying the Conventions are applied universally.[97]

Whilst the drafters may never have intended that this provision should obligate High Contracting parties to ensure compliance by third-parties where they have

[96] J Pictet (ed), *The Geneva Conventions of 12 August 1949. Commentary IV Geneva Convention* (ICRC Geneva 1958), Article 1 (the other three commentaries contain similar statements).

[97] ibid.

no direct relationship with the potential victim; it is clear that the choice of the word 'ensure' was 'deliberate' and was 'intended to emphasize the responsibility of the Contracting Parties,'[98] and was not intended to be interpreted narrowly. The ICRC commentary on the paragraph concludes that 'Article 1 is no mere empty form of words, but has been deliberately invested with imperative force. It must be taken in its literal meaning.'[99] Its literal meaning would surely encompass ensuring that people in the care of agents of the State are protected from abuse in violation of the Conventions, in so far as this is possible.

Similarly the effective control jurisdictional test applicable to human rights treaties may encompass protection of persons in the care of the State party, to the extent that this is feasible, where the vulnerable persons are under the direct control of the force, for example in detention, or are in locations that fall within the established exemptions to the territorial principle of jurisdiction, such as ships, prisons, military camps. Arguably this obligation also encompasses protection of persons against whom there is a specific and imminent threat, and whose care the force has assumed, for example political leaders to whom the force has extended its protection, or local personnel working for the force, such as translators.[100] However, as noted above, the ECtHR has stated that it will not review acts and omissions relating to Chapter VII operations.

5.3 Protection of the Local Population

The extent of troops' obligations to provide protection to the local population outside of its own areas of direct control, (such as its prisons and military camps) is difficult to assess. Certainly troops that do not have effective control of the area cannot protect civilians from every human rights abuse, however grievous. However, where troops are witness to crimes against humanity, or are aware of such crimes and are in sufficiently close proximity to be able to respond, and have the capacity to do so, the local population, the international community, and in

[98] ibid. [99] ibid.

[100] Hasan Nuhanovic who was working for the UN as an interpreter at the compound of the Dutch peacekeepers in Srebrenica is seeking damages in tort from the Netherlands. On the day the enclave fell, his father, mother and brother were at the compound. On 12 and 13 July, the father acted as the representative of the refugees in meetings with the Dutch commander Karremans and Bosnian-Serb military leader, General Mladič. As such he was considered to be under UN protection. On 13 July, the Dutch acting commander Major Franken, assured the mother and the brother that they too could stay at the compound because of the protection received by Hasan and his father. But later that same day, by Franken's order, the mother and the brother were handed over to the Bosnian Serbs. The father chose to leave with them. Dutch peacekeepers brought them to the gate—and watched while the brother and the father were separated from the mother. Witness hearings were held in 2004 *H. Nuhanovic v de Staat der Nederlanden* 28 October 2004, Hof 's-Gravenhage (Court of Appeal, The Hague, Witness Hearings). Court Hearing June 16, 2008. Decision, rejecting the applicants claims, 10.9.2008 LJN: BF0181, Rechtbank 's-Gravenhage, 265615/HA ZA 06–1671.

many cases the troops themselves, will expect peacekeepers to try and stop such atrocities.

International human rights law does not normally extend to this situation because there is generally insufficient basis to hold that the contributing State has jurisdiction (absent other criteria such as those discussed above, for example where the State has effective control of territory).

It is unclear to what extent Article 1 of the Geneva Conventions encompasses an obligation on troops to ensure respect for the Conventions, in cases where violations are being perpetrated against the local population but outside the direct control of the force. It is the current view of the ICRC and other commentators that Article 1 obliges the High Contracting Parties to respond to such violations but it is not clear what the implications of this are for peacekeepers. Under the Peace Support Operations Working Draft Manual Doctrine for African Military Practitioners,[101] '[s]hould members of a PSF who are designated as combatants witness war crimes, but take no action to stop them, they themselves become party to that war crime.'[102] Even where the mandate of forces is limited to self-defence 'not to intervene when confronted by wide spread abuses to basic human rights and ethnic cleansing, may be regarded as a dereliction of military duty.'[103] The UK and NATO peace support doctrines are more equivocal on this issue. However, where the force has a mandate to provide protection (it is the norm now for peacekeeping mandates to include authorization to protect civilians) and the host-State is unable or unwilling to respond in sufficient time to protect the lives of the persons under imminent attack, it ought to be best practice to require peacekeepers to respond, if they have the capacity to do so. This would be in line with the principle of Article 1 and also with the expectations generated by deployment of a peacekeeping force.

Whatever the exact scope of the obligation in common Article 1 of the Geneva Conventions, the words 'to ensure respect' must be clear enough to any soldier in non legal terms and they undoubtedly encompass a moral imperative not to ignore serious abuses of the rights of local people (which presumably most soldiers would feel anyway): but a moral obligation without a legal framework to guide the force (and its political directors at the UN or other mandating authority) on how to implement that obligation is likely to lead to frustration, and psychological stress that may lead to serious misconduct by some troops. The report by the Netherlands Institute for War Documentation (NIOD) did not examine specific allegations of misconduct by Dutchbat but it did observe that the troops were suffering from 'peacekeeper stress,' brought on in part by the lack of clarity with regard to their

[101] '*Peace Support Operations: A Working Draft Manual for African Military Practitioners*' DWM 1–2000 February 2000 <http://www.iss.co.za/Pubs/Other/PeaceSupportManualMM>, produced as a result of a workshop held at SADC Regional Peacekeeping Training Centre in Harare, Zimbabwe, 24–26 August 1999.

[102] ibid [0245]. [103] ibid [0346].

responsibility to provide protection to the local population. The report argued that the kind of stress this causes can have a dehumanizing effect on troops:

Being forced into a spectator role as a third party in an environment that is characterized by violence and a violation of human rights can have drastic consequences for individual soldiers. Soldiers can come into conflict with themselves if they have to observe excesses, especially if they are prevented from acting by the Rules of Engagement. Such experiences consist of a mixture of guilt, compassion, powerlessness, frustration, fear, anger and hostility.

This complex of often simultaneous emotions is referred to by the term bystander anxiety. This symptom occurs if people are not in a position to do anything about the violence in the surroundings. It is therefore particularly important for soldiers to know exactly what task derives from their mission, what position they have to take as a third party and how they are to interpret concepts such as neutrality, impartiality and humanity.[104]

The description by witnesses in a class action brought by survivors of Srebrenica against the Netherlands and the United Nations, of Dutch troops witnessing terrible atrocities without reacting or reacting with laughter supports the conclusions of the NIOD investigation that troops were suffereing from shock and emotional dissocciation. Plaintiff Subašić said that:

[Mladić] asked a young boy how old he was. The boy told him that he was eleven. To that Mladić said that in six years he could be a soldier and that he had to go with them. The young boy was then grabbed, taken out, and taken away. I told this to my husband and he told it in turn in English to one of the soldiers that children were being removed. The Dutch soldier looked at him and said only, 'So what.'

The Serbs began at a certain point to take girls and young women out of the group of refugees. They were raped. The rapes often took place under the eyes of others and sometimes even under the eyes of the children of the mother. A Dutch soldier stood by and he simply looked around with a walkman on his head. He did not react at all to what was happening. It did not happen just before my eyes, for I saw that personally, but also before the eyes of us all. The Dutch soldiers walked around everywhere. It is impossible that they did not see it.

There was a woman with a small baby a few months old. A Chetnik told the mother that the child must stop crying. When the child did not stop crying he snatched the child away and cut its throat. Then he laughed. There was a Dutch soldier there who was watching. He did not react at all.

I saw yet more frightful things. For example, there was a girl, she must have been about nine years old. At a certain moment some Chetniks recommended to her brother that he rape the girl. He did not do it and I also think that he could not have done it for he was still just a child. Then they murdered that young boy. I have personally seen all that. I really want to emphasize that all this happened in the immediate vicinity of the base.[105]

[104] Netherlands Institute for War Documentation *Srebrenica 'A Safe Area': Reconstruction, Background, Consequences and Analyzes of the Fall of a Safe Area* (2002) pt II, ch 8, s 13 'Peacekeeper Stress' (footnotes omitted).

[105] *Mothers of Srebenica et al v the Stat eof the Netherlands and the United Nations* Rechtbanke's-Gravenhage 295427/HA ZA 07-2973, Writ of Summons, [244].

Another plaintiff reported:

> I wanted on 12th July 1995 to fetch water with my sister from a house that stood close to the factory, and to do so I had to cross a corn field that was in front of the house. I saw bodies lying there without any heads. My sister, who was walking in front, dragged me away. Dutch soldiers were standing only a short distance away and I cannot believe that they did not see it.
>
> During the rest of 12th July 1995 I saw Dutch and Serbian soldiers walking about together. I heard a Serbian soldier ask a Dutch soldier in Serbian whether the Dutch soldier was interested in a girl and he offered him a girl. The Dutch soldier said nothing back.
>
> I was later with my niece close to a group of Dutch soldiers. The soldiers were handing out sweets. My niece asked a Dutch soldier in English what was happening and the soldier said that whatever it was, it was not good for us. He then began to laugh. We went back to my mother. It began to get dark and we heard screams from the direction where the men and boys from the factory had been taken.[106]

The NIOD report in discussing the psychological effects of 'bystander syndrome' comments that it can:

> manifest in the creation of a pure 'survival mentality' and being as detached as possible from the outside world. This attitude serves to put the surroundings 'at a distance' so as to prevent a fundamental disruption of the arrangement of a person's own conceptual and experiential universe. The original goal of creating a psychological distance is therefore self-protection in a broad sense, although the self-protection can also become a goal in its own right. The distance is usually created by starting to consider people in the outside world as beings from a different category from oneself. This can even apply to people who are in principle powerless and even victims of extreme violence.
>
> . . . In the extreme case, such a negative view can lead to dehumanization, which means that a certain category of fellow humans is no longer treated as human. It is then becomes understandable and even acceptable that other standards and values apply to the 'dehumanized,' inferior group. In theory this also increased the risk of misconduct towards this group. This process was described by a former Dutchbat member: 'Perhaps it was also because the Muslims looked like animals, and sometimes also behaved like animals. Filthy and rotten. After a while that is what you start to call them. "I am going to fetch the cattle" is the way you talk about them.'[107]

The report specifically notes that the lack of clarity in the mandate and in the ROE with regard to responsibilities towards the population of the 'safe area' declared by the UN, contributed to the psychological stress of the troops:

> It was therefore risky that there was no clear vision in the Netherlands Army during Dutchbat's mission on the question of how Dutchbat was to deal with situations that could occur in practice, and that much would depend on improvization. This was partly because the Rules of Engagement did not contribute to clarity on the way in which

[106] ibid [245].

[107] Netherlands Institute for War Documentation *Srebrenica 'A Safe Area': Reconstruction, Background, Consequences and Analyzes of the Fall of a Safe Area* (2002) pt II, ch 8, s 13 'Peacekeeper Stress'.

Dutchbat was to position itself in the enclave. This again created the opportunity for different commanders to interpret the position of the battalion in different ways: the result was confusion among Dutchbat members regarding how they understood their duties, and misunderstandings among the NGOs with which they had to cooperate.[108]

A reporter for Der Spiegel interviewed a Dutchbat soldier, Gerald Verhaegh, ten years after the fall of Srebrenica, who said that he:

> had to turn his helmet and bullet-proof jacket over to them [the Serbs]. But he didn't fear for his life. Others were forced to strip down to their underwear. Then dressed as UN soldiers, the Serbs could more easily convince the Muslims to go with them.[109]

Verhaegh also told the reporter that 'we realized the Serbs had taken pretty Muslim women into building. But they barred us from entering it.'[110] A witness to some of the crimes committed at Srebrenica reported that:

> The Serbs did whatever they wished. A sort of tape was stretched across the road just about where the 'Blue Factory' and the zinc factory were. The Dutch soldiers stood in front of it and no-one was allowed to pass. At that moment a Chetnik, slightly older than my oldest son, spoke to me. He looked like Rambo, with a cartridge belt across his body. At first I did not recognize him but I remembered him when he told me that his name was Željko. He asked me where my family was, in particular my husband. I told him that he had been killed by a shell. He offered me a cigarette. While I smoked it he told me that there could be, and here I use the Bosnian word, a 'Kurban'. This stands for ritual slaughter. At that he walked to the tape that had been placed by the Dutchbat soldiers and sliced it through. Željko spoke to one of the Dutch soldiers, who stood by the tape. This soldier was then struck in the face by Željko with such a hard blow that the soldier's helmet fell off. The Dutchbat soldier then had to give his weapon to Željko. The Dutchbat soldier blushed red but did nothing. He appeared scared and allowed this to happen to him.
>
> I later saw Serbs stab an old man. This happened under the eyes of a Dutchbat soldier. This was the same Dutchbat soldier from whom Željko had taken the weapon. The Dutchbat soldier did nothing this time also. He stood there and just watched.[111]

It is obvious that this kind of response by UN forces to atrocities is damaging to the reputation of the UN both locally and internationally. It is also damaging to the peacekeepers themselves; a high proportion of Dutchbat soldiers that were present when Srebrenica fell have needed psychological help, in some cases years of counselling.[112] Such humiliation of an elite fighting force (as Dutchbat was intended to be),[113] in the face of such horrific crimes, is a far cry from the ideals

[108] ibid.

[109] A Schröder, 'A Dutch Peacekeeper Remembers Genocide' Der Spiegel, July 12 2005 <http://www.spiegel.de/international/0,1518,364902,00.html> Accessed July 31, 2008.

[110] ibid.

[111] *Mothers of Srebenica et al v the Stat eof the Netherlands and the United Nations* Rechtbanke's-Gravenhage 295427/HA ZA 07-2973, Writ of summons, Witness Kolenović, [245].

[112] ibid ICTY Tribunal Update 'Dutch peacekeepers to return to Srebrenica' <http://www.iwpr.net/?p=tri&s=f&o=325295&apc_state=henh> Accessed July 31, 2008.

[113] Netherlands Institute for War Documentation *Srebrenica 'A Safe Area': Reconstruction, Background, Consequences and Analyzes of the Fall of a Safe Area* (2002) pt II, ch 5, s 2, 'The planning for the dispatch of the Airmobile Brigade'.

of peacekeeping expounded by Dag Hammarskjöld. In 1964, UN forces in the Congo were reminded that they:

serve as members of an international force.... Protection against acts of violence is to be given to all the people, white and black. You carry arms, but they are *only* to be used in self-defence. You are in the Congo to help *everyone*, to harm no-one.[114]

These words communicate a sense of pride in the UN, in its aims and ideals and in the discipline and courage of the 'international force' deployed to secure those aims, in particular the protection of 'all people.' As early as the 1960s Hammarskjöld argued that the principle that the use of force must be restricted to self-defence could not justify standing by in the face of serious atrocities committed against civilians. In such circumstances 'emphasis should be placed... on the protection of the lives of the civilian population in the spirit of the Universal Declaration of Human Rights and the Genocide Convention.'[115] Neither of these instruments creates obligations directly binding on individual soldiers but, in conjunction with the 'responsibility to protect' norm, they do contribute to a moral responsibility on contributing States and on the UN to authorize their forces to stop such crimes if they are in the area and have the power to do so.[116] The Report by the Secretary-Generals' High Level Panel on Threats, Challenges and Change noted that it is now widely accepted that the self-defence norm is sufficiently broad to encompass use of force in the face of genocide and crimes against humanity but there is not yet consensus amongst the UN Member States that this is so, or at any rate on the scope of permissible response.[117] However, since 1999 it has been the norm for peacekeeping mandates to authorize protection of civilians that are in the immediate vicinity of the force and that are facing imminent and serious risk of being deliberately attacked and abused.

6. Sexual Violence

One area of protection responsibilities that is of particular concern in modern armed conflict, and that requires an especial effort to combat, is sexual violence.

[114] Press Release CO/15 July 19, 1960; GIAD Draper, 'The Legal Limitations Upon the Employment of Weapons by the United Nations Force in the Congo' (1963) 12 International and Comparative Law Quarterly 387, 399.

[115] Annual Report of the Secretary-General on the Work of the Organization, June 16 1960–June 16 1961, 16th Session, UN Doc A/4800, 11.

[116] As noted above Louise Arbour has argued that the 'responsibility to protect' norm may also create legal responsibilities for States that are in a position to act: L Arbour, 'The responsibility to protect as a duty of care in international law and practice', Review of International Studies (2008), 34, 445,453.

[117] Report by the Secretary-Generals' High Level Panel on Threats, Challenges and Change '*A More Secure World: Our Shared Responsibility*' <http://www.un.org//secureworld>, [212]; United Nations, Report of the Secretary-General on the implementation of Security Council resolution 340 (1973), UN document S/11052/Rev. 1, 27 October 1973.

Rape has been a feature of armed conflict of thousands of years but in recent years the scale and brutality of sexual violence in armed conflict appears to have increased markedly. Major General Cammaert, now retired but formerly General Officer Commanding the Eastern Division of MONUC, has commented that it 'has probably become more dangerous to be a woman than a soldier in an armed conflict.'[118] The sexual violence perpetrated in some conflicts today is no longer a bi-product of war but a means of waging it and its effects persist long after peace processes have been concluded. In part this is because of the increasing use of attacks on civilians as a method of war and attacks on women and children are particularly devastating for the survival of the community; but it is also because of pervasive beliefs both amongst local militias and war lords, and on the part of peacekeeping forces, that abuse of women is inevitable and to be expected in war; and therefore to be viewed as collateral damage rather than as a factor contributing to the social and economic instability that fuels and perpetuates conflict. Rape and sexual violence are a means of decimating a society socially, culturally and economically. Women who have been subjected to the kind of brutal rapes and other sexual assaults that are now common in some conflicts often die; if they survive they are unable to work, unable to support their children, are usually ostracized from their community, and may suffer seriously debilitating health problems. HIV and irreparable fistulas are a common consequence.

Dallaire's description of the cruelty of the sexual violence perpetrated in Rwanda is almost too unbearably horrific to repeat; but it is important to draw attention to the extreme nature of the violence because historically there has been a tendency to underplay the seriousness of sexual exploitation and abuse in conflict and post-conflict society. In his book Dallaire describes how at first he 'sealed away from his mind' all the signs of sexual brutality:

> But if you looked, you could see the evidence, even in the whitened skeletons. The legs bent and apart. A broken bottle, a rough branch, even a knife between them. Where the bodies were fresh, we saw what must have been semen pooled on and near the dead women and girls. There was always a lot of blood. Some male corpses had their genitals cut off, but many women and young girls had their breasts chopped off and their genitals crudely cut apart. They died in a position of total vulnerability, flat on their backs, with their legs bent and knees wide apart. It was the expressions on their dead faces that assaulted me the most, a frieze of shock, pain and humiliation.[119]

90% of all females above the age of 3 in parts of Liberia have been raped.[120] A 2008 report concluded that 'there was no place and no time of day or night where

[118] P Cammaert, speaking at the Security Council meeting leading to the adoption of SC/RES 1820 19 June 2008; S/PV.5916, 9.

[119] R Dallaire, *Shake Hands with the Devil* (n 15), 430.

[120] AM Goetz, (UNIFEM) Wilton Park Conference 914 *Women Targeted or Afflicted by Armed Conflict: What Role for Military Peacekeepers?* 27–29 May 2008 Text of Speakers' Presentations, 2.

adolescent girls [in Liberia] could be considered safe.'[121] A majority of victims were under twelve and some of the rapes were exceptionally brutal gang rapes.[122] Up to 50% of women and girls in Sierra Leone have suffered some form or threat of sexual violence during the conflict.[123] In the DRC, three out of 4 women in parts of the Eastern Kivus have been raped.[124] Women dare not sleep in their homes at night and dare not go out to their crops on the outskirts of their villages by day. They 'live in fear, so they live in the bush. They expose themselves to diseases: malaria, gastro-enteritis. It's cold at night. All of this claims lives.'[125]

Sexual violence in conflict and post-conflict situations may be widespread and systematic, part of an organized campaign, or widespread and opportunistic, perpetrated with apparent impunity in traumatized conflict and post-conflict societies. All are serious violations of human rights and, if committed in an armed conflict, war crimes. Sexual abuse that is widespread and systematic may also be a crime against humanity and may even constitute genocide. The UN has a responsibility to protect women and children from abuse of this nature, and has undertaken to do so.[126] Moreover given that the nature of peacekeeping and peace support 'is such that the strategic objectives will normally relate to the establishment of a secure, stable and self-sustaining environment for the local population, the nation and the region,'[127] it is essential that the UN (and other organizations involved in peacekeeping) have a clear policy on protection from sexual violence and abuse.

Whilst most sexual abuse in armed conflict is perpetrated by local militias or government forces, sexual abuse by peacekeeping personnel is also known to be widespread and heavily under-reported.[128] Save the Children UK in its 2008 report *No One to Turn to: The under-reporting of child sexual exploitation and abuse by aid workers and peacekeepers* states that the scale of abuse by personnel working for international organizations is 'significant' and that although it exists in all international organizations peacekeepers are the most likely perpetrators.[129]

[121] S Lewis, Wilton Park Conference 914 *Women Targeted or Afflicted by Armed Conflict: What Role for Military Peacekeepers?* 27–29 May 2008, Text of Speakers' Presentations, 13.

[122] ibid.

[123] AM Goetz, Wilton Park Conference 914 *Women Targeted or Afflicted by Armed Conflict: What Role for Military Peacekeepers?* (n 120), 2.

[124] ibid.

[125] 'DR Congo: Rape Happens We Are Human Beings' *Mail and Guardian* 13 November 2007.

[126] S/RES 1674 28 April 2006; S/RES 1820 19 June 2008.

[127] Ministry of Defence, Development, Concepts and Doctrine Centre, *Draft UK National Doctrine that will replace JWP 3–50 The Military Contribution to Peace Support Operations* (n 3), [0112].

[128] C Csáky, *No One to Turn to: The under-reporting of child sexual exploitation and abuse by aid workers and peacekeepers* (Save the Children UK London 2008), 12; P Cammaert, Wilton Park Conference 914 *Women Targeted or Afflicted by Armed Conflict: What Role for Military Peacekeepers?* Text of Speakers' Presentations, 8.

[129] C Csáky, *No One to Turn to: The under-reporting of child sexual exploitation and abuse by aid workers and peacekeepers* (n 128) 8.

Sexual abuse by peacekeepers ranges from visits to brothels (many working girls are trafficked and almost all are economically and socially vulnerable); the purchase of sex for small amounts of money or 'an egg'; sexual slavery of women and children and the purchase of women as 'housemates'; the fathering of children by women living in the local community (who will often be rejected by that community); rape of adults; attendance at events at which women and girls are publicly raped; the trafficking of women and girls; the filming of children for pornographic purposes; sex with children ('often it will be between eight and ten men who will share two or three girls');[130] and the rape of children.[131] The Save the Children report also states that although the charity:

> did not set out to explore the reasons why perpetrators of abuse are disproportionately represented among DPKO, our own fieldwork, as well as other reports, point to certain factors. Peacekeepers are capable of exerting particular influence over the communities in which they serve, especially over children and young people. This is largely due to the fact that they are armed and provide much-needed physical security within contexts of extreme fragility. Furthermore, peacekeeping forces contain a significant number of military personnel with discriminatory attitudes to women.[132]

Sexual abuse is still often viewed on the one hand as a domestic problem, the product of local culture and the effects of war (in so far as it concerns local actors); and on the other hand an ordinary consequence of deployment of many men away from home in military surroundings, (in so far as it involves participation of peacekeeping personnel). Whilst some UN commanders are beginning to take sexual abuse seriously and have taken innovative steps to try and prevent it (for example some forces have been prohibited from carrying money or food when on patrol, thus reducing the opportunities for buying sex)[133] the Lessons Learned Study undertaken on behalf of the UN DPKO into sexual abuse by MONUC in 2006 reported that the:

> general climate in which investigations were conducted in MONUC in the first months was one of considerable suspicion and a degree of defensiveness on the part of MONUC

[130] 14 year old boy in Côte D'Ivoire quoted in C Csáky, *No One to Turn to: The under-reporting of child sexual exploitation and abuse by aid workers and peacekeepers* (n 128), 6.

[131] C Csáky, *No One to Turn to: The under-reporting of child sexual exploitation and abuse by aid workers and peacekeepers* (n 128); S Martin, *Must Boys be Boys: Ending Sexual Exploitation and Abuse in Peacekeeping Missions* (Refugees International 2005); N Dahrendorf, *Sexual Exploitation and Abuse: Lessons Learned Study, Addressing Sexual Exploitation and Abuse in MONUC* (UN DPKO Best Practices Unit March 2006); Wilton Park Conference 914 *Women Targeted or Afflicted by Armed Conflict: What Role for Military Peacekeepers?* 27–29 May 2008; M O'Brien, *Overcoming boys-will-be-boys syndrome: Is prosecution of peacekeepers in the International Criminal Court for trafficking, sexual slavery and related crimes against women a possibility?* (Master Thesis University of Lund 2004)

[132] C Csáky, *No One to Turn to: The under-reporting of child sexual exploitation and abuse by aid workers and peacekeepers* (n 128), 8.

[133] N Dahrendorf, *Sexual Exploitation and Abuse: Lessons Learned Study, Addressing Sexual Exploitation and Abuse in MONUC* (n 131), 19.

staff, at all levels. Whilst the SRSG [Special Representative of the Secretary-General] and the DSRSG [Deputy Special Representative of the Secretary-General] welcomed and supported the initiative, rumours of witch-hunts abounded, as did assertions that the office[134] was purely cosmetic to save the credibility and image of the mission and of the SRSG.[135]

Sarah Mendelson in her report on *Peacekeeping and Human Trafficking in the Balkans* for the Center for Strategic and International Studies observes that:

> the events in the UN Mission in Congo share many similarities with previous peacekeeper involvement in trafficking in Bosnia and Kosovo. Specifically, sexual violence against women and girls during war is again perpetuated by international peacekeepers. 'What should be totally unacceptable has become the norm. This brutal consequence of sexual violence is what paves the way for rampant sexual exploitation and abuse by [UN Mission in Congo] personnel.' The UN system has once again been dysfunctional in responding to these allegations...'Most military... think it is unfair to penalize soldiers who pay for sex since they have no other reasonable means of engaging in sexual relations in the mission area.' Again, the UN mission has policies in place regarding sexual exploitation and abuse but which 'most military' view as 'unduly broad and very unrealistic'.[136]

Refugees International reports that sexual exploitation and abuse tends to be viewed in terms of sexual behavior only and not as a problem of abuse of power,[137] but as one Liberian woman said:

> [t]hese girls that [peacekeeping soldiers] go off with are just children. They cannot reason for themselves. They are hungry and want money for school. The peacekeepers give them that. But the peacekeepers are adults. They should act responsibly.[138]

Commanders tend to focus on what they believe are their soldiers' 'rights' and not those of the victim. Mendelson comments that many KFOR commanders seemed unaware that prostitution is illegal in Kosovo; that prostitution has largely developed to supply the demands of the Kosovo Force and that 'the vast majority of women and girls used for these purposes are trafficked.'[139] She cites a NATO lieutenant colonel based in Kosovo in 2000 who explained to her that:

[134] Office for Addressing Sexual Exploitation and Abuse established March 2005 to address allegations of sexual abuse. The Office was transitioned into a Conduct and Discipline Team in November 2005. A number of other missions now have Conduct and Discipline Teams attached to them.

[135] N Dahrendorf, *Sexual Exploitation and Abuse: Lessons Learned Study, Addressing Sexual Exploitation and Abuse in MONUC* (n 131), [7].

[136] SE Mendelson, *Barracks and Brothels: Peacekeeping and Human Trafficking in the Balkans* (Center for Strategic and International Studies February 2005), 67–68 (Internal citations omitted).

[137] S Martin, *Must Boys be Boys: Ending Sexual Exploitation and Abuse in Peacekeeping Missions* (n 131), 5; One senior US military commander is reported to have described a US Department of Defense Report into trafficking in the Balkans as an example of government 'waste, fraud, and abuse': Statement made on June 9, 2003, at EUCOM (European Command); Cited in SE Mendelson, *Barracks and Brothels: Peacekeeping and Human Trafficking in the Balkans* (n 136), 21, 45.

[138] S Martin, *Must Boys be Boys: Ending Sexual Exploitation and Abuse in Peacekeeping Missions* (n 131), 5.

[139] SE Mendelson, *Barracks and Brothels: Peacekeeping and Human Trafficking in the Balkans* (n 136), 32.

[t]he commanding officer may be thinking, 'This guy [his soldier] is happy and he is happier if he had a half hour with a beautiful 17-year-old— whether he knows she is forced or not—he is happier—he will do his mission better. . . .' The commander can be a great guy but maybe he will turn a blind eye and think that boys will be boys.[140]

These arguments are similar to those of militia commanders in the DRC and elsewhere who say, as Colonel Edmond Ngarambe of the Democratic Forces for the Liberation of Rwanda has done:

this thing of rape . . . I can't deny that happens. We are human beings. But it's not just us. The Mai Mai, the government soldiers who are not paid, the Rastas do the same thing. And some people sent by our enemies do it to cause anger against us.[141]

Over the last five years the UN has made a concerted effort to address sexual exploitation and abuse in armed conflict whether by local militias or by its own forces. In 2003 the Secretary-General published a Bulletin on *Special Measures for Protection from Sexual Exploitation and Sexual Abuse*, setting standards of conduct for UN forces, which prohibits any 'actual or attempted abuse of a position of vulnerability, differential power, or trust, for sexual purposes' or any 'actual or threatened physical intrusion of a sexual nature, whether by force or under unequal or coercive conditions.'[142] Specific examples of sexual exploitation and abuse that are prohibited include 'exchange of money, employment, goods or services for sex, including sexual favours or other forms of humiliating, degrading or exploitative behaviour,' and sexual relationships between United Nations staff and beneficiaries of assistance, since these are based on 'inherently unequal power dynamics,' and 'undermine the credibility and integrity of the work of the United Nations.'[143] United Nations staff are obliged to create and maintain an environment that prevents sexual exploitation and sexual abuse, and if a staff member develops concerns regarding sexual exploitation or sexual abuse by a fellow worker, he or she must report such concerns.[144]

In January 2005 the UN established a joint Task Force on Protection from Sexual Exploitation and Abuse, to be managed by the Department of Peacekeeping Operations and the Office for the Coordination of Humanitarian Affairs. The Secretary-General also requested the Permanent Representative of Jordan,[145] His Royal Highness Prince Zeid Ra'ad Zeid al-Hussein, a former civilian peacekeeper, to undertake a detailed report on the problem. The Zeid Report *A Comprehensive Strategy to Eliminate Future Sexual Exploitation and Abuse in United Nations Operations*, published in 2005, recommends that the standards set out in the Secretary-General's bulletin on *Special Measures for Protection from*

[140] ibid 34.
[141] 'DR Congo: Rape Happens We Are Human Beings', *Mail and Guardian*, 13 November 2007.
[142] UN Doc ST/SGB/2003/13 9 October 2003.
[143] ibid [3(2)].
[144] ibid [3(2)].
[145] Jordan is a major troop contributing State to UN peacekeeping missions.

Sexual Exploitation and Sexual Abuse should be incorporated into the memoranda of understanding (MOU) signed by the UN with troop-contributing States and that troop-contributing States should be obligated to ensure that they are binding on the military members of their national contingents.[146]

In June 2007 the Special Committee of Peacekeeping operations approved a new draft model MOU, which incorporates a number of measures intended to improve compliance with the UN's zero tolerance policy.[147] It includes a commitment that UN personnel will always report all acts involving sexual exploitation and abuse and will never commit 'any act involving sexual exploitation and abuse, sexual activity with children under 18, or exchange of money, employment, goods or services for sex.'[148] It also includes a number of provisions to improve accountability. For example, if the government of the contributing State has prima facie grounds indicating that any member of its national contingent has committed an act of serious misconduct, it is required to inform the United Nations without delay and forward the case to its appropriate national authorities for the purposes of investigation. Further:

> In the event that the United Nations has prima facie grounds indicating that any member of the Government's national contingent has committed an act of misconduct or serious misconduct, the United Nations shall without delay inform the Government. If necessary to preserve evidence and where the Government does not conduct fact-finding proceedings, the United Nations may, in cases of serious misconduct, as appropriate, where the United Nations has informed the Government of the allegation, initiate a preliminary fact finding inquiry of the matter, until the Government starts its own investigation.[149]

The Government is required to provide the United Nations with the findings of its investigations. If the Government does not notify the UN within 10 days from the time of notification by the UN, that it will start an investigation, the Government is considered to be unwilling or unable to conduct such an investigation and the United Nations may initiate its own administrative investigation.[150] Troop contributing States will continue to have exclusive jurisdiction as regards criminal charges but the 'Government assures the United Nations that it shall exercise such jurisdiction with respect to such crimes or offences.'[151] The draft MOU was approved by the General Assembly on July 24 2007;[152] but it has yet to be implemented.

[146] Comprehensive review of the whole question of peacekeeping operations in all their aspects A/59/710 24 March 2005, 4.

[147] Annex to Report of the Special Committee on Peacekeeping Operations and its Working Group, A/61/19 (Part III), New York, 12 June 2007, [3–4].

[148] ibid Annex H (new annex to be inserted at the end of Chapter 9 of the model MOU).

[149] ibid [7(2)]. [150] ibid [7(1)]. [151] ibid [7(3a)].

[152] The Resolution entitled 'Comprehensive review of the whole question of peacekeeping operations in all their aspects' was contained in a report from the Fourth Committee (Special Political and Decolonization) A/610/409/Add 2; 'General Assembly Adopts Recommendations on Peacekeeping Operations, including United Nations Standards of Conduct' GA/10605 UN Press Release.

Following the publication of the Zeid Report the Special Committee on Peacekeeping Operations recommended the development of full-time personnel conduct officer positions in field missions, and many missions now have a conduct officer. However, Save the Children's Report of 2008 clearly shows that, despite the UN's zero tolerance policy and radical initiatives to implement it, abuse of children is still widespread amongst peacekeepers. This suggests that the UN's efforts to combat it have yet to have a significant effect; and if abuse is still prevalent amongst peacekeepers there is little chance of them taking action to improve protection from abuse by local armed groups. Conduct officers need to be proactive in finding out what is going on, informing people about their role, and encouraging reporting; otherwise the result of campaigns to prevent sexual abuse may amount to no more than a public relations exercise that may drive the exploitative conduct underground rather than stop it. The persons most likely to be abused by peacekeepers are orphans and children separated from their families, who do not have enough to eat, have no money, and do not have anyone to protect them or to make a complaint on their behalf.[153] Young girls are also afraid of rejection by their community:

> The reason why most girls are not confident to report is that the message will go straight to the community that she is not a girl any more, that she is spoiled, and no one will want to marry her and no one will look after her. So she just keeps quiet.[154]

Some children 'are scared they might be killed by the perpetrator.'[155] Governments may discourage local communities from protesting because they don't want problems with the mission, which may bring much needed assistance.[156]

The UN Department of Peacekeeping is committed to ensuring all peacekeepers are trained in gender and sexual abuse issues. Since sexual violence is a major weapon of warfare, sexual abuse training should not be a peripheral topic but should be integrated into the mainstream of military training; all peacekeepers need to be aware that protecting women and children is one of the major tasks that they will have to confront if their mission is to be successful. Moreover, many soldiers witnessing the widespread and extreme sexual violence prevalent in some wars may be deeply shocked and may need to be prepared psychologically and practically for how to deal with it. Power-point presentations immediately before deployment, or in the first week or two of deployment when soldiers have a thousand adjustments to make to their new environment, are insufficient on their own. Sexual abuse training should include case studies, debates, and films, and should be part and parcel of all army training from the very beginning on a regular basis, along with

[153] C Csáky, *No One to Turn to: The under-reporting of child sexual exploitation and abuse by aid workers and peacekeepers* (n 128), 7.

[154] Young girl Southern Sudan quoted in C Csáky, *No One to Turn to: The under-reporting of child sexual exploitation and abuse by aid workers and peacekeepers* (n 128), 13.

[155] ibid (Young boy).

[156] ibid 16.

training in international humanitarian law, and relevant human rights law. There should also be mission specific training in dealing with sexual exploitation and abuse; this should include information about the prevalence and nature of sexual abuse in the area, information about who to contact if they encounter abuse, and details of local NGOs providing support to abused women.

Stephen Lewis, Co-Director Aids-Free World, Boston, has suggested that peacekeepers, because of the need for heightened awareness when they are deployed into an unknown and violent situation, tend to develop a sense of intuition of what is going on in the local community, and he argues that they should put this insight to use in order to provide protection:

> Peacekeepers aren't mere passive observers of the human family. Peacekeepers move into a country; they learn its social architecture; they watch the roiling political terrain on a day-to-day basis. They come to know the foibles, to know the extremes, to know the anomalies. More often than not, they can tell when trouble is brewing. They can intuit when men might hurtle out of control. They have the pulse of the culture. When it unravels, they're there to bear witness. I'm saying that when patterns of sexual violence emerge, peacekeepers are rarely surprised. In some cases, they alone have anticipated the atrocities in the offing. And with that knowledge comes obligation. With that insight comes responsibility. It isn't enough to stop the shooting when the raping continues apace. The only worthwhile armistice restores peace for the entire population, male and female.[157]

The need for vigilance in relation to sexual violence is true not only of missions deployed into conflict but also missions deployed to monitor a peace agreement or assist in securing post conflict stability. Major General Festus Okonkwo, now retired but formerly force commander of AMIS, and of ECOWAS in Liberia, states that during post conflict activities peacekeepers tend to focus on issues such as disarmament, demobilization, reintegration and elections; but sexual violence does not stop at the end of hostilities.[158] Some combatants seem to regard it as a form of compensation for what they lost or didn't gain in the war. Okonkwo cites one militiaman in Liberia who said during disarmament 'since we have lost the battle, we should at least win the beautiful women.'[159] Peacekeepers need to be trained to be aware of this likelihood and to be vigilant in looking out for it. Whilst some sexual violence is perpetrated in public spaces, much of it goes on in places and at times when troops would not normally be present, such as peoples' homes.

Security Council resolution 1820 on Women, Peace and Security[160] adopted unanimously on 19 June 2008 provides a strong base on which to develop

[157] S Lewis, Wilton Park Conference 914 *Women Targeted or Afflicted by Armed Conflict: What Role for Military Peacekeepers?* (n 121), 14.

[158] Security Council meeting leading to the adoption of SC/RES 1820 19 June 2008; S/PV.5916, 33.

[159] Major General Festus Okonkwo, 'Protection of Women Civilian in Practice: Operational Case Study 1: Liberia', 9 Paper presented at Wilton Park Conference 914 *Women Targeted or Afflicted by Armed Conflict: What Role for Military Peacekeepers?* 27–29 May 2008, 9 [12].

[160] S/RES 1820 19 June 2008.

proactive measures to improve the protection of women. The Council made it clear, for the first time, that sexual violence is an issue relating to international peace and security and not simply a domestic crime. It stressed that sexual violence, 'when used or commissioned as a tactic of war in order to deliberately target civilians' or 'as a part of a widespread or systematic attack against civilian populations,' can 'significantly exacerbate situations of armed conflict and may impede the restoration of international peace and security.' It also affirmed that effective steps to prevent and respond to such acts of sexual violence 'can significantly contribute to the maintenance of international peace and security,' and it expressed its readiness 'to, where necessary, adopt appropriate steps to address widespread or systematic sexual violence.' It demanded 'the immediate and complete cessation by all parties to armed conflict of all acts of sexual violence against civilians with immediate effect' and demanded ' that all parties to armed conflict immediately take appropriate measures to protect civilians, including women and girls, from all forms of sexual violence.' It also encouraged:

troop and police contributing countries, in consultation with the Secretary-General, to consider steps they could take to heighten awareness and the responsiveness of their personnel participating in UN peacekeeping operations to protect civilians, including women and children, and prevent sexual violence against women and girls in conflict and post-conflict situations, including wherever possible the deployment of a higher percentage of women peacekeepers or police.[161]

The Secretary-General stressed the importance of Resolution 1820 in paving the way for strong mandates:

[w]hen the Council adopts resolutions with strong language on sexual and gender-based violence, the United Nations can respond more forcefully. Let us ensure that all future mandates have clear provisions on protecting women and children in conflict situations.[162]

[161] ibid; Major General Cammaert believes that 'The deployment of female military and police personnel proved to be effective. A critical mass of women in peacekeeping missions can enhance confidence-building with the host community by presenting an organisation that looks more like a civilian society than a military occupation force.' P Cammaert, Wilton Park Conference 914 *Women Targeted or Afflicted by Armed Conflict: What Role for Military Peacekeepers?* 27–29 May 2008, text of presentation, 11; He reiterated the point at the Security Council meeting leading to the adoption of SC/RES 1820 19 June 2008; S/PV.5916, 10; Comfort Lamptey the first Permanent Gender Advisor in the UN DPKO argues that that' in a lot of countries women who have been subject to gender-based violence feel more comfortable talking to a woman...In many countries where women have been raped by men in uniform, they are more comfortable talking to another woman than men in uniforms. Having women in the field who are well-trained may be able to respond to women who have been violated': B Schoetzau 'Women Peacekeepers Can Work With Female Victims, Set Example for Male Colleagues' Voice of America 12 March 2007; Secretary-General Ban Ki Moon acknowledged this at the meeting leading to the adoption of Resolution 1820 on Women, Peace and Security and requested Member States to send more female troops' promising to ensure 'that the maximum number are deployed as quickly as humanly possible.' Secretary-General Ban Ki Moon, speaking at the Security Council meeting leading to the adoption of SC/RES 1820 19 June 2008; S/PV.5916, 4.

[162] Secretary-General Ban Ki Moon, speaking at the Security Council meeting leading to the adoption of SC/RES 1820 19 June 2008; S/PV.5916, 4.

Resolution 1794 of December 2007 strengthening MONUC's mandate is an example of a strong mandate in relation to sexual violence. In it the Security Council emphasized 'that the protection of civilians must be given priority in decisions about the use of available capacity and resources' and also *requested*:

> MONUC, in view of the scale and severity of sexual violence committed especially by armed elements in the Democratic Republic of the Congo, to undertake a thorough review of its efforts to prevent and respond to sexual violence, and to pursue a comprehensive mission-wide strategy, in close cooperation with the United Nations Country Team and other partners, to strengthen prevention, protection, and response to sexual violence, including through training for the Congolese security forces in accordance with its mandate, and to regularly report, including in a separate annex if necessary, on actions factual data and trend analyses of the problem.[163]

This is a detailed *request*, not merely an authorization, to pursue a comprehensive mission-wide strategy to strengthen prevention of abuse and protection and to provide regular reports on what they are doing and whether it is achieving its purpose. Similar provisions should be included in all peacekeeping mandates and should be regarded as a blueprint for protection provisions relating not only to sexual violence but to all serious abuses of human rights. It is only by adopting strong measures such as these and applying them as standard norms across all missions that real progress on the responsibility to protect (both specific and general) can be made. However, strong mandates are not enough on their own: in May 2008, five months after the adoption of Resolution 1794, Dr. Denis Mukwege, head of the Panzi Hospital for survivors of rape and sexual violence in the Eastern city of Bukavu in the DRC, reported that although the steady flow of raped women has slowed since the Goma accord[164] it continues in shocking numbers and it was also reported that 'the UNICEF staff in the field agree that things are still in the realm of nightmare for women, who live lives haunted by the fear of being violated, tortured, mutilated, infected with HIV.'[165]

7. Conclusion

In the wake of Rwanda and Srebrenica, the Brahimi report recommended that 'peacekeepers—troops or police—who witness violence against civilians should be presumed to be authorized to stop it, within their means, in support of basic United Nations principles,'[166] but acknowledged practical difficulties

[163] S/RES 1794 21 December 2007, [5] [18].

[164] Signed January 23 2008 between President Kabila and a number of armed groups.

[165] S Lewis, Wilton Park Conference 914 *Women Targeted or Afflicted by Armed Conflict: What Role for Military Peacekeepers?* (n 121), 14.

[166] Report of the Panel on United Nations Peace Operations A/55/305-S/2000/809 August 21 2000, [62].

in implementing this presumption as a principle. The report was cautiously received and although greater efforts have been made to improve the protection of civilians in armed conflict both at UN level and through developments in national peacekeeping doctrines, the extent of peacekeeping forces protection obligations remains controversial. Where forces are in occupation or exercise similar levels of effective control over territory they have a legal obligation to restore law and order and to maintain respect for fundamental human rights. Similar obligations apply to forces in localized areas subject to their authority and generally regarded as within their State's jurisdiction such as its prisons, embassies and military camps, wherever they are located. Forces also have an obligation to ensure the security of persons within their immediate control, such as detainees. There is much less clarity regarding the scope of peacekeepers' obligations to provide protection outside of these situations. However, it is clear that the effectiveness of a peacekeeping mission is likely to be seriously undermined if they fail to provide the local population with protection from crimes against humanity and other similar abuses. There may be circumstances in which providing protection to some potential victims may threaten other humanitarian objectives, for example food aid may be blocked. However, requiring troops to stand by in the face of conscience-shocking acts violates the rights of the troops themselves as well as constituting an abandonment of the local population. It is also likely to undermine the general success of the mission by reducing 'campaign authority' or 'perceived legitimacy' and contributing to poor troop morale. The UK's most recent *Draft National Doctrine on the Military Contribution to Peace Support Operations* suggests that a mission's 'perceived legitimacy' in the eyes of the local community may:

> be lost if the PSF doesn't meet local expectations; for example, if local parties question why the PSF does not respond to breaches of the mandate, does not enforce international laws and takes no action to control major abuses to basic human rights such as ethnic cleansing. A loss of 'perceived legitimacy' may result in an escalation of violence, sustained opposition to the PSF and a possible loss of control.[167]

Arguably therefore peacekeepers have both a moral obligation and a practical incentive to respond to serious abuses of the fundamental rights of the local population; and should be prepared and trained to do so.

[167] Ministry of Defence UK, Development, Concepts and Doctrine Centre, *Draft UK National Doctrine that will replace JWP 3–50 The Military Contribution to Peace Support Operations* (n 3) [0226].

6
Conclusion

Since the early days of peacekeeping the protection of civilians has been a matter of concern; but the failure to prevent the mass killings in Rwanda and Srebrenica triggered intensive efforts to tackle the gross human insecurity that many people have to live (and die) with. The key position of human security as an aspect of international peace and security is now recognized.[1] The UK's draft new peace support operations doctrine notes that the requirement to constrain all military techniques 'should not be confused with a minimalist approach but is the basis of a philosophical approach to the use of force, which limits its application to what is necessary to achieve the desired outcome.'[2] It argues that 'the real or actual success' of a peace support operation 'is related to the human security of the local populace and achieving a situation in which violence is reduced to levels that are acceptable to the local population.'[3] Moreover:

In cases of clear breaches of the mandate, the flaunting of international law and the abuse of human rights, the use of force, if authorised by the ROE, may serve to enhance the credibility of the PSF locally, nationally and internationally. It may be that the use of force reduces local consent, but if this can be isolated, wider national consent may be promoted. In certain circumstances, wider consent may serve to marginalize spoilers and make them vulnerable to the use of force.[4]

As the report on *The Fall of Srebrenica* observes:

When the international community makes a solemn promise to safeguard and protect innocent civilians from massacre then it must be willing to back up its promise with the necessary means. Otherwise it is surely better not to raise hopes and expectations in the first place, and not to impede whatever capability they may be able to muster in their own defence.[5]

[1] Secretary-General's High Level Panel on Threats, Challenges and Change *'A More Secure World: Our Shared Responsibility'* A/59/565.

[2] Ministry of Defence, Development, Concepts and Doctrine Centre, *Draft UK National Doctrine that will replace JWP 3–50 The Military Contribution to Peace Support Operations* (MOD Shrivenham 16 April 2008), [0207].

[3] ibid [0113].

[4] ibid [0211].

[5] Report of the Secretary-General pursuant to General Assembly Resolution 53/55: *The Fall of Srebrenica*, UN Doc A/54/549, 15 November 1999, [502–504].

Nevertheless force is force, a fact that creates major difficulties; trying to distinguish protective force from force for other purposes is inherently problematic. For example, in a statement to the Security Council on 21 June 2005, Under-Secretary-General for Humanitarian Affairs, Jan Egeland, welcomed 'the more robust peace-keeping being developed in the DRC where MONUC is using the protection of civilians as an overall concept to guide operations.'[6] However, whilst the more robust approach taken by MONUC in recent years has improved the security situation for many people in the DRC; it has also been alleged that MONUC has participated in operations in which excessive force has been used against civilians. Moreover, where troops are in a position of power and use force robustly the potential for personnel to abuse their position is increased. Peacekeeping mission personnel, both military and civilian, have frequently exploited local people, often for sex, but also for money and for 'tithes' on the communities' wealth, such as gold and diamonds. Whilst only a minority of personnel are involved the problem is widespread in virtually all missions, including the MONUC mission that Jan Egeland praised so highly in his 2005 statement to the Security Council. To be effective, use of force to protect civilians should not be simply added on to a mandate but needs to be incorporated into a deeper commitment to civilian protection as intrinsic to the function of peacekeeping.

This requires a significant rethinking of the purposes and principles and peacekeeping in line with the major changes that have developed in the late twentieth, and particularly in the twenty-first century, with regard to the UN's role in the maintenance of international peace and security. Peacekeeping was originally regarded as a means of managing tensions between the major powers so as to reduce the possibility of war between them. Human rights were regarded as an important but largely separate limb of the UN's Charter mandate. Today it is accepted that the maintenance of human security is an integral aspect of the UN's role in the maintenance of international peace and security. The core principles of the collective international 'responsibility to protect' have been endorsed by both the Security Council and the General Assembly. One means of carrying out this responsibility is through peacekeeping, which can play a role in prevention; in reaction to crimes against humanity and war crimes; and in rebuilding a community's security after a period of gross insecurity.

[6] Jan Egeland, 'Statement by Under-Secretary-General Jan Egeland to the Security Council on the protection of civilians in armed conflict', UN Department of Public Information, 21 June 2005; See also Gareth Evans, 'Making Idealism Realistic: The Responsibility to Protect as a New Global Security Norm' Address to launch Stanford MA Program in International Policy Studies, Stanford University, 7 February 2007 <http://www.crisisgroup.org>; VK Holt and T Berkman, *The Impossible Mandate? Military Preparedness, the Responsibility to Protect and Modern Peace Operations* (Henry L. Stimson Center Washington September 2006) 5; VK Holt, 'The military and civilian protection: developing roles and capacities' in 'Trends and Issues in Military and Humanitarian Relations' eds. V Wheeler and A Harmer, Humanitarian Protection Group Report, March 2006, 53.

Sexual violence in conflict and post-conflict situations provides a paradigm example of extreme human insecurity and the UN's efforts to improve its response to it can, and should, provide a blue-print for its approach to other serious abuses of human rights. Sexual violence is a special problem, requiring special expertise, but it is also one amongst many serious human rights abuses that take place in conflict and post conflict situations. In the face of the appalling cruelty and decimation of societies through sexual violence there is now growing pressure to require peacekeeping missions to reject a culture of tolerance of sexual exploitation and abuse and to hold commanders accountable if they fail to make the necessary efforts to do so. Failure to prevent sexual violence has been linked in part to a tendency to regard the problem as a domestic one (a fault or backwardness in the local culture) alongside an unwillingness by commanders and their troops to regard sexual exploitation and abuse by peacekeepers as a serious issue exacerbating the problem. Similarly, the failure to prevent the genocides in Rwanda and Srebrenica have been linked in part, not only to failures at the Secretariat and Security Council level, but also to a lack of respect for the local community amongst some peacekeepers together with poor leadership in dealing with intolerance and racism within the force. In addition peacekeepers' training has often been focused almost entirely on military skills and IHL has been treated as only a marginal element, often 'presented in a half-hearted and "touchy-feely" way that makes instructors appear out of contact with reality.'[7]

The UK's 2004 Peace Support Operations Doctrine emphasizes that all actors involved in the operation must maintain:

the highest possible standards of professionalism, compassion, and regard for the higher aims of the campaign, both on and off duty. Through Status of Forces Agreements (SOFAs) or other special agreements the PSF [Peace Support Force] may enjoy certain immunities relating to its duties. Notwithstanding this, its members must routinely

[7] R Murphy, 'International humanitarian law training for multi-national peace support operations—lessons from experience', 840 International Review of the Red Cross, 953, 957; Some of the Dutchbat troops only training in peacekeeping (as distinct from other types of military operations) prior to deployment to Srebrenica, 'consisted of a video tape (lasting approximately 25 minutes) on the history of the UN, including the Dutch participation in UN operations. A text was also included as a commentary to the slides. This part was supposed to be rounded off by a discussion, which in practice did not happen because no one had sufficient background knowledge of the conflict.' Netherlands Institute for War Documentation *Srebrenica 'A Safe Area': Reconstruction, Background, Consequences and Analyzes of the Fall of a Safe Area'* (2002) pt II, ch 8, s 2; the Dutch soldiers 'were fed with prejudices' (ibid, ch 8, s 3); the simulation training exercises for Srebrenica were based 'on completely stereo-typical ideas' with part of the brigade 'acting out the role of "beggars and traffickers" from the local population.' (ibid, ch 5, s 7); video recordings showed the 'roles of Muslim men were played in white robes and with turbans on their heads... holding prayer chains in their hands, while shouting 'Allah' and reciting texts such as 'You are disturbing our prayers!' and 'Allah will punish you!" whilst those acting out the Bosnian Serb soldiers were 'usually portrayed screaming, lashing out and stamping their feet....[and] always wearing a Russian fur hat.' A Field notebook was issued to all personnel deployed. The section on local culture 'stated that "the population of the former Yugoslavia is extremely proud... Many are short-tempered. Although they are basically friendly, they easily take offence."' (ibid, ch 8, s 3).

respect the laws and customs of the host nation and must be seen to have a respectful regard for local religious and secular beliefs. This latter point is particularly important where local religious or cultural beliefs may consider behaviour routinely acceptable to members of the international community as culturally or socially unacceptable. Such a perception would undermine Campaign Authority. It is important that PSF [Peace Support Force] commanders act to ensure that common standards of behaviour are recognized and implemented across the nations contributing to a PSF.[8]

To achieve this requires:

All personnel to develop a detailed understanding and respect for the law, religion, customs and culture of the range of actors engaged in the PSO [Peace Support Operation] complex, particularly with regard to the indigenous population. Ideally intelligence activity will inform the training process, and constant effort will be needed during a PSO to ensure that responses and actions remain culturally appropriate and are perceived as intended. Through the sensitive action of individuals or groups within the PSO complex, mutual trust and respect can be developed... Campaign Authority is improved markedly by investing research, planning and training to accord with this principle. A culturally astute and responsive PSO will increase the prospect of success.[9]

The type of force needed for a successful peace operation described in these guidelines is very different from the picture associated with the allegations regarding troop misconduct and troop attitudes in Rwanda,[10] Bosnia-Herzegovina[11] and many other missions since. The alleged abuses that occurred in those operations have in common a marked lack of respect for the local population. A culture of disrespect and misconduct directed at the local population is unlikely to inspire much effort to provide protection when that same population is under attack. To deploy troops with sufficient sensitivity and awareness to meet the standards set out in the UK guidelines requires investment in training and intelligence resources.

Since 1999 the majority of peacekeeping mandates have authorized the protection of civilians, in the immediate vicinity within force capabilities and with due

[8] UK Ministry of Defence, Joint Warfare Publication (JWP) 3.50 *The Military Contribution to Peace Support Operation* (2nd edn, The Joint Doctrine and Concepts Centre Shrivenham 2004), [306].

[9] ibid [323].

[10] According to UNAMIR's commander, Brigadier-General Dallaire, some of the Belgian troops had little respect for the local population and he notes 'dozens of disciplinary infractions' including being drunk on patrol; being disrespectful to officers from other contingents 'especially officers of colour'; being absent without leave; fraternizing with the local women; inappropriate unauthorized use of military helicopters (which caused them to be fired on); disobeying direct orders; abandoning individuals that they had been specifically charged to protect; and 'put[ting] themselves before the mission.' He writes that 'They seem to view the mission as a sort of Club Med where their recreational and vocational needs were to be met and where any training they undertook was designed to help them meet the paratrooper evaluation they would face when they returned to Belgium. This serious deficiency in leadership, coupled with disciplinary problems and the lack of mission specific training created conflicts between the mission, the RSF, and the general population.' R Dallaire, *Shake Hands with the Devil* (Arrow Press London 2004), 183–185.

[11] See Chapter 3.

respect for the primary responsibility of the host State in protecting its population. In addition Security Council resolutions such as 1820 on Women Peace and Security (2008), 1674 on the Protection of Civilians in Armed Conflict (2006), and Resolution 1314 on Children in Armed Conflict (2000),[12] can be used to shed light on less than clear protection provisions in a mission mandate. The UK's most recent draft peace support operations' doctrine recognizes that in addition to mission responsibility to protect, which may arise where a force is deployed with 'a primary specified task of responsibility for the physical protection of civilians,'[13] all peacekeepers, whatever the nature of their mission, have a general responsibility to protect.[14] Thus the case for peacekeepers taking their 'protective' role seriously, and for respecting human rights more consistently, seems to have been accepted in principle. However, as Major General Cammaert has pointed out, in order to be effective in providing protection peacekeepers must not only have a clear mandate, strong ROE, sufficient armament and be well-trained; 'equally important is the willingness of United Nations commanders to take swift decisions.'[15] Essentially the commitment to protection needs to be internalized and implemented; probably the most effective means of achieving this are through a combination of leadership, training, and persuasion of the relevant political agencies that effective protection of civilians by peacekeepers enhances the likelihood of success of the operation and is also likely to further the mission's perceived legitimacy both internationally and locally.

[12] S/RES 1820 19 June 2008; S/RES 1674 28 April 2006; S/RES 1314 11 August 2000.

[13] Ministry of Defence, Development, Concepts and Doctrine Centre, *Draft UK National Doctrine that will replace JWP 3–50 The Military Contribution to Peace Support Operations* (n 2), [3A24].

[14] ibid [3A23].

[15] P Cammaert, speaking at the Security Council meeting leading to the adoption of SC/RES 1820 19 June 2008; S/PV.5916, 10.

Index

References are to page number and footnotes, e.g. 121n indicates a footnote on page 121